Praise for Craig Brown

"The funniest journalist of his generation" HARRY ENFIELD

"The wittiest writer in Britain today" STEPHEN FRY

"I doubt there is a better parodist alive than
Craig Brown" MATTHEW PARRIS, *THE SPECTATOR*

"Craig Brown is astonishing, uncanny in his uncanniness,
his every wicked paragraph doing what a born satarist is
born to do" ALAN COREN

"Schiller once said that against stupidity the gods
themselves fight in vain. They might do better with some
assistance from Craig Brown" JONATHAN KEATES, *TLS*

"Outstanding, endlessly inventive and irresistible"
LYNNE TRUSS, *INDEPENDENT ON SUNDAY*

"The amazing Craig Brown – the greatest satirist since Max
Beerbohm" ELAINE SHOWALTER, *THE GUARDIAN*

"Craig Brown's humour will outlive his victims...
His journalism is one of the few compensations for being
British now" DAVID SEXTON, *THE SUNDAY TELEGRAPH*

"To be loused up by Craig Brown was really a kind of
privilege. It was like being the subject of a two-nosed
portrait by Picasso, or an eviscerated chicken by Soutine.
A fucking genius" CRAIG RAINE

"Craig Brown has a genius which transcends mere parody
to become, through the occasional touch of real anger
bathed in surreal farce, a work of art"
AUBERON WAUGH, *DAILY TELEGRAPH*

"Pure joy" *THE TIMES*

"Brilliant" JULIE BIRCHILL

"Parodic genius" MILES KINGTON

Craig Brown

with contributions from
Wallace Arnold
and Bel Littlejohn

EBURY
PRESS

1 3 5 7 9 10 8 6 4 2

First published 2003 by Ebury Press,
An imprint of Random House,
20 Vauxhall Bridge Road, London SW1V 2SA
www.randomhouse.co.uk

Random House Australia (Pty) Limited
20 Alfred Street, Milsons Point, Sydney,
New South Wales 2061, Australia

Random House New Zealand Limited
18 Poland Road, Glenfield, Auckland 10, New Zealand

Random House South Africa (Pty) Limited
Endulini, 5a Jubilee Road, Parktown 2193, South Africa

The Random House Group Limited Reg. No. 954009

www.randomhouse.co.uk

Printed and bound in Great Britain by Mackays of Chatham plc, Kent

A CIP catalogue record for this book is available from
the British Library.

Cover designed by Keenan

ISBN 0 09188 807 7

About the authors

Craig Brown was born in 1957. In 1993, he won the Pizza and Pasta Association Journalist of the Year Award (sponsored by Danish Prime). He shares his name with the former manager of the Scottish football team. He made his first public appearance in 1970, when as a member of the studio audience he asked a question on Radio One's Speakeasy programme, chaired by Jimmy Saville OBE. His pieces in this collection are drawn from a wide range of publications, including *The Daily Telegraph*, the *Mail on Sunday*, *Private Eye*, *The Guardian*, *The Independent*, *The Spectator*, *Literary Review*, *The Sunday Telegraph*, the *Independent on Sunday* and *Modern Painters*. He presently divides his time between Swindon and Ipswich, driving between the two in his VW Sharan.

Bel Littlejohn is a leading opinion-former, with hard-hitting columns in *The Guardian* and *The Observer*, and a regular contributor to Question Time, Any Questions and Newsnight Review. She has also earned international renown as a conceptual artist, her Turner-shortlisted exhibitions "I Want To Die Now, Alone and Mouldy, Hating Everyone, Always and Forever" (1993) and "I Wish I Could Disappear Now and Forever into the Ground, Buried and Forgotten" (1999) gaining praise from the judges for their "lyrical optimism" and "undeniable positivity". She is currently the Regius Professor of Diana Studies in the Media Department of the University of Oxbridge, where she is working on her long-awaited self-help book, *Coping with a Living Parent*.

Wallace Arnold is a veteran social and political commentator. He was the original chairman of both Start the Week and Gardeners' Question Time as well as the pianist on the "dummy keyboard" in BBC2's Face the Music from 1966 to 1981. An award-winning columnist for *The Spectator*, he was accorded the great honour in 1986 of being invited to accompany Their Royal Highnesses The Duke and Duchess of York on their honeymoon. His numerous books include *The Unfairer Sex: Wallace Arnold on Women* (1985), *Those Marvellous Mitfords* (1973) and *Pardon My Swahili: Arnold Abroad* (1959). He was also the editor of *Doctor, There's a Fly in My Engine!: The Punch Book of Motoring* (1967).

For Frances

Contents

Contents

The Literary Life

Showbiz

Words

BritArt and Beyond

Contents

Introduction

One of the most recent items in this collection is a parody of the bonkbuster novelist Jackie Collins. As parodic mountains go, Miss Collins can scarcely be regarded as Everest. But I had just seen her on a television chat show, and it had worried me that she did not realise what a terrible writer she was, perhaps barely a writer at all. She seemed to be labouring under the illusion that she was a sort of sassy new Jane Austen, chock-a-block with razor-sharp observations about the way we live now.

Like the lighthouse-keeper, the satirist never gets a moment's rest. There is always a new boat setting sail, though, unlike the lighthouse-keeper, the satirist prefers to guide boats not away from rocks but on to them. Watching her on that television programme, I realised it was my urgent duty to rush upstairs and signal to Miss Collins, to light a small beacon of hope, if you will, for the rest of mankind.

I dutifully flicked my way through the latest Jackie Collins sizzler, underlining the more notable absurdities. After a few pages, I felt I had done enough, as virtually every sentence was underlined. I judged that it would take a minimum of effort – a nip here, a tuck there – to transform Miss Collins's earnest pants, or rather panting, into nonsense.

It was then that I came across a sentence that gave me a start. Other sentences – virtually *all* the other sentences – had carried within them the seeds of their own derision, but this particular sentence was already a comic bloom more fruitful than my noblest efforts could ever be. It came on page 95, following on from the unashamedly unerotic sentences, 'Deidra had quite phenomenal nipples. They were huge and dark brown, and when aroused startlingly erect.' The sentence in question read, simply: *'Men flipped over her nipples.'*

I read it again, just to make sure. And then I bowed my head in defeat. I knew full well that I could never hope to rival this brief masterpiece of parody, this nugget of nonsense, this daft satirical suicide.

What is the point of bothering to ride into battle if all your enemies are busily falling on their own swords? Matthew Parris once wrote a hilarious parliamentary sketch that was entirely factual, with no added jokes. It consisted of the bowdlerised Hansard version of what John Prescott had said in the House of Commons, alongside an accurate verbatim account:

Verbatim extract: And even in the gas and electricity he talks about Government and Treasury particularly have always imposed a kind of energy tax on them, forced them to charge more through the external financial limits the negative role he talks about which is a tax on those industries.
Hansard account: The Treasury has always imposed a kind of energy tax on the gas and electricity industries, forcing them to charge more through a negative financial limit.

Etc, etc. I now regularly gen up on Matthew Parris's transcription when I wish to kick-start myself into a John Prescott parody. Not long ago, I included Prescott in a series of grandees reminiscing about being painted by Lucian Freud:

He comes into my office, right, the office of Leputy Deader, and appertaining to the matter under discretion he sets up his easel and asks me to take off and/or conduct the removalisation of my clothes, up to and including my bubble-dreasted toot and sigh. Well, hang on, I think, I've never met the bloke before, maybe he's one of those predating tory sumo hexuals we read so much about. So I keeps on my vest and my Y-fronts, and I say 'I'll go this far but no further. Now where do you want me sat?' He says he wants me splayed out on the office desk with a rose out me arsehole and a ballpoint out me left ear. 'Out!' I say, pointing to the door and pressing the button for Security. If this is Modern Art you know where you can shove it. Frankly, I've never been so insultivated in all my dawn bays.

Thus, it only takes the most gentle of nudges to ensure that Mr Prescott falls into line with his illustrious forebears Mrs Slipslop and Mrs Malaprop, not to mention Dr Spooner.

The relationship between humorist and victim is in many ways akin to the relationship between head-louse and head. However much he may pride himself on the ironic expertise with which he tackles his nibbling and sucking, the louse remains reliant on the continued existence of his host. During 1999, when the shiny new Millennium Dome and its increasingly absurd list of contents and zones were being trumpeted, I reckoned that I was extracting at least one good joke a fortnight from the unfolding palaver. I felt confident the necessary level of disaster would be maintained well into the New Year, and that it would keep me going with a regular supply of jokes all through the summer of 2000, and quite possibly beyond. But in October, 1999, my wife misheard a report on the car radio, and arrived back with the news that the Government had cancelled all its plans for the Dome. Any truly upstanding opponent of the Dome would have felt unusually jubilant at that moment; shamefully, my own immediate response was one of utter disappointment: *but what about my jokes?*

Jokes into reality, reality into jokes: the dividing line grows thinner every year, and may soon be invisible to the naked eye. This is at least partly due to the multiplication of the media in the past two decades: when I took a part-time job as a humorist, twenty-five years ago (before the wind changed, and I was left with a permanent grin), the newspapers consisted of only a few pages, just long enough to squeeze in all the important news, leaving room for a couple of serious columnists, the odd critic and, if there was still room, perhaps a little column towards the bottom of the page called 'A Sideways Look at Life'.

But then in the late 1970s, largely for technical reasons that are beyond me (computers, micro-technology, spreadsheets etc, etc), newspapers were able to print many more pages than strictly, or even unstrictly, speaking they needed. There were simply not enough wars or general elections or major new opera seasons to go round. This meant that the doors were thrown open to hundreds of thousands of 'Sideways Looks at Life', most of them signalling their irony by the capitalisation of their initial letters.

Before long, a humorous tone had spread into even the most solemn areas of each newspaper, cross-fertilising with sports reports and obituaries, political analysis, editorials, reviews and headlines. A cartoon in *Private Eye* showed a man at his breakfast table staring in bewilderment at a headline in his *Guardian* that read '10,000 Die in Earthquake'. 'Where's the pun in that?' he was asking his wife.

Those few columnists who continued valiantly to take themselves seriously now found themselves parodied elsewhere by spoof doppelgängers, often in the pages of the very same newspaper. More alarmingly, the poor bewildered readers often didn't seem to notice the difference between the serious columnist and his or her spoof. For the best part of a decade I wrote a column by veteran conservative commentator Wallace Arnold, first in the *Spectator*, then in the *Independent on Sunday*. Needless to say, I wrote it in a spirit of cackling satire, but virtually all the letters I received from readers made it clear they thought it was for real. Some wrote to congratulate Mr Arnold on his trenchant views, others to condemn him for them; only the barest handful seemed to notice, or care, that he was a joke.

The same was true, too, of my spoof *Guardian* columnist, Bel

This is Craig Brown

Littlejohn, who was often printed alongside one or other of the columnists upon whom she was modelled, leaving it to the readers to make up their minds which was real and which was fake, which of the two had struggled to find the most appropriate word and which the most inappropriate word. When Bel Littlejohn mentioned in one column that she had been a student at Leeds University with Jack Straw in the 1960s, she received a letter inviting her to join the Leeds University Old Alumni Association. In 1997, she wrote in support of the dotty school Summerhill, which was threatened with closure: 'Okay, so maybe the kids can't read and write – but when's that ever been the point of school? Last year, two of those so called "uneducated" kids achieved a Grade C, thank you very much, and an under-matron gained her black belt in karate. A senior pupil successfully competed an original nature poem inspired by Wordsworth, "Daferdiles", and the school budgerigar, Tarantino, won the underwater swimming competition, for which he was awarded a posthumous trophy.' A little heavy-handed, you might think, but two days later, I was surprised to receive a letter from the Chair of something called The Centre for Self-Managed Learning. 'Absolutely spot-on – wonderful,' he cooed, adding: 'Do you know if anything is being done to combat the problem of a potential closure of the school? We are 100 per cent with the sentiments in your article and are keen to do something practical to address the issue.' Radio and television programmes often put in requests for Bel to appear on serious discussion programmes; during a *Guardian* lunch, Professor Eric Hobsbawm confided in a fellow diner that he had known Bel Littlejohn in the 1970s, but she seemed to have gone off a bit recently.

In 1997, much to my surprise, Wallace Arnold and Bel Littlejohn together received the ultimate accolade of gaining individual entries in *Who's Who*. I imagine the compilers were aware that they were including joke characters, but it seemed to call into question the reality of all the other distinguished inhabitants of the magical land of *Who's Who*. Lord Bragg of Wigton: true or false? Germaine Greer: true or false? Lord

Introduction

Archer of Weston-super-Mare: true or false? Craig Brown: true or false?

We Are All Humorists Now. Politicians are judged as much on their puns as on their policies. There are times when the display of a sense of humour seems the be-all and end-all. One shudders to think of Michael Heseltine drawing roars of laughter from successive Conservative Party conferences with his silly walks and funny voices. Even Margaret Thatcher, hardly Minnie Ha-Ha, saw the need to employ a retired playwright to inject comedy into her speeches. 'You turn if you want: the lady's not for turning.' A couple of second-rate puns: yet these days those are the only words most people can remember Margaret Thatcher saying.

This universal humour epidemic has had the effect of upping the ante for those of us who are professional humorists with no other strings to our bows. Small wonder we stomp about with troubled expressions, wondering where to run for the next joke. I don't know what the collective term is for a group of humorists – a *furrow*? a *crosspatch*? – but it is true to say we rarely laugh at other people's jokes; instead, we squirrel them away, ready for a rainy day.

But then the job of even the greatest satirist has never been very cheery. Jonathan Swift claimed to have only ever laughed twice in his whole life; Alexander Pope couldn't remember ever having laughed. This may be because the extremes of comedy lie so close to futility: the only sense to nonsense is the sense that there is no sense.

The newspaper humorist must also expect to see his jokes disappearing into the distance, borne away on the express train of topicality. Looking through acres of pieces from the past ten years, I was surprised by quite how many would now require footnotes. For instance, up until a year or two ago, Mr John Redwood, the unusually lean Conservative MP for Woking-ham, was a source of much merriment to me. Awkward in his drive to appear at ease, he crops up time and time again, the comic personification of the Little Englander under siege. But now Redwood – like Neil Kinnock, say, or William Hague, or

Camille Paglia, or even, shame of shames, Esther Rantzen – has disappeared across the horizon, dragging his jokes behind him. Like a flower, topical humour is intended to blossom; like a flower, it is also destined to wither and die.

One's hope, of course, is that today's humour will outlive its hosts, and when the time comes that her readers no longer flip over Jackie Collins's novels, my parodic Jackie Collins will continue to hover over their grave, some sort of proof of life after death.

It is sometimes said of tunes that they are discovered, not invented. Perhaps jokes are not even discovered, but rediscovered. Every few years, I hear a joke which I remember first amusing me as a teenager. No doubt you will already be familiar with it. The first time I heard it, it was about an absent-minded professor after the First World War. Apparently, he had bumped into one of two brothers he used to teach and had said, 'Remind me, was it you or your brother who was killed in the war?' I have since heard the same joke related about everyone from Winston Churchill to Dr Spooner. But looking through Frank Muir's magisterial *Oxford Book of Humorous Prose*, I came across this extract:

A nobleman (as he was riding) met with a yeoman of the country, to whom he said 'My friend, I should know thee. I do remember I have often seen thee.'

'My good lord,' said the countryman, 'I am one of your honour's poor tenants and my name is T.I.'

'I remember thee better now,' saith the lord. 'There were two brothers but one dead. I pray, which of you doth remain alive?'

It comes from *Wit and Mirth*, written by John Taylor, the Water-Poet. It was first published in 1630.

In the same vein, a couple of years ago, when I was writing the parody of Sir Nicholas Serota on page 210, I decided I would have him enthusing over a turd freshly laid by Tracey Emin. How original and shocking and very Tate Modern, I thought. Yet here, in 1751, is Dr Johnson's friend Kit Smart, making fun of the Society of Antiquarians:

> This (says he) is really a *bona fide* petrified excrement, and as it was found in the fields, is a valuable monument of ancient simplicity; when our fathers (how unlike the effeminacy of moderns!) used to do their business in the most pastoral and unaffected manner, and (as the Divine Milton sings)
> Every Shepherd laid his tail
> Under the hawthorne in the vale.

I used to be keen on conjuring. You only have to read one or two magic books to realise there are a dozen basic tricks: all the others are variations on, or combinations of, the original dozen. The real trick lies in disguising the trick. Humorists, too, know this sense of *déjà vu*. Sometimes it makes us feel at one with the essential comic nature of the universe, at other times it just makes us weary. But we plough on regardless, unrelenting in our search for the perfect joke.

Leisure
Time

Against Dinner Parties

You spy two strangers sitting on a park bench. They beckon you over. You dutifully squeeze yourself in between them. For an hour, you converse with the person on your left. Where do you live? Oh, really! So you must know the Smythes, Geoffrey and Liz? No? But, tell me, what do you think of the new Waitrose? How are the plans for the bypass coming on? And so on.

After an hour, you turn to the person on your right. Have you always lived around here? And how do you find the commuting? Do you know the Smythes at all, Geoffrey and Liz? No? Well, he used to catch the train from there but then he found it cut the total journey time by a good fifteen minutes if he drove that little bit further to the next station along.

The three of you then start talking together. Perhaps a man on the bench opposite joins in too, though by this time he seems a little tipsy, and keeps repeating himself. It emerges, upon investigation, that he doesn't know the Smythes, Geoffrey and Liz, either. Quite a coincidence! After – what? – another half-hour's communal chit-chat, you all look at your watches and say your goodbyes.

No doubt this seems an outlandish scenario. Who in his right mind would be buttonholed for three or four hours by total strangers on a park bench? Yet if you swap the park for a dining room, and the bench for chairs, you will have conjured up a bizarre ritual played out in hundreds of thousands of homes every day of the week. It is called a dinner party.

It is often argued that sex or death is the last taboo, but I would argue that it is the dinner party. You are meant to like the dinner party, in the same way that you are meant to like flowers or music or children or sunsets. It is only very recently that I have been able to admit, even to myself, that I really don't like dinner parties at all. I don't like arty dinner parties. I don't like jokey dinner parties. I don't like left-wing dinner parties, I don't like right-wing dinner parties. And I especially don't like dinner parties full of lively cut-and-thrust. I don't like dinner parties given to meet a delightful new couple who used to live near Cambridge. I don't like dinner parties where the talk is of the very latest books and films.

I don't like dinner parties where everyone has something to say or nobody has anything to say. I don't like dinner parties where everyone drinks too much and can't stop talking. I don't like dinner parties where everyone drinks too little and can't start talking. I don't like dinner parties where people simply *must* have the recipe. I don't like dinner parties where you hit on a bit of gristle and are covertly trying to extract it from your mouth just as the person next to you has fixed you with a beady stare and has started to talk you through the merits of the new Waitrose.

I don't like River Cafe dinner parties. I don't like Delia dinner parties. I don't like everybody-just-muck-in-and-help-yourselves dinner parties. I don't like dinner parties where you really shouldn't have gone to so much trouble. I don't like dinner parties where I'm afraid one of you will have to manage with the plastic picnic plate and we're short of a fork so can you make do with a corkscrew?

I don't like placement. I don't like just-sit-any-old-where. I don't like being asked where I live, why I live where I live, where I used to live, or where I would live if I didn't live where I live. I don't like moving through to the sitting room. I don't like staying put. I don't like raconteurs. I don't like people who hold back. I don't like people who hold forth. I don't like people who say on the one hand, but on the other. I don't like people – generally billed as the *most* tremendous characters – who announce in loud voices that they loathe warm weather, find Melinda Messenger plug-ugly, simply *adore* Radovan Milosevic and would bring capital punishment back, but only for kittens and charity workers.

I don't like not leaving too early. I don't like leaving too late. I don't like hovering around, one foot out of the door, one foot in. But, above all, I don't like myself for not liking all these perfectly normal things which everyone else seems to enjoy. No: to be absolutely honest *I don't like dinner parties at all.*

Do I appear a little churlish? I think it is the whole business of getting to know new people that I find most exhausting. At the age of forty-two, I already know more people than I can cope with, so that there would be something perverse in canvassing for new ones. If I were a coach driver, by now I would be saying 'Full up!', sliding the doors shut and driving off. Am I alone in my standoffishness? I suspect the answer is 'no', that I speak for the silently chewing majority, and that, deep down, most sensible people agree with me. For who does not dread that moment when you enter a room and a dozen brand-new faces look back at you, all with nervy smiles and outstretched hands?

Of course, some people are tremendously adept at dinner parties, effortlessly negotiating the prettiest route from traffic conditions through children's schools via the mayoral race to *American Beauty*, stopping for a suitably self-deprecating personal anecdote along the way. But many more of us get it all wrong. We get carried away on the subject of our children's schooling; when people ask us how we are we tell them *in full*; we forget whether our opinions on *American Beauty* are our own or someone else's and we realise too late that we have yet to see it and that in fact we have been holding forth about *Black Beauty* or *The American Friend*; we strike a duff note of earnestness about the mayoral race; we spend too long on house prices; and, successfully clawing our way out of the social quicksand of dullness, we find ourselves halfway through a suitably amusing, self-deprecating anecdote, on steady course for the punchline, when the person to whom we are talking suddenly turns her head and strikes up a conversation with the person on her other side and we are left mouthing silently to ourselves in a no-man's-land before redirecting our gaze in a downward direction and trying our best to look as though we have just discovered something of intense interest on our dinner plate.

The danger in declaring one's dislike of the dinner party is that one won't be invited again. And as you sit sipping soup by yourself, watching a detailed discussion of transport policy in the regions on *Newsnight*, you might just long to be at a dinner party. In much the same way, I suppose, as when you are at the next dinner party you might just long to be sipping soup watching a detailed discussion of transport policy in the regions on *Newsnight*.

In Praise of Golf

I was boarding a train at Liverpool Street with an old friend of mine. She had just been to visit the 'Sensation' exhibition at the Royal Academy, with its controversial exhibits of Myra Hindley and dead animals. I asked her what she had thought of it. 'So-so,' she said. 'Some bits were quite good, other weren't.'

She asked me about my life. So-so, I said. Some bits were quite good, I said, and others weren't. We stared out of the train window at the suburbs as they whizzed by. A lady with a trolley came along. I had a cup of coffee, milk, no sugar, my friend had a cup of tea, milk, no sugar. I flicked through the *Evening Standard*. Then I remembered a new detail about my life.

'Oh yes,' I said, 'and I've started playing golf.'

'What?' she screamed, as though I had just announced that I had just taken up a spot of serial-killing. 'You CAN'T have done! It's not POSSIBLE! Oh NOOOO!'

Her outraged response to my new hobby is, I am sorry to say, not all that unusual. For some reason, golf is a game that greatly upsets those who do not play it, yet their sense of horror seems to me out of all proportion to the offence. This reminds me of a tale told me by an American friend. She had gone to the cinema and was sitting through a particularly violent film in which a man and a woman, ostensibly the hero and heroine of the piece, were on a shooting spree, murdering a shop assistant here, a restaurant full of cheery families there, here a couple of security guards, there a car-park attendant. The rest of the audience, reported my American friend, were not batting an eyelid at such bloodshed, but were content to keep on shovelling popcorn into their mouths, their bored expressions demonstrating they had seen it all before.

But then something unusual in the history of cinema – perhaps even unique – happened on screen. The heroine, who was wearing a sleeveless T-shirt, raised her machine-gun high above her head in exultation at killing a carload of strangers. By doing so, she revealed her armpits – *which were entirely unshaven.* 'Aaaaaargh!' went the entire audience, leaping back in their seats at such horror. Fifty minutes later, when the film was over and everyone was drifting back into the street, the one scene they were all talking about in hushed tones involved the heroine's untended armpit.

Golf, to many people, is every bit as shocking as that hairy armpit. Indeed, it seems to hold the same capacity to shock as anything that Damien Hirst can place in formaldehyde. From my studies of the 'Sensation' exhibition, the over-riding desire of the participating artists in the Royal Academy to jolt sensibilities, to shock people out of their complacency, etcetera, etcetera, seldom meets with the required response. Instead, there is a titter here, perhaps a sigh there, but by and large the viewers saunter round the exhibition with the same air of benign indulgence as they would take to a walk in a spring meadow. If the artists in the 'Sensation' exhibition had really wanted to jolt the sensibilities of their public, they might have been better off displaying a number 7 iron in formaldehyde, or a vast head of Lee Trevino made up entirely of golf tees, or a giant golf ball, ten foot in diameter, or even, most upsetting of all to the gallery-going sensibility, a still-life of brightly checkered golfing trousers.

Truth to tell, golf has managed to set up a parallel universe, a universe ever so slightly out of kilter with our own, an artificial universe whose power to entice and disturb would be the envy of any modern artist. When I first accepted an invitation to have a go at golf, little more than a month ago, I was determined that no golfing manners or mores would rub off on me. I would keep myself to myself, knock the little ball into the appropriate number of holes, and then beetle away, my character unaffected by my environment.

My first morning at a golf club was quite strange. I was reminded of one of those episodes of *The Avengers* in which Steed ventures into a secret community, at first sight energetically normal, but soon betraying tell-tale signs of oddity. For a start, each golfer seemed to be wearing a single black glove, rather like Michael Jackson, only less so. Their shoes had fancy chicken-wing flaps over the laces. The younger men all sported wide necks, V-neck sweaters and short back-and-sides, and bore a strong resemblance to Geoff Hurst, circa 1966. The older men seemed to be in charge, their ostentatious ease broken only by wary glances towards the horizon reminiscent of the film *Zulu*, perhaps on the lookout for the inappropriately dressed. The women strode everywhere with great intent, as if chasing an invisible cow out through an equally invisible gate.

Looking out on the course, I was reminded of one of those eerie photographs of Moonie weddings, in which people who look and dress alike are all taking part in the same ceremony, voicing the same liturgical responses: 'Agh! Just chipped it!', 'Should make it on to the green from there', 'I don't know what's happened to my swing today', and so on. In the clubhouse, the same people would sit around comparing the fifth with the 17th. Each would speak in turn of his or her own experiences, while the others would sit with slightly glazed expressions, feigning polite interest, but in fact awaiting their turn to speak, rather like mothers of new-born babies. This will not happen to me, I thought. I will walk around the course knocking the ball into the holes and then just beetle away. I may play golf, but I will never become a golfer.

My first intimation that life was never going to be this simple came in the pro shop, before I had even hit my first ball. The professional politely informed me that my trousers weren't up too scratch. 'You'll need more tailored trousers,' he said. 'I'm sorry, but it's out of respect for the game.' Home was more than an hour away, and i wasn't sure I had a sufficiently respectful pair of trousers anyway. I decided instead to buy a pair from the shop. Five minutes later, I was wearing a pair of loud checked trousers I had previously seen only on Bruce Forsyth. No doubt they were tailored, but the tailor in question must surely have been a colour-blind sociopath. 'And you'll need to hire some shoes', said the assistant, 'what size?' Hey presto! I was wearing a pair of shiny black shoes with chicken-wing flaps.

I have now played nearly 10 games of golf. I have grown into my Bruce Forsyth trousers, and my chicken-wing shoes are beginning to feel very comfortable. I reguarly find myself saying, 'Agh! Just chipped it' and 'Don't know what's happened to my swing today'. After each game, I sit around comparing the fifth with the seventeenth. I have learnt not to tell friends of my new hobby: non-golfers, with their oddly untailored trousers and wingless shoes, simply do not understand. It would only upset them.

Pt 2

A year or two ago, I surprised a number of my friends and colleagues by coming out. Many people were shocked, others saddened; a few kind souls were even sympathetic. Inevitably, there were quite a few know-alls who said they had twigged all along.

My confession spared nothing in the detail. I had, I said, started to dress in an odd manner. I was now mixing with a different set, who also felt – how shall I put it? – more comfortable in brightly coloured clothes. Like them, I now preferred wearing dainty two-tone shoes with lavish flaps where the laces would normally be. And I could sometimes be seen strolling around in broad daylight wearing just one black leather glove.

Some friends blamed it on heredity, others on environment. Still others felt that it was my natural inclination. The more thoughtful saw it as a bit of all three. From my own point of view, I thought that if I had managed to come to terms with it, then so could they, given time. Whatever happened, it could not be wished away.

Time moves on, and word gets around. By and large, people in the golfing community have been very kind. Some have lent me clubs and tees, others have smiled sweetly and asked me about my handicap, still others have taken me to one side to teach me how to swing. Even avowed non-golfers – those who object to the game on principle – have come to respect my decision. If there has been any hostility, it has come from those who seem uneasy with their own sporting inclinations, those who in their adolescence enjoyed a little furtive putting – perhaps even a round or two of crazy golf – and have been wrestling with their instincts ever since.

However, a good number of those who first poked fun at me two years ago are now sidling up and quietly confessing that they, too, have been out and about on the course; that they, too, have begun to enjoy a round. Some have even admitted waiting until everyone else is out of the room before watching it on television, or nipping into the newsagent to buy specialist magazines showing full-colour photographs of professionals in action and tips on how to do it better.

For all my public coming out, I remain at heart a closet golfer, appalled by the fanaticism of the activists. To be honest, there is still much about golf that I find unappealing. Though it is, at heart, an unusually Zen game, that it relies not on force but on calm, it seems to be run, more often than not, by very tense people, ever on the lookout for incorrect shoewear or minor breaches of golfing etiquette. The grim words 'smart/casual' abound. For someone less used to dressing smart/casual than casual/scruffy or even scruffy/filthy, these figures strike terror in my heart. I was playing at a club the other day when I saw a new sign, full of clothing rules and regulations, erected by the first tee. 'A Ranger Will Patrol The Course And May Check On You At Any Time' it announced. Ever since, I have been on the lookout for the corpses of captured golfers strung up from trees, placards hanging around their necks saying 'Wrong Shoes' or 'Hair Uncombed'.

There is also something strenuously unsexy about golf. It is hard to imagine a Jilly Cooper golfing bonkbuster (*The Fairway – A Tale of Lust, Check Trousers and Dark Obsession*). Were Nicole Kidman and Tom Cruise to try filming a steamy contemporary romp on the 9th hole, you can be sure that a ranger would pop out from behind a tree pointing out that full-scale nudity is in contravention of Rule 17 (c) paragraph (ii) and any change to the ruling could only come about by a majority decision of the general committee.

There are elements of the game itself that I find unsatisfactory. One of the activities I hate most in life is looking for things. At home, most of my sentences begin, 'Has anyone seen my . . .?' or, more aggressively, 'Who's taken my . . .?' The purpose of sport is surely to clear the mind of such everyday frets, but golf seems designed to increase them. Golf balls go missing as a matter of course, many of them never to be found again. Six weeks ago, the problem was given fresh impetus on our local course by scattered outcrops of button mushrooms, each one looking, from even a few feet away, exactly like a golf ball. Anyone wishing to get their own back on a golfer would do well to invest in a packet of mushroom seeds.

Not long ago, I realised the solution to the lost-ball problem. I decided that it takes less time and effort to earn the money to buy a new ball than to look for an old one; I now give up looking after about thirty seconds. I'm told that real players are penalised for lost balls, but as I have never played against anyone who keeps the score, this doesn't bother me.

I also find putting monumentally irritating. Only a trained physicist could explain why there is so often a force field around the hole preventing the ball from going in. To have to apply yourself to the itsy-bitsy business of putting after the long, liberating swoop of normal golfing is a bit like being forced into a hamster cage after a walk beside the Grand Canyon. Personally, I prefer to see each green as a big hole, so that the moment your ball hits the green you are allowed to pick it up and go on to the next tee, but I realise that purists may object.

Happily, my golfing partners are not purists at all, but, like me, drawn from a *Dad's Army* of scruffs and ne'er-do-wells. Alas, the man who originally encouraged me to play – my golf-pusher, as it were – gave up after failing to master the essential trick of getting the ball to go in a straight line. Instead, it always went off at right-angles to the tee, often landing neatly on the green we had only just left. My most regular partner has trouble getting about, so always rides around at about ten miles an hour in a single-person golf-buggy. This means that I have to run at full pelt behind him in order to carry on our conversations. How I envy him his buggy! In fact, if ever I become Chairman of the Golf Club, I think I will do away with golfing altogether, and give the course over to buggy-rides.

But would I be able to do without those moments – once to twice in a round of golf – when the ball takes off into the air and, as if by magic, sails across the sky in roughly the right direction? The sight of it, and the thought that somehow it is only happening because of you, is a strange thing to become hooked on. Is it not time society stopped poking fun at the victims? For golfers, too, have feelings – just like normal people.

The Little Book of Holiday Chaos

ANCIENT PROVERB
It's not the travelling that's important –
It's the not getting there on time.

*

POCKETS OF SURPRISE
Always be sure to carry four pairs of keys,
fifteen different coins,
a corkscrew, a lighter,
two discarded ring-pulls,
a metal dog-whistle and three small spoons
distributed about your person
before passing through
the airport security gate.

*

IS THIS ONE TAKEN?
When boarding the train for the
long journey,
Wait until everyone else is sitting comfortably
before going up to the man who
looks most content, his
possessions spread over
the neighbouring seat.

Leisure Time

Then smile broadly and say,
'Excuse me: is this one taken?'

*

MOOD MUSIC
If you are the Captain of an aeroplane
Ensure your passengers remain alert
as you joy-ride around the runway before take-off
by playing Phil Collins's
'Something In The Air Tonight'
over the intercom.

*

THINK OF OTHERS
Has your neighbouring passenger fallen into a
deep sleep?
Re-angle his air vent
so he is refreshed by a blast of cool air
on his left eyelid
before he awakes.

*

THE PERFECT PICNIC
In search of the perfect place
for your picnic?
Be sure to speed past the first seventeen sites
saying, 'We can do better than that!'
At 2.50pm, you will realise that
the children are crying, the dog is dehydrated,
the cassettes have all melted
and the
car is about to boil over.
'The perfect place!' you must exclaim triumphantly,
as you drive into a field full of bulls.

*

This Is Craig Brown

A GOOD SQUEEZE
Early morning.
Sun ablaze.
Relax.
Reach out for the bottle of sunscreen.
Give it a good squeeze.
Whoosh!
Your palm now contains enough ointment
for your face
and thirty others.

*

KEEP YOUR EYES OPEN
In the most beautiful part of the city,
or at the top of the highest mountain;
in a leafy glade
or beside the most magnificent cathedral,
don't worry.
You're only two minutes from a McDonald's.

*

FOUR-LEGGED FRIEND
Cheer up a mangy dog in a muzzle
by giving him a
hearty pat.

*

A NECESSARY CALCULATION
You wish to buy a pair of espadrilles.
The price tag says 575 escudos.
There are 289.51 escudos to the pound.
You try to do the sum in your head.
switch to a pencil and paper,
then nip back to your hotel
for a pocket calculator.
Ah! Good news!
Less than £2 for a pair of espadrilles!

You rush back to the shop.
They're out of your size.

*

ROOTS
Don't forget your roots.
On holiday, always remember
what the time is
in the UK.
So that when your family is relaxing over lunch
You can glance at your watch and say,
'At home, *Birds of a Feather* would be just starting.'

*

A GRASP OF THE LANGUAGE
Never let a foreign menu show you up.
Point with a self-confident smile
at the seventh dish down.
And sit back, ready to enjoy your
Fritters of Raw Squid and Whole Chillies in a Jellyfish Puree.

*

AWAY FROM IT ALL
A little village in the Dordogne.
The office seems a million miles away.
But who's that waving hard at you across the street?
Why, if it isn't
Frank from the Fifth Floor
And
Maureen from Accounts.

*

LE MOT JUSTE
Never mind that the ticket-seller
the hotel receptionist, the courier, the shopkeeper
and the air stewardess
all speak fluent English.

This Is Craig Brown

They will be delighted to linger while
you flick through your selection of phrasebooks
in search of
Le Mot Juste.

*

LIFE IS A CAROUSEL
When picking up luggage
from the airport carousel
remember to
grab the handle of your heaviest bag
as it whirls round, sending others flying
as you struggle
to keep up with it.

*

A SOUVENIR
A hand-crafted porcelain model
of a peasant woman in brightly coloured
traditional dress
performing a customary pirouette
will lend colour
to even the most sober mantelpiece.

*

MEMORIES
'Terry up to his tricks on a donkey!
Our room, seven down and three along!
Jemima with a pigeon in the background!
The sun setting over the taverna!
That's the lovable José, just out of shot!
The nice couple from Bristol we met in the second week!
Whoops! Geoffrey takes a tumble!'
With over 350 slides still to go,
the neighbours already show signs of getting to grips
with your recent holiday.

Bel Littlejohn: Sorry!

Remember, remember, the 5th of November. Or so the old saying goes. How could I forget? How could I bloody forget?

Last year, I was trying to grill a polenta and salsa sausage on the fire in our garden when I singed the tip of the middle finger on my left hand. I tried to be strong, if only for the kids' sake.

'Okay! That's it!' I said to them, fighting back the tears, hoping against hope that my face wasn't betraying my panic. 'Someone please put that fire out! Everybody inside! Now! I'm sorry, but no more Guy Fawkes ever again! I'm sorry, but I am not, I repeat *not*, going to live with an annual fire hazard!'

(Incidentally, I'm a great believer in that little word 'sorry'. It means so much to people. Just as an experiment, I counted up the times I employed it yesterday. The final total was five: 'Sorry, Sue, but that sniffing has got to stop', 'Sorry, but my decaff still hasn't arrived', 'I'm sorry, Sue, but no, you must provide your own Kleenex', 'Sor-reeee! My mistake! I should have known you weren't to be trusted, Jim!', 'Look, I'm really sorry, Sue but I'm going to have to ask you to do that in the toilet').

But back to fireworks. Sorry about that! (There I go again!) In common with most of my friends I placed a blanket ban on fireworks in 1986, after everything had gone so wrong at Chernobyl. For the next twelve years, we successfully

26

improvised our own form of safety-first fireworks – just as much fun, and a lot less expensive – using brightly coloured paper and going 'whoosh!' through our teeth.

But stupidly, I bowed to the forces of conservatism and let my kids revive the bonfire tradition. But never again – not after that truly terrifying incident with the singed fingernail, to say nothing of the ruined polenta and salsa sausage. A friend suggested indoor fireworks for this year. Some friend! I pointed out that, quite apart from the potential fire hazard, indoor fireworks such as 'Puffing Billy', in which a cardboard clown appears to be smoking, are a disgraceful attempt to entrap juveniles into the global cigarette culture. Speaking personally, I've made all my office, car and home environments all smoke-free zones, and, sorry, but I have no intention of letting Puffing Billy flout the rules.

So this year, we are going to celebrate Guy Fawkes night indoors, without any form of fire hazard. Instead, we're going to have a stove-based fondue, during which I'm going to read a selection of my new poems on the theme of Night and Fire, with time for questions and discussion afterwards. Actually, both kids say sorry (!), they might not be able to make it this year, thank you very much, but my lovely friend and colleague Sue has promised to drop round, if she feels up to it.

But will she be bicycling? I was deeply saddened when Sue admitted she doesn't wear a safety helmet. I told her she was dicing with death, that it was as crazy not to wear a safety helmet out cycling as it would be to make repeated calls from a mobile phone, now we know the all-pervading cancer risk.

We were in the wine bar round the corner at the time. 'Can I get you another, Bel?' asked Sue, stretching over for my empty glass.

'Sit yourself down, Sue, love,' I said, in my gentlest voice. I then looked her straight in the eye and had it out with her. 'Sue, love,' I said, 'how many units are you drinking each week?'

Frankly, her reply knocked me backwards. 'Two or three glasses of wine a day,' she admitted.

I was shattered. 'Have you considered seeking advice, Sue,

love?' I said. 'I think it might be time for you to confront your problem. Let's fact it, Sue – we both know that two or three glasses a day constitutes a *serious condition*. Don't you listen to You and Yours, Sue?'

Perhaps it's got something to do with living in the shadow of the millennium, but one helluva lot of my friends seem to be flouting the health and safety recommendations laid down by experts. For instance, at our local indoor tennis courts I am the only one who bothers to wear a helmet, and I've noticed that a number of people still reach blindly for the butter, regardless of cholesterol. Wrestling, boxing and horse-riding are still permitted by Tony, but I can't believe it will be long before he comes to his senses. Let's hope history remembers the next hundred years as the Century of Safety First – and let's pave the way by banning sparklers. Sorry!

The Society of Pedants

After I mentioned the Society of Pedants, Mr Little from Bristol wrote in pointing out a grave error. 'We could never call ourselves the Society *of* Pedants,' he wrote. He went on to explain that they – or, rather, *it* – were – or rather *was* – originally known as the Society *for* Pedants, 'since the society of pedants is what we enjoy while at a meeting and the society for pedants is the group we would wish to join'.

But over the years, he went on, the Society came to believe that few prospective members were truly pedants, since they did not make a living from their pedantry. 'We therefore decided to rename ourselves, after a secret ballot, the Society for the Promotion of Pedantry,' he concluded. 'I hope this clears up the confusion.'

Alas, I must inform Mr Little that in pedantic circles things move quick, or quickly. Three days ago, I attended the weekly Woden's Day meeting of the Society. Members were due to debate whether its title should be changed from 'the Society for the Promotion of Pedantry' to '*The* Society for the Promotion of Pedantry'.

Before the main debate could begin, the Chairman – or Chair – informed us that there were a number of outstanding matters to clear up, before being overruled by a majority of members who said that, on the contrary, there was a number of outstanding matters to clear up. 'Next week's cinema outing is to *The Golden Bowl*, the adaptation of Henry James's famous novel,' he said. 'This will be followed by a short meeting in which you will be able to vote for a motion declaring it not as good as the original, followed by an opportunity to list its key mistakes and anachronisms.'

'On a point of order, Mr Chairman.' A tall woman at the back had raised her hand. 'On a point of order, should that be not Henry James's famous novel but Henry *James'* famous novel?'

'Strictly speaking, that's not a point of order,' replied the Chairman. 'It's a point of information.'

'In this day and age,' began a man in a beige cardigan. At the sound of this explosive phrase everyone perked up. 'In this day and age, I wonder if one is able to strictly call *The Golden Bowl* a *famous* novel at all?'

A cry of horror erupted in the hall. 'I must ask the gentleman in the beige cardigan to leave the hall,' said the Chairman. 'We cannot sanction a split infinitive.'

'I refute your suggestion that this is a cardigan,' retorted the offending gentleman. 'A cardigan buttons, or, if you will, unbuttons, to the waist. This garment buttons only a quarter of the way down, to just above the chest. So it is not a cardigan in the strict sense of the word but a jersey, even though that aforementioned island is not, strictly speaking, its country of origin.'

There followed a heated discussion over the speaker's use of the word *refute*: some thought he meant *deny*, while others believed he would have been better off employing – or at least using – *confute*.

'On a point of information, Chairman.' The speaker was a woman with a bun in her hair, by which I mean not a woman with a small, sweetened, bread roll or cake (often with dried fruit) in her hair but a woman whose hair was drawn into a tight coil at the back of her head. 'On a point of information, I must point out that in the original novel *Frankenstein* was not, as is commonly supposed, the monster, but rather the inventor of that monster.'

A murmur of approval swept – metaphorically – around the

room. We pedants always appreciate being reminded of the F-point, even if it hasn't been raised. 'May I also add,' continued the woman with the bun, 'that, contrary to popular mis-conception, King Canute was only too well aware that he could not hold back the tide.'

'Your statement did not require that superfluous *"also,"*' interjected the Chairman, 'for it means "in addition": if you say "May I also add" you are, in effect, saying *"May* I add add". I'm not sure that this was what you meant to infer.'

'Imply! Imply! Imply!' the entire hall – or, at least, all those contained within it – chanted at the Chairman. He left in tears, knowing as well as anyone that the incorrect use of the world 'infer' has always been a resigning matter.

After three hours fifty-nine minutes twenty-three and a half seconds had passed, the time came to debate the central motion, That the Name of This Society Should Be Changed from the Society for the Promotion of Pedantry to The Society for the Promotion of Pedantry.

'But what exactly do we mean when we say that someone is a pedant? Are we saying, in effect, that he – or she – is a pedal-operated pleasure boat?' asked a Scotch man, that is, a man who worked for Teacher's.

'No. That is a *pedalo*,' replied the Treasurer. 'Of course, it is possible that a pedalo might be operated by a pedant, and if it was then to be defined solely by its movements it could claim – probably through a lawyer, since pedalos are unable to speak – that, in this specific instance, a pedalo would also, to some extent, be a pedant. Or one might imagine a pedalo in a children's story – say *Peter the Pedalo* – in which the author had contrived to give him – or her – a pedantic character but —'

There followed a lengthy debate over whether or not imaginary inanimate objects could be classified as pedants, and, if so, whether they should be admitted to the Society, or The Society. The proceedings went on for ever. Well, not literally *for ever* . . .

A Holiday Primer

I am a traveller
You are a sightseer
He is a tourist.

We accompanied our children around the splendid sixteenth-century cathedral
You took your children around the splendid sixteenth-century cathedral
They dragged their children around the splendid sixteenth-century cathedral.

Our mountains towered majestically
Your mountains blocked out the sun
Their mountains were a positive death trap.

My hat is charming
Your hat is amusing
What does he think he looks like?

I am able to enjoy myself
You are very game
He isn't afraid to make a fool of himself.

My soup is chilled
Your soup is stone cold
His soup hasn't been heated up.

32

This Is Craig Brown

Our children enjoyed *pommes frites*
Your children ate french fries
Their children stuffed themselves with chips.

Our sea was great fun
Your sea was fine for the experienced swimmer
Six tourists died in their sea last summer.

I keep in touch with the office
You are a workaholic
He is a show-off.

We have a guide
You have a tour-leader
They have a courier.

Our hotel is full of facilities
Your hotel is a bit modern
Their hotel should be completed by next year.

I have a villa
You have a house
He has a maisonette.

I am a mountaineer
You are a climber
He is a rambler.

We are greeted by the head waiter
You are recognised by the head waiter
They are watched by the head waiter.

Our children are in high spirits
Your children are letting off steam
Their children are an utter nuisance.

Leisure Time

I cut a dash
You are unmistakably English
They stick out a mile.

We met some marvellous local characters
You were buttonholed by street-traders
They never managed to shake off the beggars.

Our garden was sheltered
Your garden was shady
Their garden was in the basement.

I am fluent
You get by
He is a show-off.

Mine is a rural hideway
Yours is a rundown barn
His loo doesn't flush.

I get what I want
You kick up a fuss
He throws his weight around.

I caught the sun
You forgot the sunblock
He's gone bright red.

Our restaurant was five star
Your restaurant was overpriced
Their restaurant was pretentious.

We concentrate on our food
You enjoy the silence
Their marriage is on the rocks.

We bargain for *objets d'art*
You buy bric-a-brac
They purchase souvenirs.

I barter
You haggle
He argues.

I can still fit into these old trunks
You are holding in your stomach
He should wear a shirt.

We find it pays to buy a case or two of fine wine
You fill your boot with booze
They are alcoholics.

Our village is within easy reach of the motorway
Your village is just off the motorway
Their village in on lane three.

We relish the local seafood
You get by without meat and veg
They never want to see another squid in their lives.

We don't stick to a rigid schedule
You refuse to make plans
They end up with some nasty bites and gyppy tummy.

I am keen
You are competitive
He just has to win.

We took it slowly
You managed to get there eventually
He mistook the N120 for the E348 and ended up stuck on the
M2736 interchange for three hours.

A Century of Progress

Let's celebrate the very real progress we have made in the course of my lifetime.

For instance, it's hard to believe it now, but I remember a time when on arrival in a hotel one was presented with what looked like a credit card. This, it was explained, would enable you to open your bedroom door, all one had to do was insert it in the slot, wait for a red light, insert it again, wait for another red light, attempt to open the door anyway, find it still locked, insert the card again, wait for another red light, try banging on the door, worry that this was not your room but someone else's, insert the card again, this time very slowly, wait for another red light, return to the reception area, be issued with another card, and begin the whole process all over again.

Clearly, this was one area of everyday life which was crying out for technological innovation. At last the breakthrough came in the shape of the 'hotel bedroom key', brilliantly designed to be inserted into a 'keyhole'. With one easy twist of the wrist, the door would be opened and the room would be yours. Before long, all leading hotels in the country had converted to this cutting-edge technology.

Other technological advances over the past few decades have been every bit as welcome, changing the fabric of our lives on a variety of levels. Youngsters today can hardly believe their ears when one tries to convince them there was a time, not all that long ago, when simply to do one's shopping one was obliged to get into a car and drive miles to a vast sort of warehouse known as a 'supermarket'. There hundreds or even thousands of other people would be sullenly pushing their trolleys up and down aisles and picking machine-packaged goods off the shelves, with no assistance whatsoever. And these youngsters also find it hard to believe that these 'supermarkets' were owned by just four or five conglomerates!

Needless to say, change simply had to come: the British people are notoriously independent and are not prepared to be bossed around in this way. Before long a bright spark came up with the idea of the 'small corner shop', a more modest, independent unit, conveniently situated on or near the high street, in which help from the proprietor would be mixed with friendly chat. Hey presto! Overnight, shopping became an enjoyable experience, and people wondered how they ever got along without the modern convenience of the corner shop.

And there have been major advances in the area of clothing since I was a lad. Take footwear, for instance: I remember the days when adults and children alike were forced to clump around in vast, luridly coloured wodges known as 'trainers', often as high as they were wide and as wide as they were clumsy, desperately ugly and giving the wearer the uncomfortable feeling of walking around on a sea of dead jellyfish. Looking at old photographs of us all wearing them, it's hard to believe that we could have stood it for so long – but of course in those days we knew no better. Children today are the beneficiaries of great design strides in the footwear industry: the 'gym shoe' that followed on from the unwieldy 'trainer' remains a miracle of simplicity, and ideal for sporting activity, while the equally lean and practical 'walking shoe' freed a new generation to walk around in style and comfort.

Perhaps the greatest area of technological innovation in my lifetime lies in the field of writing and research. I remember when I was starting out just how difficult it was for one person to find out anything and write it down. The writing alone required an extraordinarily complicated and unwieldy piece of machinery known as a 'word-processor', complete with all types of accessories such as 'printers' 'disks' and so forth. The instruction manuals alone would often go on for literally hundreds of pages. Small wonder that when the two instruments we now know as the 'pencil' and 'paper' were invented, they took off in such a big way. Inexpensive, user-friendly and splendidly portable, the pencil was set to take the world by storm. After early jitters with the basic technology – it was a short while before the 'pencil sharpener' was invented – the pencil soon ousted the cumbersome 'word processor' from its position of dominance, though one or two examples of the machine may still be seen in the Victoria and Albert Museum.

Similarly, it is worth remembering that before the advent of the book, Western civilisation was heavily reliant on the old 'Internet'. This meant that if ever one wanted to look up a simple piece of information – the number of rings around Saturn, for instance, or the fourth wife of King Henry VIII – one was forced to type all sorts of dots and coms and UKs and www's into a special machine before ploughing through various 'sites', the majority run by sub-literates with interests confined largely to pornography and conspiracies, before alighting on an answer. But the book released us from all that: within seconds, one could simply pick up an encyclopaedia, look up 'S' for Saturn or 'H' for Henry VIII and – Bob's your uncle! – the answer would miraculously appear before your very eyes.

In retrospect, it's hard to know how we managed to find any free time at all in days gone by. In the years before the advent of the test card, if you chanced to turn on a television in the morning or afternoon you would be greeted by a studio full of disgruntled men and women explaining their presence in the studio on childhood traumas of one sort or another. This would invariably be followed by an excitable man with a beard talking a nervy woman though the best method of cooking a vegetarian lasagne. They were bleak years indeed. But then someone high up in television hit upon the brilliant idea of putting on nothing but a test card throughout the daytime, allowing viewers to bypass other people's childhood traumas and vegetarian lasagnes.

Entertainment beyond the home has also improved by leaps and bounds. It wasn't so many moons ago that those who wished to watch pop stars were obliged to go to 'rock festivals' in order to sit outside in the mud in the pouring rain in the hope of catching a glimpse through finely tuned binoculars of a band onstage a quarter of a mile away. But then someone came up with the bright idea of offering pop fans comfortable seats in warm theatres with good views of the performers, and that was the last we ever ever heard of Glastonbury or Reading.

We should never allow ourselves to forget quite how primitive things really were in the old days. Technology still had miles to go. For instance, windows in trains could not be opened, so that passengers sat in zombie-like states of airlessness throughout their journeys. Car windows, too, were haphazard, for they were then at the mercy of complicated Heath Robinson electrical systems that worked only every now and then. But then some bright spark came along and invented a handle for opening car windows, and driving became a pleasure.

And how many young people are aware of what happened before the arrival of the moving bicycle? We are now so used to cycling from A to B that it is hard to imagine the time when bicycles – then known as 'exercise bikes' – were fixed to the ground, often in windowless cells known as 'health clubs'. Today, we take for granted our ability to bicycle through town and country, seeing all the sights and taking in the fresh air. But our ancestors were forced to bicycle on the spot, going nowhere, surrounded only by other sweaty bodies. Imagine the worldwide joy at the invention of a bicycle that could actually be pedalled from place to place!

Other sporting breakthroughs followed: for centuries, even the most energetic oarsmen had never managed to get a boat to move across a gymnasium floor – but overnight they discovered that if the boat was placed on a stretch of water, it could be rowed through pretty countryside for literally miles and miles. And walkers, too, found that they could travel to places beyond the fast-moving rubberised strip of pavement next to the coffee machine. Soon they were walking over hill and dale, free to go wherever they pleased.

Many youngsters find it hard to credit that, not all that long ago, we were once forced to stand in enclosed boxes, jam-packed with strangers, just to travel from one storey to the next. But then the invention of the staircase revolutionised every-thing: suddenly, we were able to go up or down floors when we wanted, and at our own pace, with no need to be crammed into moving cupboards, which would invariably go down when you wanted them to go up and up when you wanted them to go down.

Things have also changed for the better in the workplace. In retrospect it seems crazy, but in the old days if one telephoned someone who worked in an office – perhaps with an enquiry about a service on offer, or to book a ticket for a show – one would be answered by a machine. The machine would then tell you to press a selection of buttons, any combination of which would transfer you to another machine, which would then ask you to wait in a queue while forcing you to listen to a medley of Andrew Lloyd-Webber tunes.

Finally, the machine would transfer you to something called 'Voicemail' which was a sort of electronic wastepaper-basket. Three cheers, then, for the person who invented the answerable telephone. Like so many brilliant inventions, this one was stunning in its simplicity: a telephone which could ring in an office and be answered by a human being. Inevitably, there was the odd Luddite who argued that we could not just sit back and watch poor Lloyd-Webber starve, but the wind of progress prevailed.

Other great discoveries of the twentieth century were almost as simple. Take eating, for instance. It seems strange now, but when ordinary middle-class people felt hungry they used to be obliged to assemble between certain hours at noisy communal depots known as 'restaurants'. There they would be forced to pay three or four times the cost of the food in order to sit hugger-mugger with total strangers. Things might have gone on like this for ever, but one day, like a flash of lightning, someone was struck by the thought that it might just be possible *to cook at home*. The experiment worked, and within a matter of years people were enjoying whatever they wanted, whenever they wanted, by themselves, in the comfort of their own homes, for a fraction of the previous cost.

But the technological strides of the twentieth century have not only been towards greater convenience; the arts, too, have benefited from the tremendous wealth of inventions. Long ago, artists were restricted to working with banal, everyday objects such as dead sheep or beds or bricks. These objects left no room for empathy, beauty or imagination: the more skilled artist might bisect the sheep, or untuck the bed, or place one brick on top of another, but there was little he or she could do to make any real impact.

All these cold, dull, hand-me-down *objets trouvés*, were revolutionised with the invention of 'paint' on 'canvas': suddenly, the artist was able to make an imaginative and intellectual leap, and to convey, through brushstrokes, an emotional response to the world around him. The Tate Gallery, for so long a sort of antique warehouse for the last gasps of traditional art – old fridges, upside-down pianos, stuffed sharks, etc – overnight became a buzzing treasure trove of this new and challenging art form. Sadly, the varied subtleties of these new-fangled 'paintings' proved too shocking for those brought up on old-fashioned 'conceptual' art. Some of them would stand in a state of shock in front of a canvas by an artist such as Turner, shaking their heads and muttering, 'But that's not art – the ship isn't *real*.'

Atchoo

Rarely in my – *aaa* – life have I – *aaaaa* – heard quite so – *aaaAAATT* – many people – *CHOOOO!!!* – sneezing. Add to – *akakakakak!* – this a disproportionate number of – *waurgwaurgwaurg!* – coughers of all melodies and – *mkmkmkmk-BLARG!* – volumes and I think we can safely say that we are experiencing one of the – *BLARGATCHOOMKMKMKM-KAKAKAKBLAAATCHOO!* – noisiest winters since records began.

Were I the government health officer charged with gauging the cough-factor every December, I would make a beeline for school nativity plays. These are the coughers' open day, the throat-clearers' jamboree, the annual get-together for everyone suffering from anything from a bit-of-a-tickle through I-can't-seem-to-shake-it-off all the way to – *BLAGAGAGABL-WAAAAWRGH!* – full-blown consumption.

Before the curtains go up, there is coughing galore, accompanied by a descant of sneezes. A smattering of the more uncouth parents even make that nasally noise like a lorry reversing – *gggrrrrggggrrrrgggg* – leaving nothing phlegmy to the imagination. But one comforts oneself by assuming that they are all busily getting it out of the way in time for hush at the appearance of the first shepherd.

And for a minute or two, there is indeed a fair measure of quiet, as the shepherds and sundry livestock file onstage and the parents cast aside their ailments in favour of the greater anxiety of identifying which of the sheep, if any, is theirs. But then the woman just in front of you closes her eyes and throws back her head. At this most touching of moments, she is planning to sneeze! All eyes swing away from the angel and towards the woman – but then she tactfully pinches her nose with her thumb and forefinger and performs a couple of those internalised sneezes – *ggnnff! ggnnff!* – which for some reason I find even more irritating than the more showy full-blasters. There is something sneaky and covert about them, something all too reminiscent of those underground nuclear tests to which the French are so drawn.

This first internalised sneeze acts as a starting pistol. After a few seconds comes the unmistakable crickle and crackle of sticky papers being wrenched any-old-how off sucky-sweets. To your right, a man's head blows up like a balloon as he tries to suppress a tickle. Suddenly, in the far corner of the school hall, a father leaps to his feet and exits through the swing door, discreetly deciding to perform his coughing fit out of hearing of the audience. Sadly, the swing doors seem to have been fitted with loudspeakers, and his medley of hacks, splutters, whoops and wheezes – *akakapwarwhooo-eeeargargarg!* – causes necks to crane away from the sheep, shepherds, angels, etc, towards the little square glass windows on the swing doors, as everyone strains to catch a glimpse of the phantom cougher.

Now there is no holding back. Anyone who has been gestating a cough through the day now gives birth to it. Six and a half minutes into the Nativity, and we are overtaken by a cacophony, or cacoph-coph-coph-ophony. All the carols – 'Oh Cough All Ye Faithful', 'Loud Night', 'Bark the Herald Angel' – take on new lives of their own.

Sir Ralph Richardson once said that acting is the art of keeping a large group of people from coughing. This suggests we all have a certain amount of control over exactly when we cough. This is borne out by those little gaps between pieces in classical concerts which are generally filled with an immediate chorus of throat-clearing, so much so that a Martian landing in a packed concert hall might imagine that the people onstage had come to watch the massed choirs in the auditorium as they barked like border terriers. So widespread is this in-concert coughing that the Royal Festival Hall now includes in its programme notes advice to patrons to stifle the noise of their coughs with handkerchiefs, and/or to buy cough lozenges from the kiosk in the foyer. Perhaps in future years they might consider having a special All-Coughers Day, on the lines of the Last Night of the Proms, with everyone – audience, orchestra, conductor – coughing along together.

In all my years of watching television, I have never seen anyone sneeze or cough onscreen, other than in an ironic ahem-ahem sort of way. This suggests we do indeed have mastery over our sneezing and coughing. Harold Pinter seemed to side with this view when he complained recently that British audiences cough maliciously in his plays; or perhaps they are so attuned to coughing in the pauses of classical concerts that, like Pavlov's dogs, when confronted with a Pinter pause, they are unable to resist.

My tolerance for coughs is confined exclusively to my own. Throughout November virtually everyone I knew was coughing except for me. Though coughers tend to look beadily around them, their bulging eyes on the lookout for sympathy, I look back in irritation, sure that they are just seeking attention and that there is nothing that a little bit of self-control couldn't put right. But a fortnight ago, I too began to cough. Suddenly, I was brimful of sympathy for myself, but it was mixed with a strange form of pride, for I found myself growing annoyed if anyone else's cough sounded even marginally worse than my own. I now take my cough with me everywhere, so that everyone can appreciate it.

'Dry or throaty?' said the lady in the chemist's when I asked for cough mixture. I felt that this division was far too simplistic for something as varied and glorious, and that to ask 'Dry or throaty?' of my cough was like asking 'Light or heavy?' of a Beethoven symphony. More than any other ailment, a cough becomes a companion, sometimes quiet, sometimes noisy, but always with a life of its own. It is like living with a Mr Hyde version of yourself, an alter ego that is liable to bark indecipherable abuse at the drop of a hat. I suspect this is why some people are so sheepish when it comes to coughing, clamping their mouths shut and letting their faces go bright red – anything to keep the madman under lock and key.

In the deep mid-winter, long, long aaaaa-tchoo! The sound of the season is here, with its unique conjugation: I have flu, you have a cold, he has a slight sniffle; we are laid low, you are taking it easy, they are skiving. And where to go to enjoy our coughs and our colds? At this time of year, there's really nothing quite like a pantomime.

Wallace Arnold Takes a Trip

I note a sinking feeling in the old tum that it is fifty years to the day since a bespectacled boffin clad in white overalls invented LSD, as it has come to be known. Might I make a confession? Back in the sixties, while still a young man making my way in literary London, I found myself partaking in this least reliable of substances.

For hour upon hour, sprawled upon a leather armchair, not knowing whether I was coming or going, I witnessed the strange, unearthly apparitions of thespians, politicians and authors barking at me from every corner of the room, some on the floor, some on the ceiling, but all talking in high-pitched screeches of their successes and achievements, their weird, strangely distorted faces framed by psychedelic ties bursting with every hue under the sun. Nothing new there, of course, for this was the Garrick Club on a regular Thursday evening. But what, I found myself wondering, would the same thing look like under the influence of drugs?

Something within me yearned at that moment to escape from the narrow confines of the Garrick into another world, a world beyond anecdote and opinion. My old friend and dousing partner Aldy Huxley claimed to have discovered – and I quoth – 'eternity in a flower, infinity in four chair legs and the Absolute in the folds of a pair of flannel trousers'. I found myself longing to share his vision, for up until then the only thing I had ever managed to discover in the folds of a pair of flannel trousers was a piece of half-sucked barley sugar, discarded in error.

I then remembered that during a pre-prandial stroll, I had been approached by a hairy creature – male or female, I know not! – who had urged me to 'tune in, turn on and drop out' before handing me a most mysterious dot. Might this be my route to Huxley's Absolute? Against my better judgement, I decided to swallow it, right there in the Garrick Club.

Here is a small selection of the notes I scribbled haphazardly over the next five and half hours:

6.15pm: I – Wallace Arnold! – feel myself transported into a realm beyond my wildest imaginings! I look at my trusty pipe and it has turned into two trusty pipes, both puffing most smoothly. I think I have discovered the Absolute!

7.25pm: I – Wellbred Armhole! – find myself floating, floating, floating! I have now landed in the vegetable selection on the central table of the Garrick dining room! To my surprise, my body has transformed itself into a Brussels sprout! . . . Oh, no! I have just been speared with a fork by my old friend and quaffing partner Kingsley Amis, who is in the midst of a pricelessly waspish anecdote about a very dear old friend! . . . Agh! He is swallowing me! . . . Oh no! I find myself sitting in his stomach, unable to hear the punchline of his waspish anecdote! This must be what they mean by a 'Bad Trip' . . .

9.30pm: Who am I? Wishful Ankle, Intergalactic Chameleon! I look down at my feet, but they are no longer my feet, they are stretchy pieces of elastic, and my hands – my hands – they are thin and silky and all pink with mint stripes! I realise I have become a Garrick bow-tie, stretched around the neck of my old quaffing partner Robin Day! And he always claimed that he wore *real* bow-ties, not ready-mades! *The horror!* While regaling the assembled company with an anecdote about his legendary encounter with Ted Short, Robin has let a spot of gravy dribble down his neck and on to me! I am STAINED! STAINED! STAINED!

10.55pm: At last, I am 'coming down'. I struggle to adjust myself to the normal world. Thank goodness no one suspects I have been "high". I am now behaving quite normally. The Duke of Edinburgh – estimable fellow – enters the room and looks around. I want to reassure him that all is well with his favourite broadcaster so I approach him, man to man. 'My name,' I said. 'My name is Waxy Angel. I am a beautiful strange tulip, sent from heaven to make you happy. Smell me!' The Duke turns around on his heels and leaves the room without a word. I feel sure he didn't suspect a thing . . .

Dread words. Indeed. Never again, never again. From now on, I stick to the port, the brandy and the large gins. At least you know where you are with them, or my names not, or my name's not . . . MEMO TO SELF: INSERT NAME IN MORNING.

120 Years To Go

Even before I saw the front-page photograph of Lily, Daffodil, Crocus, Forsythia and Rose, I always found groups of cows a little creepy. Even without cloning, they all do the same thing at the same time, shuffling around and staring back at one in a weirdly choreographed manner, like a slovenly end-of-the-pier dancing troupe, the Black and White Minstrels gone to seed.

With their big eyes and vast foreheads, cows also have a knack of making you think they know something you don't know. As they chew away with such showy nonchalance, they give the impression of meditating on the larger issues of existence, issues lost to fly-by-night human beings in the hurly-burly of everyday life.

Posing for their group photograph, Lily, Daffodil, Crocus, Forsythia and Rose looked strangely unrelated. There was none of the ain't-life-grand leaping in the air one has come to expect from beauty queens or pop groups, none of the man-of-the-world, well-pressed-suit look of heads of state at summit meetings. Should these cows not have been over the moon at the prospect of a bonus 50 per cent more years to live? Or was the thought of so much extra life weighing heavily on their minds?

Another ten years of eating nothing but unwashed grass; another ten years of trudging around in mud; another ten years of incessant queuing for the indignity of having one's udders pummelled; another ten years of trying to outstare human beings as they skitter nervously away.

The Great and The Good

It is, I think, an idea that should also give the rest of us something to chew on. If the results of the cow-cloning could be transferred to humans and the ageing process in our cells were also to be reversed, then we could live for anything up to 200 years. At first sight, this might hold some appeal. It would certainly give us plenty of time to brush up on our Italian, and with an extra 120 years or so we could definitely get to the end of *Midnight's Children*. We would probably get round to visiting quite a number of countries that now seem only *quite* interesting – New Zealand, say, or Luxembourg – and in well under a century we're bound to be able to change the plug on that old lamp in the spare room.

An extra 120 years should easily prove long enough to make amends with that great-aunt you have neglected for far too long: you could even pencil in a nice lunch in eighty-two years time, and if, when the time came, something more interesting had come up, you could have a bit of a re-jig and move it on another fifteen or twenty years.

All well and good, but it doesn't take long before, like Lily and Daffodil and co, one begins to entertain second thoughts. Family Christmases, for instance, can be a sufficient burden without a hundred years worth of extra relatives to worry about. Christmas at Balmoral would be particularly trying. With the process of rejuvenation already in full swing, Queen Victoria would still be going strong with a full nineteen years to go before her 200th birthday and King Edward VII, George V, the Duke of Windsor and King George VI would all still be milling around, kicking their heels. With all their attendant spouses there wouldn't be much room for anyone else, so that our own Queen and her family, very much the youngsters, would have to make do on put-you-ups.

Similarly over-extended get-togethers would be echoed throughout the land. Present-buying, never easy, would be virtually impossible (did I buy great-great-great-great-great-uncle Charles a cardigan last year, or am I confusing him with great-great-great-great uncle James?) and the possibilities for family arguments would be so many and various that they would be erupting in every corner of every room at every minute.

Scientists say that, all things being equal, women will be giving birth at the age of eighty. Presumably this means that most people will not take the plunge into marriage until their seventieth birthday beckons, and the average age for a first divorce will be ninety or so. Stages of life will no doubt be prolonged to fill the allotted time. Twelve-year-olds will still be wearing nappies, sixteen-years-olds will be toddlers, and adolescence will start in the mid-twenties and go on until the mid-forties.

Middle age will last roughly a hundred years and a mid-life crisis will descend on men like a thunderbolt as they reach their hundredth birthdays; for the next ten or fifteen years these centenarians will be squeezing into jeans, wearing leather jackets and trying to chat up pert young eighty-five-year-olds. Eventually, they will learn to come to terms with their mortality, and before long they will be signing up for relaxing Saga holidays for the over-150s.

'You are born into an empty field and you die in a dense forest' goes an old Russian saying. It is hard to imagine quite how dense that forest will have become after 200 years. Think of the accumulation of library books unreturned (all biographies will be twice as long), of letters unanswered, fines unpaid, friends unphoned, cupboards unsorted, rubbish unbinned, chores untackled, resolutions forgotten and promises broken. To put it all in perspective: anyone hiring a video in, say, the early months of the year 2010 and forgetting to take it back until late October 2130 will be liable for a fine of anything up to £89,000 – *and it may not even have been worth watching in the first place.*

It is often said of people who grin a lot and talk loudly that they are 'in love with life'. But can even the most passionate love affair hope to survive 200 years? So much of life's interest comes from novelty. There are new faces in the newspaper, new places to visit, new things to buy. It may be hard to face a world in which, for instance, Edward Heath would be looking forward to another eighty-odd years in active politics, and David and Victoria Beckham would shortly be unveiling their seventy-seventh complete change of image; a world in which we are thinking of taking our nineteenth holiday in Hobart, Tasmania, or in which, on our 142nd birthday, we are presented with our twenty-second juice extractor, and we are still expected to look delighted and say thank you. I rather think that, by the time our three score years and ten and ten and ten and ten and ten and ten and ten and ten and ten and ten and ten and ten and ten are over, we may all look as shattered as Lily and her chums.

Mega Summer Reading
With Jackie Collins

The dressed-to-kill guy walked into the five-star-rated top LA go-to-be-seen restaurant Giovanni's, a fabulously expensive Gucci shoulder bag draped over his shoulder. All eyes swivelled as he entered.

He had the buttocks of Mick Jagger and the nose of Warren Beatty. The jawbone of Michael Douglas, the pecs of Sylvester Stallone. And the crotch of Bruce Willis.

And they were all packed into his Gucci shoulder bag.

His name was Sam Sadisto. Hollywood's latest secret sado-serial killer.

A ruthless, mass-murdering kinda guy.

The kinda guy who butchered top mega-stars. Just for kicks.

And the kinda media moghul who wholly owned top international media corporation MegaMovies.

The kinda guy who knew he could get away.

With murder.

Over the other corner of Giovanni's sat petite, huge-breasted, gypsy-haired, mega-buck Hollywood superstar Andrina Glitzz, who looked like Madonna with a touch of J-Lo, mixed with quite a bit of Jane Russell and Rita Hayworth when they were still alive and topped off with Sharon Stone. *Jeez, was that babe hot.*

'Shit shit shit shit shit shit shit!!!!!' sobbed Andrina. Giovanni had forgotten to place her customary three pinches of salt on her single lettuce leaf – and there was nothing she could do about it.

Her companion, thrice-married Hollywood dark-haired fading mega-hunk, Jake Bronze, felt his gorgeous chest hairs rise up and wave, like a warm blue Carribean ocean composed largely of hair and painted brown.

His career on the skids since his last movie bombed, his chest hairs acted as so many finely turned antennae to the emotions of other people. At that moment he sensed something was wrong with Andrina.

'Whassup?' he intoned, thrusting his five-fingered hand below the VIP corner table and letting it shoot up her lip-pink Armani micro-skirt with gold detailing. Andrina moaned. She felt powerless to push him away. She was hot as Santa Monica in August. To hell with lettuce. *Oh God*, she moaned, *this is amazing*.

Jake Bronze had the longest tongue in the whole goddamn business. Still sitting at the table, he released it from his over-size mouth.

It snaked feverishly down his chest, turning outwards past the expensively laundered crisp white tablecloth, straight along the length of the bottom of the solid teak table, and up Andrina's perfectly chiselled inner thighs before coming to rest on her red-hot diamond-studded $25,000 black lace thong.

Jeez! she gasped. Her phenomenal nipples sprang to attention like the magnificent guards in their busby hats she had seen only last summer outside Buckingham Palace, London, England, the priceless piece of highly desirable real estate owned by world-famous ruthless property tycoon Queen Elizabeth Two.

Over the other corner of the restaurant sat gorgeous, natural, body-to-die-for Maribella Slinkkke. Ever since her mom died in the act of saving her from the path of an oncoming train when Maribella was only three years of age she was through with being hurt.

Since that day, Maribella hated violence, just hated it. *Hated it*. She was through with being hurt. These days, she couldn't see a head being snapped off another human being by an oncoming train without flinching somewhere deep inside.

'Huh!' grunted John Travolta-lookalike top Hollywood director triple-Oscar winning Salvatore Franco. He had no need of words.

'Huh?' replied Maribella, quizzically. She was through with being hurt.

'Huh,' confirmed Franco, firmly.

'Huh,' agreed Maribella, good-naturedly.

'Huh!' exclaimed Franco, defiantly.

Huh, thought Maribella, thoughtfully, *I'm through with being hurt*. Yup. One thing was for sure.

She was through with being hurt.

Over the other corner of the restaurant, fading 39-year-old mega-star Pasta Vermicelli fingered her vastly expensive, expertly prepared sushimi with her long, aquiline toes.

Ever since top Hollywood surgeon bespectacled Jack Lemmon lookalike Dr Mike Decent had so expertly fixed those wrinkles around her fingers, she now had the beautiful smooth hands of a ten-month-old baby girl, even if it did mean she had to eat with her feet.

'You're sure I now look as good as it gets?' she had begged Dr Decent as he stripped off the plasters from her head, hands and chest.

She stared down at her naked body with mounting excitement.

She now had the gorgeous bosoms of Marilyn Monroe. One on either side of her own.

'Four breasts! It's *so* the very latest mega-fashion in cosmetic surgery!' Dr Decent assured her, warmly.

How can I thank him enough, thought Pasta, her eyes riveted to his huge crotch as it swayed gently in the breeze beneath the thin covering of his expensive Harrods of London pure cotton trousers.

Leisure Time

Now Pasta Vermicelli sat in Giovanni's, her cleavages proudly displayed over the top of her Versace all-in silken double-mesh body-stocking, waiting for the gorgeous, highly intelligent man who had made her young again, this mega-handsome but vastly intelligent phenomenally endowed yet brainy man who had gained a double first in sums at Harvard – without even trying.

Sam Sadisto cast a cold ruthless eye over the mega-glamorous Giovanni's A-list celebrity clientele.

With the other eye, he took a long, hard look at the machete he was hiding in his manly palm.

Who would be his next Hollywood mega-victim?

In the far corner, Andrina Glitzz was going down on mega-hunk Jake Bronze over a $72 plate of fresh linguini, specially flown in that day from Rome, Italy.

In the opposite corner, big-new-thing Salvatore Franco was smearing his main-course portion of finest beluga caviare over Maribella Slinkkke's thrusting ass, his tongue wrapped round her body, prolonging her orgasm and sending her past the point of no return, making her cry out – HUH! HUH! HUH! – for him to stop.

Yup. *She looked like a girl who was through with being hurt.*

In the remaining corner of the top restaurant, legendary sex symbol Pasta Vermicelli was pleasuring legendary surgeon Dr Mike Decent while his long fingers expertly renovated her left eyelid with a skill born of a lifetime's experience.

Evil tycoon Sam Sadisto thought long and hard. Who would be his next mega-victim?

One thing was for sure.

It'll take my legandarily mega-sad reader 532 pages to find out.

The Great
and the
Good

The Diary of HM Queen Elizabeth II

Sunday

A hectic week ahead. After church, Mr Lucien Freud, who is a painter, arrives to paint another portrait.

He is quite old.

When I ask if he likes corgies, he tells me he does.

Good, I say. I ask him if he has been painting long.

He tells me he has.

How interesting, I say.

He doesn't reply.

Otherwise precious little small talk. He tells me he paints pictures, mainly. A lovely hobby, I say.

I might have asked him if he wouldn't be awfully kind and paint over the crack on the bathroom ceiling, but I forgot. They tell me he can be desperately expensive, so I think we've got off lightly!

Freud is not a name you hear very often.

At lunchtime, I open a new day-care centre in Warrington. They kindly present me with a 'pizza'.

I thank them, and assure them that I will wear it when I get home, if I can make it stay on. A piece of pink ribbon might do the trick.

MONDAY

In the evening, Edward and his wife arrive. We all shake hands.

She has fair hair.

'Hello, mummy,' he says. 'We were just passing so we thought we'd just drop by to say hello.'

I say hello.

'Hello,' says his wife.

'You remember Sophie, of course,' says Edward.

'Of course,' I say, making her feel at home. 'Have you come far?'

She says she hasn't come all that far: they live quite near Windsor.

She starts stroking a corgi. 'That's Patch,' I say. 'He's a lovely lovely boy, aren't you, Patch? Yes, you are – you're a lovely, lovely, lovely boy! Who's a lovely boy, then?' Patch loves a little chat. I suppose we all do, really, when you think about it.

I turn to Edward. 'Have you had a busy day?' I ask him. 'Do you live nearby?'

Philip comes into the room. 'You know Sophie, of course,' I say. But I'm afraid to say Philip is in one of his moods!

'I thought I b***** told you No Filming in the Palace,' says Philip, snatching a tiny little camera device from out of Edward's hand.

'Oh, be like that then,' says Edward. 'Some of us have a job to do.' He leaves with his wife, shutting the door behind them with quite a bang. 'I do hope you have a safe trip home,' I say.

At this time of year, as the days begin to grow longer, it is nice to keep in touch with one's family.

TUESDAY

I receive my Prime Minister, a Mr Blair. He informs me of his plans for revitalising the National Health and modernising the railway system.

'This is all very interesting indeed,' I say.

'Thank you,' he says.

'You're obviously put a tremendous amount of thought into it,' I say.

'Yes,' he says.

'Railways are still very popular,' I tell him. 'They are

particularly useful if people want to get from A to B and for one reason or another they don't have their driver.'

'You've hit the nail on the head,' he says.

After fifty years as their monarch, I have a wealth of knowledge and experience to offer my Prime Ministers.

'And hospitals form a vitally important part in the health of the nation,' I tell him, adding, 'Though important as hospitals are, they wouldn't be as effective without doctors and nurses – not to mention patients.'

I have had quite a number of Prime Ministers during the course of my reign. One of them was a woman. The others were men.

Mr Blair is busy telling me about nursing shortages in central London when the clock chimes.

I convey to him our meeting is at an end by making a subtle incline of my head, holding out my hand and saying, 'Have you got far to go?'

I think my Prime Ministers appreciate the sense of continuity that only a monarch can give them.

As he leaves, I notice that one of Mr Blair's shoelaces is almost undone. I tell Philip about it in the evening. He roars with laugher. He reminds me of the occasion on which the Bishop of Norwich stepped backwards, fell over and broke his ankle while taking a service at Sandringham. Needless to say, by this time we are both in absolute fits!

WEDNESDAY

A reception at B.P. for leaders of the Commonwealth, many of them in colourful national dress. They love bright colours, particularly shiny coloured beads. They shake my hand with a natural sense of rhythm.

I observe that most of them have a far keener sense of history and tradition than many of their British and European counterparts – they bow quite beautifully and treat me with the very greatest respect and devotion. This is no doubt that we in the West must move with the times, but there is always a danger that we are moving too fast, and losing something very precious in the process. In this day and age, deference should never be a dirty word.

'May I present the President of Somalia, ma'am,' says my Foreign Secretary.

'And where are you from?' I ask him.

'Somalia, ma'am,' he replies, with a deep bow.

'That must be very convenient,' I say.'Though it must be frightfully hot.'

It is conversations such as these, conducted between friends in the family of nations, that constantly afford me hope that a better world lies ahead of us.

This evening, my son Andrew turns up. He is divorced. 'I was just passing by so I thought I'd just pop in to say hello,' he says.

'Have you been waiting long?' I say, setting him at his ease. 'Have you done this sort of thing before? Keep you busy, do they?'

Who's Who

Was there ever such a happy book?* It is so long, so detailed, with a greater range of characters than anything yet dreamed up by the South American magic realists, and yet every page sings of triumph and joy, of success and achievement and lives fullfilled.

Harvey Proctor, who will be best remembered as the author of *Billericay in Old Picture Postcards* (1985), has been the director of Proctor's Shirts and Ties since 1992. John Ernest Douglas Delavalette Browne has been Managing Director of Falcon Finance Management Ltd since 1978, while Ernest Saunders MA has been President of Stambridge Management ever since 1992. Happily neither Sir David Frost nor President Nelson Mandela ever had to go through the trauma of a divorce, for they have only been married once, and it is reassuring to see that both Kurt Waldheim and President Mitterand had such uneventful wars.

One or two of the characters do not play ball, but they are in a tiny minority. All we are told of the mysterious (Sir) Felix Roland Battan Summers, 2nd Bt, cr. 1952, for instance, is that 'he does not use the title and his name is not on the Official Roll of Baronets'. In contrast, the life of the 7th Earl of Lucan seems a lot fuller, furnished with a date of birth, a wife, children, parents, an education and a spell in the army, though alas no recreations and no address, just the delicately parenthesised

Who's Who A&C Black, 1995

62

italics beneath his entry – (*The Earl has been missing since Nov. 1974*).

Such glimmers of mystery and suspense, of secret lives lived between the lines, are what make *Who's Who* so compelling. In no other work are all the characters permitted to write their own stories, and retrospectively to plot their own destinies, jigging the facts and figures about from year to year, leaving this out, putting that in, rather like a painter returning again and again to improve his self-portrait. Back in 1986, Peter Bruinvels described himself as an MP. Come 1988, thrown out by the electors of Leicester East, he became: 'Management consultant: Director, Aalco Nottingham Ltd since 1983'. This year, he appears as 'Principal, Peter Bruinvels Associates, media management and public affairs consultant, founded 1986; news broadcaster, political commentator and freelance journalist'.

It must be hard to know what to leave out. Dame Barbara Cartland bites the bullet, and puts in all in, from 'designed and organised many pageants in aid of charity, including Britain and her Industries at British Legion Ball, Albert Hall, 1930' through 'carried the first aeroplane-towed-glider-mail in her glider, the *Barbara Cartland*, 1931' to a complete list of all her novels (22 last year alone), with separate sections devoted to Sociology (*Be Vivid, Be Vital, Men Are Wonderful*, etc), Philosophy (*Touch the Stars*), Biography (*Polly, My Wonderful Mother*) and Autobiography, the most recent being *How To Write Like Barbara Cartland, Vols 1 and 2* (1994). Sir David Frost is similarly never backward in coming forward, least of all here, where his entry contains his own name repeated no less than forty-five times – David Frost Live By Satellite from London, 1983, David Frost Presents *Ultra Quiz*, 1984, and so on. Looking through his long list of achievements, it is hard to know which of them one should feel most regret at missing. Personally, I swing between 'Elvis – He Touched Their Lives' (1980), 'Frost Over Canada' (1982) and 'Abortion – Merciful or Murder?' (1975).

Less public figures find it harder to signal the living, breathing personalities waving beneath the avalanche of posts acquired. For them, the spot marked 'Recreations' must come as a mixed blessing – too dull (Reading, Walking, Music) and you sound like all the others, too offbeat and you sound either pious ('keeping friendships in constant repair') or arch ('thinking about writing the Great British Novel') or both ('Mother Earth'). Sir Ronald Millar lists 'All kinds of music, all kinds of people', which immediately makes one want to send The Beastie Boys round to his house for a jam session, Meanwhile, Andrew Neil has increased his recreation over the years from the off-putting 'Dining out in London, New York and Aspen' to the proportionately more off-putting 'Dining out in London, New York, Aspen and the Cote d'Azur'.

Intimations of marital tension may be daintily plucked from the opposing recreations of married couples. Virginia Bottomley says 'family' which includes her husband, while Peter Bottomley says 'children', which excludes his wife. Why should Peter be a recreation for Virginia, but Virginia not be a recreation for Peter? Actually, I think the reasons are perfectly obvious, but it is interesting to see the evidence presented so forcefully. Similarly, though Lord Archer of Weston-super-Mare numbers his recreations as 'theatre, watching Somerset play cricket (represented Somerset CCC in benefit match, 1981; Pres., Somerset Wyverns, 1983)', his wife Mary numbers hers as 'village choirmistress, cats, squash, picking up litter'. This raises a number of questions. Does the village choirmistress know she is Mary Archer's recreation? Who creates the litter that Mary spends her leisure hours picking up? Or is it a metaphor? Of the ho-ho recreations, the most over-used must surely be sleeping, named by, among many others, Terry Jones, Jeremy Paxman, Roy Hudd, David Lipsey of *The Economist* and Lord St John of Fawsley (who combines it with 'appearing on television', which goes some way to explain his recent drawling, droopy-eyed performances at all hours of day and night in defence of the Royal Family). There are one or two recreations, however, which make one view their practitioners in a new light. I never knew that David Bowie was a keen skier, for instance, or that the mad-eyed astronomer Patrick Moore composes music for the xylophone. Indeed, anyone wishing to test the enthusiasm of Sir Ronald Millar might do worse than purchase him the 1979 waxing *The Ever Ready Band Plays Music for Patrick Moore*.

The prize for the most tortured recreation goes to the playwright Edward Bond. It used to be 'the study of physics, because in physics the problems of human motives do not have to be considered'. However, after I sneered in print at such galumphing, he has now extended it, adding '. . . for the benefit of newspaper reporters: this is a joke, as anyone who had attended a rehearsal with actors would know'. We can only hope that Mr Bond's long-awaited excursion into comedy is not too far off.

Bond can be counted among those avowedly anti-elitists who have boldly managed to hold their noses long enough to fill in the entry form, some for so long that by the end they must have been gasping for breath. Pat Arrowsmith 'pacifist and socialist' awards herself 27 lines, Tony Benn 24, Dennis Skinner ('good working-class mining stock') 9, Professor Eric Hobsbawm 19 and 'Hero of Socialist Labour' Georgi Alexandrovich Zhukov, *Pravda* columnist since 1962, double-holder of the order of Lenin, 31. But at least Pat Arrowsmith, alone among the 29,000 included, mentions her spells in prison – 'awarded Holloway Prison Green Band, 1964', no less. She is similarly uncagey when tackling her private life: '*m*. Mr Gardner, 11 Aug 1979, separated 11 Aug. 1979; lesbian partnership with Wendy Butlin, 1962–76'. For me, such frankness knocks spots off the mealy-mouthed entry of Jeanette Winterson ('partner: Dr M. Reynolds').

The essential question to be asked of *Who's Who* is whether or not the editors have achieved their stated aim of recognising those whose 'prominence is inherited, or depending upon office, or the result of ability which singles them out from their fellows in occupations open to every educated man or woman'. I would say they have a success rate of 80 or 90 per cent, which is pretty good going, though in some areas their choices appear far more random than in others. On foreign soil, and in particular among foreign politicians, they are nervy and hesitant, hitting the small fry, but missing the big fry. Many dictators and ex-dictators are excluded – no Castro, no Saddam, no Amin, no Bokassa, no Gaddafi – while some of their underlings are in. Chairman Deng Xiaoping is out (should one address him as Chairman? have I spelt his name right? – who can tell me, if not *Who's Who?*), but Zhao Ziyan, the General Secretary of the Chinese Community Party is in. Perhaps Deng couldn't be bothered to fill in his form, whereas Zhao simply leapt at the opportunity; if so, wouldn't it be wiser for *Who's Who* to earmark foreign politicians for compulsory inclusion, however brief, just as they do our own home-grown politicians?

Other exclusions suggest strangulated cries of 'oh, my God, must we?' at the final editorial meeting. No Cilla Black, no Paul Gascoigne, no Noel Edmonds, yet the minor lyricist Don Black is in, and so are the quizmaster Bamber Gascoigne and Mr John Edmond, the Professor of Marine Geochemistry at the Massachusetts Institute of Technology. Prominence linked with youth poses a particular problem. When sportsmen have been around long enough for inclusion, they have also been around long enough to retire. This produces peculiarities: this year, Torvill and Dean are finally in, just as they are on their way out.

If there is a bias, it is, perhaps unexpectedly, towards poets and professors. Any British poet who has sold over 1,000 copies stands a good chance (Carol Ann Duffy makes it this year) and there are professors galore. Indeed, it is hard to find a page without a professor: pages 36–7 offer a choice of no less than six Professor John Andersons alone.

But these are quibbles. *Who's Who* is a book of unrivalled interest and amusement on all sorts of different levels. Page 1156, for instance, offers us brand-new characters with the gorgeously Firbankian names of Harry George Lillicrap, Sir Edouard Lim Fat, Professor Lim Pin, Sir (John) Gordon (Seymour) Linacre, Rambahadur Limbu, Edward Horace Fiennes Clinton, the 18th Earl of Lincoln, and – perhaps the happiest name in the entire volume – The Rt Rev. Edward Flewett Darling, Bishop of Limerick and Killaloe.

Reading such a page, or, indeed, any other, it is hard not to feel in some eerie way that these are the Beautiful, and the rest of us are the Damned, and that *Who's Who* is a slightly more jaunty Raft of the Medusa, everyone on it frantically waving their CVs in the direction of the ship of immortality as it sails away over the horizon. When Dame Barbara eventually drops off, I suppose there will be room for a good ten more, or twenty if they each agree to be modest. But we must all await our turn, and I'm afraid to say that, for this particular raft, it is definitely not women and children first.

Poky

From *The Diaries of Woodrow Wyatt, Volume 11: The Missing Month*

April 1st: The trouble with staying in places like Windsor Castle is that you so rarely meet anyone of interest. Bumped into the Reagans as I was going up the stairs. Dull little couple. He's making a goodish stab of being President of the USA, she has a reasonable figure but eyes too far apart. Feel sorry for the pair of them. Should I put him on the board of the Tote? It might give him something to do.

April 2nd: I collar Reagan over a brandy and give him some advice. 'A lot of people tend to forget,' I say, 'that America's a very big country.'

April 3rd: Time to leave Windsor. I worry over a point of etiquette. How much should one tip the Queen? As we leave, I pop a shiny new 50 pence piece and a used betting slip into her hand. Her smile is radiant.

April 6th: I hear Alan Clark is keeping a diary he intends to publish. Disgraceful! The man is an utter cad, and has no place in society.

April 8th: Norman Lamont drops by. He asks for my advice. I tell him that Britain is a relatively small country. 'America, for instance, is far larger,' I add, 'particularly if you include Texas.' We decide he should stay in Britain. It's pretty easy to become Prime Minister, I say: in fact, hardly worth the effort. I myself came within spitting distance when I was Parliamentary Under-Secretary of State, only to decide it wasn't worth the extra bother. But Norman remains mustard-keen. 'Do you know Queen Elizabeth the Queen Mother?' I ask him. 'A dear friend. She could probably arrange it for you if you're really that desperate. I'll mention it.'

April 12th: Queen Elizabeth the Queen Mother to dinner. As usual, I have gathered some intellectuals to entertain her: Tony Quinton recites 'Alfred and the Lion', Asa Briggs does his Shirley Bassey impersonation and Isaiah Berlin does a turn on spoons. Over brandy, I ask after her elder daughter, whom I was instrumental in getting into her present post in the early 1950s. She says she is doing well, and enjoying the job. I wait for a suitable lull and then mention that Norman Lamont might be interested in becoming Prime Minister in a year or two, adding 'and he's really not bad at that sort of thing'. She says she'll look into it, but for the moment, if Norman's after something to keep him occupied, the hedges at Clarence House could do with a jolly good trim.

April 15th: I telephone Mrs T. As ever, she wants to hear what I have to say on world affairs. 'Australia is ginormous and completely surrounded by sea,' I tell her, 'but Switzerland is the opposite.' I end by telling her she's the greatest Prime Minister this country has ever had. 'I can always count on you, Woodrow,' she says. 'You're the only person who tells me the truth.'

April 16th: Dinner v. boring. I was telling people of my close friendship with Queen Elizabeth the Queen Mother, recounting amusing anecdotes such as the time I mixed her a dry Martini and she said, 'You mix an excellent dry Martini, Woodrow', but no one was listening. Instead, they were hanging on to every word of some frightful foreign bore with a beard at the other end of the table. 'Who's the beardie?' I hissed to my neighbour, a reasonably attractive woman with big elbows. 'Alexander Solzhenitsyn,' she replied. 'But is *he* a personal friend of Queen Elizabeth the Queen Mother?' I replied. 'Well, is he?'

April 17th: President Deng Xiaoping has decided to relax state control, opening the way for a more capitalist system.

The Great and The Good

Exactly what I told him to do in my *News of the World* column last Sunday. He owes me a favour. I wonder if he has a job for Lamont up his sleeve?

Apirl 18th: Phone Mrs T. Tell her she ought to do something about that ghastly airport near Windsor. 'Heathrow?' she says. 'That's the one,' I reply. 'So bloody noisy.' I tell her my friend Queen Elizabeth the Queen Mother finds the noise an awful bore when she's staying at the Castle, 'But it might be all right if they got rid of those planes.' Mrs T says that planes are an important part of any airport. Remarks like this make me worry she's controlled by her civil servants. 'Ah, well, you're still the finest leader in the history of the Western world, Margaret,' I tell her. 'You're so frank, Woodrow,' she replies. 'You're always bringing me down to earth.'

April 20th: We have bought a new puppy, Spot, who is quite simply not housetrained. Time to pull strings. I telephone the Master of St Swithin's, Oxford, and ask if he'll take Spot on in some sort of undergraduate capacity and knock a bit of sense into him. He tells me that to his knowledge they've never had a puppy at St Swithin's before, but he'll see what he can do. I tell him there's a dinner with Queen Elizabeth the Queen Mother in it for him if he succeeds. He seems to brighten up.

April 22nd: I phone Mrs T, who wants my advice on New Zealand. I look it up. 'Small island, English-speaking, somewhere near Australia, butter galore,' I say. I then tell her the latest news: Norman Lamont told me Heseltine had told him that Leon Brittan had said Mayhew thought that Jim Prior had heard Nigel Lawson was pretty sure Geoffrey Howe had said Norman had been telling me things that Mrs T had told him. 'Typical Heseltine,' she says, 'always making trouble.'

April 23rd: Cigar goes out mid-puff. Furious, I put a call through to Fidel Castro, but without success.

April 24th: To Chatsworth. Poky.

April 25th: Sit next to the Duchess of Devonshire at dinner. Very, very common.

April 26th: The Master of St Swithin's College rings to ask if Spot could muster a grade 6 in latin O-level. 'I'll ask him and get right back to you,' I say and put down the phone. I immediately telephone the King Pin of the O-level examiners, introduce myself and invite him to a slap-up dinner with my friend Queen Elizabeth the Queen Mother. I phone back the Master of St Swithin's. 'I think we can get Spot a grade 5,' I say with confidence.

April 27th: To a dinner party at George Weidenfeld's. I'm at my witty and candid best. 'You're a very fat person who serves execrable food and drink,' I tell him. He then rounds on me, saying he has never heard anything like it in his life, and that he didn't have to ask me to his dinner party and I didn't have to come. Really! Some people have the most terrible manners.

April 28th: To Jeffrey Archer's. He wears a bow tie, puffs on a huge cigar and proceeds to boast of his friendship with Queen Elizabeth the Queen Mother. The man's an obvious charlatan.

April 30th: Spot is accepted as an undergraduate by St Swithin's, Oxford. Dropping him off on his first day, I mention to the Master that we've been rather hoping he'll get a chance to row for his college. The Master tells me that as far as he knows they've never had a puppy rowing for the college before. I happen to mention that there's a place on the board of the Tote coming up. The Master thinks for a while, and says there's really no reason why Spot shouldn't make a very useful cox, just so long as he can produce the necessary swimming proficiency certificate. On my return home, I put a call through to the Chairman of the Board of Swimming Proficiency. 'I was wondering if you've ever had the chance to meet my dear friend Queen Elizabeth the Queen Mother?' I ask.

Mohamed Fayed's All-Time Greatest People To Do Business With

1) COLONEL MUAMMAR GADDAFI

The Colonel he very very nice man, very good man, man never bomb nobody, even if you placing top-class quality bomb in his hand, he say, 'Hey! I no having this top-class quality bomb, what I have do with bomb, I have no one to bomb today, why you give me this dratting bomb when I don't need, eh?'

The Colonel, he have beautiful skin, same as Kate Moss but lots better, no holes, no crinkles, no nothing, his skin have win all top awards, I giving him Harrods own-brand executive moisturiser for heterosexuals, top-class product for Colonel to having keep skin top-tip condition, okay? The Colonel he also have wearing Harrods pashmina round head to keep beautiful black thick hair from bleaching.

And he love his people so much, they having no poverty, no begging, no shanty towns, all luxury houses, Harrods Gold Card, the lot, 'cos he say to drattin poor and filthy beggars you shove off, you no wanted in my beautiful country, you take your bloody shantys someplace else, you choose have mess up my country, I throw you in dungeon till you quit begging, okay, is deal.

2) COUNT DRACULA

He no homo, he no government stooge, he ordinary people. Okay, so he live in coffin and drink blood of virgins, but what bloody hell wrong with that? Prince Philip, he drinking blood of virgins all in snooty Royal cocktail which they serving at so-called garden parties for all snobby friends, so why they no prosecute him is what I want to know? Count Dracula is great guy believing in God, wearing top-of-the-range cloak, 100 per cent pure silk, now available in red and black, he give thirty-five years good employment to the masses of the ordinary decent vampires, why you attack him? Is because poor guy Transylvannian? Is Establishment cover-up. Are you filthy Blairite lying racist?

3) DR CRIPPEN

Lovely guy, he never killing his wife, no way. Before she die, his wife, she has saying, 'I want to see my very good friend Mohamed.' So, man of people, I go to her and she say with her dying breath, 'Mohamed,' she saying, wordy for word, I write it down, 'Mohamed, is Establishment cover-up. My husband excellent doctor, never cross word, always the gentleman, best hubby in the world, he no poisoning me, no way, Mohamed, I poison myself to *make it look like he poisoning me.*' But I wanting to no more, so I say, 'Buy why, Mrs Crippen, why you do this to this lovely guy?' and she take second dying breath and saying me, 'I am being MI5 agent, Mohamed, I am being paid by top brass to having killed myself.' And with that, she die.

4) DR HANNIBAL LECTER

Hannibal, he great man, he personal friend of al Fayed, he victim MI5, MI6, MI7, the lot, conspiracy to discred, they say he eat human flesh but is all bullshot, he have eat nothing, he just little bitty peckish, is all. He shop Harrods Food Hall, nothing but best for Dr Lecter, he demand to assistant, 'I gourmet, that's what I have wanting!' and he point to what is in assistant's hand. But assistant, he have look worried, so I say, 'Spot-spit! Give gentleman what he want, man! He VIP customer! He want eat what's in your hand, you give him, okay?!' And assistant say, 'B-b-but what is in my hand is . . . my other hand!'

So I say, stop nancy about, you give Dr Lecter other hand, he busy man, top quality, very hungry, he only want nibble, why you deny him nibble, you homosexual?

Next day, sadly I have dismiss assistant. 'We no have one-handed assistants in Harrods Food Hall,' I say, 'It no look professional.' Okay, so he make big fuss, sue me have unfair dismissal, whatever, he probably homosexual, boyfriend Blair, we settle out court, I don't want get hassle, waste my time, I want have do my duty for my country, the people, the masses, the poor people who feed from my charity store.

5) KING RICHARD III

King Richard, he personal friend Mohamed, he not withdraw Royal Warrant from top people store Harrods, no way, he proud to shop with Mohamed, he having buy all his pillows at top people store Harrods, he man honour. The Princes in the Tower, what have that to do? People make big fuss, say 'Poor Little Princes, hoo-boo, hoo-boo', but why they never asking what so-called Little Princes doing wrong, eh? They MI5 agents, they nuisance, they no good two-timing little midgets, they start smear campaign against Richard, he has get own back. But he no hurt Little Princes, no way, you have no proof, you say that then you liar, what you talkin' is total rubbish, you get out my store, okay, or I call security. I am say exactly what happen, okay? Harrods spokesman, he have issue statement on behalf Little Princes, he say, 'I spoke with Little Princes this morning, they fine, they say, "We no bloody smothered to death by Uncle Richard, no way, media conspiracy, bunch of gangsters, he great guy, so Mohamed, we sitting up in bed really happy, breathing well, enjoying Harrods breakfast, full English, now piss off".'

6) CAPTAIN HOOK

Peter Pan, who this guy, he nancy-boy, he having wear green body stocking and silly hat with feather, why he no got to decent classy outfitters, dress like proper man, he have no dignity, instead he ponce about, all baby talk, worse than Tories, who this bloody Tinkerbell, what kind of name that, so I say to Peter Pan, 'Is about time you bloody grew up.'

But Captain Hook he old friend of Mohamed, posh pal, pedigree chum, naval officer, he run top ship, all crew sleep in luxury cabinets, no riff-raff, this is leadership you know, we do excellent business, treat me like Head of State. We supply Hook's ship with luxury planks. You say Hook make people walking luxury plank? Is rubbish, garbage, who told you that? You work for M25?

Wallace Arnold: Vulgar, Vulgar, Vulgar

It was at that delicious time of day immediately prior to luncheon. Our very select Reading Group sat in the library of the Travellers Club, mulling over the business of the day. We had, as you will soon gather, been enjoying a magisterial new tome on a particularly knotty social problem.

Whither Kosovo? 'You can tell by his haircut that Milosevic is a nouveau,' quoth I, adding ruminatively, 'No gentleman would ever ask his barber for such fancy scissor-work. And do I detect the tell-tale curls of a blow-drier at hand? I rest my case.'

'But surely one can blow-dry one's hair yet still remain a gentleman?' asked my young confrère Simon Heffer, no stranger, methinks, to the henna jar.

'The last gentleman to blow-dry his hair was King Edward VIII,' I opined, 'and look what happened to him.'

The others purred agreement. 'Vulgar, vulgar, vulgar,' said my old friend and quaffing partner Lord Charteris, stirring his coffee employing only his penis, as is correct.

'Pardon me,' chimed in Hughie Trevor-Roper, 'but King Edward VIII was no gentleman. His father and his grandfather both sported beards. No gentleman has ever sported a beard. I rest my case.'

'But did his family not date back to the Normans, Hughie?' asked Roy Strong, a novice in these matters.

'I don't care whether they date back to the Freds, the Sharons or the Kevins, they are fearfully common,' snapped Hughie, dipping the end of his necktie into his coffee and sucking on it in the approved manner. 'Look at the Queen Mother! She might have stepped from behind the bar at the Rover's Return bearing a half-pint of lemonade shandy!'

'The Rover's Return?' quoth young Heffer. 'I'm afraid you've quite lost me there, Hughie'.

'And what on earth is a lemonade shandy?' quoth I. 'A motor-car, is it? Or some sort of household gadget?'

'"*Gadget*", Wallace? "*Gadget*"?' spluttered Roy Strong. 'I trust you are employing the word with a fair dollop of irony! No gentleman *ever* says the word "gadget", you know!'

'Vulgar, vulgar, vulgar,' chipped in Charteris.

'One's revulsion towards the word dates back to the days of Sir Sidney Gadget, the nouveau riche Victorian entrepreneur,' elucidated Roy. 'The moment it was discovered that he had invented the toothbrush, society dropped him like a hot brick.'

'Just as they had dropped Sir Algernon Brick, less than two hundred years earlier,' added Heffer. 'Neither he nor his wife, Lady Cynthia, ever recovered.'

How very stimulating our reading group discussions can prove! We had all, you will have gathered, been inwardly digesting J. Mordaunt Crook's magisterial new work on *The Rise of the Nouveaux Riches*. As you might imagine, it had served only to increase our vigilance against this ongoing social problem.

'Of course, the Bricks were forced to change their name, in the hope that they might one day be accepted back into society,' said Hughie, 'but they chose badly and their ploy failed miserably.'

Roy's ears priced up. 'To what did they change their name?' he asked.

'Sir Algernon and Lady Cynthia Toilet,' explained Hughie with an ill-concealed grimace.

The Great and The Good

At this point, the library doors swung open. A young couple strode in, all over-pressed clothes and eager smiles. 'Vulgar, vulgar, vulgar!' muttered Charteris. It was HRH Prince Edward, escorting his fiancée, Miss (Msssss!) Sophie Rhys-Jones on a whistle-stop tour of the club.

'Don't look now,' hissed Heffer, puckering his lips, 'but I think he's holding her hand!'

'Eeyurgh!' we all groaned in unison.

'No man and woman should ever hold hands,' said Trevor-Roper, 'unless, of course, the gentleman is on his deathbed, his will is about to be read, and no qualified doctor is available to take his pulse.'

The royal couple continued to scurry about the library, blissfully unaware that they were the objects of our social analysis. 'I see the Prince wears tassles on his shoes,' I whispered.

'Tassles were invented by Rodney Tassle in the late eighteenth century,' hissed Roy Strong. 'The family still live at Tassle Castle in Rutland, but they're never invited out.'

'No doubt the pair of them will wave after their wedding,' said Hughie. 'The Windsors are always waving. They don't know any better.'

'Vulgar, vulgar, vulgar!' confirmed Charteris, picking his nose with thumb and forefinger, in the approved manner.

The Beatles Anthology

Ringo: It's hard to remember now but basically we had this car, well, it was more of a lorry. A small lorry. Somewhere in between a small lorry and a car.

George: A van. We had this van. In some of the history books historians may say it was a small lorry but that's historians for you. Bullshit. Total bullshit. It was a van.

Ringo: In those days, you had to like stop for petrol when your tank ran out. By tank, I don't mean it was a tank. Not a real tank. It wasn't. It was more of a van. But it had a tank for the petrol. These days, no one worries about petrol. Cars are chauffeur-driven. But this was the early sixties.

George: We thought we were going to run out of petrol because we'd forgotten to fill it up.

Paul: Running out of petrol! A lot of madness went on in that van! As usual, it was yours truly who noticed the arrow was near to empty, and it nearly did me in. I thought, 'Whoa, this could be it. We could run out of petrol, man,' so I'm like, 'Right, guys – we've got to stop at the next petrol station.'

Ringo: It was like, we almost ran out of petrol. Bloody touring lark! But we didn't because there was a petrol station just round the corner. It was pretty far out. I remember thinking something. But it was a long time ago, and I forget what.

Paul: This lyric came into my head like from out of nowhere, and I couldn't get it out. 'Van, van van – c'mon baby, let's drive my van.' A real old rocker. Originally, it had a verse about nearly running out of petrol, but there's like no rhyme for petrol.

Ringo: 'cept 'metal'. And 'kettle'.

Paul: In the past, John's taken all the credit for 'Van' and I kept shtum about it for some time but historically it was mine and that's a fact. Sorry, John! Sorry, old mate!

George: The thing about being in a van is, like, it's basically on wheels. Not like a house, say, or—

Ringo: A wheelbarrow. A wheelbarrow's not on *wheels*. It's like just got the one.

George: What I mean is in a van you're never still, you're always going. Unless you've stopped, of course. Traffic lights, parking, blah, blah.

Ringo: Or for a pee. Or stopped for a pee. One of the all-time great Beatles peeing-by-the-side-of-the-road stories happened when—

George: What I want to say about being in a van is that, it's, like, 'Hey, I'm *in* this van, but the van isn't like *in me*.' And that's an amazing level of consciousness to be at. All the rest is just bullshit, just bullshit. All the governments and all the people running around the planet doing whatever they're doing. It's just a total waste of time. Or that's what I remember thinking at the time. At least it's what I *remember* remembering thinking, but now I've like mainly forgotten.

Paul: So when it came to recording 'Van' we are in the studio, and the others were kind of sitting around and that, and I'm like, 'Hey, guys, let's get this whole thing on the road,' but whaddyaknow, I'm like as usual the only one who's got his act together, so I just record it by myself. (*Sings:*) 'Oooh, van, van, van. C'mon, baby, let me by your va-a-a-an!' And it's like an instant classic, the song everyone remembers from that year. And I'm happy that the others got the credit for it, but sometimes, I'm like 'Hey, guys, hang on – let's not forget who really did it?!' yeah! Rock 'n' roll! Wooh!

George: That's just Paul's way, really. He has this way of, I mean, like telling what he wants to tell and I'm not blaming him for that because though over the years it may have kind of annoyed us, I think we're used to it. But for the history books it's best that people know it was me who was inspired to write a song about that van and not just that van but all vans everywhere, even the vans that aren't yet vans but are like, just bits of metal not yet struck together, or like vans-to-be. And like out of nowhere I wrote this song, 'Van Vanu Vishnu Van' and round the time of the Double White I recorded it with just this sitar and this cushion in the middle of this great empty space. And it totally knocked me out. But the others said the Double White was too short to include it on. They were often like that, and I'm like, 'I've had it up to here, man.'

Paul: But fair's fair, we always let him have his three minutes on each album, and he'd already like used them up. But that's our Georgie boy! Sense of humour needed here you know! Bless him!

George: So I later put the twenty-three minute version on my triple solo concept album, and now every day I have Beatle historians come up and tell me it's better than anything the Beatles ever did together, so I'm like reconciled. It's like a that-was-then-and-this-is-now kind of thing.

Ringo: Another great van story was when George and Paul were both planning to drive the van, I don't know where, it was definitely somewhere, but that's not the point of the story, the point is they couldn't find the keys anywhere! It was pretty far out, because in those days no one ever lost the keys to anything. Especially not a van. So after looking around for them for two or three minutes – a lot of time in those days – we eventually found them, I forget where. And so we set off to where we were going. And I guess we must have got there, because I'd remember if like for some reason we never. Classic!

George: Ringo had his sixth shag in the back of that van.

Ringo: My seventh. I've often seen it referred to as my sixth but it wasn't. It was my seventh.

Paul: We sat round looking at them, 'cos Ringo and this bird were like having it off over the bit with the spare wheel in it and we'd had a puncture so we had to wait and we thought we might as well watch. Donovan watched too. People like that. Billy Fury. Freddie and the Dreamers. The Swinging Blue Jeans. They all watched. You see, it was the sixties.

Ringo: I took LSD in that van. It blew my mind. I looked round and thought 'Hey! This is a van!' and then I woke up and it was. I've never thought the same about anything ever again. Was it a van? It was somewhere between a car and a small lorry. I'd guess you'd call it a van. John would've known.

George and Paul: John who?

Rivers of Bloop

We shall not see his like again. His like again we shalt not see. Again shalt we see not his like.

He wath indeed a giant among men, one of the greatest intellects of this or any century, perhaps even the greatest of them all. Travelling to Westminster on the London Underground, he would make it a rule to translate his request for a ticket from English into Portuguese, from Portuguese into Urdu, from Urdu into Taiwanese and finally from Taiwanese back again into English before delivering the final result into the expectant ear of the ticket salesman. Only three times in his long career did that message come out faulty; on the first occasion, he arrived at Ongar; on the second, at Putney South; and on the third he did not arrive anywhere at all, for he had inadvertently mistranslated his request to the London Underground sales staff for a ticket to *My Fair Lady*, a popular musical comedy at that time enjoying a lengthy run in the West End.

Few of us who were privileged to meet him will lightly forget his rigorous command of the language. 'How do you do?' I remember saying to him as we shook hands upon first being introduced.

'It is with regret that I must needs inform you, sir, that your question is expressed improperly,' he replied. 'For the only true answer to "How do you do?" is perforce "How do I do what?" which is itself, as you will now note, and as many have noted before you, another question. A question answered by a question is a question destined to remain unanswered, thus rendering redundant the question in question. You ask me how do I do; I tell you, sir, that how I proceed to do that which I am desirous of both doing and, later, having done is neither here, nor, in the absence of its presence here, there. I must therefore ask you to extend to me the courtesy of withdrawing your initial question, for the knowledge it is desirous of eliciting is itself contained in its original expression.'

At this point, my wife came up. Sensing an awkward hiatus in our conversation, I introduced her to the great man. 'How do—' she began, and before I could stop her she had continued with her question, '— you do?' Five minutes later, she was still nodding her head attentively through each of his subordinate clauses.

His command of English was, of course, the most impeccable any of us ever encountered. None knew better than he that English is best expressed in reverse. Or, to put it another way, in reverse is English expressed best; than he none knew better. Later at that same meeting, I asked him if I could get him a drink. His answer was peerless both in its courtesy and in its reversed English. 'A drink you could indeed get me,' he said. 'Wine red, in glass or beaker served, would greatly me please.'

He was a man of tremendous passions, never shirking from his duty of spying storms ahead, even on a cloudless day. Few who were there will ever forget his famous 'Rivers of Bloop' speech, in which he bitterly attacked standards of typing in our secretarial colleges. And indelible on the memory, too, lies his impassioned belief in the British Empire. As late as 1985, he was submitting detailed plans to the Cabinet Office for the conquering of the Galapagos Islands employing a submarine, a rowing boat, three lilos and a penguin costume. He forcefully argued that the animals on the Galapagos were to all intents and purposes British. 'The armadillo, even as she walks, carries about her person the knowledge that Britain is not as Nineveh and Tyre. For within her shell lurks that profoundly British sense of a mother country. Within her armour plating, buffeted by centuries of supping off rocks, she feels no country other than Britain to be her home. Indeed her very being seems, in a very real sense, to shout out, "I, too, am desirous of the rule of British law; even I, the common armadillo, wish to enjoy the uncommon force of British logic." And with that she goes scratching for another bug, unimpeded in her resolve.'

His intellect cast a formidable shadow over his contemporaries. His passion lay in sums. He was capable of bringing a dinner party to a halt simply by turning to his neighbour and saying, in his precise, mesmeric, tones, 'Three hundred and thirty-three divided by seven add nine take away twelve multiplied by fifteen now take away the number you first thought of and the answer is seventeen.'

He thrived on debate. On one occasion, upon overhearing a fellow passenger on his beloved London Underground commenting, 'Every cloud has a silver lining,' he issued a detailed nine-minute refutation, lasting from High Street Kensington to St James's Park.

His argument went as follows. As clouds are formed of vapour, they are capable of evading the noblest attempts of even the most skilled seamstress to furnish them with a lining or any sort; that as a lining by definition is made from loose fabric, silver would be singularly inappropriate for the job; and, finally, that, even if this were not the case, were all clouds to be equipped with that self-same silver lining, they would be rendered inoperable, and the consequent climatic damage to crops and animal life would be ruinous not only to Britain but to lesser nations. Never again was the gentleman in question ever to venture the opinion that every cloud has a silver lining; indeed, from that day on the poor fellow stopped travelling on the Underground altogether.

His dress was at all times distinctive and idiosyncratic, and always inextricably linked to his deep sense of occasion. Once, while wearing the appropriate headwear to celebrate the anniversary of the Battle of Balaclava, he walked into a high street bank only to be arrested on charges of attempted robbery. Shod in gumboots, he would annually wade to and fro in the Palace of Westminster, calling on all those present to observe with him fifteen minutes silence for the dead of Waterloo.

The Great and The Good

The most hurtful accusation thrown at him by his political opponents was that he was in some way a 'racialist'. For this there was no evidence whatever beyond his predictions of wars between the races, his approval of a constituent who predicted that in twenty years time the black man would have the whip hand, and his insistence that no one should be prevented from discriminating between black and white. In fact, he was always most courteous to those few immigrants he encountered, entertaining them with a selection of up-tempo numbers from *Porgy and Bess*; rumour had it that he even regularly performed incognito with the popular song-and-dance troupe The Black and White Minstrels.

He would never refuse a cup of tea, promptly syphoning off the liquid in order to decode the pattern in the tea leaves. And what patterns he discovered! Forty years ago, he predicted that closer links with Europe would result in Swedish becoming Britain's first language by the turn of the century, by which time smorgasbord would be compulsory in all our schools. That this nightmare scenario has not come about owes everything to the power of his warnings. And, like smorgasbord, his memory is not only indelible; it is also inedible.

Wallace Arnold:
Pinochet in Belgravia

It was only the other day. An intimate group of us had gathered at My Lady Thatcher's home in Belgravia for another delightful trip down Memory Lane. The drinks had been served, the nuts circulated, and My Lady was enjoying her usual pint mug of Teacher's through a straw.

'I'll never forget how you gave those wretched miners a run for their money!' chortled Lord McAlpine, chewing on a cashew.

'And you taught those nurses and firemen a lesson they'll never forget, ma'am!' chipped in young Heffer, to a brief burst of applause.

'And what about the wretched doctors and steelworkers?!' laughed my old quaffing partner, Lord Sherman. 'You certainly forced them to put a sock in it, eh, Margaret?!'

'Happy days!' purred Lord Young.

'I do welcome these debates,' concluded Margaret, sucking up the last drop of Teacher's before emitting a ladylike burp. 'Top-up, anyone?'

'Ding-dong!' It was the doorbell. My Lady looked at her watch. 'That'll be Augusto!' she said, perking up. 'Now there's a man who knows his own mind! Heffer – the door!'

A flash of red hurtled through the room as Heffer scuttled to the door. We all craned out necks for a first glimpse of our esteemed visitor.

The Great and The Good

'Out of my way, carrot top!' General Pinochet marched into the house, giving Heffer a playful swipe on the head with the sheath of his sword. He then strode forcefully up to where My Lady was sitting, slammed his heels together and gave her a full military salute. 'Margaret, my dear!' he screamed. 'You've never looked lovelier!'

Two of the General's bodyguards clad from top to toe in chunky balaclavas elbowed their way past my Lords Tebbit and Archer bearing two sackfuls of gifts. The General proceeded to unpack each one.

'Two dozen red roses, very, very costly!' he announced, handing them to My Lady. 'A 100 per cent cashmere shawl, also very costly! One executive-style hamper from Fortnum and Mason containing four gift-wrapped champagne flutes in Waterford Crystal! Four front stalls tickets to a Thursday matinee of *Starlight Express*! Two silver foxes, ready-strangled for their luxurious prestige fur! Five hundred duty-free Benson and Hedges! Four fully automatic torture-tongs and some electric cable to silence any subversives in our midst! And finally my dear Margaret – a very special box of Milk Tray for a very special lady.'

I think I'm right in saying that by the time he'd finished his presentation, there wasn't a dry eye in the house. The General's kindly reputation had preceded him, of course, but we were nonetheless tremendously moved by this display of generosity.

'I d-d-don't often b-b-blub,' croaked dear old Alan Clark, removing a monogrammed silk hankie from his upper pocket and dabbing at his eyes, 'b-b-but this time, Aug-g-gusto, you've surp-p-passed yourself, you l-l-little p-p-poppet, you!'

Margaret, too, was visibly moved. 'I don't know how to thank you enough, Augusto,' she said, taking a prolonged slurp through her straw.

'My only thanks are to be found in your appreciation of my undoubted generosity,' he said. 'For instance, whenever you wear your 100 per cent cashmere shawl, you must think of me, your little Augusto! And whenever you use these fully automatic torture-tongs and this length of electric cable on your opponents, you must remember the dear old friend who gave them to you!'

At this point, an awkward hush fell upon our tight-knit community. 'Frankly, we don't have an awful lot of torture in this country, Augusto!' quoth I, adding, to put the poor chap at his ease, 'More's the pity!!'

'On the other hand,' said McAlpine, 'it seems a dreadful shame to waste such a thoughtful present.' So saying, he picked up the tongs and fingered them lovingly, adding, 'Surely there must be *someone* in this room who's just a *teensy bit* subversive. Come on! Own up!'

It was I who broke the silence. 'Didn't My Lord Archer drag his feet a bit on the miners' strike?' I suggested.

'I never!' countered Archer. 'But Norman here once told me he was dead against the poll tax!'

'Come outside and say that!' said Norman. At this point, we all realised that the atmosphere was becoming a little unpleasant. I think we all knew that if we were to enjoy General Pinochet's well-intentioned gift, we would have to look to someone beyond the narrow confines of our group. But who?

Margaret sighed wistfully. 'It seems ages since we've seen dearest Heseltine,' she said. 'Does anyone have a number for him?'

Kenneth Tynan's Diary

2 August 1973

Contemplate suicide. Look in diary. Princess Margaret[1] to dinner tomorrow. Decide against.

9 August 1973

Dinner for Princess Margaret. She is really quite extraordinarily small. Without her shoes, she would be officially reclassified a dwarf. Jill Bennett[2] mistakes her for an occasional table, places an empty glass on her head and drawls for more. Princess Margaret becomes fearfully upset, so I try to draw her back into the conversation.

'Do you not agree, Ma'am,' I say, 'that Chairman Mao's[3] Cultural Revolution is simply the most marvellous thing that has happened in years? How one wishes one were an adorable little Chinesey peasant at this time!' The Princess burps wittily, then follows it up with the most delicious yawn. All perfectly timed, as one would expect of royalty. As Noel[4] once noted, she really is the most exquisite yawner.

Across the table, Mick McGahey[5] is having a fearful row with Debo[6] about workers' ownership of the means of production.

[1] Cousin of the Queen.
[2] Tempestuous wife of dramatist Alan Bennett.
[3] Leading Chinese parliamentarian.
[4] Noel Redding, Rolling Stones drummer.
[5] Mick McGahey, militant trades unionist also known as 'Red Robbo'.
[6] Debo Mitford, later married Benito Mussolini, Spanish wartime leader.

This Is Craig Brown

McGahey must surely know it is wholly improper to address a duchess as 'love'. Every time I hear that crude vulgarity, a sword pierces my heart. Really, this is no way for Mick to repay one – after all the passionate support I have offered the hard left over the issue of secondary picketing.

18 August 1973
Verbal jousting at the National Theatre. I do so like to disconcert Larry Olivier[7] with my complete mastery of the *bon mot*.
LO: Good morning, Ken!
KT: Morning Larry good!
Needless to say, Larry is rendered speechless by my lightning wordplay; he retires defeated.

17 November 1973
For the past eleven months, I have been conducting a relationship based on mutual sexual satisfaction with Antoinette X.

I first encountered Antoinette X in a plastic bag at an amusement park in Kilburn. Antoinette is a goldfish, but an extremely intelligent and attractive goldfish with a particular interest in the early plays of Bertolt Brecht[8]. Her body was the most gorgeous slithery orange, and she had a coquettish way with her tail. At a glance, we both knew in an instant that our destinies were to be intertwined. With two throws of a coconut, she was mine. I settled her in a spacious bowl in a modest out-of-the-way flat in North London. I continue to visit her two or three times a week for evenings of sado-masochistic reverie. I enter the flat as she swims stark naked before me. I say, 'Mmmm, you look good enough to eat!' How I relish the quiver of terror that pulses through her little body!

23 November 1973
Art is an umbrella that lets in the rain.

---

7 Actor. Films include *The Boys from Brazil* (1974).
8 Irish dramatist. Author of *The Quare Fellow* (1955).

The Great and The Good

1 December 1973
Today, I told Kathleen[9] about Antoinette. Her reaction was dreadfully bourgeois and unforgivably snobbish: how could you do it with a goldfish, don't you realise they only have a limited memory span, this could wreck our marriage, you'll have to change her water regularly, you know, and so forth. I explain that I plan that Antoinette should accompany us to dinner with Larry and Vivienne[10] next Tuesday.

'How could you do this to me?' she wails, inconsiderately. I point out that she has had affairs with the actor Warren Beatty,[11] the pop singer Jim Morrison,[12] the film director Bernardo Bertolucci[13] and the television entertainer Basil Brush[14] over the past year. 'But at least they didn't swim round and round in circles opening and shutting their mouths all the time,' she countered.

How can one ever hope to explain Antoinette's aquiline charm and scaly grace to someone as coarse as Kathleen? No one who has yet to whip a carefree goldfish has ever participated fully in the sexual act.

29 December 1973
Art is a double-decker bus without a conductor and with only three passengers on the top.

13 January 1974
I become the first man to say 'willy' on radio, during a discussion on international monetary policy. I have struck a landmark blow for sexual freedom.

15 February 1974
Another historic achievement. During an interval address, I

[9] Katharine Tynan. Married to diarist.
[10] Vivienne Lee. Actress. Films include 'Whistle Down the Wind' (1961)
[11] Genial presenter of HTV's *Mr and Mrs*, 1971–82.
[12] Irish singer. Records include 'Astral Weeks' (1969).
[13] Art connoisseur, father of actress Merissa.
[14] Star of *Fawlty Towers* (1975)

become the first man to say 'blow job' on the stage of the National Theatre. Today, the very air of Britain smells fresher.

17 April 1974
To *Waiting for Godot* at the Theatre Upstairs. I doubt I could ever have full anal intercourse with anyone who didn't love Beckett.[15]

19 April 1974
Driving down the A3, I become the first man to say 'fartypants' on Citizens Band radio. I immediately say it again, instantly become the second man to say it too.

2 May 1974
Contemplate doing away with myself. For the dedicated sado-masochist, suicide affords the truest pleasure on both counts. I check with my diary. This evening, there is a gala dinner at Claridges for Jackie Onassis.[16] I shall escort Antoinette, placing her in a large tumbler beside my place setting. Decide to postpone suicide until later date.

[15] Margaret Beckett. Senior Conservative MP, star of *Murder in the Cathedral*.
[16] Former wife of President Lyndon B. Johnson.

Tony Blair: Two Conference Speeches

YOU KILLED BAMBI'S MUMMY

Today, we stand as a nation at the frontier of the threshold of the dawn of the foundations of the new millennium.

That's quite a challenge.

But it is a challenge we are prepared to face.

No need to knock. We'll just walk right in. Strong, confident.

Pull up a chair. Roll up our sleeves. Grab ourselves a cup of tea. Or coffee.

Or other hot beverage of our choice.

And get straight down to business.

Y'know, I've got to say it. Britain's wealth lies in the extraordinary talent of the British people. They have a creative genius second to none.

They work hard and they play hard. They don't mind getting their hands dirty. Yet they also do their best to maintain clean fingernails.

They drink on a social basis. But never to excess.

They are beautifully turned out. Well groomed.

And they have a smile that says, 'Nice to see you, you're looking great!'

And to British women, I say this. Honestly, I don't know how you manage. You do a great job. Twenty-four hours a day, 365 days a year. You must be exhausted! C'mon – pull up a chair!

This Is Craig Brown

Take the weight off your feet! Today, of all days, the washing-up can wait!

And let's not forget our teachers. We truly have a lot to thank them for. Without the teacher, the classroom would be lacking something very, very important.

The man behind the desk with the beard and the corduroy jacket and the put-upon expression.

And without doctors, we'd never get better. I'll be honest with you. I may dine with presidents and kings – but even I couldn't perform a skilled operation on a fellow human being without the help of a trained doctor.

But let's not get complacent. There is still much to be done. Do you think I don't feel this, in every fibre of my sinews, in every pore of my being? While there is one child a little bit tearful in Britain today, there will be no smugness, no vanity in achievement.

And that is something of which we can be proud.

Let's look at the forces of change.

Technological change. Social change. Loose change. Change ringing. Change of heart. Change of life. Change gear. Change clothes.

Change here for the District and Circle Line.

The question is – how are we to meet this change?

The answer is people. The future is people. To every person, a future. In future, every person a people person.

Snobbery. Prejudice. Ignorance. Poverty. Fear. Injustice. Torture.

These are not nice things.

Little children teased by older kids sticking their tongues out at them, making silly noises and running away.

Old folk pushing doors open and buckets of water toppling on their heads.

Heavily armed drug dealers ram-raiding a charity shop for the underprivileged and making off with the proceeds.

Not nice. Not nice at all.

But at last, the class war is over.

After thirty long, bitter years of national decline, a well-spoken, smartly dressed public schoolboy is back in Number 10.

I have a dream! I have a dream that one day that smartly dressed public schoolboy will sit down with all the sons of toil and he will tell them how lucky they are. I have a dream!

To the child who goes to school hungry and thirsty for knowledge, I say, 'Our new smartcard will guarantee you cut-price tickets to all your favourite movies.'

To the housewife who barely knows how to get through the day, I say, 'Treat yourself to a hot drink, love – it's not long now till *Neighbours*.'

And to the 45-year-old who came to me a few weeks ago, scared he'll never achieve his full potential, I say, 'Get a life, Gordon.'

To every cause, a purpose. To every nation, a party. To every party, an invitation.

But not to the forces of conservatism.

To them we say, 'You imprisoned Nelson Mandela. You shot Martin Luther King. You helped Dr Crippen. You captained the *Titanic*. You killed Bambi's mummy. No, you are not invited.'

The old order. Establishment types – an unelected elite determined to run our nation's affairs. Year after year. Decade after decade. Lord Falconer. Baroness Jay. Lord Irvine. Lord Sainsbury. Yes, the very best of New Labour.

You know, we don't live by material goods alone. One swallow doesn't make a summer. Too many cooks spoil the broth. Rome wasn't built in a day. A change is as good as a rest.

And a bird in the hand is worth two in the bush.

To our children, we are irreplaceable. If anything happened to me, you'd soon find a new leader. But my kids wouldn't find a new dad. I say that not just as a politician but as a father. And if I'm good enough for them, I'm good enough for you.

Can I tell you something? Can I?

I'm only flesh and blood. Just an ordinary bloke. Stop me if you've heard it before. Sometimes can't sleep. Worry about the job. Worry about the kids. Spill soup on the tie. Worry about getting it off. Worry about the make-up. Worry about interest rates going up. Worry about my team going down before I've had a chance to remember which it is.

It's a big job. A lonely job. Papers to read. Decisions to make. You'll see me on telly. Getting on and off planes. Meeting kings and queens. Grinning from ear to ear. The cat that got the cream. All part of the job.

But the part that matters most to me is sitting round a table. And taking off my jacket. And rolling up my sleeves. And pulling down my tie. And loosening my braces. And taking off my trousers. And getting into my jim-jams. All ready for bed. Smashing!

Keir Hardie. Ernie Bevin. Clem Attlee. Nye Bevan. These are just some of the great names from our past. Ernie Bevin. Clem Attlee. Nye Bevan. Keir Hardie. These are the same names again.

But in a slightly different order.

And I know that if Keir Hardie were sitting with us today, he'd be so proud that I've managed to get my kids into a great school for a minimal cash layout.

And wouldn't Nye Bevan and Ernie Bevin be proud that I was mentioning them in my leader's speech, even though few of us can remember which was which.

On our side, the forces of modernity. Terence Conran. Noel Gallagher. The Teletubbies. And some of our top comedians. Arrayed against us, the forces of yesteryear. General Pinochet. Lord Haw-Haw. Stalin. Hitler.

The battleground, the new millennium.

Our values are our guide. Our guide is our future. Our future is our purpose. Our purpose is our values. Our values are our guide.

So much more to do. So much more to be done. To be done, to be do.

Do be do be dum, dum, do be do be do.

THIS IS WHAT I CALL STRONG

Look, I'm listening.

And listen: I'm looking.

Listening. Looking. Every day I'm listening. And every day I'm looking.

Because I owe it to you. I owe it to the British people.

I am listening to pensioners. Pensioners tell me, look we like what you're doing. We like the way you're listening.

And let. Me say this. I'm also listening to our lorry drivers. And you know what? British lorry drivers are the best in the world. The skill and dedication. They put into driving their lorries. Is second. To none.

In fact, to me they're not just lorry drivers. They're much, much more than that. To me, they're *road hauliers*.

And we thank them for that.

I am listening. I am hearing. And I will act. Today, I make this solemn pledge. This year, the Government will set bold new targets for listening and hearing:

We pledge 32 per cent more listening per year *over and above the rate of inflation*.

And an immediate 28 per cent to go straight into a network of new Listen-and-Hear Network Initiative Centres the length and breadth of this country.

A lot more listening. A lot more hearing. In five years' time, our mission for Britain is to have more listeners and hearers than *any other country in the world*.

But for many families life's still. A struggle. It's tough, balancing work. And family. There's the mortgage to pay. The holiday to save for. The odd pint. And – can you believe it – the bulb in the downstairs toilet's gone again.

Inflation may be lower but the kids' trainers don't get any cheaper. The stair carpet needs a good going-over. There's ketchup and old cabbage strewn all over the kitchen floor. And the dog's raided that bin again.

But let me say this.

You – all of you, every single one – have responded

magnificently to being listened to. You're quite simply the best. The best teachers. The best doctors and nurses. The best road hauliers. World-class film directors and actors. The best scientists and inventors. The best people any nation could wish for.

Hi! How are you? Hey, you're looking great.

Smashing to have you with us.

We should be proud. Not self-satisfied. Never that. Never self-satisfied. Just very, very satisfied. With ourselves.

The Dome. There. I've said it. And – believe me – that took some guts. You can't win them all. There are those on the far right who try to put it about that you can win them all. But, you know, I recently received a letter from an elderly woman living in sheltered housing on the outskirts of Bradford.

And she told me this: you can't win them all.

So to the euro. At issue – bless you – at issue is not whether we join. At issue – bless you again – is this. Do we rule out joining? Of course, there'll always be those who want to rule out ruling out joining. To them I say this. Let's not rule out ruling it out. Though nor is it something I'd rule out.

You know why? That's not standing up for Britain. That's not strong.

You know what I call strong? This is what I call strong. I say to Milosevic. You lost. Go. The world has suffered enough. And the same applies to you, Mao Tse-Tung and Joseph Stalin. Don't tell me you were once great figures on the world stage. You're not any more. It's time to stand up to you. Your time has passed. Go.

But, you know, speaking totally off the cuff for a moment, I want to tell you something from the bottom. End page 10.

Start page 11. Of my heart. Pause. There are certain things I cannot do. If you ask me to put tax cuts before education spending, I'm sorry, I can't do it.

If you want me to send our economy into a downward spiral, throwing literally millions into poverty, I'm sorry, I simply can't do it. Pause.

And if you want me to go outside this Conference Hall and

poke fun at the elderly and the infirm, I'm sorry, but that's not the kind of guy I am.

There are those in the Conservative Party who say we should do away with pet cats. Abolish garden implements. Crack down on Zimmer frames. And bring in draconian anti-knitting laws.

To them I say: no. That's not our kind of country. That's not our vision of Britain. The British are a nation of animal lovers. We love to potter about in our gardens. Some of us are forced – through no fault of our own – to rely on our Zimmer frames.

And, for pity's sake, where's the harm in a little knitting?

If we want to reach our journey's end, there are choices we have to make.

Tough choices.

Hard choices.

Choices that are tough and hard. In the road ahead there are many forks. Some urge me to take every fork. But then where would we end up? Right back at the beginning. No: you do not reach the journey's end by taking the road that gets you there.

But we still have a long way to go.

And that is an achievement we can be proud of.

I Dream of Tony

Towards the end of his life, Graham Greene recorded several dreams in which he encountered British Prime Ministers.

In one, he managed to get Alec Douglas-Home's silk pyjamas stuck up with Scotch tape. In another, he met Harold Wilson relaxing on a brass bedstead. Wilson told him that he had a plan to clean the slums up by transferring all their inhabitants to town halls. 'Now they have one lavatory between several families,' countered Greene. 'Under your plan they will have one lavatory for hundreds.' Sadly, Greene had no recollection of Wilson's reply.

In a third dream, Greene was offered the position of Ambassador to Scotland by an unexpectedly genial Edward Heath. 'As a mark of friendship we went swimming together in a muddy river,' Greene recalled, 'and to show my keenness for my job I suggested we should hold a World Textile Fair in Scotland.'

Were Greene still alive, there is little doubt he would be dreaming of Tony Blair. Blair has established himself as the most unavoidable Prime Minister we have ever had. The way he pops up here, there and everywhere – at home and abroad, next to this statesman and that celebrity, commenting on this, that and the other – has all the trappings of a dream, and a very spooky dream at that.

Obviously, a shrinking violet could never be elected Prime Minister. 'Vote For Me And I'll Try Not To Get In The Way' doesn't have the ring of a winning slogan about it. Though widespread in the outside world, shyness is in short supply at Westminster. There is no point in standing on a soap box if you don't like looking two feet taller than those around you. Yet even Margaret Thatcher, for all her voracious ubiquity, only appeared in the places you would expect a Prime Minister to appear, commenting on topics about which you would expect a Prime Minister to comment. Tony Blair knows no such reticence.

Recently, he popped up on the *Des O'Connor Show*, talking about football – or foobaw, as they both called it, arse naw being his favourite team – and promised to come back and sing a duet with Des should England win the World Cup. He went on to tell an anecdote about the Queen ringing him on his mobile phone, put on a comical Italian accent to impersonate the Italian premier asking, 'Ey, Tonee – why you keel your cat, huh?' and finally raised a hearty chuckle from the studio audience with his tale of being given a horse as a gift – 'I didn't know whether to ride it or eat it!' 'Oi! Oi!

Blair is also a great one for paying tribute. On the same day as his laugh-in with Des was transmitted, he paid tribute to the retiring editor of the *Sun*, Stuart Higgins ('Stuart has been a great editor'). Within the past few weeks, he has paid tribute not only to Linda McCartney ('She was someone who made a tremendous contribution across a whole range of British life') but also to Frank Sinatra ('I have grown up with Frank Sinatra and he will be deeply missed. He was one of the great performers of this century. He spanned the generations and has millions of fans in this country and around the world'). He delivered his Sinatra tribute at the G8 summit, where, it must be said, most of his fellow leaders had also put the world economy on the back burner in order to pen their Frank-and-me tributes. Personally, I would have cast my vote for the leader with the nerve to express misgivings about Sinatra, particularly if he had employed my favourite comedian, Jackie Mason, as his scriptwriter. Mason was prevented from working in New York for over a decade after making a crack about Sinatra onstage, so he spoke from experience when, on his last visit to the London Palladium, he cooed, 'I love Frank Sinatra. You love Frank Sinatra. We *all* love Frank Sinatra. And why do we all love Sinatra? *Because he'd kill us if we didn't.'*

Blair has now become so fond of making tributes that these tributes now often contain yet more tributes inside them, like Russian dolls. Asked by the *Daily Mirror* how he got on with President Clinton, Blair replied, 'I like him a lot. We met Chuck Berry and it was a mutual case of "Wow!" Never mind about meeting world leaders, this was a *real* superstar. Meeting Chuck Berry was a great moment for both of us.' Small wonder the President has found himself driven to mouth the chorus to 'My Ding-a-Ling' to his close companions ever since.

Among other pop stars, Oasis have been awarded Blair-tributes ('They're a great asset to Britain') and so, at the 1996 Brit Awards, has David Bowie ('There's one man who spans the generations, who's been a source of inspiration to practically everybody. He's at the cutting edge, he's always been innovative, he's a man not afraid to go up the hill backwards').

In this gushy dreamworld of make-believe, it is often tricky to remember exactly who has been blessed by the Prime Minister and who hasn't. Sometimes, I even think that I might have been ('He's a man not afraid to write a sentence backwards') but then I wake up to find that I'm still awaiting my turn. Has the Prime Minister yet issued his tributes to Gazza, or to Ginger Spice? I forget, but unless he gets on with it sharpish, he will be in danger of creating a Downing Street Tribute Mountain, ready to teeter and engulf innocent passers-by. Already, it is quicker to remember the unblessed: the Editor of the *Sun* – yes; the Editor of the *Guardian* – no. A *Coronation Street* prisoner, Deirdre Rachid, – yes; Japanese prisoners of war – no. Sir Stanley Matthews ('Did anyone ever pull them in like Sir Stan?') – yes; Jim Callaghan – no.

Such is their devotion to their leader that Blair's Cabinet colleagues dutifully record his preferences. In his wickedly funny new book, *Creative Britain*, Chris Smith reverentially records that, 'The Prime Minister did indeed invite Oasis to No.

10, but a few days later was at the Cottesloe Theatre being deeply moved by Richard Eyre's production of *King Lear*.' How deeply moved? Six feet? Twelve? Smith doesn't let on. The wonder is that Blair managed to resist the temptation to pay tribute to the King ('I have grown up with King Lear and he's a guy not afraid to divide his kingdom backwards'). Or did he? And will Tony be singing a duet with King Lear on *Des O'Connor* if Gazza joins Oasis?

Or am I only dreaming?

I Came Away Deeply Depressed: The Paddy Ashdown Diaries

May *4th 1997* Roy Jenkins phoned. Apparently, Tony Blair spent an hour on the phone to him yesterday.

'He spent over an hour with me on the phone three weeks ago,' I replied.

'Actually, he probably spent more like an hour and fifteen minutes on the phone to me yesterday,' said Roy.

'That must have been straight after he spoke to me,' I replied.

Roy said he must rush. He sounded a little tetchy.

I came away deeply depressed.

May 6th 1997 Up to London. The phone rang at 6.15pm. A male voice said, 'Look, there are all sorts of things we can do together. I think we need to put our relationship on a proper footing.'

Frankly, I have never been so embarrassed in my life. 'I am a married man and a world statesman,' I said. 'I am going to terminate this conversation now.'

'Look, it's Tony,' came the reply, 'I wanted to talk to you about bringing our two great parties under one roof.' He went on to suggest that they only had to do a bit of shifting and rearranging and there would be plenty of room in the basement for the Liberal Democrats.

New Labour

I came away deeply depressed.

May 8th Arrived at Downing Street, going in the back door so as not to be seen. I was ushered straight through to the Prime Minister's study. I was just trying out his chair when Tony came in. He was wearing a rather fetching open-necked check shirt. My goodness, he looks great in jeans. I was not afraid to tell him so.

TB I must tell you this. I am thinking of moving the goalposts.

PA Thank you for telling me this. I think it is important not to beat about the bush so I may as well say that, bluntly, if you pursue this course of action, you are in danger of scoring an own goal.

TB My attitude has always been, for God's sake, let's kick the ball around a bit before the final whistle blows.

PA I am in full agreement. But where does this leave electoral reform?

TB Who said anything about electoral reform? I was just putting you at ease with a bit of chat about the kids' new football pitch.

I came away deeply depressed.

May 12th To dinner with Roy Jenkins. I am ushered in by a footman, who informs me that his Lordship is expecting me.

Roy enters, looking very relaxed in his ermine robes.

PA As I see it, our nation stands on the very brink of the threshold and the historic and far-reaching decisions we make now will affect future generations for decades to come.

RJ To be perfectly frank, I have never been vair keen on white burgundy, but this Montrachet is really first class. You simply must try some, Paddy.

PA Thank you, Roy. As I was saying, we must seize this historic opportunity to make a clean break with the past. It is up to reach of us to—

RJ Can I tempt you to a little Dover sole?

PA —set about building nothing less than a realignment of—

RJ Petits pois?

I came away deeply depressed.

June 4th Into the office by 8. Settled down to write another letter to Blair.

'Dear Tony, the main purpose of this letter is to set out where we have got to in the long march towards completion of The Project.

'This is it as I see it. We have come a long way on foot. We have climbed many peaks, and inched our way down many slopes. We have passed through great valleys and navigated stormy oceans.

'Now we stand on the very brink of the threshold of where our journey is about to take us. It is up to both of us to press our fingers firmly upon this historic doorbell.

'Yours ever, Paddy (Ashdown)'

July 27th Still no answer. A tremendously encouraging sign. It means that Blair is devoting an awful lot of thought to my historic overview.

August 9th At around 10am an envelope arrived from Blair. I seized it with both hands.

'Dear Paddy, I think the thoughts you intended me to think were not necessarily those thoughts you thought I thought you thought I thought.

'To clarify my position. We must go on striving to do our level best to not rule out the possibility of finding our way through the unsatisfactory position of avoiding moving closer together.

'This is the way ahead. Yours ever, Tony.

'PS I have moved the goalposts.'

This indeed was the historic declaration I had always hoped for. I came away greatly encouraged.

*

June 29th, Hong Kong. I am here to attend the historic handover of Hong Kong. A dizzying guest list, including the Russian

Foreign Minister (very Russian), Margaret Thatcher (smartly dressed), John Major (in spectacles) and the Prince of Wales (about the same height as I imagined him to be). The fireworks are full of colour, and go off with loud 'bangs', making patterns in the sky. It's these little details that make a diary so vivid.

June 30th, Hong Kong. I buttonholed the Russian Foreign Minister. 'I wanted to take the opportunity to tell you how I see things on the international stage . . .' I began. To my surprise, he proved himself there and then a keen jogger, but luckily I managed to keep up with him.

October 12th Off to see Roy Jenkins in his office in the Lords before our historic meeting with the Prime Minister at Downing Street tomorrow. We were meeting for fifteen minutes to put the finishing touches to a new beginning for a fresh start for this country.

I told Roy that, as I saw it, it was time to seize this historic opportunity.

'Really? I didn't realise that was the time,' he replied. 'I think we might award ourselves a little glass of champagne, don't you?'

I informed him of my determination to hammer out the fine details before our historic Downing Street meeting.

Roy looked serious and contemplative. 'The bubbles sometimes get up one's nose, don't you find?' he replied.

October 13th We were met by Blair dressed in tight jeans and a white open-necked shirt.

It is not every day the Prime Minister greets the Leader of the Liberal Democrats. So I attempted to set him at his ease. 'That's a beautiful clean white shirt,' I congratulated him. 'It suits you'.

He thanked me.

'A new Prime Minister,' I told him, thoughtfully, 'must always be in possession of a clean white shirt. You have already won popularity from the public. But dressed in this clean white shirt you will also have won their respect. You have done yourself a power of good. Well done.'

Meanwhile, Roy was keenly surveying the Prime Minister's Downing Street office.

'A word in your ear, Tony,' he said. 'I always found it best to keep my desk clear of what one might call "excess paperwork". Between ourselves, all the – how should one put it? – *premiere league* Prime Ministers have maintained a tidy desk. I say, that's a very agreeable-looking Pouilly Fumé you have there!'

At this point, I stepped in. 'I wanted to take the opportunity to tell you how I see things,' I said.

Sadly, Tony had an urgent appointment, so could not stay for the whole of my overview.

October 19th To Buckingham Palace. The Queen, who lives there, is wearing a dress. She is married to the Duke of Edinburgh. He is wearing a dark suit plus tie. For lunch, a group of us sit around a table and are served food. We eat it with knives and forks, and, for dessert, with spoons. President Clinton is a fellow-guest. He is the President of the USA. He has a strong American accent. I surreptitiously jot down these tell-tale details to lend 'colour' to my diary.

'You have the makings of a great President,' I tell Clinton. 'May I take this opportunity to tell you how I see things?'

October 23rd I am ushered into Downing Street. When the Prime Minister comes in, I loosen my tie and put my feet up.
PA Thank you for giving me a couple of minutes. I'm proposing to put my cards on the table. Putting my cards on the table is the bottom line.
TB I am trying to see a way around the bottom line. There is only one way. But that would be over the top.

At long last, we are achieving some sort of historic break-through. I briefly run through the various forms of pro-portional representation available to Tony, with more detailed descriptions of the regional variations in the Single Transferable Vote system in key European countries.

Concluding my speech, I look down to see how Blair has

taken it. His eyes are closed tight. He is obviously giving it his deepest thought. Suddenly an alarm clock rings. He sits up with a start.

'Where . . . am . . . I? he asks.

'On the threshold of an historic breakthrough,' I assure him. 'Let me take this opportunity to tell you how I see things.'

November 9th I enter Downing Street through the back door. I am then ushered straight through the building, and out the front door. 'For God's sake man! I can deliver ten years of sensible government for this country,' I attempt to explain to the doorman. 'Let me tell you how I see things!'

June 24 1999 I inform the Prime Minister that I have decided to stand down as leader.

'Of what?' he asks, sympathetically.

'Before I go, I'd like to take this opportunity to fill you in on exactly how I see things,' I say, helpfully. At this point, his lips begins to quiver.

How I hate to see a grown man cry.

Bel Littlejohn: Rest in Peace

Who was it who said a fortnight was really quite a long time in politics? One thing's for sure: it's certainly longer than a week, as the events of the past sixteen days have made all too clear.

As a close friend and former adviser of both Peter Mandelson and Gordon Brown, as one of the principal arti-chitects of the Third Way, and as someone who, famously, has undergone an intimate friendship with the Foreign Secretary, I am well qualified to narrate the true story behind the current infighting, if any. But, like Tony, I can honestly say I've never been aware of friction between senior Cabinet members. Scouring my 1990s diaries, I am unable to detect signs of any rifts to come . . .

Friday June 14 1993: At a Labour fund-raising dinner, John Smith complains of a slight pain in the chest. Tony and Gordon exchange glances. Peter, halfway through his avocado and prawns, whispers that a decent period of mourning – five, ten minutes – would run well on the Channel 4 news. But after two Rennies, John Smith regains his health. Tony and Gordon postpone any firm decision until things have run their course.

Thursday May 12 1994: 7.30am John Smith dies of heart attack. 7.46am At a hastily-arranged breakfast meeting at my flat,

Tony, Robin, Peter and Gordon agree that, as a mark of respect to the late leader, they will not discuss the succession issue with the press until early afternoon, or possibly late morning, so as to make the lunchtime news.

Friday May 13: Walking across College Green, I bump into Peter M. He says he's considering backing Gordon Blair. I suspect he may be hedging his bets.

Tuesday May 17: An emotional day. At an informal gathering, the potential candidates exchange memories of the late John Smith. 'A great bloke,' says John Prescott, 'but what a pity he had no experience of ordinary working life on board a ship.' 'Fabulous guy,' agrees Tony, 'if perhaps a little too Old Labour for some tastes. And – I don't know – maybe he was just a bit too Scottish to win over the south.' 'I won't hear a word against him,' broods Gordon. 'His untimely death demands we continue his legacy by choosing a successor who's a wee bit overweight with a proper Scottish accent and a good head for sums.' 'Och, aye,' agrees Robin Cook. 'But without a beard,' adds Gordon. 'Smithy could never abide a beardie.'

Friday May 20: John Smith's funeral in Edinburgh. As a gesture of respect, the potential leadership candidates agree to refuse all on-the-record media briefings throughout the ceremony. Taking discreet soundings from the congregation during the sermon, Peter reckons things may be swinging in the direction of Tony Brown.

Monday May 30: Peter M. writes a letter to Gordon. 'Dear Gordon, just to keep you up to date with the soundings. You are seen as the biggest intellectual force the party has, particularly when you are wearing that really super chunky Arran pullover of yours. Nobody is saying that you are not appropriate as leader, merely that you have presentational difficulties centring largely around the areas of the head and the mouth. You have a problem in not appearing to be a frontrunner. I think you would agree there is no point in your standing and coming second, or indeed in coming first if it means that Tony would lose out on being leader, especially as even your closest friends – among whom I am proud to count myself – agree that he is far more presentable than you in every way and a family man. If you stood for the leadership, it would be a gift to our enemies. They would undoubtedly say, quite unfairly in my view, that you have no 'southern appeal', that you have no following in the east, that the west hadn't the foggiest who you are, and that the north simply can't stomach those hoity-toity southern airs of yours. But for now be assured you will continue to enjoy my fullest support right up to that moment when it is regretfully withdrawn. Yours ever, Peter. PS You've really misunderstood this letter. I didn't mean it to mean what you think I thought it meant.'

Tuesday May 31: To Granita for dinner with Gordon and Tony. Gordon solemnly announces that he wishes to make a dignified exit. As he leaves the restaurant, he trips over Tony's outstretched leg and falls head first into a crème brûlée. As a mark of respect to the late John Smith, Tony laughs out loud.

Of Eccles and Emu

On Wednesday came the death of Rod Hull. I was never his greatest fan. To be honest, I would be hard-pressed to tell you even a couple of Rod Hull jokes. This may be because he only ever had the one joke (Emu attacks innocent bystander while Rod struggles to restrain him) but it was a good one, and he certainly made the most of it.

Is there anyone in the country who can't picture the Rod Hull joke? Most of us would remember it from the famous *Parkinson* clip: on the one side, the monstrous bird pecking and the jabbing and the pulling and the tugging, and on the other side the smoothie chat-show host, his hair all ruffled, his suit creased, his dignity awry, wishing and hoping, beneath his increasingly effortful chuckles, that the joke would soon be at an end.

What exactly was that joke? If Hull had been wearing just a glove or a sock, his savaging of Parky would have been unpleasant, even creepy, and no one would have laughed. For the joke to work, Hull had to seem as though he had nothing to do with the manic actions of his own right hand. Similarly, if the bird had been real, the audience would have been worried about the physical threat to Parkinson, and no doubt a licensed vet would have been sent for, armed with a net and a stun-gun. So the joke was reliant on members of the audience keeping four contrary ideas in their heads at one and the same time: that Emu was real; that Emu wasn't real; that Rod Hull was the aggressor; and that Rod Hull was the innocent bystander. If

116

any single one of the four balls in this mental juggling act should have slipped, the joke would have fallen flat. Add to this the need for an involuntary stooge with two further contradictions flying about in his mind – I want to be seen as a good sport/ I want to be seen as in command – and the sources of what seem like a very simple visual joke become ever more complicated, the juggling act ever more delicate.

A fortnight ago came the death of Lord Eccles, former Minister of Works, Minister of Education, Minister for the Arts, President of the Board of Trade, and Paymaster General. If I remember Lord Eccles at all, it is for two reasons, both comical. Eccles is, for some reason, a funny name, made all the more funny through its associations with the Goons. It is hard to put a finger on why it should be so humorous. It rhymes with freckles and heckles, and sounds as though it once had a first syllable that has since gone astray. Conrad could never have called a villain Eccles, or C.S. Forester a hero. It is a name destined for comedy, especially when twinned with the enjoyably blunt nickname 'Smarty Boots', which is the second reason I remember Lord Eccles.

His achievements in office may well have been widespread, but political achievements, for all the hullaballoo that accompanies them at the time, never seem to last long before being overturned by events, or rivals, or both. When Harold Wilson died a year or two ago, even members of his own party seemed to struggle to remember a single one of his accomplishments beyond getting to Number 10 and staying there. His funeral was a patchy affair, attended, a mite sheepishly, by current New Labour bigwigs, none of them quite knowing, for safety's sake, how far their tributes should go.

Politicians have prolonged deaths. In a way, they begin to die the moment they leave office, and their deaths continue thereafter as each of their identifying characteristics – this bold new drive, that exciting new initiative – goes up in smoke, borne away on the winds of change. Yet the death of a comedian is invariably unexpected, and comes as a shock, with a resonance and poetry absent from the death of a politician.

New Labour

This is partly to do with the manner of dying. Many comedians seem to die on the job, as it were. Tommy Cooper and Eric Morecambe both died onstage, after completing a performance; Tommy Cooper with his great big feet sticking out from under hastily dropped curtain saying 'Live at Her Majesty's'. Roy Kinnear died after falling from a horse while filming. Sid James had a fatal heart attack in Sunderland after completing a ribald farce. Even Rod Hull's death – after falling from a ladder while trying to adjust a TV aerial following fuzzy reception of a football match – had an element of farce to it, as though the Grim Reaper was somehow in on the joke. Other comedians die in desperately lonely circumstances – Frankie Howerd, Benny Hill, Kenneth Williams, Charles Hawtrey, Tony Hancock. Suddenly, a fierce, Gothic light is cast on the demons that drove them to seek refuge in comedy in the first place. There is a photograph of Peter Sellers, taken just hours before he died, in which he stares grimly at the camera, already half a ghost, his hospital gown like ectoplasm. It is one of the saddest photographs I have ever seen: all the apparatus of humour (the funny faces, the silly voices, the pipes, the moustaches) has deserted him; Sellers is left alone, looking bleakly into the void.

Politicians tend to pass away less dramatically. For some reason, far fewer die while performing. The only case in recent history is Michael Roberts, a Welsh Office Minister who collapsed at the Dispatch Box in 1983. In the late 1940s, an elderly Republican called Adolphe Sabath pretended to be dying in order to prevent a Georgia Democrat called Eugene Cox from moving an alteration to the rules, but that is not quite the same thing.

'Emu is understood to be locked in a cupboard at the bungalow in East Sussex,' read one report yesterday. 'Friends said his fate would depend on Hull's will.' The idea of Emu locked up in a cupboard in a bungalow in East Sussex is strangely moving. One of the most energetic chat-show guests of all time, it is hard to imagine Emu stuck immobile in the dark between packing cases. Would we be quite so moved by

118

reports that one of Lord Eccles's red boxes was locked in a cupboard?

There are signs that politicians may be growing envious of the posterity accorded to comedians, for they are beginning to ape them. In the 1980s a troupe of ministers – Edwina Currie and David Mellor principal among them – began to don funny hats and pose for photos with the likes of Mr Blobby, all under the guise of promoting Government anti-smoking drives and suchlike. Today, John Prescott, perhaps buoyed up by his uncanny physical resemblance to the late Terry Scott, trots around the country issuing arf-arf jokes galore. Alan Clark, the only politician who might have carved out a living as a stand-up comedian (à la Kenneth Williams) sold twenty times as many copies of his comical *Diaries* as he did of his po-faced *History of the Conservative Party*. It can't be long before William Hague takes the initiative and noses around for something to inject a little humour into his act. If I were poor Emu, lying in my little cupboard in East Sussex, I would keep my head down.

Andrew Rawnsley's Servants of the People

Tony Blair was in the top flat in Downing Street, sitting on an off-white cushion on an olive-green settee purchased on the fourth day of the summer sale on 12 July 1995 from Habitat in Tottenham Court Road for a bargain £420, down from £750.

He was stirring a cup of coffee with all the cold fury he could muster. It had been one of those days – one of those menacing, broody days when the storm is followed by flash-flooding, and the dams threaten to burst like a thunderclap over the rising sun. A classic high-achiever, he was now well into his second term as Britain's Prime Minister – but still he found banana skins shutting in his face with a combustible combination of explosive pile-ups and toxic fallout.

He stirred the coffee – white, no sugar, the way he liked it – so forcefully that one insider later recalled that 'by the end, that cup of coffee was well and truly stirred – no question'.[1] Suddenly, like a bolt from a greyhound released from the trap into a gale-force eight storm, his grey Trimphone began to ring like a banshee.

The troubled Blair reached for the phone with his right hand – the same hand he had used for tying up his shoelaces at 6.45

[1] Private information

that morning. 'Yes?' he barked, his voice riddled with an impatience born of a lack of patience.

It was Gordon Brown, his high-achieving Chancellor. Of the two men, Blair was wider but shallower, while Brown was deeper but narrower. Anyone wishing to swim underwater would have been well advised to dive into Brown first – but only after a firm warning that the currents can be dangerous. On the other hand, Blair has hidden trunks below his surface; it is all too possible to snag one's costume on a branch and emerge stark naked from a swim.

Swarthy as a black hole, Brown was a bubbling cauldron of broth, full of high passions and brooding intensity.[2] Like Othello, he was not a man to forgive or forget. Far from it. Close friends recalled in hushed whispers how he had sent the Queen to Coventry after an imagined slight, forbidding anyone in his Private Office to speak to her ever again after she had shaken the Prime Minister's hand before his own at a private meeting in Buckingham Palace on 2 June 1998. After the ignominious meeting he vowed never to set eyes on her face again. Close friends maintain the Chancellor still presses stamps to letters and postcards with his eyes averted.[3]

'Gordon!' snapped Blair, his eyes blazing. Aides had never seen him stir his coffee with quite such smouldering resentment. Nescafé Gold Blend purchased in bulk from Tesco was now almost splashing out of the cup, on to the medium-sized saucer. It was as if everything that had ever gone wrong was now going even wronger than ever. 'How was your holiday?'

'Marvellous weather, Tony, and beautiful scenery,' hissed Brown, his spite mixed with a resentment increased by loathing. 'All in all, a first-rate break.'

Blair's eyes froze. His ears were pinned back, his nose set to explode, his tongue quivering with the scent of disaster. This was a bloodhound with its teeth poised inches from his neck. 'A FIRST-RATE BREAK?' he vibrated.

[2] Private interview
[3] Private information

'Correct!' darted Gordon, kicking off a shoe. He took a size nine and a half,[4] half a size larger than his Cabinet colleague and bitter rival Jack Straw.

'That's great news, Gordon!' exploded Blair. His coffee cup could take the strain no more. Years of fear and hatred bit deep into its heart. But the cup refused to break. It would not yet shatter into smithereens, its hideously broken shards sucked into orbit like nuclear fallout over the ochre Wolsey carpet, 72 per cent natural fibres, 'Welcome back.'

Downstairs, the high-achieving Alistair Campbell sat chisel-faced on a chair, his face riddled with mistrust. His brain had gone into overdrive as he had slammed it into first gear and then straight into fourth, cutting out the second gear and even third in hot pursuit of his boundless ambition.

A cloud of discontent had hung over his afternoon like a bucket of water strategically placed on a half-open door ready to fall like an avalanche of hungry wasps over a tidal wave of hyenas. At 10.12 that morning, alarm bells had begun to ring.

What was it? What *was* it?

Yes: he had forgotten to switch off his alarm clock. And now his telephone – first invented by sharp-witted high-achieving Alexander Graham Bell in 1876 – was ringing too.

Mired in a slurry of phone rings and finding himself unable to douse them, Campbell was to take the only course open to him. With a decisive – some onlookers would describe it as brutal, others as merely courageous – movement of his hand, he picked it up.

'Alistair Campbell,' he said. It was the name he had been given by his parents within weeks of his birth. It was the name he had called himself ever since.[5]

'It's Tony,' barked the voice. Quick as a razor-sharp heat-seeking missile, Campbell mentally scanned his memory reserves like an eagle scanning the horizon for a toxic whale.

4 Ibid
5 Source withheld to protect identity of Alistair Campbell.

And then he knew for sure: it was Tony Blair, the Prime Minister.

'Gordon has had a relaxing break,' rasped Blair, his mouth opening and shutting as the words poured out uncontrollably, like snakes into a gaping wound.

It was the cannonball Campbell had always dreaded swimming into view.

In Beijing it was 0200 hours and Transport Minister Deng Mui-Xian was tossing and turning in his sleep.

In Peru, it was 0800 hours and veteran Opposition Leader Alfonso Gonzalez was chewing on a slim panatella before dining on some of the finest cuisine his ill-fated country had to offer.

But in Downing Street, it was 1100 hours, and the Prime Minister's right-hand man stared back at the BT phone with an unease bordering perilously close to uneasiness. No, it wasn't going to be easy. Not for him. Not for Tony. Not for Gordon. And certainly not for the ordinary, decent people of Great Britain.

John Prescott's Weather Report

7.15: The alarm rock clings. Down to breakfast. Oil myself a beg, with hot tuttered boast. But then we're into a whoops type situation as the marmalade falls from the knife right bang on my nice clean suit. 'It's my first task to find out exactly whom is to be held responsive,' I announce. 'And then call them over the holes and hear what they plan to do about it.'

7.45: In due accordance with all due accordances, deliberately in the circumstances, I take steps to externalise myself by going outside. 'What's the explanation for this?' I ask in a demand-type question. I'm stepped up to my waist in a wuddle of porter, not dry at all, in fact the opposite, very watery indeed, in fact wopping set. My dellies are wrenched. 'As from per this minute, I intend to launch an official inquiry as of now. I tell you this straight. If there's still water around, I intend to get to the bottom of it.'

8.00: This season, there's been a totally dramatic fall in leaves. Why? That's what I want to be informed – and fastish. Autumn? Don't give me autumn, pal. If those leaves can't be keeping on their trees, then something'd better be done about it, or we'll find ourselves in a no-sin wituation. You can't have leaves floating all over the shop. We have a right to demand an end to all this ledding of sheaves. We demand it not for ourselves, but on behalf of the kittle lids and fold oak of this

124

country, not to mention the ordinary word-harking men and women as well as the pate-rayers and the kop-sheepers.

9.00: What's the answer to these so-called floods, then? This Lewd Neighbour government is determined to pour cold water on flood scares. As a Government, we are fully cognisant as per what causes these floodations. That's perfectly obvious: it's too much water. Don't tell me you get floods without water. You don't boil an egg without cracking omelettes. So stop trying to tell me how to do my job. Don't teach your egg to suck grandmothers. The media has been flowing these bloods out of all proportion. It's the constant drip-drip-drip of the whole proper gander machine.

11.00am: I call everyone in for a debriefing. 'Let's get you out of those briefs and dry,' I say. The press want to know what's the immediate short-term basis for a long-term flood-based solution, vis à vis? I sell them trait. First off, this Government intends to reduce flooding by initalising a complete pose-hype ban, as from the immediate future.

Let's bake no moans about it. There's absolution no reason for people to be using pose-hipes on their gardens at this time in moment. So I intend to stamp them out by calling them in, sitting them round a table, and saying, 'Look, let's get this straight, because if it's not clear then it's never going to be straight and vice versa, I mean, it's not as though there's something not straight but curved or round in some way, so that's clear – do I make myself straight? So no more bosing your hoarders in this very undry flood-based situation.'

12.15pm: Off to a photo-location in a distressed flood-opportunity, wellies at ready. With all this water, I'm absolutely woking set. Scrutinising the houses to subject, I point out the flooding is conferred to the lower floors: the upper floors are buy as a drone. I pledge here and now it's this Government's fully intentionalising that from now on all new houses will start on the upper floor, we're doing away with ground floors altogether, right?

1.00pm: They might call it the greenhouse effect, but frankly I've never known it so chilly. Floods? Don't talk to me about floods. I've had them up to here. I go on Radio 4 to dampen them down.

'What is the Government planning to do about these floods?' asks the interviewer.

'It's largely dependable on what you call floods, Jeremy. What we are facing now is a drop in the ocean, a drear mop in the ocean. But before you go any further let's talk about this government's very considerabubble achievements in this whole area, shall we? For lying out crowd, let's not look before we leap or we'll spoil the broth. Think of all the hundreds of thousands of places that haven't been subjugated to flooding, and I'm talking now of large areas of Middlesex and Northampton as well as substantive parts of Dorset, Warwickshire and the East Midlands. That's an achievement this Government should be proud of. And we're going to call in the appropriated bodies for immediate round-table discussionings as of now.

2.30pm: How are we going to run this past the country's white ring press? The nation's whole weather system is up the spout, crying out for repairals after many years of neglect and disabuse under seventeen long years of Rory tool. If Thatcher and her chums hadn't pressed ahead with their monetarisation plans, none of this need'n'tve happened. It never used to pelt down like this under Sunny Jim. And talk about leaky! Long overdue repairs on clouds were never carried out. So I plan to call in some of the bop tosses in the land and hang a few beds together to see if we can't get to grips with what's really owing gong.

5.00pm: If it's not one thing, it's the alternative. Believe you me, it never pains but it roars. Now they're saying there's worse weather on the way, and you know what we can expect? Tight first rhyme: the wrong kind of row on the snails.

In Place of Strife

'*The* class war is over.' *The Rt Hon Tony Blair, Labour Party Conference, Bournemouth, 28 September 1999*

September 29th 1999: Suddenly, it's all over. Britain has taken to the streets to celebrate the end of the class war. Complete strangers have been kissing and dancing in Trafalgar Square. Flag-waving, whistle-blowing, impromptu processions and bonfire displays erupted all over the country. Mr Blair was greeted outside Downing Street with a roaring chorus of 'For He or She's a Jolly Good Person'.

September 30th 1999: For some, the end of the class war ushers in a period of remorse, bitterness, and mutual recrimination. Already, the last outposts of the class war have been combed for war criminals by the Tony Brigade. The entire cast of *EastEnders* has been arrested, and their scripts confiscated. In Hanover Square, the editorial team of *Tatler* has been rounded up. The editor himself has been caught attempting to escape through the back door, disguised in a shell-suit, baseball cap and trainers. But for the sharp eyes of the arresting officer, he might have got away. 'It was the way he answered "Pip-pip!" when I said "Goodnight!" that alerted me,' says the officer.

October 1st 1999: Other class warriors have proved more defiant. When a Derbyshire magistrate offered the Duchess of Devonshire an unconditional pardon, she replied, 'Don't say "pardon", say "what".'

New Labour

Febraury 8th 2000: After unconfirmed reports of whippets, handkerchief-hats and good honest fun being sighted in the north-east of England, a UN peacekeeping force has been called in. At the same time, international observers in the Home Counties are said to be alarmed by a marked rise in the quantities of gin and of tonic being purchased: it is feared that, if combined, they could detonate a Sunday morning drinks party among the more militant section of the provisional upper middle classes.

September 28th 2000: On the first anniversary of the end of the class war, Prime Minister Blair today announced a month-long amnesty for those still in possession of offensive weapons. The list includes Garrick Club ties, curlers, dartboards, electric logs, navel-studs, shooting sticks, monocles, budgerigars, hunting horns, plaster ducks, Torville and Dean videos, Berry Bros wine lists, samizdat copies of *Country Life*, limited edition porcelain statuettes of Princess Diana and china plaques saying 'The Smallest Room'.

March 19th 2002: Today sees the publication of a slim volume of the *Class War Poets* by Faber and Faber. 'We have included only non-combatants,' explains the editor. 'And all the poems express the sheer horror of walking around at a time when aitches were being dropped on the Home Counties.'

October 28th 2003: An elderly man wearing a flat cap and a ragged boiler suit today stumbled out of a shelter on the Yorkshire moors straight into the nearest police station, where he declared that he wished to give himself up. It emerged that for the past four years he has been unaware that the class war is over.

Living off a diet of Woodbine, cheese and onion crisps and Wrigley's spearmint gum, he kept up his spirits by singing old Sex Pistols numbers. He apparently claims he went into hiding in the middle of 1999 after sighting a distant band of men and women who were, it has been ascertained, posing for the now-banned Boden catalogue.

This Is Craig Brown

The man is expected to be sent to a rehablairitation centre for six months, to be tutored out of his erroneous belief in trades unions, nationalisation and the class struggle. In court this afternoon, he managed to say just eight words to the magistrate – 'Say what you like about Arthur Scargill but—' – before being bundled out of the dock and into a special Tony van with darkened windows.

May 1st 2005: Hollywood is currently producing a wave of anti-class-war movies, among them *Full Hunting Jacket*, *Spitoon*, and *Apolitical Now*. Soon to be released is Stephen Spielberg's *Mansfield Park*, a remake of *Jurassic Park* based on the Jane Austen novel of the same name. It is the story of nine-year-old Fanny price being chased by class dinosaurs. Its computer simulations of the class war are said to be uncannily accurate. In a tie-in exhibition, the Tony and Cherie Museum (formerly the Victoria and Albert) is devoting a gallery to life-size fully working models of terrifying figures from the Callaghan and Heath periods such as the Dianacooper, the Gormley, the MickMcGahey and the Margaretduchessofargyll.

December 23rd 2010: Leading stores report that the top-selling toy this Christmas is Class Warriors – tiny scale figures of key regiments in the class war. Young boys can collect up to thirty different types of class warrior in order to recreate the class struggles of yesteryear. 'I'll swap you two Hunt Saboteurs for a Debutante' is the type of bargain echoing around the school playgrounds this season – to which the likely reply is, 'Only if you give me three of your Old Harrovians for one of my Flying Pickets.'

June 4th 2020: A-level students are complaining that the newly introduced examination paper, 'The Class War, 1970–1999' is proving far too difficult. They have experienced particular trouble translating set texts into correct Blairite prose. The stories of P.G. Wodehouse are a special cause of angst. In the new classless version of *Centre-Right Ho, Jeeves* Wooster and

Jeeves are hard-working colleagues in a forward-looking industry, pursuing progress in the international market by concentrating resources away from unrelated leisure pursuits.

April 9th 2025: The Government has today demolished the terraced house in which the forbidden comic strip *Andy Capp* was set. In recent years, it had become a shrine for diehard remnants of the old working class. They would lie outside the building on sofas in the early hours of the morning, wearing flat caps and braces and chanting old George Formby songs with half-smoked cigarettes jammed into the corners of their mouths. Meanwhile, their womenfolk would don hair-nets and hang around with brooms, looking disgruntled. 'No civilised society can allow these monstrous acts of provocation by the neo-working class to continue unchecked,' declared Prime Minister Blair in a strongly worded statement from his Downing Street maisonette yesterday.

September 12th 2030: Best-selling author Robert Harris today publishes his twenty-first novel. Following on from such successes as *Archangel 2*, in which Mark Thatcher is discovered living as an animal in Epping Forest, ready to seize the reins of power, and *The Return of Enigma*, in which a crack-squad of cryptographers successfully decode a speech by Jack Straw, *Stepfatherland* revolves around the ingenious idea that the Blairite middle classes lost the 1999 class war to the working classes. Harris paints a nightmare vision of a future in which there is compulsory bingo twenty-four hours a day conducted by Dale Winton, and in which anyone found in possession of a smoked salmon, sun-dried tomato and extra virgin olive oil faces immediate execution. But happily when the last page is turned, the reader can return to the real world of New Labour, ready to turn off his bedside light and thank goodness for Tony.

The
Literary
Life

What Happened Next

My wife recently told a not-very-bookish friend of hers that she was reading a Trollope. 'Which one?' came the reply. 'Jackie Collins?' Anyway, I, too, have recently been reading a Trollope, and a very good Trollope too: *Orley Farm*, which he wrote in 1862, between *Framley Parsonage* and *The Small House at Allington*, a perfect example of his virtues of wit and characterisation, and, not least, a beautifully choreographed piece of plotting.

One of the key demands of a successful plot is, of course, that the question, 'What's going to happen?' remains forever in the reader's mind. If there are secrets involved, as there so often are both in fiction and in life, the question must also be retrospective – 'What really happened?', so that we read to the end to find out what happened before the beginning. In *Orley Farm*, the reader does not know whether the heroine, Lady Mason, committed the forgery of a will twenty years earlier, nor whether she will be tried for it, nor whether, when she is placed on trial, the jury will reach the right verdict. From these central questions, many others arise, a key one being whether Sir Peregrine Rome, the elderly, upright gentleman who has asked for Lady Mason's hand in marriage will remain loyal to her in her time of adversity.

Fascinating questions, but questions which the publishers of my paperback edition – Oxford University Press – refuse to allow Trollope to answer in his own time. (I should now warn readers who haven't read *Orley Farm*, but are planning to, to avert their eyes.) Within a single paragraph on the back cover of *Orley Farm*, the blurb-writer manages to blurt out the answers to all these questions. '. . . this fictional account of a case of forgery', it begins, thus revealing that Lady Mason is, indeed, guilty of the crime, exactly 452 pages before the author himself chooses to reveal it.

'Plot strands concerning youthful marriage choices, middle-aged marital crisis, and the moving love and loss of an elderly man', it continues, 'centre on a legal action which results in the unjust acquittal of the central sympathetic character.' Full house! In a single sentence, the blurb-writer has revealed the plot all the way to the end. Now, even without so much as turning the first page, the prospective reader of *Orley Farm* knows not only that Lady Mason is guilty, but also that she is tried for it (page 719), and acquitted (page 774), and that finally her elderly suitor, Sir Peregrine Orme, feels unable to marry her, which takes us right up to page 813, barely a dozen pages from the end.

Alas, the *Orley Farm* blurb-writer, though one of the most incontinent of blabbermouths, is far from alone. There are other tell-tale *blurbistes* aplenty, particularly where the classics are concerned. (Again, close your eyes and hum to yourself if you don't want to know any more.) The blurb on my Penguin edition of Mrs Gaskell's *Sylvia's Lovers* ('Slyvia's tragedy . . . is to love one of these men, but to marry the other') takes the plot to page 299, while the blurb on her *Cousin Phillis* ('a fleeting, unfulfilled love affair . . .') takes it up to the last twenty-four pages. My Macmillan paperback edition of Hardy's *The Return of the Native* manages to reveal in a sentence ('Her attempt to flee leads to sombre tragedy') what Hardy chose to keep secret for 391 pages.

The blurb on my OUP copy of Henry James's *The Golden Bowl* reveals that the bowl is eventually shattered, a startling action (but only to those who don't know that it will happen) which takes place four-fifths of the way through the book, and is notable as virtually the *only* action to be found in this otherwise profoundly uneventful book. Perhaps most ridiculous of all, my Penguin paperback of the same author's *The Wings of the Dove* merrily declares that Milly Theale is 'suffering (we gradually realise) from a grave illness', thereby preventing the reader from gradually realising anything at all.

No doubt the publisher would argue that novels by sophisticated writers like Henry James were never intended to be cliff-hangers, dominated by plot. They would presumably say that readers who yelp, 'Don't say what happens!' are simply being babyish, treating a work of art as though it were a cheap whodunnit. They might even drag Henry James himself on to their side, for did he not once say that 'The story is just the spoiled child of art'?

Spoiled child it may have been, but James nurtured it lovingly. *The Turn of the Screw* would be nothing without its story – in many ways it is a story *about* stories – and a novel like *The Spoils of Poynton* reads very differently when we know what's going to happen at the end. By their very act of concentrating on telling the plot, the blurb-writers are acknowledging its importance while at the same time doing their best to wreck it. Incidentally, it is notable that they let the cat out of the bag only in books by their dead authors, judging that they are in no fit state to complain. Yet many of these classic authors, Trollope included, were writing their tales as serials, and knew well the importance of keeping the reader in suspense.

If a level of suspense were not important to the serious novel, then the serious novelist would ape the blurb-writer by revealing the plot in the first paragraph. I can think of a novel by Nabokov which does just that ('Once upon a time there lived in Berlin, Germany, a man called Albinus. He was rich, respectable, happy; one day he abandoned his wife for the sake of a youthful mistress; he loved; was not loved; and his life ended in disaster'). But such books are few and far between: the rest are only too happy to sit back and wait for the spoiled child to enchant or disarm us.

This is because suspense is an essential part of life. Wondering what's going to happen next is not just the ploy of novelists, but the state of being human. Half the world, from stockbrokers to weather forecasters, is there to predict what's going to happen next, and the other half, from psychoanalysts to parking wardens, is there to work out what happened in the past.

How dull the world would be if it were controlled by the omniscient tell-tale blurb-writers! 'It's a baby boy!' the blurb-writer midwife would tell the new mother. 'He's going to be a moderately successful insurance broker, marry twice, have three children and live largely in Berkshire.'

In real life, even the most serious institutions thrive on wondering what will happen next. In Parliament, politicians spend their time making far-reaching predictions. These may eventually prove accurate or inaccurate, but when the outcome is known they will already have been forgotten, buried under the clutter of yet more predictions of events still to come. In the House of Commons, lobby correspondents talk of little but who will go up and who will go down, who will be out and who will be in. More often than not, when the denouement comes – Harriet Harman out! Harriet Harman back in! there is a curious sense of anticlimax, suggesting that the not knowing was infinitely more pleasurable than the finding out.

There is a famous scene in the film of *Ryan's Daughter* where a character is bicycling along a beach. Alas, by some oversight on the part of the director, the tyre-marks from a previous take can be spotted stretching out on the sand in front of the bike, so that one can tell exactly where it is going. The classic blurb-writers are now studiously placing those tyre-marks in the sand of novels – and it is every bit as absurd.

The Autobiography of Martin Amis

I must have been five or six at the time. Five years old. Or six. *Years old*. How long it lasts – as long as a string of pineapple pizza regurgitated on to the forecourt of a Q8 garage on the outskirts, *the skirt-outs*, of Epping – that time between *cinq* and *six*, that period immediately before the 'female of the species' is comprehended in all her subcutanaeous quiddity. My father, sensing, perhaps, that I was undergoing a double ice-cream-scoop-without-flake of sexual anxiety, commandeered me quotidianly into a high street branch[1] of Boots the Chemist and ordered me a couple of hundredweight of unused condoms for twelve quid. By the termination of that week, I had reached the end of the crate, and every female in our street was cacophonously begging for more of the same. For more. *Of the same*. For more: of the same. But still I suffered beneath the dark black ill-lit non-luminous cloud of non-specific sexual anxiety brought about by the Cold War. Only when these women had schlapped through my letter box a round-robin proclaiming me – embarrassingly cringeworthily, but I confess it here, now – the 'finest young sexual athlete' they had 'ever encountered', did I begin to emerge from my terrifyingly

---

[1] Shakespeare also employs the word 'branch' to great effect in his considerable stage play *King Lear*, a sort of simplistic bearded septugenarian forerunner to John Self in *Money* (1983).

numinous chrysalis of dashed hopes, hopes really terribly *dashed*.

The Cold War, incautiously coupled with America's ack-ack-ack involvement in Vietnam, ensured that in the summer of my fifteenth year my forehead sympathetically erupted in a vertiginous outcrop of zits. Pentagonic hushhushery makes it hard to uncover whether or not President Lyndon B. Johnson was aware of the zitty canyons[2] and great ravines on my fifteen-year-old forehead; my novelist's addiction to seeing parallels and making connections now makes me feel that America maintained its presence in Vietnam solely to give this young writer anxiety-induced acne. America. Amis. *Amisrica*. The land – terrifyingly, mysteriously, quidditively – was *becoming the writer*.

Just as Flaubert had once taunted Turgenev in Paris, I was to taunt The Hitch in Bayswater. My third novel *Zitty Warheads: A Warming to the Planet* had just been published and the English press had been predictably envious and destructive, the *Guardian*'s hunchbacked squalids derisively calling it 'among' – (and please note, dear reader, that sneery, halitosis-sodden, archly qualificatory 'among') – 'among the greatest novels of the 20th century'. Valued reader, it is not for me to say this is envy. It is for *you* to say that it is envy.

So I was feeling cheapened and soiled, chasteningly taken aback by a spite-filled entity I had once thought I understood: England. The Hitch and I were in a burpfarty willybumcrack dive off the Portobello Road and drinking like men – one half of Skol leapfrogged swiftly by another, two packs of salt and vinegar, heavy on the salt, don't hold back on the vinegar, *mush*, then another half of Skol, this time with a desperate slash of lime, followed by a Pepsi, all black, no ice – when I rasped

[2] I recall that when I first encountered the Grand Canyon, some sixteen smegma years later, I felt immediate empathy for a force of nature similarly endowed; though of course the Grand Canyon has yet to publish a major novel.

that, *fuckitman*, I preferred early Conrad to later James and middle Nabokov[3] to either of them. The Hitch immediately puked into the pocket of a passing paediatrician and snorted vomitoriously that middle James could beat early James and late Nabokov hands down, *ansdarn*.

'Come outside and say that.' The words shinned out of my mouth like a nuclear siren signalling the decimation of a world boorishly encyclopaedic in its slavish variety. On the ashpuke streets wheezing with urine-drenched tramps, The Hitch and I squared up to one another, eyes unblinking, *like men*. I flexed my arms; The Hitch flexed his. *GO!* Hands working faster than the speed of travelling luminous energy, we began to trade smacks, all the while singing, 'A sailor went to *sea sea sea* to see what he could *see see see* and all that he could *see see see* was the—' By this time, we were biffing our way through it full pelt. But (the rapid strokes of the writer's mind) I got to the end – 'bottom of the deep blue *sea*[4] *sea sea*' – before him, and The Hitch collapsed, fighting for breath like a man fighting for breath, his defeat ameliorated by his knowledge that with his hands and his rhyme he had just been a participant in the tumescent whirligig of twentieth-century literary history.

Innocence. Experience. My mother was innocent. Then experience came, and she experienced it.[5] And then she got her innocence back. Having first experienced innocence, she then lost her innocence to experience. Once experienced, this innocence became innocent of experience. But she knew that this was innocence; and put it down to experience.

Though his airy tailoring left much to be desired, I have no little

---

3 See later chapter on Nabokov's magisterial use of the semi-colon in *Pale Fire*.

4 Like Conrad, I have always found the sea terrifyingly powerful, and inarguably *liquid*.

5 I remember the egregiously envious smile that came over John Updike's lips – liplike and lippy – when he congratulated me on my use of the word 'it' in *Time's Arrow* (1991).

sympathy for Jesus Christ – for he, too, suffered crucifixion on account of his fame.[6] The combined terrorism of the self-styled media in this sordid little offshore island has forced me into the position of being the most celebrated man in Britain today, and the sheer brutal burden on the quiddity of the writer is crushing. These days, I cannot walk through my own home without someone recognising me, and when I go out to the shops to buy, say a cardboard spermbank of milk, I only have to remove my shades and say 'A pint of milk for Martin Amis – that's me' and I am recognised without warning. 'Ewe dat Mar In Ay Miz, innit?' blurts the sweatsodden shopkeeper as he claws at my loose change. I hope this makes the 'gentlemen' of the British press – remorselessly interviewing me over two, three, bumfucking *four* pages every time I have a new book out, then stabbing me repeatedly with their shopworn superlatives – very happy indeed. Very happy. *Indeed*. But Christ's books, perceptive and with a certain post-diluvian charm, if somewhat stagey, remain rightly celebrated today – judicious testaments, like my own, to the permanence of a writer's worth. Of a writer's *sublunary* worth.

6 And he, too, was the famous son of someone famous.

Bel Littlejohn:
Margaret vs. Antonia

Suffer? Of course I do, but not half so much now as when I was a teenager, reading my way through the early novels of Margaret Drabble. In many ways, Drabble taught a whole generation of women how to feel, and, more crucially, how to feel depressed.

There's an unforgettable scene in one of her middle period novels, I forget which. The heroine, Angelica, is contemplating suicide while preparing an avocado dip for a theme dinner party for close friends. The theme is misery. It's the 1970s, so when the guests turn up they're all bankrupt and very sad. By 9.00, the avocado dip is exhausted. They all are. For two pages, no one says anything while the author homes in on the pattern of the tablecloth – a depressing mixture of interlocking triangles, in many ways just like life.

To break the silence, the heroine's friend Paul, a psychiatrist, mentions it's raining outside. Next to him, Sally, a polytechnic lecturer, takes the news badly and has a breakdown. Sally's ex-husband, Phil, blames Paul for mentioning the rain. 'How could you be so callous?' he asks.

'Chicken cooked in a brick with rosemary, anyone?' asks Angelica, struggling to wipe away the accumulated tears of two failed marriages.

Teddy, the failed merchant banker, bursts into a fit of near-hysterical weeping. Angelica blames herself for forgetting that

Teddy's first wife was called Rosemary. Rosemary left Teddy for Phil, who had deserted Sally after that fling with Paul. To alleviate the tension, Angelica turns on the radio. News comes through of the miners' strike, a major earthquake and two or three plane crashes. 'And it's still only 1974,' thinks Sally. 'We've got another six years to go until the eighties – and who's to say they'll be any better?' She opens the oven and takes out the lemon souffle. Storm clouds hover over it.

Powerful stuff, and, as ever with Drabble, it captured the mood of the nation at that time. A lot of people were crying into their avocado dips that decade. So I await her very latest novel with the keenest anticipation. But – whoah, Bel! – the subject of today's column is not Margaret Drabble, novelist. It is in fact, Margaret Drabble, younger sister of A.S. Byatt. And my message to them is this: a great big hug can make all the difference, believe me.

I think I was one of the first to notice the onset of their sibling rivalry. It was at a book-reading at the Hay-on-Wye Literary Festival back in '83. Margaret was reading a beautifully sensitive passage from her seminal novel about the sixties, *Choking to Death*. She had just got to the crucial bit where Hermoine asks Gladwyn exactly what Celia thinks of Patricia's affair with Marcus, and in particular how it will affect James and the kids. The lecture theatre was hushed in expectation. Suddenly – SCRUNCH SCRUNCH SCRUNCH SCRUNCH – all eyes turned to the back, where Antonia Byatt – SCRUNCH SCRUNCH SCRUNCH SCRUNCH – was tucking into a king-size packet of Golden Wonder crisps. By the time Antonia had got to the bottom of the packet, James had run off with Gladwyn, Celia had had a breakdown and Hermione had departed with Patricia to find her real self in India.

Of course, it may have been pure bad luck. For Chrissake, even Susan Sontag sometimes enjoys a packet of cheese and onion. But just two months later, I was to experience another intimation of this sibling rivalry. Antonia Byatt had come to read from her novel-in-progress before an invited audience for a special edition of the *South Bank Show*. In suitably hushed tones, Melvyn introduced her as one of the finest English novelists of her generation. She came on to much applause in a free-flowing cerise dress and headed for an armchair carefully positioned in the centre of the station. With impeccable dignity, she sat down, but then – PHWAAAAAARRRRPPP! – the most embarrassing of all noises emerged from her seat, followed by unearthly giggles from the back row. A full investigation by *South Bank Show* security staff unearthed a used whoopee cushion secreted upon the chair some minutes before. When the giggles had died down, their perpetrator was revealed as none other than the speaker's sister, Ms Drabble.

Similar incidents followed. In 1992, as Byatt walked to the platform at the Guildhall to collect her Booker Prize, *The Late Show* cameras caught the merest glimpse of a 'Kick Me' placard sellotaped to her back, the tell-tale flourish of the 'K' suggesting Drabble up to her old tricks again. And the last time I saw Margaret, at a platform reading of her latest novel at the Lyttleton Theatre, I was surprised when a grand piano fell headlong from the roof, landing within inches of her feet. Five minutes later, Antonia Byatt was seen in the theatre restaurant ordering a three-course dinner with jelly to follow, a pair of sharp scissors glinting in her breast pocket.

In the Footsteps of Graham Greene

The sun lay mellow in the trees, puddles were strewn like so many small pools of water and the Adriatic was as damp as it had ever been that frosty July morning when distinguished novelist Graham Greene – just over halfway through his eleventh best-selling work of fiction – was in the middle of enjoying sexual intercourse with his mistress beneath the voluminous seventeenth-century papal robes of Pope Pius IX, fresh on that morning.

Roughly twenty-nine minutes earlier, the world-famous author, his bright blue eyes (two, one on either side of his nose, both working in unison) absorbing all around them, like a pair of those bright blue bathtime sponges available until November, 1977, through all major retail outlets of Boots the Chemist, had been admitted to the Vatican with his indefatigable lover, Catherine Walston, for a privileged audience with Il Papa.

Down the far end of the Sistine Chapel, the two of them spotted God's representative on earth, resplendent in his ornate vestments. The Pope had never looked more infallible than he did that December afternoon. Noticing, with his novelist's eyes, that there was plenty of room for two more beneath the Holy Father's chasuble, Greene was overcome by the need to take Catherine, again and again, beneath its shady folds.

143

Diverting the Pope's attention by throwing a pebble at a life-size statuette of St Barnaby – itself a mortal sin – the two waited until he was looking the other way before nipping headlong beneath his vestments. Within seconds, they were at it like rabbits. 'Where are our two distinguished visitors from England?' ('Questa il due distinguo visitoria pasta linguini alle Inghlesi?') they heard the Pope exclaim to a passing cardinal as, down below, Greene's fluid eye continued to pour itself over Catherine's well-sprung breasts. For the rest of the world, this was literature in the making.

Satiated after undergoing somewhere between five and a half and six simultaneous orgasms, literature's most famous lovers rested awhile beneath the Pope, catching their breath and adjusting their clothes while relaxing, as lovers do, over the half-bottle of vintage Bollinger that Greene had smuggled in with him. Just a few feet above them, they could hear Il Papa sending out a search party for them. Finishing off their champagne, they crept out of the back of the cassock, brushed themselves down, and circled round to the Pope's front, their heads bowed in supplication, ready for the papal blessing. 'It was at that moment,' Greene later explained in a letter to Catherine, 'that I came to understand the theological heart of Manichean dualism, and for that I shall ever be grateful to you.'

In that passage, he was, in fact, writing about an entirely separate incident, but he could just as well have been writing about this one, if it ever happened, which it may well have done, had either of them been in the Vatican at the time, which they almost definitely would have been had they not been elsewhere. But what is certain is that Greene had enjoyed liaisons with some of the most alluring women of his day, among them top Hollywood actress Betty Boop, up-and-coming young saint Bernadette and the darkly attractive divorcee Cruella de Vil. At that point, Greene was nursing the wounds of an affair with Maria von Trapp, who had walked out on him after opening a brown paper package wrapped up with string only to discover a box of pornographic snapshots of

Greene engaged in indecent acts with a Gaiety Girl. Catherine Walston provided him with the solace he so craved, and together they discussed the Albigensian Heresy while eagerly licking each other's bodies. Their affair was like a ferocious storm at sea: wet, tempestuous and rocky, drinks flying everywhere and both parties suffering from wind; but like a ship athwart the waves, Greene was soon bobbing up and down again. Those early stages were to inspire the poem, 'St Iganatius Loyola' which scholars were to rate as one of Greene's greatest intellectual and spiritual journeys into the very heart of Catholic theology:

> *I dulled my soul deliberate to forget*
> *Our arguments thru' darkened glass*
> *On Dominian views of Grace while you*
> *Let me take you up the arse.*

Whether Catherine Walston enjoyed riotous lesbian affairs with a wide variety of willing partners in an increasing number of contorted positions designed for the prolongation of unimaginable ecstasy while her husband was busy mowing the lawn we have no means of knowing. What is certain is that she did not mow the lawn herself. As Greene's biographer, I, too, am not unused to passionate affairs with some of the world's most tempting yet fickle young ladies. And like Greene, I, too, am an inveterate traveller, braving forest and desert in order, like *Sons and Lovers* author T.E. Lawrence, to satiate my intense curiosity. Did Greene himself participate in these kinky Sapphic romps? The world of letters would remain imprisoned in its own bookishness until I could come up with an answer to this critical literary question. I simply had to find out whether that self-same lawnmower was still in operation. There is no mention of a lawnmower in Greene's great novel, *The End of the Affair*, in which the author's alter-ego Andrex unravels down the stairs before his mistress's very eyes. This suggests that, full of Catholic guilt, he was ashamed to acknowledge its major role in his own sexual adventures. These were my thoughts as

The Literary Life

I boarded the 10.42 am train from Kings Cross to Godalming on a misty February day late in August.

On arrival at the lawn, I began a one-man police-search-style investigation with a fine-tooth comb, looking for any remaining condoms bearing the Greene imprint that may or may not have been hurled from an upstairs window some fifty years before. The minutes ticked by, but after more than six minutes of obsessive searching, I had still found nothing but grass. Once again, the novelist, essayist and master spy had eluded me, his natural heir, the 'burnt-out case' of one of his most prescient titles.

Over the years, Catherine was to conduct many sexual adventures in a wide variety of locations: with Colonel Mustard in the lounge with the spanner, with Professor Plum in the kitchen with the dagger, and perhaps even with Miss Scarlett in the hall with the lead piping. But to the end of her days, she was never to forget the time she spent with the Reverend Greene in the conservatory with the length of rope. To Catherine, it was more than just a game.

Glaciers, Fingernails and Bulgarian Folk Dances

I was prowling around a second-hand bookshop earlier this week when I caught sight of a bright red twenty-volume work, selling for just £30. It was called *Arthur Mee's Children's Encyclopaedia*. At random, I picked up Volume 7A. It began with a full-colour illustration of 'Flower-like Creatures of the Sea', before launching into a couple of thousand words on 'Electricity, Our Servant'. Next, under the heading 'Wonder' came answers to an extraordinary array of questions, among them 'Where does our breath go?', 'Why do we forget what happened to us when we were babies?', 'What happens when a foot goes to sleep?', and 'How many British Isles are there?' Incidentally, the answer to this last question was surprising: 'over 5,000 if we take all the smaller islands and islets into consideration'.

Next came 'The Policeman – What He Is and What He Does', including a photograph of four sturdy young constables studying traffic problems, 'Culture and Sport in Czechoslovakia', a wide selection of Wordsworth's verses on childhood, the sheet music to 'Pussy Cat, Pussy Cat, Where Have You Been?', a fairy tale from Germany called *Undine of the Lake* and a long chapter on 'Architecture in the 19th and 20th Century'. And I had still only reached page 100 of one volume!

I paid my £30, and staggered back to our house bearing two heavy boxes of the encyclopaedia, one under each arm. I have a penchant for reference books bordering on megalomaniacal. Reference books on my shelves include *The Encyclopaedia of Aberrations* (L is for Laughter, Fits of; Lesbianism; Letheomania; Logorrhea; Lycanthropy; and Lying), *Three Steps to Heaven: an Encyclopaedia of Untimely Deaths in the Music World*, and the 1981 *Book of Predictions* (by 1992, a cure for cancer, the common cold and viral ailments will have been found, 1,000,000,000 Soviet citizens will have been destroyed in a pre-emptive nuclear strike by the USA and the word 'Nevernester' meaning 'a person who will never marry or own a home' will have established itself as a vital part of everyday speech).

I confess I had bought *Arthur Mee's Children's Encyclopaedia* partly to satisfy my rather arch craving for the camp and the anachronistic. In this respect, it came up trumps. Much of it reads like a highly effective parody of a Victorian children's encyclopaedia. Some of the photographs are gloriously, almost sublimely, dull. My favourites include 'Celery prepared for sale in a shop', 'How to play the mouth organ', 'Two smiling Australian Aborigines standing before an enormous ant-hill' and 'A Bulgarian folk dance is performed in national dress in the main square of the town'. Mr Mee's interest in folk dances, sea anemones and glaciers borders on the pathological. Glaciers, it emerges, are quite remarkably unphotogenic, but Mr Mee is never put off by such hiccups.

Though the overall tone is one of wonderment, occasionally a hint of the subversive creeps in. For instance, in the section titled, 'Some Unusual Pets' comes the suggestion, 'Why not try a dormouse, for example? With its reddish-brown coat, furry tail, and large dark eyes, the dormouse is a handsome little animal, which is easily kept indoors . . . Another unusual pet is the squirrel . . . Rats are fascinating little animals to keep as pets and quickly become very tame.' But as I leafed through each successive volume, my overwhelming sense was of a document from a lost world, as separate from our world today as the tomb of Tutankhamun or the lost city of Atlantis. One picture caption reads, 'Americans like their cold drinks really cold! A smiling coloured boy delivers a block of ice'. A chapter titled, 'Larks and Other Winged Charmers' begins, 'A song at heaven's high gate from the throat of a skylark seems the crowning glory of a hot summer day.'

When was this encyclopaedia compiled? No volume carries a date of publication; I had been imagining it to have sprung from the pre-war period. As I read on, however, I came across references to the early 1950s, then to the mid-1950s, then to the late 1950s. The most recent reference I found was to the end of 1962. This meant the encyclopaedia must have been published as late as 1963 – the year of my sixth birthday. Imagine my astonishment! The *Arthur Mee's Children's Encyclopaedia*, so quaint, so Victorian, so full of enthusiasms of yesteryear, had in fact been written not for my grandfather, nor even my father, but for me.

Reading on, I felt that those of us who were children in the 1960s had somehow let poor Mr Mee down. Today, I know nothing of how bathroom soap is made, and I haven't a clue how a periscope works. What are our fingernails for? What was the phoenix? What is 'laughing gas'? When we are looking at a rainbow can other people see the other side? I cannot answer a single one of these questions; yet I can give you the real names of Dave Dee, Dozy, Beaky, Mick and Titch, a good half of the names of the Great Train Robbers and I can recite, without recourse to a crib sheet, the entire staff of Crossroads Motel, circa 1966, with positions held.

Arthur Mee's Children's Encyclopaedia may at times be comically earnest, but it is all underpinned by a belief in a child's unquenchable curiosity in the world and its inhabitants. Volume 3B carries a chapter, 'More Philosophers and Thinkers'. Under the heading 'A Simple Little Man Who Taught Profound Philosophy' there is a picture of Immanuel Kant. 'Picture to yourself a dwarf-like figure little more than five feet high, with a deformed shoulder, a hollow chest, and feeble, stick-like limbs' begins the essay, 'Place upon this body a fine head. Then imagine a weak, piping voice proceeding from thin lips. Such was Immanuel Kant, so far as the outward man was concerned. But the soul of him was grander. He was youthful, cheerful and even gay of heart; he was witty; and in all respects he was unaffected, sincere and high-minded.'

Funny though it may seem to read of Immanuel Kant in such storytime terms, the fact remains that, by the end of the essay, any child will have a clear idea of his thoughts and character, and all told in the most memorable manner.

Though I shy away from reading or writing 'Why Oh Why' articles, in which everything that happens is viewed as symptomatic of general decline, I do feel a pang at the passing of Arthur Mee. Nowadays, children are more likely to spend their Saturday mornings watching minor Radio 1 celebrities throwing custard pies at one another than to find themselves introduced to the world of philosophy. In those few moments when information is allowed to peep into children's television, it does not concern what fingernails are for, or the song of the skylark. Rather, it is about where Mr Blobby is next appearing, or the very latest on Liam Gallagher's favourite food. The child's natural sense of wonder and curiosity is being erased. If you watch children's television on any channel, you will find that the only lesson children are being taught is that they already know more than enough. It all makes one yearn for Bulgarian folk dances. Yes, and even glaciers.

Collateral Thinking

If Edward de Bono is remembered at all, it will be for coining the phrase 'lateral thinking' in 1967, a key year for fluffy terminology. Ever since, he has been paid a fortune to fly around the world and explain what on earth it means.

The secret is, of course, that it means nothing at all. There is no difference between 'lateral thinking' and 'thinking'. But de Bono has the great salesman's gift of being fluent in the international language of gibberish. At the same time, he realises that stupid people love to be dazzled by things they don't quite understand. This means that for thirty-odd years he has been able to earn a living – $30,000 a whack, if his biographer is to be believed – by standing up at conferences spouting yet more gibberish in an attempt to explain his original gibberish.

His ham-fisted way with language ('Edward mistrusts words,' says his biographer) has been a great help in spinning out this process of befuddlement. In this new book, he defines lateral thinking as 'a means of escaping the dominant main track to form a new perception which is logical only in hindsight'. Come again? Take a closer look, and you will see that this means nothing at all. In an earlier book, *Conflicts*, he wrote that 'we cannot conceive of new concepts until after we have conceived of them', adding that 'If "something" happens then "something else" will happen'. Again, under the heading 'Thinking is a two-way process' comes the following *apercu*:

151

'It has been implicit all along that the map-making style of thinking is a two-stage process: 1st. Make the map. 2nd. Use the map.'

His books are full of such banalities, all togged up in abstract words to look like profundities. He is particularly keen on initialising everything, so his books are riddled with acronyms such as OPV and EBS and APC and SITO, printed alongside pseudo-technical words like structure and framework and tools. It all looks impressively high-minded until you realise that the initials stand for Other People's Views, Examine Both Sides, Alternatives, Possibilities and Choices, and Supranational Independent Thinking Organisation. Personally, I plan to make a million with my Cognitive Research Approach Plan, teaching Strategic Happiness Intercognitive Theory.

Breaking Out of the Box* reads more like a PR puff than a biography. The author, who has previously written books about Catherine Cookson and *Emmerdale*, rates de Bono as a major league philosopher, or, to put it another way, a Truly Wonderful Artist and Thinker. De Bono's work, he says, 'represents a major contribution . . . to our knowledge of how the brain works'. He further enthuses over de Bono's integrity, charisma, brilliance and so on; when he runs out of superlatives, he chases after fresh suppliers. 'What Edward de Bono is doing to teach people how to think may be the most important thing going on in the world today,' says someone called Professor Gallup. 'De Bono stands alone totally and goes it alone totally,' drools Professor Norah Maier, who is billed as 'sometime Professor at the University of Toronto School for the Very Able', a joke title if ever there was one.

Well, one of us must be wrong. Personally, I would rate him as a thinker slightly lower than a Tellytubby, to whom he bears a striking facial resemblance. For whenever de Bono strays outside his chosen realm of pseudo-science, he stands revealed as a buffoon.

**Breaking Out of the Box – The Biography of Edward de Bono* by Piers Dudgeon (Headline)

This Is Craig Brown

Some time ago, in one of his numerous books (his biographer claims he writes each one in under a week, but they read a lot more hasty than that) de Bono claimed that if you applied lateral thinking to the process of shaving, you should keep your razor in one place and move your face around it. This was what originally alerted me to the fact that there was more wisdom to be found in a Bonio than in de Bono.

His biographer details one or two other schemes of de Bono's, all equally daft. For instance, his stated solution to parking problems is to allow people to park for as long as they like, provided they leave their headlights on. This, he maintains, would encourage them to return as soon as possible. Like many of his ideas, it sounds good for roughly five seconds, but then the novelty begins to evaporate, leaving only confusion behind. If ever this scheme were to be implemented, every street would be filled with a continual glare, and half the cars would be abandoned with dead batteries, causing even more blockage, while the other half would be fitted with independent light generators by their canny owners.

Or take his plan to number the pages of a book from 200 to 1, rather than from 1 to 200. This, he explains, is so that you can tell at any moment how many more pages you have to go. All well and good, but he obviously doesn't consider the idea worth applying to any of his own books, nor, indeed, does his biographer.

His solution to the Northern Ireland problem is equally full of holes. He claims that when he met Gerry Adams, he suggested that instead of surrendering the IRA's arms, he should sell them on. 'I said, if the IRA sold them they are beyond reach, you have got the money, you could buy them back again if you need them or you could distribute the money.' This is simply not thinking, laterally or otherwise: how can the arms be simultaneously both 'beyond reach' and ready to buy back? And who would the IRA sell its arms to? Obviously they wouldn't sell to the Government or any of its allies, as none of them would be prepared to sell them back. This would mean that they would have to sell them to like-minded terrorists, which would defeat the whole point of the exercise.

But the dafter the message, the more money de Bono rakes in. His biographer is particularly impressed by de Bono's wealth, twice listing all his various properties – collateral thinking? – including islands in the Bahamas, Italy, Australia and Ireland, apartments in New York, Venice and Sydney, houses in Norfolk, South Kensington and Malta and 'an apartment in Albany, Piccadilly, one of the most prestigious addresses in Central London'. Oooh!

What Dudgeon terms de Bono's 'unique lifestyle' is further fleshed out with a list of his celebrity friends, dragooned into attending his parties by 'Julie Pomirska, who now runs a global party circuit for her boss'. The list includes the actor Michael York and his wife Pat ('who have become very close friends'), the astronaut Buzz Aldrin and his wife Lois, Eric Idle, Herbie Hancock and Ron Jones, who, we learn, is the 'composer and conductor of the theme music to *Star Trek: The Next Generation*'.

These all sound very B-list to me (the unfunny Python, the second man on the moon, the composer to the *Star Trek* follow-up). Nevertheless, they are a step up from some of de Bono's earlier supporters. Though his biographer discreetly mentions Robert Maxwell only in passing, the portly tycoon was instrumental in de Bono's success. In the official Maxwell biography written by Joe Haines in 1988, de Bono is happy to praise Maxwell for playing 'the key role' in selling his thinking courses around the world. De Bono repaid this debt by including Maxwell as one of the business visionaries interviewed in his book *Tactics: The Art and Science of Success*, an unusual number of whom were to end up on the wrong side of the law.

If the life and career of Edward de Bono can teach us anything, it is that no one ever lost money blowing his own trumpet. '. . . and within twelve minutes they had solved the problem, saving the company $10 million' is the way a typical sentence ends. On page 247, de Bono even takes credit for his part in bringing down the Berlin Wall.

This Is Craig Brown

In the most revealing passage of all, de Bono reveals his belief that all human decisions are grounded in fear, greed or laziness. It must be said that his own career seems singularly free of fear or laziness. So what does that leave?

Showbiz

Celebrities on the Wall

At Luigi's in Covent Garden, Simon Dee, flushed with the success of *Dee Time*, is looking more youthful than ever. Just around the corner in PJ's Bar and Grill, the Oriel College first eight rowing team of 1932 stand brim-full with fresh-faced confidence. And who is that jolly group in the upstairs corridor of the Gay Hussar, still enjoying a joke after twenty years in each other's company? Why, if it isn't Sir Peregrine Worsthorne, Lord Hailsham and Sir Rhodes Boyson, all enjoying the pleasure of each other's company over a relaxing glass of wine.

The celebrity photograph – preferably signed, and topped up with a gracious compliment ('You're delish! Elaine Paige') – has long been a mainstay of restaurant walls in Britain. In less easy-going countries, the choice of celebrity remains sadly obligatory. In Cuba, for instance, even the non-smoking sections of restaurants are generally blessed with photographs of President Fidel Castro, while in Kenya a full colour photograph of the well-fed yet still uncheery features of President Arap Moi is de rigueur, particularly if the restaurant wishes to stay open. But in Britain, the choice of celebrity is the responsibility of the restaurateur, and the restaurateur alone.

If the restaurateur is himself a celebrity, then the choice is made all the more easy. When I lived near Liss in Hampshire, I would occasionally drop in to a pub called the Jolly Drover, which was owned by the ex-England cricketer Godfrey Evans. The walls, the bar, even the slot machines, were all adorned with photographs of Evans in his whites, and there, serving behind the bar, was Evans himself ('Morning Godfrey!'), ready at all times to reminisce to one and all of the days when he kept wicket for England.

The Page Three girl Sam Fox – or 'former Page Three girl Sam Fox', as she has since become – once owned a restaurant in Tottenham called Sam's; it was decorated almost entirely with engagingly posed photographs of the proprietor. For a short while in the late 1970s, the British boxer John Conteh owned a restaurant called JC's. The photographs on the walls were all of celebrities who enjoyed the honour of sharing his initials, among them Joan Collins, Jimmy Cagney, Jack Charlton, Jim Callaghan, Jimmy Connors and Jimmy Carter. In a welcome nod to good taste, a signed photograph of Jesus Christ was nowhere to be seen. Incidentally, though JC's has long since disappeared, a signed photograph of John Conteh still hangs in the bar of the Piccadilly Hotel, Manchester, an establishment particularly rich in such treasures.

Bill Wyman's Kensington restaurant Sticky Fingers is a shrine to twenty-five years of the Rolling Stones, of whom, judging by the photographs, Mr Wyman himself was always the most prominent member. Similarly, walkers in the Savernake Forest chancing upon the Savernake Hotel may be surprised upon entering to find themselves in a bar called the Green Room, chock-a-block with dramatic photographs of Shakespearian and Jacobean heroes in varying degrees of misery, all of them played, over the years, by the hotel's proprietor, the actor Richard Johnson.

Those restaurateurs who are not themselves blessed with fame – and, even in these days of the TV chef, they still form the majority – must rely on the chance visits of appreciative celebrities to keep them in signed photographs. Alas, celebrity visits to little-known restaurants in out-of-the-way places tend to be few and far between, so the restaurateur must learn to accept whoever comes his way. Thus, the Putney Tandoori in south-west London proudly displays a signed picture of Mr David Mellor, the local MP. Yet Mr Mellor must have visited many a more fashionable restaurant and never once been asked for his photo. Chelsea's La Famiglia, the restaurant to which he used to escort his companion Miss Antonia da Sancha, possesses not a single photograph of either of them. Instead, it has Albert Finney ('Okay, Alvaro, I'll pay – Albert'), Joan Collins ('such great lasagne!') and an energetic black and white shot ('thanks for the good food and the good times') of someone called Kenny Moore (nearly but not quite the more famous Kenneth More) who comes into that mysterious and beguiling category of the unknown celebrity.

What happens when the famous sink back into obscurity? Do restaurants maintain a system such as Madame Tussaud's, whereby once a celebrity transmutes into an ex-celebrity – when the politician loses his seat, the pop star croaks his last, the soap opera star comes a cropper in a fire – their photographs are quietly removed from the wall, to be replaced overnight by more up-to-the-minute stars of *Question Time*, *Top of the Pops* or *EastEnders*? Quite the opposite. Restaurants up and down the country form a sort of celebrity heaven, within which the forgotten stars of yesteryear will forever shine, pictured at their moment of greatest glory, their smiles never more sunny, the twirl beneath their autographs never more exuberant. For many years after the demise of the SDP, and way after Madame Tussaud's, with a bit of melting and a few deft chops, had transformed Lord Jenkins of Hillhead into Take That, the Westminster restaurant L'Amico remained happy to display a signed photograph of the Gang of Four, still busily thrashing out their bold new policies over a mould-breaking luncheon.

For me, photographs in restaurants only really come into their own when their subjects have fallen out of kilter with the times, when the whim of fashion has left them behind. I would prefer to sit beneath a photograph of, say, Freddie 'Parrot-Face' Davis than David Beckham, Diana Dors rather than Naomi Campbell, Harold Wilson rather than Tony Blair. Luigi's has a particularly ripe (or stale, if you would prefer) collection of such celebrities taken in their prime, when their worlds seemed so fresh, their boundaries endless; alongside the young Simon Dee is the young Rudolf Nureyev, and a little further down is the young Patricia Hayes. Encrusted forever upon a restaurant wall, the celebrity's star never fades, his smile never droops, his swagger never slows to a shuffle.

The tradition of the celebrity photograph is not new; nor is it confined to the more cheap and cheerful establishments. London's oldest restaurant, Rules, sports a signed portrait of its most illustrious customer, King Edward VII. Outside the downstairs loos at Cliveden there is an extraordinary array of grainy shots of past guests standing in the drive or in the garden, among them T.E. Lawrence, Queen Marie of Romania and George Bernard Shaw, though none at all of those more jaunty guests who brought Cliveden back into the public eye with such a bang in the summer of 1963.

Personally I prefer grand celebrities stuck on the walls of cheap restaurants, or, even better, cheap celebrities on the walls of grand restaurants. In Rodos, a nice little Greek restaurant near Centre Point, Dustin Hoffman makes a surprise appearance in no less than four different photos – placing a fork in his mouth, with the proprietor's wife on his knee, with the proprietor's son on his knee, standing with his arm around the proprietor. The restaurant is situated just around the corner from the theatre, where Dustin Hoffman made his West End debut as the Merchant of Venice.

For a restaurateur, being close to a celebrity's stamping ground is half the battle won. Opposite Kensington Palace is an unassuming café called Diana's Diner, which was, indeed visited by the Princess of Wales, on one occasion with her two sons in tow. In return, the Lebanese brothers who own the café have a Princess of Wales calendar hanging on the wall, together with countless photographs of her, one of them properly autographed.

Other celebrities will always be associated with a particular restaurant, whether they like it or not. Since 1926 Karl Marx's old house in Dean Street has been home to the plush Italian restaurant Leoni's Quo Vadis, which now pullulates with captains of industry tucking into expense-account meals, a living rebuff to Marx's belief in the historical inevitability of the demise of capitalism. Customers are allowed to view the room in which Marx worked, though sadly there remains no signed photograph of him beaming merrily on the restaurant wall ('You're delish! – Karl'). Instead, there is a photograph of the more voluptuous if less hirsute Sophia Loren, a one-time regular at Quo Vadis, after whom the chef has named a chicken dish.

Lending one's name to a dish must be the ultimate aspiration of all those who peer from restaurant walls. One or two historical figures have achieved such eternal peace – Omelette Arnold Bennett is still served in the Savoy, Dame Nellie Melba inspired Escoffier to create both peach melba and melba toast, and pumpernickel is so called because Napoleon once said that it was fit only for his horse ('Pain pour Nicole') – but few living celebrities, man or beast, seem guaranteed such edible immortality. So far, there is no Pork Hattersley, no Worsthorne Buttie, no Cod Jeffrey Archery, though for a time L'Amico served Spaghetti Gorbachev, containing smoked salmon, beluga caviar, cream and vodka, to commemorate the Soviet leader's 1987 visit there as the guest of the British Labour Party.

Among contemporary British grandees, the only one to have a dish named after him seems to be the publisher of *Sunday Sport*, Mr David Sullivan. The David Sullivan on the menu at his favourite restaurant, the Phoenix Apollo, just off the Bow flyover in Stratford, consists of a pot of tea with a three-tiered doileyed tray laden with Quality Street chocolates, After Eight mints and KitKats split into individual bars.

Though absent from most food guides, the Phoenix Apollo has cornered the market in photographs of a particular type of celebrity, with over 300 different photographs of famous customers hanging on its walls. 'We've got Telly Savalas, we've got Nigel Benn, we've got Frank Bruno, Danny Baker, loads of Page Three girls, we've got all the *EastEnders*, Marvin Hagler, we've got Terry Marsh, both the *Birds of a Feather*, we've got Gazza – how many more do you want?' the owner asked when I spoke to him about his collection. He takes the photographs of the celebrities ('most of them become personal friends') when they dine at his restaurant, 'otherwise some people wouldn't believe they've been here'. His favourite exhibit is a gold bottle shaped like the World Cup inscribed 'It's a crying shame' by Paul Gascoigne. 'I value that more than anything,' he adds.

Few celebrity inscriptions are as pithy as Gazza's. Most have the wooden feel of compulsory jocularity that is more commonly to be found on plasters surrounding broken legs. A selection from Joe Allen's illustrates the point. 'Jo – It's a pleasure to be up on *this* wall!' writes the actor Henry Winkler. 'Upstaged by Sondheim!' writes the impresario Hal Prince, pictured arm in arm with Stephen Sondheim. 'Us Joe Allens stick together – Joe Allen', writes a Nasa astronaut, also called Joe Allen. Others don't even try to raise a smile. 'Thank you for all your help. Cheers. Phil' writes Phil Collins on his old drumskin, now owned by the Hard Rock Café.

In the old days, only the more presentable pop stars – Frank Ifield, Russ Conway, Tommy Steele – could ever hope to find themselves upon a restaurant wall. But now fame is all, and, once you can prove your celebrity, there is no need to wear a tie, or even trousers. It is hard to imagine any smart restaurant admitting someone who looks and behaves like Keith Richard, unless of course he actually is Keith Richard, in which case it's free meals all round, the management only too anxious to commemorate the visit of the great man with a signed photograph, elaborately framed. Motcomb's, a portly old restaurant in Knightsbridge, boasts a photograph of Keith Richard in a leopardskin shirt holding a cat (with a view to skinning it?), while the solemnly trendy Pied à Terre in Charlotte Street sports the Richard Hamilton picture of Keith Richard and Mick Jagger in handcuffs in 1967, charged with the possession of illegal drugs. Keith Richard is also to be found in Sticky Fingers and in the Hard Rock Café. At this rate, it can't be very long before the Connaught begins to serve Pommes Frites Keith Richard beneath his full-colour signed portrait ('Cheers, Keith').

The Day I Didn't Make Love to Marilyn

Colin Clark, brother of Alan, is soon to add to the mountain of books about Marilyn Monroe with My Weekend with Marilyn. It purports to be a memoir of his heroically standoffish encounter with the twentieth century's sexiest actress.

'Four hours! Aren't we going to make love, Colin?' says Marilyn. 'Will that give us enough time?' To which Clark sternly replies, 'Oh, Marilyn, you are a naughty girl. We are not going to make love, okay?'

This is the English way of doing things. We have better things on our minds than a night of passion with Marilyn Monroe.

DR DAVID STARKEY

'Aren't we going to make love, David?' she purred cattily, pulling back the bedclothes.

But I had seen these tactics before. 'A typically fatuous invitation, if I may say so, Miss Monroe,' I countered with a smirk, buttoning up my blazer and donning a waterproof for added protection. That certainly put her in her place. I was determined to push my advantage home.

'As a – correction: *the* – leading constitutional historian of our age,' I continued, 'I must frankly declare I have no interest *whatsoever* in accepting your characteristically ill-phrased invitation. Hands off, Monroe! In fact, I put it to you, Miss Monroe, that you are incapable of formulating an invitation commensurate with my status! But that's Americans all over! Pah! Game, set and match to Starkey, methinks!'

Touche! She never asked me again! And they say she died of a broken heart!

SIR TERENCE CONRAN

'Aren't we going to make love, Terence?' It was an enormous privilege to be the recipient of such a truly delicious invitation. This sort of thing gives one – and let's not forget those one works with, we're very much a team – the most terrific *buzz*.

I had initiated the process of removing, folding, ironing and tidying away my necktie, jacket, shirt, etcetera in preparation for 'the main event', as it were, when I glanced over at the bed upon which the naked Marilyn lay.

Something was troubling me. 'I'm sorry,' I said, 'but really one should never *ever* allow five pillows on a bed. Two, four or six, yes. But one, three or five – no. Even numbers only. Anything else is so desperately . . . *uneven*.' I then embarked on a painstaking rearrangement of the pillows so that they would catch the morning light at an angle of approximately 45 degrees.

'Aren't we going to make love, Terence?' It was an offer no less tempting for being repeated. Alas, while removing my Italian shoes – the laces were woven by a simply *marvellous* little man on the harbour at Porto Ercole – I noticed a small scuff just off-centre from the toe of the left one. 'Patience is a virtue, Marilyn!' I said, adding, 'I'll just deal with this.' I then got down to French-polishing the shoe, employing the ingredients of a delightful little lime green sachet of my own design.

'Aren't we going to make love, Terence?'

'But first let's keep things simple, Marilyn! How one *craves* simplicity!' I exclaimed, removing the busy floral curtains and improvising something rather ingenious with some loose cheesecloth fabric I had managed to find in a bottom drawer. Two and a half hours later, with everything just right, I was all set for a delicious amorous liaison.

I looked at the bed. It was empty. Marilyn was all dressed by the door, her case in her hand, looking anxiously at her watch. She wanted me to drop her at the airport.

'*Aren't we going, Terence?*'

JEFFREY ARCHER

'*Aren't we going to make love, Jeffrey?*' I looked frankly at the nude screen goddess before me. I had to tell her the honest truth. 'Oddly enough,' I said, 'that is exactly what Mae West asked me when I was invited to the Roosevelt White House to honour my achievement of becoming the first man to cross the Atlantic swimming doggy-paddle. Incidentally, Marilyn, did Winston ever tell you what my good friend the Pope said to me while anointing me Cardinal?' "Jeffrey, dear boy," he said, "Jeffrey, you're worth a million dollars!" "Cash?"' I said.

'*Aren't we going to make love, Jeffrey?*'

'First things first, Marilyn,' I said, frankly. 'The time's not 11.00pm, it's 10.30am, we're not at your hotel room, we're at the home of a close friend, we're not alone, we're in company, and if anyone asks you if this ever really happened, you're to tell them it did. Sign here!'

TONY BENN

'*Aren't we going to make love, Tony?*' In response, I drew up a request asking her politely but firmly to furnish me with proof of membership of an affiliated trades union. 'Y'see, Marilyn,' I informed her, 'we've got to stick to the issues here—'

'B-b-but Tony . . .'

'Let's keep personalities out of it, shall we? Someone had to make that bed, and someone else had to sew those pillowcases. Ye Jenkinses and ye Hattersleys might see fit to disregard the centuries-old struggle of the ordinary working people of this country for a night of passion, but I am not prepared to ride roughshod over a thousand years of organised labour.'

Eventually, we arrived at a compromise. She would remain in bed, while I would read choice passages from my *Collected Speeches (1942–56)* out loud to her. Oddly enough, Marilyn was soon fast asleep. Had MI5 been at her cocoa?

Showbiz

MICHAEL WINNER

'Aren't we going to make love, Michael?' said Miss Monroe.

I was having none of this. Not a please or a thank you, would you believe, and her clothes were spread any old how across the floor. And now she was attempting to coax me into her bed, with no suggestion of payment! To my mind, this was one young lady in urgent need of a lesson in manners.

'Do you know who I am?' I said. 'I've never been treated like this in all my life! Don't you ever expect me to come back here again! I'll have you know I'm a personal friend of the Prime Minister and I have had the great pleasure of being presented to Her Majesty on three separate occasions! Now, let me see your manager, if you please, young woman! Do you know who I am?'

The Diary of Anthea Turner

At the age of thirty-seven, I was one of the most successful women on British TV. Yes, I had mastered them all. Breakfast TV. Mid-morning TV. Lunchtime TV. Afternoon TV. Early Evening TV. Evening TV. The lot.

I was cherished in every sitting room throughout the land for my warm and sunny smile, to-die-for figure and radiant good looks. Yet inside, I was hurting.

There was one thing missing in my life.

More fame.

I was married to Pete, one of the country's top show-business managers. We shared a four-storey neo-Georgian mansion built to our own specifications in sought-after Twickenham, complete with six ensuite bedrooms, four reception rooms, a top-of-the-range electric hob and hot and cold running water.

But without a sixteen-page full-colour spread in *Hello!* magazine our marriage was a sham.

In the eyes of the world, I was the superstar pin-up who effortlessly managed to combine a bubbly outgoing personality with world-beating talent. In TV terms, I could do everything – beaming, talking, laughter to camera, looking left and right, the lot. I was so famous that I only had to issue a press release marked urgent for every news desk in the land to know what was going on in my private life.

But inside, I was pining. I had been the subject of six-page spreads. Ten-page spreads. But where was my sixteen-page spread?

And why with my sunny disposition and girl-next-door personality wasn't I being asked to front BBC's prestige flagship programme, *Newsnight*?

Outside I was bubbly.

But inside I was hurting.

I supposed I first realised that our marriage was a sham when the news filtered through that Denise van Outen had been offered the BT corporate video instead of me.

One day I burst into floods of tears and began throwing our luxury twenty-five-piece pure china crockery set from the exclusive Harrods department store in Pete's direction. Pete must have sensed something was wrong.

'There's something the matter, isn't there, Anth?' he said.

'Yes,' I choked. Before I could stop myself my tears were splashing on the luxury pure satinwood table from top people's store Conran. 'It's our marriage, Pete,' I sobbed. 'The public's lost interest in it.'

He reached out a hand. As my manager as well as my husband, he always had my best interests at heart.

'Let's prepare the press release,' he said. 'This could make a full page in the *Mail*.'

Grant was ten years younger than Pete. His recently renovated nine-bedroom neo-Tudor house was set in twenty acres of luxurious Sussex countryside, equipped with indoor swimming pool, whirlpool bath and double-fronted summer house with full barbecue facilities for entertaining business clients on warm summer evenings.

Grant and his sad wife Della seemed to enjoy all the trappings of a wealthy lifestyle. Two top-of-the-range off-road vehicles. Three daughters. Four horses. A fully integrated stereo system throughout the house. The lot. His pride and joy was the expensive hand-tufted prestige carpet in their main living room, mown every Thursday by a member of his household staff.

'My corporate clients and business contacts assure me that mine is a lifestyle to envy, Anthea,' he confessed to me one day, 'but inside I'm pining.'

'There's something the matter, isn't there?' I said.

'It's my sad wife Della,' he choked, burying his head in my cleavage for comfort. 'To me, she isn't nearly as famous as you. And let's face it, Anthea – she never will be.'

From the second our lips met, I knew that I was lost. Grant gently undressed me, strewing my expensive clothes from some of London's top designers across his costly prestige carpet.

What happened in the hour that followed was a golden time that will stay with me for ever. I was euphoric that I was now in the hands of an experienced man who knew exactly how to please a woman. 'Anthea, darling,' he whispered, his naked body pressed to mine, 'forget the press. Forget the cameras. Forget the TV. You've got to realise there's something much, much more to life than all that.'

Grant took a deep breath, and looked me straight in the eyes. *'There's a book in this,'* he sighed.

Breaking up with Pete was probably the darkest fifteen seconds of my life, but somehow I got through it. Overshadowing everything was the intense public scrutiny to which Grant and I would be subjected if we left our partners. Our private lives would be held up for examination in every newspaper and magazine in the land. Grant's sad wife Della would be portrayed as an object of pity. Wherever we went we would be photographed. We would have no rest from the searing spotlight of the world media.

It was the chance of a lifetime.

While Grant whispered sweet nothings into my ear, I stroked his naked chest with one hand and drew up a press release with the other.

Poor Della didn't know what had hit her. I genuinely felt for her. A former sad dental assistant, she sadly had no idea about anything. But Grant and I were determined to keep her from becoming any sadder, so we decided to maintain a low profile. We further decided that the best place to do it was the *Lord of the Dance* party at Wembley Arena, held in honour of top-earning dancer Michael Flatley. But hopes that we could pass unnoticed among the other guests – including fellow top TV celebrities Pauline Quirke and Dale Winton – proved misplaced.

The photographers' flashbulbs blinded us. It was like Oscars night. With a shock, I realised I was now more famous than sad, tragic Princess Diana, former best-loved gran the Queen Mother, glamorous yet untouchable and sadly now dead Jackie Kennedy and bubbly former weathergirl Ulrika Jonsson rolled into one.

I had come through another harsh lesson in the price of life on Planet Fame.

Family break-ups. Distraught kiddies. Sad Della. The whole messy business of divorce.

Yet still I was pining for something.

Worldwide serialisation rights.

Now read on, and on, and on, and on, and on.

Bel Littlejohn: Medea Studies

The transcript of a three-way discussion between Fiona Shaw, Bel Littlejohn and Deborah Warner, which took place in Fiona Shaw's dressing room in the Queen's Theatre, prior to a performance of Medea:

Deborah Warner: You said something very interesting to me the other day, Bel. You said that as Concept Designer of Medea, you had been struck by how very like contemporary icons such as Victoria Beckham and Dido she was. It's a thought that has really stayed in my mind – *reverberating* like some sort of primitive drum on a lonely hillside above Athens.

Bel Littlejohn: That's certainly very interesting, Deborah. I'm always struck by the way in which our society has put Victoria Beckham on a pedestal, and I think the same thing can be said of Medea. And though Medea strictly speaking never married a footballer—

Deborah Warner: And Victoria Beckham never strictly speaking tore her brother to pieces and left his mangled limbs on the way that Aeetes would pass—

Bel Littlejohn: Quite, so though they are different in some essentials, they are also, I think, both very *contemporary* women, trying to come to terms with the whole conflict of how to combine work with children.

Fiona Shaw: Of course, in some ways our investigation into

Medea has discovered that she was never wholly successful, at least in the eyes of society, in combining the whole work and children and leisure thing. Basically, she was forced to avenge herself by slaying the two children she had by Jason, which can't have been easy for her. It must have cut into their quality time, for one thing.

Bel Littlejohn: My researches confirm that she was under one helluva lot of pressure at the time, Fiona. Throughout my studies into the real Medea, I've found Clare Short coming to mind. They're both very modern women, very determined, very much their own people – and with the odds stacked against them. Lovely Brummie women, both of them.

Deborah Warner: And in rehearsal, we've tried to bring out that lovely Brummie side of Medea's character, wouldn't you agree, Fiona?

Fiona Shaw: Absolutely, absolutely. And of course, during the current train strike there's every reason why the contemporary Brummie women should feel even more cut off from what one might call the cultural norms of a male-dominated society than she would already. I mean, her embarkation for the traumatic return to Greece, via Iolcos, has many chilling parallels with an away day to London from Birmingham New Street.

Bel Littlejohn: I think the lovely thing about Medea is when you get to know her, she's not the warped person of popular mythology. In fact she's very normal. I've tried to bring this out in my Medea Studies course.

Deborah Warner: She is. She loves Jason, the children, the house. She's very much the happy housewife of Corinth, bless her. Her passion for Jason is so great she murdered her brother for him. That's why when Jason wants to trade her in for a younger model, it's so devastating for her. It's very much the story of Ivana Trump – and if you look hard enough you can see the whole Hillary Clinton/Monica Lewinsky thing in there too.

Fiona Shaw: There is part of him that just wants to start again and part that wants it all to be all right. What's that line in Bel's super new translation – 'A man tired of domesticity goes out'. Domesticity is tiring, at least for men it is. I just love that scene where Jason is unloading the ancient dishwasher for what must seem to him the umpteenth time, and finally he snaps at Medea that he couldn't care bloody less, he's put the saucers where the bowls usually go, and she can bloody well go and stuff it.

Bel Littlejohn: Thanks, Fiona. I was trying, in just a few hand-picked lines, to bring out the drudgery of life 2,400 years ago – and frankly I don't think much improved, even with the new Blair administration, and that's a very important point too. So when Medea says 'Things can only get better' while she slays her own children, I think I'm using a certain amount of savage irony there. It's making a very political point, and that's a good thing.

Deborah Warner: We want to challenge the audience, and that's a challenge. And of course, we want the audience to challenge us too. We want it all to be very challenging. It's trial by Medea.

Bel Littlejohn: It's like *Changing Rooms*, but instead of Carol Smillie, there's Medea – and the room is splattered with bloodgore. No wonder the neighbours are shocked. It's all a far cry from the lovely rich browns and deep, deep purples they were expecting.

Fiona Shaw: It's an image that will stay with me for the rest of my life, Bel. Thank you for that.

Clive James Meets Barbra Streisand

Clive *James:* On an earth that looks up to the stars, Barbra Streisand is the biggest star on earth. She is such a big star that she has become her own planet, and on that planet she is the rocket that will take us anywhere we want to go. And so when I was invited to step on to this rocket, I simply couldn't say no.

When Barbra Streisand sings, the world stops turning just to listen. Her high notes make you want to say 'Hi, notes!' and her low notes seem to be saying 'Hel-low!' An accomplished actress, no actress is more accomplished. And it was as her accomplice that I agreed to fly to Hollywood not on a rocket but in a plane, because it was plain that I wanted to meet her.

Barbra Streisand:

> Maremriz!
> Lak the cwarners of ma maand
> Myistyee-waaarrtered cullid maremriz
> Arft the weeeey we whirrrrrrrr.

Clive James: Barbra, you've always been able not only to sing like an angel, but also to angle your song. And, like the angler you are, you have fished for pure gold. I think it was Nietzsche himself who once said that to be Nietzsche was kinda neat, and certainly when I was an acne-ridden young boy growing up in Australia I—

176

This Is Craig Brown

Barbra Streisand: Have we started? Could someone tell me, have we started?

Clive James: Back to that time in Australia, I remember dodging my—

Barbra Streisand: Okay, okay. Let's get this over with. You got forty minutes.

Clive James: I've always been your number one fan, and, what I've always wanted to know is—

Barbra Streisand: Who'd you say this is for?

Clive James: The BBC, Barbra. May I call you Barbra?

Barbra Streisand: Thirty-nine.

Clive James: Barbra, you hit the floor running. And it turned out to be the floor of the elevator going up. So you hit the button marked 'Top Floor'. Tell us what happened then?!

Barbra Streisand: As a child, I never had a puppy. My mother could never afford a puppy. Maybe that's why I always cry when I see a puppy. For years, I thought maybe my father was a puppy. So every man I met, I wanted to put him on a lead, walk him round the park, feed him Kennomeat. Maybe that's why my relationships never lasted. If only my mother had bought me a puppy. All the other girls had a puppy . . .

Clive James: When I was a young boy growing up fatherless in Australia, I too wanted a puppy, and my—

Barbra Streisand: Maybe that's what made me determined to make it as a star. Maybe I put all my pain and frustration and love and sorrow and feeling for my fellow man into my music.

> Pyee-parl.
> Pyee-parl who need pyee-parl.
> Waar the LYAAAAAAARKIEST PYEE-PARL
> In the WOOOOORRRRRLLLLLLLDDDDD.

Clive James: You are unique, a one-off. There's never been anyone like you. How such an amazing singer could also be so . . . striking-looking is almost beyond the comprehension of a mere mortal such as myself.

Barbra Streisand: Twenty-one minutes.

Clive James: And with *Yentl* you truly made a buster that turned out to be a block. Put the two together, and you had created a true 'block-buster'. I think it was Bertolt Brecht who said—

Barbra Streisand: Yentl is a celebration of what it means to be feminine. I wanted to show women that we really do have to pull together, because, hey, we can be so powerful if we support one another. But a lot of the critics, especially the female critics, were very negative in their reaction. There's a lot of jealousy towards me among women. It's like they can't take another woman being so beautiful and yet so talented. But that's women for you, they're just not worth it. Fourteen minutes thirty.

Clive James: Barbra, 'control-freak' is not a term I like. And of the terms I like, 'control-freak' is not one. In fact, I'd get rid of anyone who used it. But some people – those jealous women – have been unfair enough to use it about you. It seems silly to mention it. And to mention it seems silly. If by 'control-freak' they mean strong, beautiful, and a wholly remarkable woman, then perhaps you are a control-freak. After all, there's no one quite as brilliant or as well-loved as y—

Barbra Streisand: Cut! Eight minutes!

Clive James: From the outside, you seem self-assured, terrific-looking, very gracious, and probably the most talented person on this planet here today. But tell me – who's the real Barbra Streisand?

Barbra: Very few people know the real Barbra Streisand. I'm a tangled mixture of shyness and insecurity, like a rose, or a diamond, or some sort of priceless songbird. If I have a failing, it's that I am too ready to admit to my mistakes. Maybe I've never wholly recovered from the experience of living in my mother's womb. I was trapped. It was cramped and damp, and at no time did I feel the walls were a colour I could live with. But that's just like my mother, to keep me shut up for nine months, unable to express myself to the world as an artist and citizen. In my movie, *The Prince of Tides,* I—

Clive James: As I saw it, that superb landmark movie was not only about the princely tide but also the tidely prince, just as the way we were was above all about the way not only that we are, but that we *were*.

Barbra Streisand: I was attempting to explore my relationship with myself. Who am I? How am I? How can I learn to love myself more? And why do I so obsessively shy away from talking about myself? Four minutes.

Clive James: Barbra may have lost an 'a' from her name, but she was certainly never on the 'b' list. She may have been as sharp as a new pin – but the notes she sang were rarely flat.

Barbra Streisand:

> LARV – sarftazun eeeeeeeezi chair
> LA-AA-ARV – fresh as the mwaw-AW-niiing air
> WAARN larv thadiz shared ba two
> AR have fow-ownd with you
> MAR pre-sherz LAAAAAAAAAARV

Clive James: Barbra—

Barbra Streisand: Two minutes.

Clive James: Barbra, you are the greatest star the world has ever known. Any future plans?

Barbra Streisand: It's still a struggle. The studios are still very, very anti-feminist and anti-semitic. For the past eight years, I've been struggling to get together a musical version of the Nelson Mandela story, but even though they know I'll be playing the title role the studios are still holding back. And it's my ambition to perform in the Acropolis, but the Greek authorities are refusing to rebuild the roof for me. Maybe it's because I'm a strong woman. Maybe because inside, I'm still that little girl. Maybe it's because I never got that puppy.

Clive James: You're such a marvell—

Barbra: Time up. Cut!

A Spiritual Overachiever

Here's a handy tip for anyone travelling abroad this summer. If you bump into Shirley MacLaine, there are five words you should never, ever utter: 'Tell us about yourself, Shirley.'

If, despite yourself, you find these words tumbling out, you'd better be sure your return ticket is open-ended. Shirley MacLaine has already written nine books telling us about herself, and there's no sign of her stopping.

Most celebrities confine their life stories to a single volume. But Shirley MacLaine believes that she has lived many times before – 'fifteen million years of life times' is her closest estimate in the present volume – so it looks as though we are in for the long haul.

Her new book* was inspired by an anonymous letter she received many years ago, imploring her to travel the pilgrim's route to Santiago de Compostela in Spain, better known as the Camino. Three years later, she received another anonymous letter, written in the same hand, repeating the same request. And so off she went.

Some 307 pages later, many readers may regret that the anonymous letter-writer did not implore Ms MacLaine to stay

*The Camino – A Journey of the Spirit by Shirley MacLaine (Simon and Schuster)

180

put with a paper bag over her head. As travel books go, it is an uphill struggle.

For instance, the third sentence on the very first page goes like this: 'By Spirit, I believe everything that we know and understand to be physically tangible and existent in the five dimensions is in fact the manifestation of a more subtle and non-visible energy that exists simultaneously.' Having read that sentence three or four times, I have a vague idea of what she is getting at. But readers who imagine they are in for the frothy memoirs of a light comic actress may be disappointed. In English terms, it is as though Wendy Craig had attempted a rewrite of Kahlil Gibran.

If time-travel really does exist, Shirley MacLaine certainly takes the concept of egomania into a previously unexplored dimension. 'Who am I?' is the question she has already attempted to answer across nine volumes and roughly 2,500 pages, and she still hasn't received a satisfactory answer. Something like 'You're a mawkish out-of-work comedienne, dear – now *shut up*!' would be pretty close to the mark.

Still in pursuit of who she really is, she says goodbye to her friends in California 'most of whom cried when I left', buys herself some earplugs, even though she 'had been told by my homeopath and acupuncturist that earplugs obstructed the meridians to the kidneys', flies to Spain, and sets off on her pilgrimage.

Shirley is not given to understatement. One would never guess from the way she goes on – 'I should be prepared to die, because to do such a pilgrimage meant I was ready to give up the old values that conflicted with my life' – that the Camino is one of Spain's great tourist routes. In her introduction, she says that for thousands of years it has been 'traversed' – one of her favourite words – 'by saints, sinners, generals, misfits, kings and queens'. But mainly, she forgets to add, by student backpackers.

She has walked only twelve and a half miles when she is already 'literally laughing with pain'. She then enjoys her first out-of-body experience while looking at some mountain flowers. 'I actually felt I had melded into the flowers until I *became* them.' A few miles on, she is visited by an angel called Ariel. Ariel says, 'Do not be afraid of your physical body.' Around this point, Shirley is struck by the realisation that 'We were each everyone and everything, and everyone and everything was us.'

It's all a far cry, then, from *Whicker's World*. Shirley picks up a walking stick from the side of the path, having first 'asked it if it wanted to walk with me'. In my experience, sticks are notoriously tight-lipped, but even though any halfway-intelligent stick would have run a mile, this one says yes, and off they set. Later that week, Shirley has come to know the stick so well that she decides that it is male 'and would know how to cross Spain by itself'.

Readers already familiar with Ms MacLaine's *oeuvre* will know that she can barely pick her nose without experiencing déjà vu. And what past lives she has had! True to her Hollywood ambitions, the God of Past Lives never seems to cast her in a walk-on role. So whereas you and I would probably find ourselves a bus conductor on the number 12 route along the Andover ring road, Shirley is always Cleopatra, or a geisha girl, or an Aztec prince, or the Tsarina.

In this new book, she has a vision of her past life as – bingo! – a Moorish girl 'with long curly black hair and skin the color of cappuccino coffee'. She also has 'the gift of healing hands'. The Giant Moor then summons Cappuccino Shirley and Her Healing Hands to cure him of impotence. As always, she emerges triumphant. 'He succumbed to the vibration of my touch and soon became aroused. His protectors left as I proceeded to consummate the healing.' But just as the breath-less reader of this new genre of literature – reinpornation – is shouting 'More! More!' (or even 'Moor! Moor!'), Shirley has yet another vision, this time of frolicking on animal skins with the Emperor Charlemagne, and bearing him three little kiddies.

She is escorted in these visions by an unlikely flunkie of Charlemagne who calls himself John the Scot. Like every Hollywood Scotsman, John the Scot has a 'ruddy, freckled face' and prefaces all his comments with 'Well, lassie'. After a number of exotic goings-on involving unicorns and UFOs, John the Scot takes Shirley into a crystal meditation hall to prepare her to leave for Atlantis (where else?) in a spacecraft piloted by extraterrestrials.

As if this was not sufficient, John the Scot now takes the opportunity to remove his top, revealing he has developed female breasts. At this point, I couldn't help thinking of Fat Bastard in the last Austin Powers movie. But there is no time for such idle thoughts – Shirley herself has begun to split in two, with one side of her chest masculine and the other feminine. 'The two thighs on the masculine side were muscular and firm. On the feminine side they were lithe and slim.'

All very well, you might think – but a nightmare when it comes to buying clothes. But by now her body has split into two separate people; she has achieved what surely must amount to the ultimate status symbol in the reincarnated community – she has become both Adam *and* Eve.

She then nobly performs her duty to the human race and has sex with herself. And what sex! 'I lifted her on to my lap, and she surrounded me with her legs . . . We actually saw the sparks of energy created by our mutual orgasms.'

By now, Shirley MacLaine has proved herself the envy of all Spanish backpackers. While these visions have been going on, she has been trudging along the hills of north Spain, exchanging pleasantries with like-minded walkers she meets on the way. A Belgian hiker stops to inform her that she was his older sister in a past life. 'It was probably true,' concludes Shirley.

Her only encounters with what she would call 'linear reality' involve Spanish journalists who dog her every move. She claims that 200 journalists and cameramen were waiting for her around every corner. Can she really be that popular in Spain? It seems unlikely. If she were walking – or even traversing – the South Downs, she would be lucky to attract a lone photographer on work experience with the *Brighton Evening Argus*.

Shirley eventually reaches Santiago de Compostela, where she humbly worries that she is 'nothing but a spiritual overachiever'. She also worries, reasonably enough, whether anyone will believe her. 'Can I prove that Lemuria and Atlantis existed? Of course not. But if I can "imagine" them in such detail, then where does that come from? The recesses of ancient creative memories?' she asks. More likely, I would guess, the recesses of ancient Hollywood B-movies . . .

Shit

In most respects, the programme for the West End production of *Krapp's Last Tape* by Samuel Beckett is much like any other. It contains full colour advertisements for widescreen televisions and expensive jewellery ('rare elegance shaped by contemporary brilliance'), brief CV's of the director, lighting designer, sound designer and so on, a few photographs of the star, John Hurt, expertly furrowing his brow, and a for-what-we-are-about-to-receive-may-the-Lord-make-us-truly-thankful essay on this most revered of playwrights.

But there is one item that makes this programme something of a collector's item. Towards the centre, a double-page spread is devoted to a selection of big-wigs, bigger-wigs and biggish-wigs saying how and why Beckett is so severe, tender, hopeful, despairing and so forth. Nothing new there. But then along comes Harold Pinter. His quote is, I would guess, unique in theatre history.

In full, it goes like this:

> The farther he goes the more good it does me. I don't want philosophies, tracts, dogmas, creeds, way outs, truths, answers, nothing from the bargain basement. He is the most courageous, remorseless writer going and the more he grinds my nose in the shit, the more I am grateful to him.

186

Book now to avoid disappointment! One can only wonder why the management has not seized the opportunity to place a choice extract ('The More He Grinds My Nose In The Shit, The More I Am Grateful To Him' – H. Pinter) above the main entrance in fairy lights.

Though there were quite a few celebrities at the first night – Dave Allen, John Mortimer, Sean Bean, Chris de Burgh – I failed to spot Harold Pinter and his wife, Lady Antonia Fraser. Perhaps they were enjoying a night in with something eggy on a tray, saving up the chance to nip along to the New Ambassadors Theatre for a little remorseless nose-grinding at a later date. Or perhaps Lady Antonia does not share her husband's hobbies. Her own quotes on the dust jackets of other people's books tend to run more along the lines of 'utterly delightful' and 'a master story-teller at the height of his powers'. In fact, I find it hard to recall a single occasion upon which Lady Antonia Fraser has recommended an author solely for his ability to grind her nose in the shit.

Or perhaps, with Samuel Beckett dead, the Pinters decided to look elsewhere for the services he once provided. 'Ding-dong!' goes the doorbell of their Holland Park mansion. 'Ding-dong!'

'Good morning, Your Ladyship! I'm your new nose-grinder!'

'Ah! Do come in! We're so grateful you could make it! I trust the traffic wasn't too ghastly!'

'Not at all, Your Ladyship. Now, as a special bargain, I can offer you philosophies, tracts, dogmas, creeds, way outs, truths, answers . . .'

'Not for us, thanks awfully! Frankly, we're up to here in truth and we've got answers galore! And as for tracts and dogmas – not to mention way outs . . . ! No – we'd just like our noses ground in the shit, if you'd be so very remorseless.'

Of course, the 's' word and its derivatives have long been a personal favourite of Mr Pinter. Back in 1950, in *A Note on Shakespeare* he wrote that Shakespeare was not only 'a traffic policeman; a rowing blue; a rear-gunner; a chartered accountant; a best man; a bus-conductor; a paid guide; a marriage-guidance counsellor; a church-goer; a stage carpenter; an umpire; an acrobat and a clerk of the court' but also that 'he defecates on his own carpet'.

Forty years on, he wrote a poem called 'American Football (A Reflection upon the Gulf War)' in which the third line was, 'We blew the shit out of them', the fourth line was 'We blew the shit right back up their own ass', the seventh line was, again, 'We blew the shit out of them', the eighth line was 'They suffocated in their own shit' and the eleventh line was, 'We blew them into fucking shit'. Mr Pinter later wrote an article in *Index on Censorship* magazine complaining that the poem had been rejected by the *London Review of Books*, the *Guardian*, the *Observer*, the *Independent* and the *New York Review of Books*, even though it was, in his considered opinion, a 'serious work, a seriously considered work'. Certainly, his present publishers seem to agree. 'His political writings,' they say on the blurb to his collected prose, 'illustrate the depth and lucidity of his views on human rights issues around the world.'

Five years ago, in an article for the *Guardian*, Harold Pinter questioned how America could continue to enforce an embargo against Cuba. 'The answer is quite simple,' he said. 'If you believe you still call the shots you just don't give a shit.' Earlier that year, he wrote a piece condemning various governments for their failure to condemn the US on this issue. 'They've probably worked out that it would be like farting "Annie Laurie" down a keyhole, as we used to say in the old days,' he concluded, adding, 'Be that as it may, the truth is plain: this is an exercise of arrogant power which stinks.'

It does not take a textual critic sifting through these various texts with a fine-tooth comb to detect a recurrent theme in his imagery. Yet the odd thing about Pinter's fifty-year-old reliance on the vocabulary of defecation is that he employs it to signal both approval and disapproval, according to whim. Thus Beckett is thanked for grinding the Pinter nose in it, yet the Americans are condemned for blowing it out of the Iraqis. At one point, Shakespeare is given the thumbs-up for his previously unrecognised ability to do it on his own carpet, and at another the Americans are reprimanded for not giving one at all.

I don't know whether the Pinters keep a puppy or not, but if so I am worried that they may be sending out opposing signals to the little fellow. To the end of her days, the late Barbara Woodhouse, who knew about these things, remained firm in her commitment to clarity. One minute, Harold Pinter feels that having his nose rubbed in it by Beckett is doing him the world of good, but the next he pities the Cubans for having their noses rubbed in it by the Americans. To Beckett, he writes a soupy bread-and-butter letter, to the Americans a strongly worded rebuke.

But there are encouraging signs that he is exploring new horizons in language. A friend of mine, a literary critic, was walking down Holland Park Avenue a while ago when he noticed Pinter marching towards him. As their paths crossed, he heard Pinter grunt a single word: 'Bastard.' Was he paying him a compliment? Who can tell?

Osama

The victory in Kabul has brought some pretty vicious infighting between correspondents to the fore. One side insists on pronouncing it Kah-bull, the other, K'bool. In between these two pronunciations, there are endless factional variations.

This would be a relatively easy problem to tackle were it not for all the other differences in vowels and stresses thrown up by the war. On Tuesday, President Bush spoke about forging a new alliance with President Poot'n. Equally, the war has revived the dispute between those who say Colin and those who say Coh-lin, not to mention those who rhyme Powell with hole and those who rhyme it with towel. I say Osurma and you say Osarma, I say bin Larden and you say bin Layden, I say Taliban and you say Talibarn. So let's call the whole thing off. Or orff.

In her biography of Anthony Blunt, Miranda Carter reveals that Blunt used to affect curious pronunciations in his lectures. He would, for instance, pronounce Milan to rhyme with Dylan. In this, he was probably just following the posh insistence on anywhere foreign being anglicised. My great-aunt, who lived on the island, always insisted on calling it Madge-orca; her generation would also have said Marsales and Lions. But just when outsiders thought they had got the trick, they would be met with its opposite: a perversely French pronunciation of an anglicised word, such as boofay or mat-ee-nay.

The English also like to hide social booby traps in their own names. It is said that when Horatio Bottomley called on Lord

Cholmondeley he was greeted at the door by a butler. 'I've come to see Lord Cholmondeley,' said Bottomley, pronouncing every syllable.

'Lord Chumley is not at home,' said the butler.

'Then would you please tell him Bumley called?' came the reply.

Satirising the English penchant for silly pronunciations of surnames, P.G. Wodehouse, or Woadhouse, as some people call him, invented a furious aristocrat by the name of Sir Jasper ffinch-ffarowmere of ffinch hall, ffinch, Yorkshire. Sir Jasper insists on the individual pronunciation of every single 'f' in his name and address – and then takes this rule even further. In the midst of a tussle, the hero Wilfred shouts, 'Give me that key, you fiend!' and Sir Jasper automatically corrects him: 'Ffiend,' he says.

The offbeat pronunciation is always handy for keeping trespassers at bay. In her biography of Georgiana, Duchess of Devonshire, Amanda Foreman points out that in the late eighteenth century the Devonshire House Circle liked to imitate Cavendish idiosyncracies of speech – 'yaller' for yellow, 'goold' for gold, 'whop' for hope, 'spoil' to rhyme with 'mile' – to such an extent that it developed into its own exclusive dialect, by the turn of the century becoming a symbol of political allegiance for all Whigs.

Upwardly mobile households on the east coast of America were keen to keep abreast of the grandest pronunciations in England, so that when the drawled 'a' – parth, barth, and so on – became fashionable in the eighteenth century, they were only too ready to latch on. But some of the grander Bostonians never quite knew when to stop: H.L. Mencken reported that up to the middle of the nineteenth century, they were forcing drawled a's upon the least likely words, including apple ('arple'), hammer ('harmer'), practical ('prarctical') and even Saturday ('Sarturday').

The Pedants Association – or rather Pedants' Association – will no doubt be anxious to get in touch with Osama, or OsARma, bin Laden, or LAYden, to sort the matter, or marter, out for once and for all. But time will always be lying in wait to pull the rug from under their feet. The original 1926 edition of *Fowler's Modern English Usage* contains this advice: 'In "HUNT HAS HURT HIS HEAD" it is nearly as bad to sound the H of HAS and HIS as not to sound that of HUNT and hurt and head.' Nowadays, it is hard to imagine even the most pedantic extremist, or the most extreme pedant, abiding by this rule.

Kingsley Amis recalled that when he was a boy everyone pronounced Edward Elgar to rhyme with sugar. Similarly, Lord Byron's name was pronounced 'Birron' by his schoolmates. Over the course of my own modest forty-odd years, pronunciation has changed a great deal. These days, anyone below the age of forty who said 'goff' or 'weskit', or dropped the 'h' in hotel would be regarded as dreadfully affected, and other dropped h's – Sir John Betjeman always said 'umour' – would now be met with utter bewilderment. And now we have to worry about Kahbool or K'bull, another cause of trouble, or trah'bull.

*　*　*

In my piece about my dilemma as to whether to pronounce Taliban Tallyban or Tallybarn and Kabul K'bool or Kah-bull and Osama Osahma or Osurma, I mentioned that in her brilliant new biography of Anthony Blunt, Miranda Carter writes that Blunt always pronounced Milan to rhyme with Dylan.

I have since received a card from Mr Geoffrey Wheatcroft. '"Milan" can never rhyme with "Dylan"' he writes, 'At least not in the latter's Welsh pronunciation (as in Thomas not Bob) which is Dullen. And "Milan" to rhyme with "Killen" isn't a pansy-traitor affectation but the old English pronunciation which I use myself when brave or drunk enough. This is proved by scansion: Shakespeare cannot have wanted the line, "Thy father is the Duke of Milan, and A prince of power" to be said MilAn, even if that's how actors playing Prospero today say it. There are plenty of other old pronunciations – Calais to rhyme with palace, Prague to rhyme with Hague – which you need to be very brave to use now but which were once standard English speech.'

My first thought on reading Wheatcroft's card was that, though, to be honest, I had no idea Dylan Thomas pronounced it Dullen, Miranda Carter was obviously referring to Bob Dylan, who, for better or worse, is the first Dylan triggered in the minds of most people below the age of fifty.

But here comes the twist: I then remembered that Bob Dylan – originally Robert Zimmerman – changed his name to Dylan in homage to Dylan Thomas. But then it struck me that, coming from the Midwest mining town of Hibbing, Minnesota, Bob Dylan probably pronounces his surname 'Dullen', just as he would pronounce his Christian name 'Barb'.

The next stage in my voyage deep into the heart of pedantry involved looking up Bob Dylan's entry in *The Faber Companion to 20th Century Popular Music*. The key passage reads: 'He immersed himself in the college folk-revival scene and he chose a new name. He later said that the name was inspired by Western hero Matt Dillon, but by 1962 he was spelling it "Dylan", in the same way as the British poet Dylan Thomas.'

This suggests that the 21-year-old Bob Dylan was under the illusion that, outside Minnesota, 'Dylan' sounded exactly like 'Dillon', whereas Wheatcroft knew better. Pop pedants will now be able to sit for hours chewing over the disarming news that the history of twentieth-century popular music would be very different had the young Geoffrey Wheatcroft, on a family holiday to Hibbing, bumped into the young Robert Zimmerman just in time to keep him up to scratch with correct English pronunciation. (Incidentally, the study of English pronunciation is known as orthoepy – a word which, strange to say, can itself be pronounced in two different ways.)

On the other hand, I am not sure I would care to accompany Mr Wheatcroft when, in one of his braver moods, he strides into his travel agent's to book a trip to Millen or Calace or, indeed, Prague to rhyme with Hague.

People who insist on correct pronunciations can be very

exhausting. I once found myself involved in a conversation with someone who pronounced the first syllable in 'sauna' to rhyme with 'cow'. No doubt she was right, and this is how they say sauna in Scandinavia, but she put me in an awkward spot. If I carried on pronouncing it 'saw-ner', it might seem like a declaration of war, but if I tried to change the habit of a lifetime to pronounce it 'sow-ner', it would make me sound silly, if only to myself. In cowardly fashion, I settled for mumbling 'it' for the rest of our increasingly cagey conversation.

Pronunciation is a stick adrift in the ocean, moving with the tide. Even the Queen doesn't speak in the same way as she did fifty years ago. Just because Shakespeare pronounced it Millen doesn't mean to say that we have to. The word we pronounce 'life' was pronounced 'lafe' by Shakespeare's contemporaries, but 'leef' by Chaucer's. Shakespeare pronounced 'clean' to rhyme with 'lane'; and 'knees' to rhyme with 'grace' 'grass' and 'grease'. And so on. If we all followed suit, we would be greeted with some very odd looks. On the other hand, if ever Geoffrey Wheatcroft chooses to introduce himself in the original as Godefroy Hwaetecroft, then the very least the rest of us can do is to smile sweetly and let him get on with it.

Dread Phrase

Perhaps every profession sees its own reflection in the world beyond. Does the salesman approach each new door in trepidation, terrified a total stranger might start trying to sell him something he doesn't want?

But the parodist is peculiarly prone to see products of his imagination wherever he turns. When I read newspaper columnists, I find it hard to believe they are not making fun of themselves especially for me. Or did I, in a moment of forgetfulness, write that piece by Germaine Greer or this piece by Jeremy Clarkson? If so, how could I possibly have been so cruel?

I began constructing parodies at prepschool, and have been doing so ever since. The prepschool is the perfect nursery for English satire, substituting parents for gargoyles and home for a detention centre at just the age when one is still young enough to appreciate it. At a Catholic prepschool run by a stout, sixty-year-old headmaster who wore the school uniform (grey flannel shorts, Aertex shirt, Start-rite sandals), my best friend Charlie Miller and I would sneak off with a tape recorder to spend hours putting on funny voices and imitating members of staff. It was a way of reducing demons to dolls, of shaping an outside world that, for the rest of the day, was doing its best to shape us: thus was born the impotent megalomania that is the hallmark of the satirist.

Of course, all speech is an imitation of speech. Only by parodying grown-ups does a child learn to speak, and every child below a certain age is an impersonator – often mercilessly embarrassing – of its own parents. The parodist never relinquishes this oddly submissive form of power, ending up practising a toytown voodoo, constructing a doll that bears some sort of distorted resemblance to his intended victim, and then sticking in the pins and bending the limbs to his heart's content.

And there are occasional signs that, through some grim and eerie process, the voodoo then takes effect, and life begins to imitate art. A few weeks ago, I was planning a parody of Tracey Emin to tie in with her Turner Prize nomination. So as not to repeat myself, I looked up a parody of her that I wrote two years ago. My parodic title for an Emin exhibition had been 'Skid Marks on Clean Linen'. I now wonder whether this parody had somehow fed itself into Emin's unconsciousness, ripe for regurgitation two years later in her bed exhibit at the Tate Gallery.

Similarly, I once wrote a *Private Eye* parody of Norman Tebbit. In it, Tebbit voiced his suspicions that Cherie Blair was not all-white. He was particularly worried about her Christian name. 'Sounds foreign to me. Cherry, yes. Cherie, no. To my ordinary English ear, the word has a peculiar, almost Eastern ring to it. Frankly, it wouldn't surprise me to find it had pitched up from India or even Pakistan . . . Of course, if the trendy new Prime Minister of this once-great country chooses to run around with an Indian wife, that is his own concern. But doesn't it get on your goat that the so-called People's Prime Minister can't come clean about his predilections? A word in your ear, Blair. Isn't it high time you forced your missus into a sari? Oh, and don't forget to lock up those valuables when she finds her way indoors!' Spookily, *Private Eye* came out on a Wednesday; in that Thursday's newspaper, Cherie Blair was photographed wearing a sari.

Parody is a knack, and, like other knacks – the knack for juggling, say, or wiggling the hula-hoop – it is best performed in a trance-like state pitched somewhere between attention and instinct. Before I write a parody, I pedantically underline and then copy out four or five pages of my target's most telling phrases. I then take a deep breath and recopy them, with a tweak here and a tweak there, rather in the manner of a drunken court stenographer. Over the years, my parodies that have attracted most praise have been those that have most faithfully reproduced the original.

On occasion, it has even proved necessary to tone down an original to make it less overtly ridiculous before it can pass muster as parody. Who, for instance, could possibly believe that this paragraph, copied word for word from Germaine Greer's collected journalism, was anything but a needlessly brutish anti-feminist parody? 'There have been doctors who loved cunt, but when they are discovered they are usually disgraced and struck off for some contravention of medical etiquette or morality. If you should hear of such a doctor, go to him. If he's not a nut, keep going to him. You'll never have such a happy and healthy cunt as when your doctor is actually fucking you. He need only be interested in it, really. Your average doctor is interested in cock because he's got one – cunt is a troublesome irrelevance, usually.'

Similarly, Tony Benn's real-life diary entry for Sunday 26 December 1976 reads: 'Caroline gave each of us a copy of the *Communist Manifesto* in our stockings, published in English in Russia, and she gave Josh a book called *Marx for Beginners* and gave Hilary Isaac Deutscher's three-volume biography of Trotsky.' This would have been far too unsubtle to publish as parody: one would have to think up something far less flat-footed than a stocking filled with the *Communist Manifesto* before anyone would even half-believe it.

And successful parody lies in the centre of this area of half-belief and half-disbelief. It is probably an echo of the state between conformity and rebellion that initially gave birth to the parodist. Like a pun, parody must resonate equally between two meanings at once. The humour is stretched between the two poles of scepticism and gullibility. If either pole topples, the joke caves in.

Thus if I write a parody of, say, Jeffrey Archer, it will only be funny if the reader can simultaneously entertain both the notions that it is Jeffrey Archer and that it isn't Jeffrey Archer. Those who think that it really is a piece by Jeffrey Archer may be impressed or depressed, but they will not be amused. And readers who only hear the ventriloquist, not the dummy, will remain equally po-faced.

Lord Archer, incidentally, is the only person to have appeared in all three of my *Private Eye* anthologies. Parody is virtually libel-proof, its rudest inferences residing in a sheltered nook between the lines. This week, it has been impossible to switch on the radio without hearing a chorus of 'Jeffrey Archer is a liar'. Regardless of what we all knew, no one has been allowed to say it until now. But in the foreword contributed by Jeffrey Archer to my second anthology, the great man complained that his own part in the creation of the assembled parodies ('up to 90 per cent, at a rough guesstimate') had gone unacknowledged. Nevertheless, he took comfort from the fact that, as the lead singer of Take That! he had led the group straight to the number one slot on seven different occasions, and that as captain of the English cricket team, he could take pride in five consecutive victories. In his diary in the new anthology he reveals that it was Sir Winston Churchill's dying wish that he become Mayor of London in 2000 ('and with that Winston passed away – but not before he had given me a useful tip to invest in Anglia TV shares').

Unlike other forms of humour, parody requires some form of empathy with its victim, even if that empathy is only linguistic. Mohamed al Fayed fills me with loathing, but the only way to construct an accurate portrayal of him was to study transcripts of his conversations, and thus ease myself into inhabiting the rhythms and patterns of his speech. I later added on everything more overtly silly or surreal, but all parody must be grounded in language, even if the texture of that language and, in al Fayed's case, its extreme colour, is known only to a few. 'I like the Queen, nice woman, very nice, woman, very good friend, for me is diamond you know, is jewel, she no bullshit, if she hear word against al Fayed she say, "You can fakh off you fakhin shit, Mohamed good man, Mohamed my friend." God save the Queen, and He will, al Fayed tell him to. He take many gifts off al Fayed. God owe al Fayed favour. Queen very nice lady. So how much she cost? We talking day-rate here . . .' and so on.

Less subversive branches of satire have the effect of painting every subject with the same thick black brush, so that they are incapable of making a moral distinction between, say, Jeffrey Archer and Adolf Hitler. The great virtue of parody is that it can reflect every shade of response from loathing to admiration. Certainly, it would make me happy if someone were spurred by my spoof of the somewhat gloomy writings of W.G. Sebald ('Above me, a seagull swooped, its wings stretched fully out, as though an unseen torturer were pulling them to breaking point . . . it continued upon its vacuous and erratic journey through a sky still glowering in fury at the ceaseless intrusion of the crazed sun. The sky loomed over me like a bright blue package containing heavy objects about to fall from a great height . . .') to go out and read them.

The most common form of parody is, of course, self-parody. It is a disease to which every columnist is prone, for it is always easier to reassemble the usual range of columnar emotions – outrage, pity, etc – than to feel them afresh. In my Wallace Arnold column, originally written as a parody of the *Spectator*, I used to insert the parenthesised expression '(Dread phrase!)' at regular intervals. Recently I came across a diary in an old 1987 *Spectator*. The writer had inserted the expression '(Dread phrase!)' after the words 'British Rail 125 express train'. Which pompous, fat-bottomed idiot wrote that? I wondered. I looked for the by-line. It was Craig Brown.

Serendipity

A poll has discovered that the favourite word of the British is 'serendipity'. A surprising choice, perhaps, but then with so many words to choose from it's hard to think of a word that wouldn't have been surprising.

I suppose I'd have guessed that the top choice would have been a pushy new shaven-headed word, freshly coined to infuriate and intimidate traditionalists, a word such as 'sorted' or 'innit' or 'saddo'. But the tweedy are in no position to feel smug: 'serendipity' is in fact a pretty modern word, new-fangled enough to be flash, even a little vulgar, like the wind-chimes its sound resembles.

Serendipity's birth can be dated to exactly 1754, when Horace Walpole coined it – or at least purloined it – from the title of a Persian fairy tale, 'The Three Princes of Serendip'. How it would have upset Dr Johnson, whose *Dictionary* was to appear for the first time the following year, to think that Serendip, the Persian name for Ceylon, or, if you'd prefer, the Iranian name for Sri Lanka, would one day be voted the favourite word of the British people.

Like so many, Johnson was upset by new words, particularly those in which he sniffed the whiff of America. He hated, for instance, the freshly coined word 'mob', which was then a recent and yobbish abbreviation of 'mobile', itself an abbreviation of the Latin 'mobile vulgus', meaning common people. He also damned newly fashionable words like 'jeopardy', 'glee' and 'smoulder' as hideous Americanisms, though he was etymologically wrong (they were in fact all old English words that had gone out of currency in Britain but, like many others – 'gotten' among them – had been preserved intact in America).

There is nothing new about the mistrust of the new. Samuel Taylor Coleridge so hated one new word that he condemned it as 'vile and barbarous'. That word was 'talented', now the mainstay of school reports written by even the crustiest of schoolteachers.

Anyone with children will know the speed with which new words – and new meanings for old words – pop up. In the past few weeks, I have heard 'shod' meaning absolutely terrible (e.g. 'Your BB gun doesn't work. It's really shod') and 'mint' meaning very good (e.g.: 'My BB gun is the best. It's mint').

In a world owned and operated by the over-15s, the under-15s have the understandable urge to coin new words of their own. Inevitably, their attraction to a new word diminishes the moment the word is colonised by oldies. A week or two ago, I used the word 'sad' in its new, or new-ish, meaning of 'socially inadequate'. My nine-year-old son winced at someone of my age employing such a young word. 'You saying "sad" is what's *really* sad,' he said.

Of course, not every fresh-faced word that pokes its head around the door of English letters is then permitted a permanent seat. It's a long time, for instance, since I've heard anyone use the word 'crucial' meaning 'splendid', yet in the early 1980s it was as prevalent as the current 'wicked!', which means the same thing. (In fact, 'wicked' itself is not quite so up to date as its users might hope: Scott Fitzgerald was using it in this ironic, jazzy manner as early as 1920, when he had one of his characters say at a dance, 'Phoebe and I are going to shake a wicked calf'.)

Trademark words such as 'Gonk' 'Filofax' 'shell-suit' and 'Tamagotchi' are destined to perish alongside the trend that gave them birth, though occasionally one of these words is able to fly free of its product's corpse. I suspect this might be true of 'anorak'. Back in the 1920s, it was a word taken from the Eskimo for a waterproof jacket with a hood. By the mid-80s, it had taken on a second meaning: it was now also a gawky social misfit with an obsessive interest in something uncool such as trainspotting or collecting stamps. This second meaning then grew so pervasive that manufacturers of anoraks were forced to rename them. In a few years' time, the original meaning of anorak may well have been jettisoned altogether.

The speed with which language changes can come as a shock even to those who live through it. In the late 1940s, when the Beatles were roughly the same age as my son, the *Daily Mail* published with a shudder a list of new-fangled American expressions it believed to be 'positively incomprehensible' to the average Englishman. These included the words 'commuter', 'seafood', 'mean' (in the sense of nasty), 'living room', 'dumb' (in the sense of stupid) and 'rare' (in the sense of underdone). Fifty years later, can there be anyone in Britain who doesn't know what they mean? In fact, nowadays most of them seem dull, almost stale, and one of them – dumb – has been overtaken many times, most recently, I think, by 'dur-brain'. (Or should that be 'duh-brain'? It is hard to know, as it is too recent for any reference work.)

My own favourite word is also still ex-directory. It is 'pimpsqueak' meaning simple. 'That's pimpsqueak!' my children say when they know the answer to a question. I imagine its etymology can be traced from 'simple' to 'pimps' via 'pipsqueak', to 'pimpsqueak'. Could it be the nation's favourite word in the year 2100? In many ways, it would seem a less radical choice than the Iranian word for Sri Lanka.

Acquainted

Over the past week, the crowds have been baying not for blood, but for tears. Having sobbed on camera and on phone-ins for Princess Diana, woman they never knew, they have been roused to self-righteous indignation when her own family has refused to follow suit. Private grief is now seen as a contradiction in terms: how can grief be private, how can privacy contain grief? The emotional reticence of the British, once so highly valued, has come to be seen as an anachronism, by turns starchy and cold.

'Acquainted with grief': I think of Kathleen Ferrier singing those words, and of how moving that phrase is, the more moving for being so buttoned-up. The more powerful the horse, the phrase suggests, the tighter must be the rein. But these days, no one is allowed to suffer in silence, to suffer within themselves. The rein must be let loose, the horse spurred on, so that complete strangers for miles around can witness all the whinnying and the kicking, the grains of sand soaring into the air.

On television on Thursday, we witnessed one of the most emotionally painful sights I have ever seen on television: the Royal Family forced into a photocall outside the gates of Balmoral, moving awkwardly like animals in a cage, the cameras whirring away, ready to capture any tell-tale signs of grief – a little hand held here, a bowed head there – for the gratification of the outside world.

I have been acquainted with grief – private grief, real grief –

this year. Two people I loved very much died after long illnesses. I would have found repulsive any suggestion from strangers that I should somehow put my grief on display, there to be shared around, like cocktail eats. I sometimes think that if Kathleen Ferrier were still alive, editors and impresarios would be telling her to change the words 'acquainted with grief' to something more open and giving, something less formal and starchy, like 'sobbing buckets' or 'dealing with emotions'.

For two years, my father-in-law was in what is known as a persistent vegetative state. It is a state so hopeless that it calls into question the very meaning of individual life and identity; any answers it provides are too grim to contemplate. For a few months, when things still looked very slightly hopeful, he was in the Rehabilitation Unit of a Bath hospital. He was surrounded by other patients, most of them with lesser, but still grievous, brain injuries. A message on the swing door into the corridor of the unit asked visitors to make sure that the door was kept closed, so that no patient could leave. Just inside the door, morning, noon and night, sat a young man in a wheelchair, presumably the victim of a road accident, his head lolling to one side, speechless and expressionless. He could comprehend enough to know that he wanted desperately to leave, but not enough to be able to do so.

That young man was in better shape than most. The majority of the others were young, barely out of their teens, the victims, I imagine, of motorbike and car accidents, their plight pathetic beyond words. Yet what I remember of that unit was love, and a love all the more poignant for being untrumpeted: the love of the nurses and physiotherapists, as they bustled about their gruelling tasks, chatting away to patients, as if to old friends; the love of the brightly coloured cards and family mementoes pinned to the walls; the love of a Gilbert and Sullivan tape, a Christmas present to my father-in-law from the staff; the love of a gang of burly, terrifyingly macho, leather-jacketed bikers sitting around the bedside of an old mate, reminiscing into his unhearing ear of past excursions, taking it in turns to hold his hand; the love of the father who sat, unrecognised, beside his son each day, and, who, in the midst of his private agony, never forgot to wave and do a cheery thumbs-up sign at another damaged young man before he left. My wife once passed this cheery thumbs-upping father in the corridor, as he was leaving the Rehabilitation Unit for the day. No longer on show, his face was streaked with tears. Public strength, private grief: his behaviour within the unit might now be condemned as that most unmodish of things, the Stiff Upper Lip; but it helped him to endure the unendurable, and it helped everyone else too.

At my father-in-law's memorial service in May we read pieces of his writing, some of it funny, some sad, all in different ways beautiful. But the most moving reading, recently reprinted in the book of his selected writings,* was a simple reminiscence:

'Of Christmases in the army I myself treasure one memory. It is of Christmas 1944, when I found myself on leave in the little Dutch town of Helmond. First I went to my billet – a small house in a side street, rather bare, shabby but neat; and a bed, with sheets! My hosts were not well off at the best of times and the war had reduced them to real want: they and their children were half-starved, their clothes were wretched, they had no soap, they lacked all luxuries and most necessities. Then I went to the divisional club and, for various reasons, got shockingly drunk. When I returned in the small hours, I had lost my key. I wakened the whole household, fell over everything in the hall, and was sick all over the lavatory. The next day was Christmas Eve. Overwhelmed with shame, I slunk out early, wandered dismally about, wrote some letters in the club and crept back at eight or so to go to bed. On the bed I found an apple, a tiny bottle of *oude genever*, a little packet of gritty biscuits, some strange tobacco, and a card, painstakingly inscribed by one of the children in English

The Odd Thing About the Colonel and Other Pieces, by Colin Welch (Bellew Publishing)

and in many colours, wishing me a happy Christmas. As it turned out, it was for me a very happy Christmas. Of all the presents I have ever had, none has seemed to me to mean more than those pitiful objects, representing as they did not only a real sacrifice, but a gesture of understanding and love. And in my bedroom, bare as it was, hung the cross of Christ.'

Those who urge the Royal Family into 'sharing' their emotions with photographers would no doubt have urged that Dutch family to hug and kiss their errant lodger, and for their errant lodger to have hugged and kissed them in return, tears everywhere, and all accompanied by a stream of Disneymania ('love ya', 'c'mon, you gotta let it out', 'you're like a mom to me, you know that', etc, etc). No doubt the same people would have urged Michelangelo to repaint the ceiling of the Sistine Chapel to emphasise the truly lovable relationship between God and Man, showing them together in a warm, manly, embrace ('Love ya, Daddy') butchly patting each other on the back. And Chardin, whose still-lifes of light gently falling on lemons and jugs are always so unexpectedly affecting, would be urged to squeeze a few lovable kiddies into the foreground of the canvas, or perhaps even a grieving mom, a lovable mutt and a few damp tissues.

Reticence is not just an artistic virtue, but a human one. It acknowledges the depth of meaning to be found in words unspoken. Lesley Cunliffe, my other great friend who died this year, had been on the brink of death for many months. Alone with her mother one night, and holding her hand, she whispered, 'Shall I slide off now, Mother?' Her mother gave her soft assent. Lesley closed her eyes. They had become her last words. I have since thought that they were a simple hymn to dignity over sentimentality, to reticence over self-dramatisation.

Today, those who yearn for howls and hugs and a feast of self-expression from the Royal Family would probably be better off running a video of an American soap opera, or of the funeral of the Ayatollah Khomeini. True grief may run too deep for surface tremors. Sometimes, there is no sight more moving, and no sight more genuine, than the reticence of the stiff upper lip.

BritArt
and
Beyond

Intensely Moving: Sir Nicholas Serota's Diary

Frankly, I welcome the bravura debate engendered by so many of our most exciting young artists. It is by turns shocking, amusing, wry and *deeply disturbing*. And this is just one of the reasons I am looking forward to next year's *My Turd* exhibition by Tracey Emin.

Emin laid her *Turd* in mid-morning – 10.44am, to be exact – on 22 November of this year. I count myself privileged to have been there when the work – rich, earthy dark browns and beiges, soft and yielding yet somehow strangely *visceral* and *concentrated* – emerged from the artist. The whole experience was, for me – perhaps even more so for Tracey – *intensely moving*.

The moment I saw it, I knew that this was something that had come from the very depths of her being, something raw and pungent, juxtaposing the old and the new, the roughage with the smooth, bold and real yet with infinite layers.

It quite literally bowled me over.

I realised then and there that I was in the presence of something new and modern and *deeply disturbing*. While Tracey Emin handled the paper with remarkable deftness, I set about confronting her new creation on my own terms. And the more I confronted it, the more I realised it would repay prolonged attention, as its layers slowly disclosed other layers. And in confronting it, I knew for sure that, yes, Emin had indeed broken new ground, bringing something very hot and very pliable to contemporary art.

My Turd has a lot to say about birth and death, a lot to say about the nature of self, a lot to say about the whole process of defecation and renewal in contemporary society, and it has a hell of a lot to say about art itself. It is almost as if, in some extraordinary way, the artist were asking us to confront the very nature of what we call 'shit'. What is it? Where is it? And who will buy it? For, studied closely, the gentle, almost classical contours of *My Turd* seem to echo the gentle curves of Poussin and Boucher, its deep dark browns and blacks gaining strength from comparison to the rich, earthy colours of Rembrandt and Goya. While firmly perched on the cutting edge of contemporary art, *My Turd* has its roots firmly buried in the past.

Advance bookings for *My Turd* have broken all records. Regardless of the critics, the public seem to welcome Tracey Emin's savage attack on the wheels of commerce and convention. To prove it, Channel 4 has already scheduled a tie-in *Turd* season, in which Waldemar Januszczak explores *The Shock of the Poo*, while minor *Turds* by Tracey Emin are already selling like hot cakes to private dealers for over £20,000 a piece and the Tate shop will soon be fully stocked with *My Turd* T-shirts, pencil-sharpeners, calendars and desk diaries. And already all the committees I chair have voted it the exhibition of the year, even before seeing it.

This all goes to show that there is a tremendous appetite, particularly among the young, for the smouldering confrontation with inner reality. Yes, art *should* shock. Yes, art *should* be ugly. Yes, art *should* set out to unnerve and confront and challenge. This is what great art has always done and will always do. Anyone with the slightest knowledge of the history of art will know that, in their day, Sizewell A and Centre Point were also dismissed by critics as 'ugly' and 'too modern'. Why, even the beautiful mushroom cloud of Hiroshima was at its opening unfairly derided by critics as 'horrendous' and – my favourite – 'an ineradicable blot on our civilisation' (!). Yet today Sizewell and Centre Point are acknowledged as seminal works, and Hiroshima continues to knock us backwards with its breathtaking force.

Of course, there will always be those who dismiss major new installations such as *My Turd* as in some way 'not art' (!). Those very same people who may happily admire the old-fashioned chocolate-box charms of a Vermeer or a Monet will hold up their hands in shock at *My Turd*.

Why? We cannot simply write off these unfortunate sections of the population as absurd bourgeois tabloid philistines with no capacity for real feeling or thought. That would be to underestimate their ignorance. It seems to me that, on a very basic level, they simply have not made the necessary effort to comprehend what Tracey Emin is trying to say through her *Turd*, what she is trying to do in this remarkable piece, with its soft, *almost floating*, lines and its peculiarly *emergent* sense of its own *turdiness*. And until they bother to make that effort, they will forever be excluded from right-minded society, unable to participate, even on the most junior level, in the world of modern art.

A word or two about myself. When I see *My Turd*, I find myself deeply disturbed. My views on the very nature of art and life are challenged.

1) Who am I? 2) What am I doing? 3) What is art? These are the sort of questions I am forced to ask. Art obliges us to answer these questions for ourselves.

But thankfully I soon get an answer to all my questions: 1) *I am Sir Nicholas Serota, Director of the Tate, Chairman of the Turner Prize, internationally acclaimed as the most important man in British art.* 2) *I am giving* My Turd *a chance to breathe.* 3) *Art is what I say it is.*

And though the questions may have been deeply disturbing, the answers give me quiet cause for satisfaction.

But many others are not, alas, quite so civilised as, after all this confrontation, I find myself to be. There are those who, seeing this work which sets out to shock, upset and disturb, write me letters complaining that they are shocked, upset my staff and attempt to cause no end of disturbance in the media. How gauche they must be to react like that!

For them, *My Turd* is just a turd. Due to lack of education in the visual arts, they are unable to place it in an historical context. Without this intercontextuality, they fail to see that by a process of evacuation and exhibition, Tracey Emin has transformed what might have been 'just a turd' (!) into *My Turd* – something tremendously powerful and sacred, a richly sourced object that will be visited and revered by anyone with a nose for art for many years to come. What wind was to Turner, and the mountain to Cezanne, *My Turd* is to Tracey Emin. Enjoy!

Bel Littlejohn:
Literally Shattered

Shattered. hattered. attered. Literally shattered. S-H-A-T-T-E-R-E-D. Even the word itself is shattered. R-E-H-T-S-A-D-T-E. All over the place, like a plate smashed in an earthquake. Suddenly, revolving on its viscous axis, the world – the dworl, the ldwor, the rldwo – doesn't seem to make sense any more.

You guessed it. I've just been to – in fact, *been* is hardly the word, *visited* probably gets you closer to the full awesomeness of the total experience – the Jackson Pollock exhibition at the Tate Gallery. It was cosmically simple, as only the most complicated things can be. I walked through the front entrance, along the main corridor, veered right. And there it was. Even to call it an exhibition does it some kind of injustice. It's not an exhibition. If anything, it's a tionhibitexh.

There's no point trying to explain it. These days, there no longer appears to be any point in arguing the matter. Those who do are worthless individuals, useful only for organ transplants. Suddenly everyone who counts is in agreement. It's official. Jackson Pollock is the greatest American artist of this or any other century. And we fortunate inhabitants of these British Isles are now in a position to savour this fascinating lurch into certainty for ourselves, from close up.

Pollock goes for something. He lurches, spins, whistles, gyrates, impacts, shakes, fragments, sips, explodes, deliberates, stabs, wipes, jerks, dabs, doodles, gobbles, thrusts, twitches, bursts, flicks, winks, cascades, grabs, pouts, points, soaps, sieves, splashes, fries, drips, bakes, quivers. And he gets it. And there is, without a whisper of doubt, something exceptionally stirring about his approach. But not stirring in the sense of 'stirring a cup of tea'. Stirring a cup of tea is hardly stirring at all when compared to how stirring this is. Pollock – Jackson Pollock – is far more stirring than that. In a way, looking at his paintings, his creations, it's as though he is stirring the whole Atlantic Ocean, stirring it with a vast great universal ladle, with all those black-blue whales and dolphins just so many croutons – and then serving it up to each and every one of us in the steaming hot bowls that are his canvases.

But first the facts. Pollock – Jackson Pollock – was, arguably, the first American who ever lived. He was the first outsider, the first man in American history to be truly dissatisfied with his lot. Before Pollock, no one had ever worn jeans and drunk too much, no one had ever left his wife for a younger woman, no one had ever lost his temper and lashed out in bars, no one had ever smashed his car into a tree and killed himself. And looking deep into his major works at the Tate, it's as though you can see all his life in a few crazed spurts of paint. Isn't that squiggle a cigarette? And isn't that mad loop of white a craving for alcohol? And what about that swirl in the corner? Might it – just possibly – be the young Jackson's childhood demons? And looked at from a certain angle, one of his greatest masterpieces, Number 1A, is the spitting image of the hawthorn bush that grew beside his kitchen in East Hampton.

Look hard at that canvas. The paint is loose and viscous. Viscous – my God, it's viscous. Viscous, but not vicious or even vivacious. Viscous, but not Viscount: whatever he was to become, Pollock always remained an ordinary American guy and never succumbed to the temptation to join the English aristocracy. Viscous, but not in the sense that cats have viscous, or Lord Kitchener had viscous: Pollock's paint was thrown on to the canvas like an anorak in stormy weather, at one and the same time protective yet foretelling showery spells ahead.

Above all, Pollock is intensely personal. Staring deep into 'One: Number 31' at the Tate, I see so much of my life laid bare. In the bottom right-hand corner, I see my mother forcing me to finish the Shredded Wheat I disliked before packing me off to the school I despised. In the middle and slightly to the left, I see Vic, my second husband, yelling at me whenever I ventured to suggest he was in the wrong. And all across the top, I see a ray of hope – the angora cardigan I knitted for myself in the winter of '69. From whichever part of the gallery you look at this extraordinary work, it looks back at you, bleakly despairing and yet strangely optimistic. As in life itself, the drips seem to follow you around the room. And no matter how much you try you just can't get them to go away. This is art that goes right through me, out the other side, and back in through another entrance. It's Jackson Pollock. It's you. It's me. But above all it's paint.

See it.

Bel Littlejohn: Wish You Were Here

Bzzzzzzzz. Bzzzzzz. Bzzzzzz.

Can you hear it? Yup – there's a buzz in the air.

Bzzzzzzzz. Bzzzzzz. Bzzzzzz. That's the only true way I can convey in simple words the feeling that comes over me whenever I walk into a fellow artist's studio with Charles Saatchi in tow. There's just this incredible buzz in the air – bzzzzzzz – and it pervades the whole atmosphere.

It was just after he visited my last exhibition, 'Why Don't I Just Dig a Hole in the Ground Jump in and Draw the Earth Upon Myself For All The Bloody Good It'll Do Me (Meditation 3)' at the Serpentine Gallery that Charles Saatchi took me on as his special art adviser. He also bought two of my best-loved pieces, the darkly comic *Nazi Scabs* – a swastika formed of all the scabs I had peeled off my body and those of my lovers in the past seven and a half years – and the dark yet comical *Drainage 8,* a montage of used Kleenex sculpted into the shape of a human nose, but a nose – ironically – with three nostrils. Ever since then I have been accompanying Charles around the country on his collecting exhibitions every Tuesday and Thursday, giving him the full benefit of my acclaimed eye. Bzzzzzzzz.

I've already been justly acclaimed as the first to spot the majority of the darkly comic new pieces that have transformed our understanding of what we mean by art. For instance, I came across the young Damien Hirst when he was still at art college. This was long before he became famous, thank you very much, and at that time he didn't have the finances to bring his major visions to fruition. When I discovered him, he was hard at work cutting a fishfinger in two with a pair of scissors and sellotaping the two halves into separate shoe boxes. 'I really wanted to do this with a slice of smoked salmon,' he explained, disconsolately, 'but I couldn't afford it.' Well, I took out my mobile, phoned round my contacts – and by the end of the afternoon we'd placed the order for one dead shark, ready sliced. And the rest, as they say, is art history.

Just recently, things have become so busy – and buzzy!! – working for Charles Saatchi that I've had to take on an assistant, Waldemar Januszczak, for expert back-up, van-hire and general admin plus a spot of cleaning. Waldemar is full of enthusiasm. He emerged from his first recce to the third-year show at Goldsmiths in love with a starkly ironic installation work composed entirely of filing cabinets, a desk and a word processor titled *Administration Knock and Enter*. It was only after Saatchi made a bid of £25,000 for the piece that it turned out to be the bursar's office, so he raised his price by another £20,000 and now it's on permanent loan to Berlin.

But then one Thursday afternoon this October, Charles summoned me and Waldemar to his gallery. 'What's the difference, then?' he asked. The two of us looked at his famous exhibits – Hirst's dead sheep, Tracey Emin's used condoms, Marcus Harvey's life-size portrait of Charles Manson formed entirely of human phlegm – and drew a blank. 'Listen!' commanded Saatchi. 'What can you hear?'

We listened hard. 'Nothing,' we replied.

'Exactly!' he snapped. 'There's no buzz! The buzz has disappeared! It's gone elsewhere! Art has moved on! It's no longer brutal and dark! It's happy and bright! It's . . . it's . . . it's The Next Move Forward! It's The New Neurotic Realism!'

Of course, Waldemar and I clapped and looked excited, but we both knew deep down that there was one helluva lot of work ahead of us. Thankfully, we managed to save some of the exhibits by painting or smiles or changing their titles to something more merry. My own *Nazi Scabs* has now been renamed *Sunny Smiles,* and we've put shades and a sunhat on Damien's shark and retitled it, *Wish You Were Here.* But most of the rest had to be wrapped in brown paper and sent round to Christie's, 'cos they were just too bleak for their own good.

Mr Saatchi's change of heart has sent shock-waves through the artistic community. Marcus Harvey was halfway through a bleakly ironic portrait of Peter Sutcliffe, but now he's had to scrub off the beard, add in some teeth and make out it's Ken Dodd. Rachel Whiteread's had to wallpaper her house and install a colour TV. But – hey, guys, listen up! – BritArt is well and truly buzzing once more. Bzzzzzzz. Bzzzzzzz. Bzzzzzzz. Can you hear it?

What Became of Turner

To: The Waddington Gallery, Cork Street
From: J.M.W. Turner.

Dear Mr Waddington,
I am an artist looking for a gallery in which to exhibit my work.
I am particularly interested in the transforming effect of light
on landscape and objects. I was wondering if I might come and
show you one or two of my works at your earliest convenience?

To: J.M.W. Turner, Maiden Lane
From: The Waddington Gallery, Cork Street

Dear Mr Turner,
Your work sounds most interesting. We are at present
organising an exhibition of young conceptual artists,
scheduled for early next year. If your interest in 'the transforming effect of light' is an installation project involving neon
strips, perhaps with the addition of several glass tubes and/or
stainless steel sheets it would suit the Waddington Gallery
well, as we have recently paid a notable amount of money for
extensive rewiring of the premises. I would be most interested
in viewing your exciting new electrical work at your earliest
convenience.
PS You mention 'objects'. Might these be corpses or skulls of
animals, or – better still – dead human beings? There is great
call for these and similar objects at the cutting edge of the

London art world at present. Recently, the addition of a dead hamster to an installation work by one of our most promising young artists (*Squeak No More: Mortality Visits the Cage*) added a further £5,000 to the asking price. The artist now has enormously interesting plans for a similar exhibit, but this time with two or more hamsters: Charles Saatchi has already expressed an interest.

To: The Waddington Gallery, Cork Street
From: J.M.W. Turner

Dear Mr Waddington,
To be honest, I use oils and watercolours on canvas. By and large, I paint landscapes, together with some interiors. There are sometimes one or two people in my paintings, and occasionally a dog, but up to this moment I have painted no hamsters, dead or alive. Nevertheless, I would love to show you my work.

To: J.M.W. Turner, Maiden Lane
From: The Waddington Gallery

Dear Mr Turner,
I admire you for your refusal to be derivative and your bold decision temporarily to turn your back on dead hamsters. Obviously, one must be original. But there are many other dead animals to choose from. You make no mention within your letter of dead gerbils, raccoons or – ideally – rats. Last year, one of our most exciting and brilliant young artists enjoyed tremendous success with his marvellously vibrant exhibition, 'We're All Going To Die One Day' in which he stuck a dead rat to twenty-three different canvases, to great profit all round. Is this something you have tried? Or, if not, is it something you might consider trying? We have it on excellent authority that the judges of this year's Turner Prize are very much on the lookout for dead rats – and they are becoming increasingly popular, too, in the burgeoning restaurant installation market.

BritArt and Beyond

To: *The Waddington Gallery, Cork Street*
From: *J.M.W. Turner*

Dear Mr Waddington,
I am sorry. I do not stick the corpses of any dead animals on my canvases, nor do I have any plans to. They are covered only with paint. But if I could show my work to you, you may well find it exciting. I have recently completed *The Fighting Temeraire*, a painting of an old sailing ship being towed to its final berth by a more modern tug. I would love to show it to you.

To: *J.M.W. Turner*
From: *The Waddington Gallery*

Dear Mr Turner,
If you could lay your hands on sections of either of the two boats in question and then reassemble them as a stunning piece of conceptual art (possible title *So That's It Then: The Ironic Paradox of a Non-Sailing Ship As It Moves Towards Death. As We All Do*) then we might be interested. We have it on good authority that the judges of this year's Turner Prize are on the lookout for young artists working with items reclaimed from scrap yards. But – really! – a simple 'painting' of the two boats is quite out of the question! But presumably you are teasing!

From: *The Director, The Saatchi Collection*
To: *J.M.W. Turner, Maiden Lane*

Dear Mr Turner,
We have heard on the art grapevine that you may be proposing to create a conceptual work employing dead gerbils and/or reclaimed metal from two derelict ships. If so, we would be very interested in purchasing such work(s) for our collection. There is increasing enthusiasm in the art world for works on video and/or in formaldehyde. Could you please let us know whether your work-in-progress would adapt to

either of these two exciting new mixed media? If so, we might think of arranging a major exhibition in time for a visit by the judges of next year's Turner Prize. Our provisional title for your proposed exhibition is 'Asphyxiated Gerbils and Scrapyard Boats: The Dried-Up Juices of Despair' which is market-oriented to appeal to our regular clients. We have already commissioned the leading art critic Sarah Kent to compose a catalogue introduction. We look forward to hearing from you.

From: J.M.W. Turner
To: The Director, The Saatchi Collection

Dear Director,
Thank you for your kind letter expressing an interest in my work. I regret to inform you that you have been misinformed. I work with paints and watercolours on canvas, and have never used asphyxiated gerbils or scrap metal in my work. However, I would be only too happy to show you my paintings, if you could spare me just a few minutes.

From: The Director, The Saatchi Collection
To: J.M.W. Turner

Dear Jo,
I enclose Ms Kent's catalogue introduction to the forthcoming exhibition of your installation works. You will note that she describes you in glowing terms as 'pitiless, morbid, grotesque, repellent, angry, sordid and uncompromising'. I am told you are interested in the effects of light on surroundings. I would be most grateful if you would let me know the wattage you require, so that our electrician can get to work. There is already a great deal of media interest in your forthcoming exhibition: Channel 4 (who are, as you will realise, the sponsors of the Turner Prize) wish to make an arts documentary about you called *The Salvaged Gerbil: The Anguished World of Jo Turner* and the *Sunday Times* magazine is keen to feature a full-colour

photograph of you on the cover, in a septic tank, naked, with 100 dead gerbils.

From: J.M.W. Turner
To: The Director, The Saatchi Collection

Dear Director,
I do not think you understood my last letter: I am a landscape painter who works in oil and watercolours. The proposals you make are sadly unsuited to my art.

From: J.M.W. Turner
To: Nicolas Serota, Director, The Tate Gallery

Dear Mr Serota,
I would very much like to find a place for my works in the permanent collection of the Tate Gallery. I would be grateful if you would take a look at them.

From: Nicolas Serota, Director, The Tate Gallery
To: J.M.W. Turner

Dear Mr Turner,
 As you may know, the Tate Gallery is always interested in expanding its collection of exhibits from the cutting edge of contemporary British art. This we do largely through the leading galleries, such as those in Cork Street, or through major competitions, such as the Turner Prize. Regrettably, through pressure of time, we are unable to monitor unsolicited work. I am sorry to say the work of J.M.W. Turner is at present unsuited to the Tate Gallery.
PS Have you tried your local village hall?

A-Z of How to Be A Significant Artist

A is for *About, What's it all.* Do not worry if, once you have created your significant work of art, you are still unsure what it is about; but do make certain that someone else is prepared to have a stab at explaining. Norman Rosenthal is especially generous in this field. Invited to explain the exhibit *The Costermonger's Stall*, shown at the Royal Academy in 1993, which consisted of a cart upon which were deposited bundles of fresh flowers, he pithily replied, 'It's about somehow a kind of memento mori of you know the world of the consumer the kind of thing he's done very very successfully within his extraordinary pieces that remind one of being in these shops in I don't know in South London or wherever you know where the vegetable markets are and the kind of giving drawing attention to their formal qualities and you know we might forget that everything has formal quality too as well as it were inherent subject quality and by looking at it in an art context it becomes different.'

On the other hand, there is no reason why you should not perform the task yourself. Interviewing himself for the book *Damien Hirst*, the artist asked himself, 'How do you see *In and Out of Love* in terms of your relationships, your experiences of love?' To which the artist himself replied, '*In and Out of Love* is the most complicated work I've made so far, it's about love and realism, dreams, ideals, symbols, life and death.' The work in question consisted of a dead butterfly stuck on to some blue paint. See also: LISTS.

B is for *Beyond itself, the ladle is up to something*. Whenever creating a work of art from kitchen implements, be sure to check that the ladle is up to something beyond itself. If you suspect that it is, but would welcome confirmation, the person to contact is Marina Warner, who is known to be highly sensitive in such matters. She certainly made a fine start rubber-stamping the work of Richard Wentworth: 'By skewing perception of an object, he helps sharpen the sense of haecceity, of the this-ness of things . . . But this-ness is not allowed to rest within its own boundaries: we can admire the beckoning shiny bowl of a soup ladle . . . but *the ladle is up to something beyond itself*' (my italics). But, alas, she was doomed to fall at the last stretch – 'And often, though we sense that it is indicating, we do not know quite what' – only to pick herself up, and stumble bravely to the finishing line any-old-how: 'Incoherence tantalises him – he wants to touch the bottom in it, because, if he can, it will cease to be coherent.'

C is for *Caption competition*. Ever since the demise of *Punch* magazine, the responsibility for operating the popular *Weekend Caption Competition* has been taken over largely by the Saatchi Gallery. Despite fierce competition from John Greenwood's *Rings and Strings and Things (No Wings, But There is Some Jelly as Always)* the annual winner is invariably Damien Hirst, whose captions can transform even the dullest objects – rows of stuffed fish, glasses or spots – into hilariously portentous jokes on the modern art market, viz *Isolated Elements Swimming in the Same Direction for the Purpose of Understanding*.

D is for *Daz*, one of many Procter and Gamble products advertised by Saatchi and Saatchi which helped contribute to the financing of the Saatchi Gallery, which then displays installation works by Hadrian Piggott, which are designed to be powerful indictments of the international soap and detergent industry. See also MARATHON and SILK CUT.

D is also for *Death*. Any work that is to be judged as significant must exhibit undertones (see IRONIC) of death. This is most easily achieved by placing the word daintily in the title (cf *The Physical Impossibility of Death in the Mind of Someone Living* by Damien Hirst). If not, it must be spotted by an astute critic. Happily, there are many critics available for the issuing of Death Undertone Guaranteed certificates for a modest sum. In 1993, Gavin Turk created a glass cube, upon the ceiling of which he placed five pieces of used chewing gum. He called the piece *Floater* and it was quickly snapped up by the Saatchi Gallery. In the Saatchi catalogue, Sarah Kent explains why: '*Floater* is a similarly ironic (see IRONIC) gesture of disaffection. A piece of chewing gum is stuck to the roof of a display case as though it were a relic, a cast of the artist's mouth . . . As with *Relic*, the subject is death and the traces we leave behind . . .'

E is for *Effort*. The art market still sets great store by effort. This means that, should your jokes (see also IRONY) lack a certain humour, you may still gain points for *effort*. A picture of a piano hanging upside down might not scrape past the beady eye of the cartoon editor of the *Sun*, but if you go to the *effort* of actually hanging a piano from the ceiling of the Tate, you will gain the approval of one and all. E is also for *Expense*, for which the same applies.

F is for *Fragonard*. Young Jean Honore Fragonard has just had his first work accepted by Anthony d'Offay. It is an installation called *The Swing* and consists of a child's swing, the bench cut in two, each of the two pieces swinging from a separate rope. It is an ironic piece about death and the traces we leave behind. It forces the viewer to confront his deepest fears, and the fears that we as a society prefer to ignore. It is also, of course, about the nature of art itself . . . (See also THE NATURE OF ART ITSELF.)

BritArt and Beyond

G is *Grappling with paradox*. Significant artists love to grapple with paradoxes, particularly if they simultaneously unleash uncertainties. 'The last colour reproduction in the Cologne catalogue shows an image of four letters, F, U, C, K, with the C facing the wrong way. The title, *Experiment in Volume*, leaves the spectator unsure of the nature of the experiment involved: word and meaning, relief and painting, depth and humour [see also: LISTS] – all from a young artist on the way to putting together a consistent and ever more clearly contoured body of work, which introduced a chilling logic into his sculpture, on the heels of warming wit' (from *Julian Opie: an introduction* by Wulf Herzogenrath, 1994).

H is for *Humour* and also for *Horn, Rebecca*. 'Oh, but our children *loooved* it' was the approved adult response to the exhibition of the works of Rebecca Horn at the Tate Gallery. This confirms that the artist has a 'childlike vision'. This 'childlike vision' could also be applied to the creators of Barbie, Ninja Turtles, My Little Pony and Dirty Fido, all of them still awaiting major retrospectives at the Tate.

I is for *Ironic*. The correct adjective to apply to all installation works without any clear point to them. I is also for *Indispensable*. Art critics are now *indispensable* to the significant artist. 'This is the first full study to appear on Wentworth,' reads the blurb of *Richard Wentworth* by Marina Warner, 'and is *indispensable* to an understanding of his work.' This means that, prior to publication of Marina Warner's book, no one could possibly understand the work of Richard Wentworth.

J is for *Jolly clever slogan*. The Saatchi and Saatchi slogan 'Labour Isn't Working', alongside a queue of people outside a dole office, was seen as a major contribution to the Conservative election victory of 1979. Within five years, the number of unemployed had almost doubled. In an attempt to reverse this trend, Charles Saatchi opened the Saatchi Gallery, containing many powerful outcries by young artists against the deleterious effect on society of a Conservative government indifferent to unemployment.

K is for *Koons, Jeff*. 'In this century, there was Picasso and Duchamp. Now I am taking us out of the twentieth century . . . I have my finger on the Eternal,' says Jeff Koons. Discuss.

L is for *Lists*. Never let your work of art leave home without its critical list. 'The exuberance and waywardness of Hume's work is a startled, funny, serious attempt to grapple with the formal, the iconographic, the ridiculous and the profound' (entry for Gary Hume in *Unbound: Possibilities in Painting*, Hayward Gallery, 1994). Every artist worth his salt should be seen to grapple with at least one of these elements; it is to Gary Hume's immense credit that he managed to pull off the entire compliment of four, with a side order of exuberance and waywardness, plus the extra critical paradox (see also PARADOX) of 'serious, funny' – full house!

L is also for significant *Levels*. How many significant levels can your art work on? And are they, as ideally they should be, contradictory? (see also PARADOX). Gary Hume scored top marks from Sarah Kent. First, she awarded his paintings a *List* ('the paintings are seductive, silent and insistently shut; emblems of our comings and goings, our entrances and exits'). And then she discovered two wholly contradictory levels in them: 'On one level they are utterly banal, on another, profound.'

M is for *Marathon* chocolate bars, also advertised by Saatchi and Saatchi. M is also for *Market research*. As Sarah Kent says, much of the work exhibited in the Saatchi Gallery is an outcry against a society that 'seeks to reduce us to ciphers, consumers and statistics'.

N is for *the Nature of art itself*. Every significant piece by a modern artist is, apart from anything else, about the Nature of art itself.

BritArt and Beyond

O is for *Odd one out.* Can you tell which of the following works by significant artists are currently on display at the Saatchi Gallery, and which are not?

a) A colour photograph of a plucked chicken performing acrobatics ('The message is Zen' – Sarah Kent)

b) A pair of size 7 boots with razor blades in their toes ('The work is an act of emblematic defiance' – Sarah Kent)

c) A goldfish bowl, the goldfish replaced with the skeleton of a sea trout ('An essentially carnivorous society is held to account for itself in terms both shocking and darkly ironic' – Sarah Kent)

d) A porcelain basin without a bowl ('Pilate's symbolic act of washing parallels our refusal to take responsibility for the suds we swill down the plug hole' – Sarah Kent)

e) A plaster cast of the artist's penis mounted on a toy steam train, in place of the funnel ('Reasserts in uncompromising terms the symbolically castrated place of the male of the species in a post-industrial society' – Sarah Kent)

f) The wrapper of a boiled sweet contains an eyeball ('The eye of the viewer is drawn, horrified, to itself, isolated and enclosed, cut off yet fiercely independent' – Sarah Kent)

(Answers: a, b and d have already been bought by Saatchi; c, e and f have not yet been created, but they will, Damien, they will)

P is for *Powerful.* Always remember to say 'Hmmm . . . very powerful' before moving on to the next exhibit.

Q is for *Questions.* Significant artists should answer questions in a paradoxical, impenetrable, ironic, etc, style, e.g.:

'What is your idea of perfect happiness?' Being miserable.

'What is your greatest fear?' Being happy.

(answers by Gilbert and George to a *Sunday Correspondent* magazine questionnaire)

R is for *Rembrandt.* Young Rembrandt Van Rijn has just had his first major work accepted by the Metropolitan. It is an installation titled *The Anatomy Lesson of Dr Tulp,* and consists of twelve 14 foot × 14 foot full colour photographs of a corpse, with the words 'LIFE IS SHIT' etched across them in felt-tip. They are, says the catalogue, 'a devastating and shattering indictment of human hope, confronting the viewer with his own mortality in an ironic yet uncompromising way'.

S is for *Social reform*. 'Art can, and should, be used to stimulate social mobility . . . to bring the aristocracy down and the lower classes up.' So far, the effect of Koons's recent exhibition on social mobility in the Cork Street area has proved hard to calculate, though the works are believed to have had a devastating economic effect, leaving those wealthy people who purchased them far closer to poverty. S is also for *Silk Cut*, advertised by Saatchi and Saatchi. Happily, Brad Lochore, a conceptual artist who 'deals with the encroachments of advertising on our judgement', is exhibited at the Saatchi Gallery.

T is for *Twix*. In the 1970s, a woman was awarded compensation after discovering a mouse's head in a Twix bar. Twix is a product handled by Saatchi and Saatchi. If she had sent the offending item straight to Charles Saatchi rather than the courts, together with a caption such as 'The Impossibility of a Good Solid Chew when Confronted by a Rodent's Head' (see also CAPTION COMPETITION) she may well have earned herself pride of place as a significant artist in the Saatchi Gallery.

U is also for *Untitled*. A great title for today's significant work of art.

V is for *Very funny*. Modern art critics have an extraordinarily well-developed sense of humour, encompassing virtually everything they see. Look out particularly for the words 'dry wit', 'laconic', as in the sentence 'His work can be laconically funny, showing a dry wit', written by Marina Warner of Richard Wentworth's *Lightweight Chair with Heavy Weights*

(1983) consisting of an office chair, with two heavy balls hanging from its seat.

W is for *What people are thinking about today*. Do keep an eye open for what people are thinking about today, so that you can then say a lot about it. 'It says a lot about what people are thinking about today,' explained the curator of the Damien Hirst show at the ICA. He was explaining an exhibit of a cupboard of medicine bottles titled *I Wanna Be Me*.

X is for *XL*. If in doubt, go for the fuller-figured canvas to fit every modern gallery. XL means 'disturbing' and 'shocking' in a way that s never could. Gilbert and George have long favoured XL, particularly in their current exhibition 'Shitty Naked Human World' at the Wolfsburg Kuntsmuseum.

Y is for *Young artists*. Young artists have nothing to learn from old artists. 'Never listen to anybody,' says Julian Schnabel. '. . . You can't listen to them because nobody knows better than you what you need to do. Most older artists are going to try to get you to conform to the standards that you are out to destroy anyway.'

Z is for *Zurbaran*. Young Francisco de Zurbaran has just had his first work accepted by the Saatchi Gallery. It is an installation called, with ironic undertones, *The Adoration of the Shepherds*. It consists of a shepherd cut into quarters, with a live sheep hanging over him upside down from a chain. It asks the viewer to confront death, and life, and the nature of art. Until last year, Francisco painted pictures, but at last he is doing works of real significance, and that's what it's all about (see ABOUT, What it's all).

Clerihews for Tate Modern

Yves Klein
Is a hero of mine
I, too, find it quaint
To smear naked ladies with paint.

Salvador Dali
Never visited Bali.
Too much sun was a risk, as
It deflated his whiskers.

Frida Kahlo
Was Mexico's Thelma Barlow.
But with an off-putting stare
And far more facial hair.

Kurt Schwitters
Is among the big hitters –
The only artist I know
To do amusing things with lino.

Joseph Beuys
Obeyed his Inner Voice
Which must have been hard
When clean out of lard.

BritArt and Beyond

Juan Gris –
(Between you and me
I don't know whether to cease
Pronouncing it Juan *Grease*).

Sarah Lucas
Unveils '8 Ways with Mucus':
Mmmm, there's no doubt she's a
Tremendous crowd-pleaser.

Lucien Freud
Is overjoyed:
The Tate's painting of the week
Is *Prickly Cactus Beside Naked Cheek*.

Gilbert and George
Are not hard to forge
If you half-close your eyes
They could be Morecambe and Wise.

L.S. Lowry
Never painted Leigh Bowery
He liked skinny men best
(Given the choice, fully dressed).

Bridget Riley
Is ever so smiley.
It doesn't get on her nerves
To be surrounded by swerves.

Gillian Wearing
Is way past caring.
And I haven't the heart
To ask 'But is it art?'

This Is Craig Brown

Chaim Soutine
Had an uneven routine
For making his mark as
The maestro of the carcass.

Alberto Giacometti
Refused a sitting to the yeti,
Stating, 'I prefer to be faced
With an 18-inch waist.'

Jenny Saville
Affords the critic a cavil:
Mightn't her model look snazzier
If she replaced her brassiere?

Damien Hirst
Is not the worst;
Jean Michel Basquiat
Puts paid to that.

My Turner Prize Dinner

It was a real privilege to find myself invited to the Turner Prize dinner after the glamorous award ceremony.

I was delighted to be placed between the Director of the Tate, Sir Nicholas Serota, and his Communications Director, Simon Wilson. As ever, Sir Nicholas was the perfect host. 'May I fill your glass?' he asked, with a very real sense of urgency coupled with restraint.

Sir Nicholas then reached for an empty bottle of wine, and poured its lack of contents into my glass. Simon leant forward and whispered, 'He is making a very important statement about something and nothing, and how nothing can emerge out of something. In this case, the bottle is something – but inside it is nothing. The whole process of pouring "nothing" from a bottle into a glass raises extremely disturbing questions about the whole nature of emptiness in today's society.'

The waiters and waitresses then arrived with our first course – or, to be more accurate, they did not arrive, and there was no first course. While everyone at the table was asking searching and relevant questions about where it was, Sir Nicholas smiled quietly to himself. 'This calls into question the whole nature of the so-called "first course". Is it first – or is it in some extraordinary way second? And is it really a course at all? Can a first course that isn't served really count as a first course in any valid meaning of the phrase? Our bold decision not to serve a first course at all has generated a lot of argument and discussion . . .'

'. . . and that must be a good thing,' added Simon.

'To be honest,' I said, 'I was feeling a bit peckish.'

At this point, the leading art critic Diana Meacher butted in. 'Passing judgement on the first course does not seem to me to be either a relevant or an adequate response,' she said. 'The whole absence-of-a-starter concept is a valid and powerful statement about the nature of consuming in the twenty-first century.'

Suddenly, there was a rumble. It came from the stomach of the prize-winning artist, Martin Creed. Obviously, this made those of us around the table tremendously excited. We all listened very, very carefully. 'His stomach is really out there on the edge of things,' whispered Simon Wilson. 'It's coming out of the whole tradition of noise-related body art. Martin's stomach is making an important statement about hunger and about food, and about the connection between the two.'

After twenty-five minutes, our empty soup plates were taken away, and a large trolley bearing the main course was brought on. 'I'm tremendously excited about this main course,' Sir Nicholas confided to me. 'It's full of all sorts of resonances and meanings.' He pointed to the empty trolley. 'It is – quite literally – nothing.'

'B-b-but,' I said, 'I was looking forward to something.'

'Absolutely marvellous!' said Sir Nicholas. 'You see, this very important main course has, in a very real way, been playing with your sense of expectation. In denying your expectation of a meal, it seems to me not only audacious, bold and witty – but it also succeeds in overturning the traditional discredited premise upon which a meal is judged – namely food.'

Did I notice a hint of self-satisfaction playing upon his lips?

Across the table, the art critic Diana Meacher was staring with her customary disarming intensity at her empty plate. 'It's bleak. And it's honest,' she said, 'but more than that – it's bleakly honest.'

Twenty minutes later, our empty plates were removed, to cluckings of approval from the critics. 'Uncompromising minimalist!' said one. 'And so bleakly nutritious!' cooed another. There was then a choice of sweets: soufflé of nothing, or no fruit salad. Most people opted for neither, or both. An expectant hush fell upon the room as the winner of the Turner Prize broke wind. Immediately, there was a sense of something very real, almost pungent in the air. 'Breathtaking!' murmured Simon Wilson, approvingly. 'It not only has resonance – but reverberation too.'

We all listened intently while Creed offered both a theory of the concept, and, more importantly, a concept of the theory. 'I was attempting to activate the whole space,' he explained. 'On one level, it entirely occupies the space, and so in a sense it's a really big work. But at the same time on another level there is nothing there.'

A few minutes later, the lights in the room began to flash on and off. 'We have come, in a very real way, to the end of dinner,' announced Sir Nicholas.

But was it dinner? And was it the end? If the dinner never began, how could it end? 'Ultimately, it makes people ask questions,' said Sir Nicholas.

'And that must be a good thing,' added Simon.

Heroes

The Unseriousness of Life: Auberon Waugh

From an early age, Auberon Waugh had his eye on the Way of the World column. A year after he first joined the *Daily Telegraph*, aged twenty-one, he applied to its creator, Michael Wharton, to be taken on as his apprentice. He was to recall his plan in his autobiography: 'I would tend his flocks, polish the shoes of his aldermen, pour sherry for his bishops, tea for his clergymen, whisky for his journalists, sit goggle-eyed at the feet of his Hampstead left-wing *penseuses* and read haikus in Japanese to his captive aesthete down a disused lead mine in (I think) Derbyshire.'

But Waugh's application was turned down. 'Michael Wharton heard me out with the exquisite politeness of an older generation, and with the same politeness, showed me the door.'

For the next thirty-odd years, Waugh would continue to nurse this strange ambition. 'If it seems presumptuous to have supposed that I could inherit the column,' he later wrote, 'I knew that the great Michael Wharton himself had announced to our shared friend, Richard West, that he had left a letter, to be opened on his death, bequeathing me the column and all its inhabitants.'

However, he was not to achieve his aim without a struggle. In the late 1980s, Wharton announced that he wished to write less. A replacement was needed but Waugh, to his horror, was not offered the job. 'In fact, I only learned the job was going when told that Christopher Booker had got it.'

For a while, Waugh resolved to grin and bear the sight of Booker 'grimacing and gibbering on the sacred ground', even though, as he was to remark, 'I cannot believe I was alone in finding his contributions an acute embarrassment.' But in 1989, after Booker had rounded on him in the column for making light of the situation in China, Waugh abandoned this charitable forbearance: 'I do not think I am particularly thin-skinned, but this high-minded lecture struck me as an unmistakable declaration of war ... On that day I started a necessarily oblique and tortuous, sometimes crablike, campaign to take over the column, the details of which I do not propose to reveal.'

His campaign met with victory. On 7 May 1990, he wrote his first Way of the World column. He continued to write it three times a week for virtually the entire decade.

Over the preceding years, in the *Spectator* and the *New Statesman* and in countless other newspapers and journals, but perhaps most memorably and graphically in *Private Eye*, Waugh had assembled his own glorious if unwilling menagerie of grotesques and reprobates on whom to practise his vituperative arts. How uncomfortably they would sit there, chained in the wings, ready to be thrust onstage and poked fun at *pour encourager les autres*.

The menagerie included, to mention just a few, the RSPCA and the RSPB ('screeching busybodies'), bats, Anthony Powell, chimpanzees ('the grossest and most revolting animals, of unpleasant appearance and disgusting habits'), Jeremy Thorpe, Tory life peers ('they tend, with very few exceptions, to give off a horrible smell'), Will Self, Cyril Connolly, contemporary poets, road safety enthusiasts, ramblers, Yorkshiremen, antifoxhunters ('bitter, power-mad crypto-perverts'), anti-smoking fanatics, Captain Mark Phillips, Shirley Williams, A. A. Milne ('whose loathsome exploitation of his unfortunate son, Christopher Robin, would surely land him in prison nowadays') and, of course, modern architects ('every time a building by Sir Basil Spence is taken down, my heart lifts up').

Heroes

To most reasonable people, such a cast list might seem admirably diverse, surmounting every barrier of class and education. For every Greg Dyke ('everything he thinks is nasty, stupid and wrong') there is an Alan Clark ('Anybody who went to public school will have recognised Clark as the sort of old boy who returns to his old school in some veteran or vintage car to impress the smaller boys'), for every Shirley Williams, a George W. Bush, for every John Pilger, a James Goldsmith. Waugh attacked the police with as much vehemence as he attacked ramblers, reserving a particular hatred for the 'punishment freaks' in the Conservative Party. 'I am convinced that intelligent educated and literate Englishmen are neither left wing or right wing,' he wrote, 'but are bored by politics and regard all politicians with scorn. That is my political creed, so far as I have one.'

Yet there is still a small, moody lobby of tut-tutters, led by Polly Toynbee, who believe him to be have been beyond the pale. 'Effete, drunken, snobbish, sneering, racist and sexist' were just a few of the adjectives Toynbee used to describe Waugh within days of his death – an odd way to repay a man who, some years before, had declared himself so enthusiastic for news of Ms Toynbee's close relationship with 'a man who looks like a squirrel' that he even went so far as to argue that their romance should be set to music. It is hard not to feel that, like people resolutely wearing too many woollies when the sun is shining, this band of sad dissenters are suffering for their intransigence. How much more free and happy they would feel were they to read his final, posthumous collection of Waugh's Way of the World columns.

If they do so with their eyes open, they will find themselves in the presence of a master of the surreal, an artist who established a unique comic persona – an omniscient, all-powerful figure, not unlike God, or at any rate a black sheep second cousin of God. Channelling current events through his strange camera obscura, Waugh creates a parallel world, a world at once more colourful and more grotesque than our own, and, of course, immeasurably funnier.

His plans to reform the world remain relatively modest: a 'Nipple Tax' on Murdoch newspapers of a penny per nipple: the dubbing of the television adaptation of *A Dance to the Music of Time*, to make it funnier; an urgent call for Cardinal Hume to ban Roman Catholics from setting foot inside the Millennium Dome; a blueprint for placing tasteful nude statutes of Chris Smith at strategic venues around the country. Though Waugh always billed himself as a practitioner of the vituperative arts, his writing had, in his later years, become increasingly benign: this volume is full of chinks of hope for the world. 'It is a glorious moment to be alive,' Waugh declares. He is delighted to note that teenagers have 'no interest in sex nowadays. Most sensibly decided that they will wait until they are thirty-six.' He also views Oxford University Press's decision to stop publishing contemporary poetry as 'certainly one of the most hopeful literary developments of our time'.

On a visit to Windsor Castle, he is thrilled to discover Her Majesty has placed three ashtrays in a state room: 'great actors and artists stood around them, puffing like steam engines'. He greets the arrival of the Blairs' baby Leo with joy, convinced that he is the reincarnation of his own Pekinese, also called Leo, who died the day before. 'His mother will find him intelligent, affectionate, loyal and utterly fearless,' he writes, before adding, 'but she might be well advised to keep him away from cats.'

His heroes in the present volume very nearly outnumber his enemies. This roll of honour seems to me notably unracist, snobbish, sexist, etc. It includes Sir John Mortimer, Major James Hewitt, the French, the organiser of the Glastonbury Festival, and Sir Elton John ('he can do no wrong, so far as I am concerned').

Of course, few of Waugh's readers would expect to follow him with equal fervour into every nook and cranny of his world view. I would guess, for instance, that those who share his dislike of modern architecture – on a point of etiquette, he once suggested that the correct way to greet an architect was to punch him in the face – would baulk at his disapproval of the police force. Nor would those who applaud his battle against facilities for the disabled ('One day, perhaps, the wheelchair motif will be adopted as our national flag') automatically join him in his stand against capital punishment. And of those who were, like him, opposed to the bombing of Kosovo, how many would subscribe to his proposed National Smack a Child Week? Unlike most columnists, who spend most of their lives sucking up to their readers, Waugh often seemed abnormally keen to ostracise the lot of them.

As Alan Watkins has pointed out, one of Waugh's great strengths as a satirist was his complete absence of restraint and good taste. He was a caricaturist, pointing his distorting mirror at a drabber reality, converting self-righteousness into comedy and bossiness into buffoonery. He also had the prose equivalent of perfect pitch. The most surreal and absurd ideas could be carried on the majestic wave of his prose, propelled from beneath by an undertow of fearless vulgarity.

Explaining his *Private Eye* diaries to a new American readership in 1998, Waugh wrote, 'If America can forget a little of its earnestness from reading this book, and learn a little bit of the unseriousness of life, I shall be a proud man. Forget that the characters were ever real people. See through the distortion of truth that life can be a much more interesting place with a tiny bit of effort to transform it.'

In his introduction to an earlier volume of Way of the World pieces, he suggested that the density and richness of material might make it an unsuitable for prolonged reading. But if you read a paragraph or two upon waking each morning, you will find that the rest of your day is pleasantly transformed, and that, as if by magic, the world has become a funnier place. Though this volume is, alas, the final chapter of Auberon Waugh's glorious day-to-day comic novel – the satiric equivalent of the Bayeux Tapestry – the world remains a happier place for having been refracted through his vision. Like the children in W.H. Auden's elegy to that other great English comic fantasist, Edward Lear, Auberon Waugh's readers 'swarmed to him like settlers. He became a land.'

Max Beerbohm, Theatre Critic

A hundred years ago, Sarah Bernhardt opened in *Hamlet* at the Adelphi Theatre. She was already a legend, and the audience and critics dutifully roared their approval. But there was one small voice of dissent.

Bernhardt had chosen to play the title role, causing the new young critic from the *Saturday Review* to dub her 'Hamlet, Princess of Denmark'. 'I cannot, on my heart, take Sarah's Hamlet seriously,' he began his review. 'I cannot even imagine anyone capable of more than a hollow pretence in taking it seriously. However, the truly great are apt, in matters concerning themselves, to lose that sense of fitness which is usually called sense of humour, and I did not notice Sarah was once hindered in her performance by any irresistible desire to burst out laughing. Her solemnity was politely fostered by the Adelphi audience. From first to last no one smiled. If anyone had so far relaxed himself to smile, he would have been bound to laugh. One laugh in that dangerous atmosphere, and the whole structure of polite solemnity would have toppled down, burying beneath its ruins the national reputation for good manners.'

The critic was the 26-year-old Max Beerbohm. He had held the post for barely a year, having taken over from George Bernard Shaw. He had come to it positively bursting with a lack of enthusiasm. 'I am not fond of the theatre,' he had declared in his very first piece. 'That a visit to the theatre can be regarded as a treat has always bewildered and baffled my imagination.'

Though Beerbohm remained the drama critic of the *Saturday Review* for the next twelve years, he never came to enjoy it. He used to dread Thursdays, when he would have to sit down and write his reviews. In his farewell article, he did not bother to conceal his jubilation. 'Is love of my readers as strong in me as my hatred of Thursdays? It is not half so strong,' he announced. 'I feel extraordinarily light and gay in writing this farewell.'

These days, Beerbohm is celebrated for all his other talents, as novelist, caricaturist, short-story writer, versifier, parodist, essayist, but his theatre criticism is mentioned rarely, and then only in footnotes. No one has ever bothered to revise Beerbohm's own low opinion of his theatre reviews. Yet reading them a hundred years on, I am struck by how fresh they are.

We all recognise the audience he describes at Sarah Bernhardt's *Hamlet*, an audience mesmerised by reputation into reverence. Biographers of great performers tend to hear only the applause, and have no means of judging its sincerity. Posterity covers actors in the embalming fluid of permanent acclaim. Reportage, written within hours of an event, is lit by a spark that has disappeared by the time the grander writer takes up his pen.

Beerbohm's talents as a theatre critic were not solely iconoclastic. In many ways, he revered Sarah Bernhardt, but he regretted the contemporary compulsion (still going strong) of eminent actors to play Hamlet, believing it had led her to betray her 'incomparable art' into 'so preposterous an undertaking'.

Beerbohm is often struck by greatness, but he is never dumbstruck by it. When Sir Henry Irving died, Beerbohm wrote a heartfelt tribute to 'that quality of mystery which is not essential to genius, but which is the safest insurance against its oblivion'. But he refused to drown him in praise ('Irving may sometimes have overdone it,' he wrote, 'but he always overdid it beautifully'), and his reservations contribute to a much fuller portrait of Irving's talents than all the gush that bore him to his grave.

'One missed the music of the verse, but was always arrested, stimulated, by the meanings that he made the verse yield to him,' wrote Beerbohm. 'These subtle and sometimes profound meanings were not always Shakespeare's own. Now and again, the verse seemed to yield them to Irving only after an intense effort, and with a rather bad grace'.

Unusually for one who classified himself a satirist, Beerbohm tended to side with the difficult and the strange against the easy and the straightforward. He loved Yeats, Synge, and, with some reservations, Ibsen. After his fellow critics had attacked a new play by Conrad, he sprang to its defence, urging them to give up their jobs. At the same time, he acknowledged that 'my gyrations recall painfully to me those of the famous bee who tried to swarm alone'.

He loathed that branch of English philistinism which is satisfied only with a rosy outlook. It is one of the advantages of journalism that it catches expressions floating around at any given time, expressions considered too transient by novelists, who have their eyes set on posterity. Beerbohm noted that West End audiences write off as 'unwholesome' and 'dreary' and 'leaving a nasty taste in the mouth' any play that does not conform to their strict standards of jollity. Has anything changed? Recently, a new Simon Gray play was refused a West End staging because a pop musical was considered less bleak and more commercial. A hundred years on, Beerbohm's observations remain as pertinent as ever.

I had always imagined that critics banging on about the *zeitgeist* were very much a phenomenon of the 1990s, but Beerbohm first complained about a barrage of *zeitgeist*-babble at a new production of *Macbeth* in 1898. At the pantomime of Humpty Dumpty, he deplored the poor quality of the jokes 'about sausages, mothers-in-law, and the other few things which are fixed by usage as being funny' and was nauseated when the principal comic man rounds off the show with the

Disneyish, 'God bless you, babies! Be babies as long as you can!'

'I do not suppose this plea for arrested development makes much impression on normal "little ones", in whom the unconscious act of growing is always accompanied by a conscious desire to be grown-up,' he concluded. 'I deplore it merely as an example of the maudlin and doddering futility of the modern pose towards children.'

For all his misgivings about the theatre, Beerbohm's hero-worship of his much older half-brother, the actor-manager Herbert Beerbohm Tree, gave him a strong feel for it. Herbert, like Max, was instinctively witty. Once, seeing a workman staggering along the street bearing a grandfather clock, he affected great concern. 'My good fellow,' he said, 'why not carry a watch?' Max's theatre criticism is full of such fun. In an essay on the art of the soliloquy, he wrote that 'Talking to oneself has this obvious advantage over any other form of oratory or gossip: one is assured of a sympathetic audience.'

But his critical mind was also very canny. At the first night, he thought *Peter Pan* the best thing J.M. Barrie had written. 'Here, at last, we see his talent in its full maturity; for here he has stripped off from himself the last flimsy remnants of a pretence to maturity.' And writing after the death of Ibsen in 1906, he acknowledges his greatness but pinpoints his key defect as misanthropy, chastising those who felt he had sympathy for women. 'His sympathy for women is a mere reflex to his antipathy for men,' he wrote. Of *Hedda Gabler*, he suggested that, far from seeing her as a strong woman, Ibsen hated her: 'She is sick of a life which does not tickle her with little ready-made excitements . . . She imagines herself to be striving for finer things, but her taste is in fact not good enough for what she gets.'

You could read a hundred academic works on Ibsen without gaining one such insight. Yet Max Beerbohm's theatre reviews haven't been in print for nearly fifty years. Why ever not?

At the Mercy of Language: Peter Cook

A year or two before Peter Cook died, I arranged a meeting between him and my editor at Century, Mark Booth. Mark wanted him to write an autobiography. They met at Rules. Peter arrived announcing that he had just finished his autobiography, and that he had it with him. 'I'd love to see it,' said Mark. Peter brought out a couple of pages of notepaper with a few rough sentences scribbled over them. 'Is that it?' asked Mark. 'I thought we might flesh it out with a few photographs,' replied Peter, his peerless lack of drive spurred on to ever greater heights by his Olympian sense of humour.

In the absence of an autobiography, a string of books about Peter Cook will appear over the next few years, some authorised by his widow Lin, others not. The first of these is Lin Cook's own collection of reminiscences from his friends.* *Something Like Fire* has a wealth of rich material in it, though one senses that quite a few contributors have, quite understandably, held back from too searching an analysis, wearing Sunday best in deference to Lin's deep love. So for my taste there are rather too many showbizzy reminiscences of a type Peter might have enjoyed parodying, beginning 'Peter *was* the funniest man in the world', and floating ever onwards on a bubbly stream of hot air. A greater sprinkling of his *Private Eye*

Something Like Fire – Peter Cook Remembered, edited by Lin Cook (Methuen)

friends might have lent a little oomph. As it is, there is no Willie Rushton, no Richard Ingrams, no Ian Hislop, no Christopher Booker, no Paul Foot.

But there is still much to enjoy, and many essays – notably those by John Wells, Stephen Fry, John Lloyd, Alan Bennett and Barry Humphries – bring back his memory with happy precision. Everyone agrees what a lovable man he was: Auberon Waugh recalls him in the company of teenagers at a school play, 'so gentle, so friendly, so ungrand and unpatron-ising'. There is also consensus on the extraordinary reach of his comic vision. To those with the nerve to pursue their analyses further, his genius for transforming everything he spotted into jokes had a touch of Midas about it: 'We clocked in, as it were, whereas Peter never clocked out,' recalls Alan Bennett. 'He was utterly at the mercy of language.'

This book shows that he was a hero – *the* hero – of his own *Beyond the Fringe* generation, the *Monty Python* generation and the Stephen Fry generation that followed it. His heroic stature combines with his sheer friendliness to ensure that all the contributors treat him as unique and special to themselves. In this they are not alone: I had lunch with him barely half a dozen times, but, in my solipsistic way, I still somehow feel qualified to write about him as though the world was composed of a joke shared only by him and me. Yet his true character remains elusive, allowing everyone to paint him in their own image. This becomes comically apparent when contributors attempt to touch on his political views. To his Cambridge contemporary Adrian Slade, ex-President of the Liberal Party, he was 'fanatically interested' in politics, and even ready to stand as the Liberal Democrat candidate for Hampstead in the 1992 election. Nicholas Luard, on the other hand, chalks him up as a Conservative with a 'contempt for socialism'. Meanwhile Elizabeth Luard recalls that 'his politics were anarchic'. On the other hand, the screenwriter Peter Bellwood believes that 'It was "the little people" who fascinated Peter, a group for whom he had the utmost affection.' Personally, I would imagine he considered politics best viewed as some sort of joke: but perhaps, like the others, I am merely reflecting my own views in his mirror.

Analysis of his comic vision by contributors is more profitable, though scarcely less disparate. It was formed early on, while he was still a pupil at Radley, and – fascinatingly – most of it seems to have been inspired by an elderly waiter at the Radley High Table who went by the name of Mr Boylett. Michael Bawtree recalls Mr Boylett 'dressed in shabby tails, grey waistcoat and tie, like a waiter in some Hungarian nightclub . . . In our arrogant way, we never stopped to think twice about Mr Boylett. He was part of the landscape. But it was Peter who took painstaking note of the man . . . The more pathetic and simple the poor man was, the more Peter saw in him an absurdist superhero . . . He used to point out that the wonderful thing about Boylett was that he was so very ordinary, so very grey, so unremarkable. Peter had a way of seeing the world through the eyes of such people, weaving around them a world of cosmic triviality.' Cook himself confirmed this view of his talent as early as 1959, in an interview for the *New Yorker*: 'Sometimes I think of old men who live in single rooms. I see them listening to their portable radio sets and charting news bulletins, which then take on great importance in their pathetic little lives. They become amusing, not because one pokes fun at them, but because they make unimportant things seem important and base their lives on false premises.'

Exasperatingly – though predictably, given his mesmerising ability as a performer – many of his jokes fail to echo their original punch when transferred to the two-dimensional world of the page. Transcripts from only quite funny old radio quizzes are unwisely reprinted at length. But now and then flashes of his real hilarity zap their way through. In his sweet eulogy, Stephen Fry recalls the time when someone on a chat show remarked to Cook that it wasn't Elizabeth Taylor's fault that she was putting on weight, it was her glands:

'I know,' he replied. 'Poor woman. There she is, in her suite in the Dorchester, harmlessly watching television. Suddenly her glands pick up the phone and order two dozen eclairs and a bottle of brandy. "No," she screams. "Please, I beg you!" but her glands take no notice. Determined glands they are, her glands. You've never known glands like them. The trolley arrives and Elizabeth Taylor hides in the bathroom, but her glands, her glands take the eclairs, smash down the door and stuff them down her throat. I'm glad I haven't got glands like that. Terrible glands.'

Fry rightly pinpoints the relentless repetition of the word 'glands' as the lynchpin of the joke: 'Hitler may have said that if you repeat a lie often enough it'll be believed,' he observes. 'Peter Cook proved that if you repeated it more than enough it'll be exposed.'

Was he happy? Many of the contributors seem almost over-anxious to insist that he was. 'The man died happy. Bless him,' is a typical conclusion. But every comedian is inextricably linked to his creations, and the seamlessness of Peter Cook's vision of 'cosmic triviality' must surely have come from somewhere deep within him. John Wells suggests that 'His originality lay in a kind of despairing boredom with the ordinariness of life.' Cook made this boredom into something comic and Samuel Beckett made it into something tragic, but the source of their inspiration is much the same.

I would like to have read more about his family: his daughters, his former wives, and, perhaps most particularly, his parents. One of only two contributors to mention his mother, Alan Bennett recalls how after her death, just a few months before Cook's own, 'he regularly referred to himself as an orphan. This seems to me so strange and uncharacteristic, both in Peter or in any man in his mid-fifties, that it made me feel that I perhaps hardly knew him at all.' I remember Peter telling me how his mother's death had cracked him up – an unusual confession from a man so free of self-pity and so reticent with his emotions. And I also remember Mark Booth telling me after their meeting at Rules that Peter had said, in all seriousness, that he could never publish an autobiography while his mother was still alive. His mother, I suspect, may be the key to a deeper investigation. Until then, *Something Like Fire* is a fitting love letter from the friends he left behind to a sublimely funny and lovable man.

A Divine Birdwatcher: Mark Boxer

I get the feeling that Mark Boxer's old friends tended to pooh-pooh the years he spent, towards the end of his life, editing the *Tatler*. Yet it seems to me that it was a post beautifully matched to his character, and that he somehow managed to turn the *Tatler* into a neat and witty reflection of the numerous contradictions within his own personality.

Only those who hold themselves aloof from real life could imagine that Mark's caricatures, for all their beauty of line and spikiness of insight, could spring from a mind immune to fripperies. I remember him telling me that once he had got someone's hair right, the rest of their face tended to fall into place. Certainly, a great many of the subjects he caricatured – Lord Lambton, Paul Foot, Kenneth Baker, Arthur Koestler, Philip Roth – might be identified from their hair alone, others – Ian Paisley, Hugh Fraser, the Duke of Kent – from their ears, and still others – Gerald Kaufman, Tom Stoppard, Terence Conran, Bubbles Rothermere (and how!) – from their clothes. 'I can never bring you to realise,' says Sherlock Holmes in *A Case of Identity*, 'the importance of sleeves, the suggestiveness of fingernails, or the great issues that may hang from a bootlace.'

Mark's art fed off his absorption in, and his ambivalence towards, high society. He was seen as a great party-goer, yet he confessed to a mutual friend that he would often find himself walking around the block three times before plucking up the courage to enter a party. He was once very sulky with me for going to interview Margaret, Duchess of Argyll without wearing a tie, yet his caricature of her – the eyes so black and as ungiving as a goat's, the eyelashes like dead spiders, the distended gash of a mouth – must have been far more alarming to Her Grace than the sight of a shabby journalist not wearing a tie. Similarly, when editing *Tatler* Mark was extraordinarily keen to get names and titles exactly right – inquisitions would be held over even the tiniest mistake – yet, as long as the name and the title were dead on, he would giggle with delight at the mischief and malice one might have poured over the correctly titled victim.

I have often thought that the puns which infected the headlines of Mark's *Tatler* represented a further outpost of this creative ambivalence, for a pun is schizophrenic, meaning two or more things at any single time, one straight, sophisticated, even snobbish, the other jam-packed with diablerie. When we were thinking of a title for a little piece on a dispute within the ranks of the Belvoir Hunt, someone came up with 'Split Belvoir'. Mark howled with laughter – his laugh sounded like a soda siphon out of control – and put it straight in.

He adored gossip, sometimes becoming so absorbed in it that it would backfire in his face. With Noel Annan and one or two others, he was once discussing which of their Cambridge contemporaries had not fulfilled his early promise. So carried away did Mark become with adding to the list that he momentarily forgot who he was talking to, saying 'and Noel Annan, of course!' But he was, by and large, only interested in gossiping about those whom he in some way admired. At one of our regular *Tatler* ideas meetings, someone suggested a profile of Lord Hanson. Mark dispatched it in two seconds. 'No point. Nothing to him. A lot of people make the mistake of thinking him interesting, but the only thing he's ever done is to be engaged to Ava Gardner.'

He seemed particularly interested in all gossip about his old employer and friend Lord Weidenfeld, for whom his fascination was unending, so much so that he once said to me that, were he ever to write a biography, he would choose Weidenfeld as his subject. He was mesmerised by Weidenfeld's success combined with his occasional revelatory faux pas in which the feet of clay poked out of the embroidered socks. Perhaps somewhere inside him Mark saw Weidenfeld as a larger-than-life caricature of himself.

In the *Tatler* of December 1987, there was a profile of Weidenfeld, printed under the punning heading – perfect from every angle – 'Publish and Be Grand'. It was written pseudo-nymously, and perhaps by several hands, but had one anecdote in it that seemed pure Mark: 'At one time, Geoffrey Keating, the Mr Fixit of his generation, used to attend Weidenfeld's gatherings as a matter of course. He fell from grace. It was explained that he was to come no more. Wandering alone one evening he spotted Harold Wilson, then Prime Minister, with his wife, and it emerged that Harold was busy but would be grateful if Keating could escort Mary to that evening's party. As Weidenfeld opened the door, his face darkened and he began, "I thought I had made it quite clear, and who is this woman?"'

Like that other great English caricaturist, Max Beerbohm (also a dandy), Mark delighted in the telling detail, the glint on the exterior that betrayed the presence of the weapons beneath. Transformed by Mark's pen, John Aspinall, for all his smart black tie, benevolent smile and frilly shirt, has the hairy hand of a gorilla emerging from his cuffs; Sir Hugh Casson has tiny little sparkles emerging from his eyes; Antonia Fraser sports a crucifix around her neck and a love heart around her wrist; Lord Weidenfeld, with tiny little feet, has eyes at right angles to one another ('For an instant, as you enter his drawing-room, it is you that George Weidenfeld is looking at over some else's shoulder' began the *Tatler* profile); and Lord Longford's head becomes curiously phallic (giving a new twist to Malcolm Muggeridge's remark that 'Frank is almost *passionately* bald'). Mark relished the juxtaposition of the base and the suave: his skill relied upon the exact balancing of the two, so that the base instinct and the suave pretence became companions, dependent yet at odds, at one and the same time.

This Is Craig Brown

After a visit to the opera the night before, Mark came into the *Tatler* office full of excitement and related a piece of gossip that was the equivalent of the gorilla hand of Aspinall. A few weeks before, he had been chatting to a dermatologist at a party. The dermatologist had told him of a new method of hair replacement which involved planting the patient's pubic hair on the bald patch. He told Mark that a senior politician was undergoing this treatment, but professional discretion forbade him from revealing which one. At the opera, Mark found that the head behind which he sat belonged to Mr (as he then was) Norman St John-Stevas. With his eye for hair, Mark had studied it carefully, and had arrived at the only possible conclusion. Pubic hair on a politician's head at Covent Garden! His joy was unconfined.

Mark aspired to worldliness, yet happily his sense of fun kept diverting him from that fateful course. In the office, he would occasionally try to be Machiavellian, but was always too innocent – almost gauche – to pull it off, hooting with laughter when the person he was plotting against made a joke, and consequently forgetting that any plot was under way. He never sacked anyone, however hard he tried.

Mark was a sort of Peter Pan figure, and with some of the vanity and petulance of Peter too. While his contemporaries may have seen his decision to take on the *Tatler* as a sign of his continued immaturity, I believe that in actual fact it allowed him to grow up without shedding his youthfulness. He developed a paternal streak towards his staff, most of whom were nearly half his age, egging them on to better things (even if it meant leaving the *Tatler*) and encouraging them to experiment, and to write with greater idiosyncrasy. Many of those who worked on *Tatler* owe him their future careers, the present editors of *Harpers and Queen*, *Mademoiselle* and *Vogue* among us. He had a zest, a capacity for delight that precluded not only the smug but also the hackish. I find it hard to think of anyone else who crackled with such life. It doesn't surprise me that the two who knew him far better than I did – George Melly and Martin Amis – both confess to dreaming that he is still alive. Even now, years after his death, I half expect that when I walk into a London party Mark will greet me with a big smile, tell me – a little brutally – that I am spreading my writing too thin, temper this by congratulating me on something-or-other, and then hiss with glee at some new piece of gossip. And if I have not seen him at a party for all these years, I still feel that he is there floating above us all, pen in hand, his half-moon glasses way down his nose, his eyes peering over us, intent, meticulous, concentrated, ready to recreate the fluffed-up feathers, the colourful plumes and the absurd chirrupings of the assembled company, like a divine bird-watcher rejoicing in his prey.

Dancing By The Light of the Moon: Edward Lear

Heaven knows why, but a month or two ago the term 'runcible spoon' came up in a conversation I was having with my mother-in-law. Like everyone else, we both knew it from Edward Lear's beautiful poem, 'The Owl and the Pussy Cat', in which:

> They dined on mince, and slices of quince,
> Which they ate with a runcible spoon;
> And hand in hand, on the edge of the sand
> They danced by the light of the moon.

But was there such a thing as a runcible spoon, or was it simply the invention of Edward Lear? As neither of us knew, I looked the word up in *Brewer's Dictionary of Phrase and Fable*. Brewer states that 'What runcible denotes is not apparent. Some who profess to know describe the spoon as a kind of fork having three broad prongs, one of which has a sharp cutting edge. However, the illustrations that Lear himself provided for his books do not support this definition. The word may actually be based on Rouncival.

I then turned to the entry for Rouncival. 'Very large or strong; of gigantic size . . . "Rouncival peas" are the large marrowfat peas, and a very big woman is (or was) called a rouncival.'

How happy Edward Lear would have been, I thought, to know that his nonsense word 'runcible' had itself given birth to yet more nonsense, all the more joyously nonsensical for existing in the tight-laced world of the dictionary definition. Caught up myself in this nonsensical pursuit, I then turned to my favourite dictionary of all, *Chambers Dictionary of Etymology*, and found, to my delight, that 'speculation among some dictionary etymologists has centred on the botanical term runcinate (1776) irregularly saw-toothed (formed from Latin *runcina a plane* but taken to mean saw) + the suffix -ible; however, this seems to be reaching as Lear used the term with indistinct meaning, applying runcible to a cat (1877), to a hat (1888) and to a goose and a wall (1895) . . .'

Then came the most magical part of the entry: 'About 1926, runcible spoon was adopted as the name of a spoonlike three-pronged fork used for eating pickles and various other foods.'

This means – if you're still with me – that Edward Lear invented the idea of runcible spoon in 1871, probably just because he liked the sound the words made; fifty years later this sound had become so much part of the fabric of the nation that someone invented a real spoon to embody the sound.

It is the mark of a great artist that after he dies his vision becomes an indissoluble part of the world he has left behind. Without doubt, Edward Lear's vision of nonsense has been incorporated deep in the fabric of our consciousness. Thus we have not only the runcible spoon, but all those artists, from *Monty Python* to John Lennon, from James Joyce to Salvador Dali, from James Thurber to Reeves and Mortimer, whose work bears the unmistakable imprint of Edward Lear.

Edward Lear was born in 1812, the twentieth child of twenty-one children born to an increasingly impoverished stockbroker and his wife. Aged four, Edward, short-sighted and ugly, was farmed out to his eldest sister to be looked after. Aged five, he developed an acute form of epilepsy – sometimes suffering several attacks in a day – that was to stay with him until his death. In those days, it was seen as a shameful condition, and throughout his life Lear would retreat into solitude whenever he felt an attack coming on: though he was a man who inspired extraordinary devotion among his friends, nobody outside his family ever realised he was epileptic.

It seems likely that his epilepsy fed both his sense of separation from society and his innate understanding of how order and logic forever teeter on the edge of mayhem. For Lear, 'common sense' was a fabrication of polite society: how could it be anything else when, several times a day, he was forced to glimpse a topsy-turvy world, a world in which:

> Sometimes I feel, but know not why, a fire within me burn
> And visions fierce and terrible, pursue where'er I turn;
> Then I forget that earth is earth, and that myself am life
> And nature seems to die away in darkness, hell and strife
> But when my phrenzied fit is o'er, a dreary hour comes on
> A consciousness of unknown things, of reason
>   overthrown.

Lear wrote those lines when he was twenty years old. He dropped them into a nonsense poem about 'Miss Maniac', but they must surely had derived from his own secret experience.

He is now probably best known for his limericks, for which he also provided those apparently effortless illustrations, so lively that they appear to dance on the page. (Like the runcible spoon, these have also taken up their place in real life: in my house, we have them as kitchen tiles.) Driven by the random demands of instant rhyme, they are all nonsense, of course, but they are not so much an absence of sense as an attack on it. Beneath their toytown merriment, they are about loners and eccentrics battling against the prescriptive commonsense of society:

> There was an Old Man of Whitehaven
> Who danced a quadrille with a raven
> But they said, 'It's absurd
> To encourage this bird!'
> So they smashed that Old Man of Whitehaven.

Heroes

'They' in the limericks, as Aldous Huxley once pointed out, represent all the duller virtues of normality; they are invariably trying to silence the heroic oddballs and assorted ill-fitting couples whose peculiar looks and obsessions set them apart. Small wonder then that when he turned his gaze to the animal world, as he often did, Edward Lear was drawn to the daffy and the doomed: the kangaroos, the pelicans, the daddy-longlegs, the owl who was in love with the pussy cat, the pobble who had no toes.

From childhood on, Edward Lear was, like his heroes, a man in constant retreat from melancholy, throwing out more and more nonsense poems to divert the wolves of depression. 'He weeps by the side of the ocean / He weeps on the top of the hill,' he wrote of himself, 'He purchases pancakes and lotions / And chocolate shrimps from the mill'. Of course, the value of Lear's nonsense verse is not remotely dependent on any critic's ability to tot up its inner torment. Far from it: the nonsense stands alone, dancing by the light of the moon, gloriously impervious to interpretation. But an awareness of the psychological impulses of the verse can only serve to illuminate the immensity of the achievement.

And this new edition of *The Complete Verse and Other Nonsense** shows the scale of Edward Lear's achievement, both as writer and illustrator. Only William Blake comes close to Lear in this twin pursuit, and to my mind Blake is the lesser genius, his verse more plodding, his drawings less free-flowing, his strangeness more contrived. Vivien Noakes, already a brilliant Lear biographer, proves herself also his perfect editor, her extensive scholarly notes not only hugely informative, but in a funny way complementing the nonsense, as though the daddy-longlegs has been togged up in a pea-green anorak.

In middle age, Edward Lear was once riding on a train when the other passengers began talking of his nonsense verse. One

* *The Complete Verse and Other Nonsense* by Edward Lear, edited by Vivien Noakes (Viking)

of them convinced the others there was no such person as Edward Lear: 'Lear' was an anagram of 'Earl', and the Earl of Derby was the true author of the poems. Edward Lear interrupted them, insisting that there most certainly was an Edward Lear 'and I am the man!' They all burst out laughing; it was only when he took off his hat and showed them his name tag that they were forced to believe him. 'And I left them to gnash their teeth in trouble and tumult,' he later recalled.

Somehow, this little story has all the makings of a Lear creation: society united in denying credit to the individual; the individual insisting on his right to be himself; and a hat stepping in at the last minute to resolve the whole shebang.

The Stately and the Homely: Alan Bennett

There are precious few contemporary playwrights one could describe as lovable. Harold Pinter, David Hare, John Osborne, Howard Brenton, Edward Bond, Dennis Potter: in each there lurks the suspicion that the dislocation in society that they see as lending their work its gravitas is simply a grandiose way of disguising some shoddier dislocation within themselves.

Harold Pinter and Lady Thatcher have rather more in common – self-righteousness, self-importance, aggression, humourlessness, and perhaps above all bossiness – than either of them would care to admit. There are so many bullies in Pinter's plays that there is little space left for any vision of a world beyond bullying. His characters are either aggressive or pitiful: remove both the kickers and the kicked, and the Pinter cupboard is bare. In this way, there is little to choose between the *Collected Speeches of Margaret Thatcher* and the *Collected Plays of Harold Pinter*. Human life, as it is known and felt, is elsewhere.

Unlike the others, Bennett is at ease with his own awkwardness, and this makes him the better playwright. He is infinitely more observant in his criticism of society than the most furious among his contemporaries, but his criticism is informed more by a love of the downtrodden than by a loathing of those who, as he might put it, 'rule the roost'. In a funny way, he is more genuinely political (though he would shudder at the term) than his more agitprop contemporaries. While they tend to allot almost supernatural powers of self-awareness to those they consider corrupt, reserving their distribution of ignorance for the innocent, Bennett suggests that something inherent in any hierarchy is to blame. 'It is a feature of institutions that the permanent staff resent those for whose benefit the institution exists,' he observes in a 1985 diary in *Writing Home*.* 'And so it will go on, even beyond the grave. I have no doubt that in heaven the angels will regard the blessed as a necessary evil.'

At one point in his diaries, Bennett criticises Lady Thatcher (who is one of his pet hates, along with Lord Hailsham, the Hayward Gallery, trendy clerics, Sir Peregrine Worsthorne and cocky Liverpudlians) for her 'want of magnanimity'. Like so much of what Bennett says, as a criticism it appears first to be rather too polite, even cosy, yet on closer inspection it is deadly accurate, and likely to convert the undecided more speedily than anything more ostentatiously 'angry'. And his own magnanimity is what makes Bennett so lovable a writer: he treasures idiosyncracy, values the embarrassed over the self-assured, the unsung over the celebrated and even – rare in any artist – the humane above the artistic. On artists' parents, he writes, 'Do it right and posterity never hears about the parents; do it wrong and posterity never hears about anything else. "They fuck you up, your mum and dad", and if you're planning on writing and they haven't fucked you up, well, you've got nothing to go on, so then they've fucked you up good and proper.'

True and funny; funny and true. The two do not always go hand in hand, but in Bennett's writing they are impossible to separate. Much of his humour comes from his juxtaposition of the high with the low, the formal with the colloquial, the theatrical with the banal. Andrew Motion is 'tall, elegant and fair, a kind of verse Heseltine'; an actor kisses a woman's breast

---

*Writing Home by Alan Bennett (Faber and Faber)

'as though if he weren't quick the breast would take to its heels'; Larkin should have been less worried about appearing on television because 'one appearance on the *South Bank Show* doesn't start a stampede in Safeway's, as other authors could regretfully have told him'. As so often with acutely funny writing, it is the words that appear to be afterthoughts to the main gist of a sentence – 'take to its heels' 'a stampede in Safeway's' 'regretfully' – that actually provide the key to the humour.

The beautifully balanced see-sawing between the stately and the homely reflects, I would guess, the essence of Bennett's own character: half north, half south; half academic, half comedian; half fogey, half rebel; his sense of amusement sitting somewhere between the two poles, feeding off his own discomfort. And his sense of humour encourages him to see inadequacy, or the acknowledgement of inadequacy, as one of the saving graces of a human being. Of an audience at Chichester, he writes ruefully, 'the same tall families, the same assurance of happiness and their place in the world', almost as though he feels sorry for them, for they will never know anything beyond assurance.

Many of the occasional writings collected in *Writing Home* – diaries, speeches, reviews, etc – are autobiographical, though in common with Queen Victoria, Sherlock Holmes, Henry James and Jeeves, each fresh glimpse of his character merely leaves one wanting to know more. Writing of his life, his favourite words are 'dull' and 'boring'. Exeter College was 'all very dull'; his school was 'dull', his childhood 'boring'. Going to the theatre, 'boredom is my great terror'. Addressing the Prayer Book Society, he confesses that 'knowing we would all be of one mind, my concern was simply not to be dull'. Yet there is not a dull sentence in the entire collection, and some of his confessions are of a type so many writers aim for, but few achieve: the dark, irrational personal revelation that opens up an unspoken – and often bizarrely funny – fear shared by one and all. 'My nightmare when blackberrying (or when I stop the car for a pee) is that I shall find the body of a child, that I will report it and be suspected of the crime. So I find myself running through in my mind the evidences of my legitimate occupation – where I started picking, who saw me park, and so on.' Unexpectedly but quite logically, the writer he most often thinks about and refers to is Kafka.

Many diary entries find him visiting church or art galleries, but he is never at ease in them: 'The same conflict in church (particularly when a service is being said) that I feel in art galleries, a need to stay and go at the same time. (Watching a sunset the same)'. There are occasional pointers to a deeper sadness ('Happier then, I reflect . . . happier almost any time than now') but these are offset by a more buoyant curiosity about other people, so that life remains unexpected, and therefore funny, and therefore worthwhile. Scattered throughout the book are little observations on the changing mores of society: 'Lent is now "the run-up to Easter"' 'Note that after a successful round even show-jumpers now punch the air', '14 March. Two nuns in Marks and Spencer's studying *meringues*'. Sometimes these observations carry a moral – he is at his most *Spectator*-ish over chumminess in church, at his least in his sympathy with the poor – but at other times they form a sort of pillow book of insight into unchronicled lives. Looking at the inscription 'He was kind' on a stone in a crematorium, he considers it 'the sort of thing women who don't like sex say of a forbearing husband'.

Up to now, Bennett's humour, his versatility, his energy, his ear for the bizarre nuances of normality and his popularity – perhaps also his lovability – have conspired to keep him on a relatively low echelon of critical and academic esteem, far below many of his clodhopping contemporaries. I doubt whether this collection will do anything for his reputation in these circles, for it contains all his qualities in abundance, and is a joy from start to finish.

In Praise of Noele Gordon

Watching Lady Thatcher's four-part series on television, I kept thinking to myself: Hmmmm, you remind me of someone. But who? The neat, tough suits; the stiff, bouncy hair; the complete self-assurance; the somewhat over-dramatic, almost camp, facial expressions; all those crises, and all that coping. Then it struck me: it's Noele Gordon.

Of course, Noele Gordon was no stranger to Downing Street herself. In 1975 – the year of Margaret Thatcher's succession to the leadership of the Conservative Party – Harold Wilson's wife, Mary, generally a shrinking violet when it came to public endorsements, wrote the foreword, headed '10 Downing Street, Whitehall', for Noele Gordon's seminal autobiography, *My Life at Crossroads*. It was only brief, but it hit the nail on the head. 'I am sure many women see Noele Gordon in the character of Meg Richardson as the type of woman they themselves would like to be – understanding, sensible, able to cope with any situation,' she wrote. 'Also, women like to look at Meg's clothes – she is always well dressed and groomed!'

Did those few, well-chosen words have any influence on the then Leader of the Opposition? We shall probably never know – Gordon, Noele, is nowhere to be found in the index of *The Downing Street Years* – but the similarities between Noele Gordon's creation, Meg Richardson, and Margaret Thatcher are so plentiful as to be uncanny.

Apart from looking, sounding and dressing the same, both Meg and Margaret had to cope as female bosses in a man's world – in Margaret's case, the cut-throat world of politics, in Meg's, the cut-throat world of Birmingham catering. Both had two children, a boy (Mark/Sandy) and a girl (Carol/Jilly) who, though essentially homebound, were forever getting into scrapes and hanging out with the wrong types. Both Meg and Margaret were married to millionaire businessmen (Denis/Hugh) who, though always on hand with sound advice, were fully prepared to take a back seat. Both Meg and Margaret exhibited a penchant for debonair types in slinky suits as their right-hand man (Cecil Parkinson/David Hunter) and both Cecil and David were to experience grave problems in their own marriages, though, to my almost certain knowledge, Cecil's wife never wounded him with a shotgun, as David's found herself doing. Margaret was voted Prime Minister on three consecutive occasions, while Meg won the *TV Times* award for 'Most Compulsive Character' on no less than eight consecutive occasions.

And, of course, both Meg and Margaret were to come to sticky ends after all that time at the top. After seventeen years playing the proprietor of Crossroads Motel, Noele Gordon was ousted on 22 June 1981. After fifteen years playing the leader of the Conservative Party, Margaret Thatcher was ousted on 22 November 1990. Both made last-ditch attempts to hang on to power (NOELE'S DESPERATE PLEA 'SAVE ME, LEW!' – *Sunday Mirror* headline, 28 June 1981) but to no avail. Both Margaret and Meg were pictured departing in tears ('I am stunned with sorrow' – Noele Gordon, 30 June 1981), though their unhappiness was not shared by one and all. Jack Straw called Margaret 'this evil woman', while the *Daily Star* ran a competition ('How would you get rid of her? Shoot her? Blow her up?') to signal Meg's demise, the £25 prize eventually going to the reader who suggested she should be beaten to death with a frying pan. Finally, both women were replaced by somewhat faceless men and both shows petered to a close. Intimates suggested that neither woman ever quite recovered from the shock of rejection, retreating behind a mask of bravado, appearing in other shows, but never finding a role of the same stature.

But Noele Gordon's spooky, Nostradamus-like artistic prescience – let us never forget that her career pre-dated Margaret Thatcher's by a good ten years – is not the only reason I have chosen her as my heroine. Hers was the most reassuring television presence of any. Like David Frost, only more so, she possessed the great gift of complete unflappability. Her public manner was professional, yet warm ('Hello, Crossroads Motel. Can I help you?'), and even in the midst of her personal crisis – one week a blackmail threat, the next a psychopathic killer on the loose – she would have a soothing word for one and all ('Why don't you put that gun away, dear? I'm sure we can sort this out in a more civilised manner. Sherry?')

People watch television to relax, and Noele Gordon was tremendously relaxing. When Noel – or was it Meg? – was on screen, you knew you were in safe hands, you knew that sets would wobble, that telephones could start ringing long after they had been answered, that posses of ruthless kidnappers, vengeful wives and mysterious lords could make a beeline for the chalets, or that – my personal favourite of all the storylines – Amy Turtle could be (falsely) exposed as the Russian spy Amelia Turtulovski, but for as long as Meg – or was it Noele? – was around, nothing could ever go really wrong: she might sigh, she might raise a sceptical eyebrow, she might even take comfort from a single schooner of medium sherry, but, my God, she would cope.

The Summer of Amo, Amas, Amat

June 1967. Ken Kesey. All You Need Is Love. Psychedelia. Make Love Not War. Tune in, turn on, drop out. Ah, the Summer of Love. We were all around back then in the Summer of Love. Mick Jagger, Marianne Faithfull and me. Timothy Leary, Janis Joplin, Mickey Dolenz and me. Iain Duncan Smith, Michael Howard, John Redwood and me. We were all affected by it, one way or another.

San Francisco was the place to be. 'If you're going to San Fran-cisco,' sang Scott Mackenzie. 'Be sure to wear some flowers in your hair. 'Cos if you're going to San Fran-cisco, you're gonna meet some gentle people there.'

Whenever I heard that song – number one in the Summer of Love – I would make plans to go to San Francisco. By way of preparation, some of us sat on the grass and picked daisies, made them into chains, and wore them in our hair. Until the sensible brown trousers of the Latin master blocked out the sun, and the stern northern voice above told us to take those darned flowers out of our hair pretty sharpish and didn't we realise we were already late for double maths and could someone please explain why we haven't heard the bell which he had rung until he was blue in the face?

The Summer of Love affected different people in different ways. It certainly made those of us stuck in ten-year-old bodies in boarding schools near Basingstoke feel that we were

272

somehow in the wrong place at the wrong time. On a scale of 1 to 10, if Paul McCartney, sitting in Abbey Road studios recording 'All You Need Is Love', scored 10 for being in the right place at the right time, then Craig Brown, sitting in double maths in Farleigh Wallop learning Venn diagrams with Mr Needham, scored somewhere in the low minus 500s.

It might be imagined the spirit of 1967 would never have managed to creep through the walls of a traditional boys' prep school near Basingstoke, and that we would all have been happily soaked in the spirit of 1940, tips of tongues nestling in the right-hand corners of lips as we diligently applied Uhu to Airfix models of Spitfires and Messerschmidts while reading *War Picture Library* comics (*'Achtung! Achtung! Donner und Blitzen! Spitfeur! AAAAAAARRRGH! Schweinhund!'*). But pop music moved like pollen through the air, finding its way through school gates, up school drives, through school doors, into even the strictest of lessons, entering the heads of little boys and causing them to dream of going to San Francisco and wearing flowers in their hair.

For instance, in the summer of 1966, the New Vaudeville Band had hit the charts with an unlikely song called 'Winchester Cathedral', which was on the tips of all our tongues that summer. At that time, major English cathedrals were rarely celebrated in pop songs, so we had every reason to expect our teachers to welcome it. Alas no: our English master, a stately gentleman who carried all his books in a shopping basket, grew furious whenever it was sung. 'What, may one ask, is WIN-Chester Cathedral,' he would harrumph. 'Or has there been a Church of England raffle, the first prize a chance to win Chester Cathedral? One never knows, these days.'

In retrospect, I realise how desperate we were that pop music should win the approval of those who taught us. At any hint of education in a pop song, we would nip over to the relevant teacher. We were upset that the Latin master showed no wish to buy the entire oeuvre of Status Quo and Procul Harum, even though their names had a hint of Latin about them.

Heaven knows why, but every Thursday we were allowed to

watch *Top of the Pops*. A barefoot Sandy Shaw would appear in a Union Jack mini-dress, singing her Eurovision topper, 'Puppet on a String'. ('You'd think with all that money she'd be able to afford a decent pair of shoes,' commented the Latin master, every Thursday.) Then Dave Dee, Dozy, Beaky, Mick and Titch would come on, singing 'Zabadak', and we would count only five people on stage. Where was the sixth? It was some time before someone noticed the absent comma: Dave Dee was just one person, Christian name and surname. Such are the conundrums with which the outside world distracts ten-year-old boarders.

The Tremeloes (or 'The Trems' as the chummier disc jockeys would call them) would follow with 'Silence is Golden' (Gowlden), at which point the Latin master would grunt: 'If only they practised what they preached.' Then we would hope to get the Beatles singing 'All You Need is Love'. By 1967, the Beatles were already far too important to sing their songs in person. Instead, they provided what was, I suppose, an early pop video of themselves in the recording studio, surrounded by hairy people singing 'Love, love, love, love, love' with sitars, joss sticks, bongo drums, kaftans, tie-dye T-shirts and strange, bulbous cigarettes. There we sat, 100 little short-haired bys in Aertex shirts, grey flannel shorts and Start-rite sandals, goggle-eyed in envy, the next day's gruelling test on *Amo, Amas, Amat, Amamus, Amatis, Amant* our sole link to that endless chant.

Others look back on the Summer of Love and recall brushing shoulders with John Lennon or a member of the Byrds or Hunter S. Thompson. Sadly, my only brush with celebrity that summer was as inappropriate as can be. The Second World War air ace Douglas Bader was due to make a speech and give out the prizes on Sports Day. I had been chosen to greet him with a programme of the day's events. His car scrunched up the gravel of the school drive. The car door – black, as I remember it, but then perhaps memory renders black all the car doors of childhood – swung open. Out came the great hero, swinging from side to side on his artificial legs. I dutifully presented him with his programme. He replied, 'Your tie's not straight, boy', and swung off in the direction of the headmaster.

Thirty-five years on, the summer of 1967 seems full of such anomalies. We may remember the Beatles Sergeant Pepper's Lonely Heart Clubs Band topping the LP charts, but in fact most of that summer it alternated with the Original Soundtrack Album of *The Sound of Music*. And the song which occupied the 1967 charts for the longest was not by the Beatles: it was 'The Last Waltz' by the lavishly sideburned crooner Engelbert Humperdinck.

Who ruled Britain? Baron Von Trapp or Sgt Pepper? During that Summer of Love, it seemed as though everyone in the country was free to choose their side apart from me. Cornered in prep school, I was at heart one of Pepper's hairy, druggy, hang-loose men, but I had somehow been captured by Von Trapp, forcibly shrunk to four feet tall and force-fed fresh air, clean knees, Aertex shirts and double maths. I was, if you like, a prisoner of war. That's my excuse. But what of Duncan Smith, Howard and Redwood? How on earth did they remain untouched by the Summer of Love? Or are they just late developers?

Wallace Arnold: The Nation's Favourite

It is often forgotten that when King Edward VIII and Mrs Simpson were conducting their clandestine romance one of their strongest mutual passions was music – and one musician in particular.

When Mrs Simpson arrived at Fort Belvedere, generally on a Friday afternoon, just as dusk was settling in, it was her custom to rush up the main staircase, over the landing and into the library. There she would go to the far right-hand corner, where she would find the then Prince of Wales's most precious possession: his gramophone.

Flick – flick – flick: with practised wrist-movements, Mrs Simpson would flick her way through the Prince's formidable collection of 78 records. Past jazz she would flick, past dance music and classical music and the big band sound, past the early recordings of King George's V's Christmas addresses, past string quartets and comical turns from the north, past recordings of Negro choirs, bassoon trios and French matinee idols. Ah! At last her eyes would alight on the one recording that she and her future husband both knew as 'our tune'. Without waiting for her lover to enter the room and take her in his arms, she would ease the recording on to the turntable. She later told friends that her heart would always miss a beat at the sound of the needle finding its way – click-click-click – into the right groove. And then the distinctive opening bars of the music – *that* music – would begin.

'CON – GRAT – U – LAAAAAAA – TIONS and CELE – BRAAAAAAA – TIONS!' It was Cliff Richard singing his famous flagship song, the song with which he was to conquer the Eurovision contest just over thirty years later. As the sound of this familiar music eddied its way up the elaborate staircase and into his second-floor bedroom, the Prince would wake up from his slumbers and a wide smile would radiate over his face, for he knew then, as he would know always, that Cliff's voice was proof positive that the love of his life had arrived home, and was eager to dance.

Thus Cliff had woven himself once more into the very fabric of our nation's story. It was not the first time, of course, that he had captured the hearts of Britain's foremost couples: a choral version of 'Goodbye Sam, Hello Samantha' had been sung by the Welsh Male Voice Choir at the wedding of King George VI and Queen Mary, and on Armistice Day 1918, the crowds who packed into Trafalgar Square had burst into a spontaneous rendition of 'Mistletoe and Wine'. Similarly, when Florence Nightingale was in search of an entertainer to lift the hearts of the casualties in the Crimea, it was to Cliff Richard she turned. And, true to form, Cliff did not let her down: his version of 'Daddy's Home' was said to have brought tears to the eyes of even the most hardened veterans, and as the closing bars drifted into the wind Cliff found himself lifted high upon the officers' shoulders and transported aloft through the cheering assembly.

Thus has Cliff Richard grown to embody the very thrust and weft and rub and hoof of Great Britain in all her vibrant, ever-youthful glory. And his influence spreads far and wide: the distinctive rhythms of 'In the Country' are echoed in the familiar bullish speech-patterns of Winston Churchill's wartime broadcasts, and even John F. Kennedy could not resist bursting into an up-temp Latin-American version of 'We Don't Talk Any More' while addressing the people of West Berlin ('Ich Bin Ein Cliffricharder') in June 1963.

To Cliff came the honour of being the inspiration behind both the first song ('The Day I Met Marie') sung on the surface of the moon, and the very last song ('Summer Holiday') played by the orchestra as the *Titanic* dipped slowly but surely below the surface of the waves.

And now . . . and now . . . (Deep breath, Wallace, deep breath. And blow. All better!) . . . And now Mr Chris Evans, no doubt speaking for and on behalf of his puppetmasters in New Labour, has decided to place a gag on Britain's greatest living treasure, denying Cliff the platform that has been rightfully his for over nine decades. Callow young disc jockeys the length and breadth of this country have followed suit, brutally snubbing one of the greatest Britons of this, or indeed of any other, century.

Personally, I do not know Sir Cliff well, though he was a good friend of Dame Edith Sitwell in the late 1930s. But I know when an injustice has been done. This is why I am now calling on you all to open your windows, lean out into the street and sing 'Living Doll' at the top of your voices. That way, even Mr Blair will be unable to claim that he cannot hear the cries of a people in anguish – and a people, furthermore, who are resolved to fight to the bitter end for Britain and Sir Cliff. You have been warned, Mr Blair: you have been warned.

Michael Parkinson Meets Victoria Beckham

Parky: In a sense, so to speak, you've done some truly amazing things in your life, would you agree, in a sense?

Posh: Seerzly, I don't ask to be in the papers, you know. It's not, like, please let me be in the papers. I mean, I don't ask to be in them. It's not as if I'm like, whatever happens I want to be in the papers. I don't ask to be in the papers, you know. It's not, like, hey, let's see if I'm in the papers today, let's, like, look through them to see if I'm in. I mean, I don't ask to be in the papers, you know.

Parky: Amazing. So would I be right in taking it then that in a certain sort of sense, Mel, you don't actually *ask* to be in the papers?

Posh: It's the meedyur. The meedyur controls what everybody thinks. A lot of people don't realise but it's the newspaper editors who say what goes into their newspapers. And the editor of the *Daily Wodever* will say, like, I demand, right, I DEMAND we have someone like really mega-interesting on the cover today to boost sales so the paper will sell more or wodever and some like office junior will say, what about one of the other Spice Girls for a change and the editor will say, like, no, they're not interesting enough I'm sorry to say it but they're a bit boring and I DEMAND Posh Spice. And that's the way the meedyur controls what everybody thinks. And I really don't need that hassaw. I don't ask to be in the papers, you know.

Parky: There's a question the whole world is asking, and in a sense I've got to put it to you. I mean, in a sense do you actually ASK to be in the papers? And on an entirely different matter, if I may – what's your husband the world famous footballer David Bockham really like as it were?

Posh: David's a very, very strong character, a really strong manly character who plays fubaw and really hates wearing women's clothes, like if I was to say, like, David, will you be wearing my lacy bra today, he'd be like, no way, what do you take me for, I wore that one yesterday.

Parky: He's not from Barnsley then?!

Posh: No.

Parky: Believe you me, you get a truly smashing chip buttie up Barnsley way.

Posh: I don't ask to be in the papers, you know.

Parky: Bit of brown sauce, salt, good splash o' vinegar, nowt beats it. Fascinating. And you've been doing a fair bit of interviewing yourself recently, in a sense—

Posh: I wanted to talk to all the famous peepaw I like really admire and ask them all the questions no one's ever asked them before. Like, I was that nervous but I asked Elton straight out when his next album was due, and I don't know how I honestly had the nerve but I walked up to Valentino, right, and asked him straight out like what it was like being a top dress designer.

Parky: That must've taken the wind out of his sails!

Posh: The sales weren't on. It was like October.

Parky: Amazing. And what did Valentino say when you asked him what it was like to be a top dress designer?

Posh: He said it was, like . . . really top.

Parky: You've got this extraordinary kind of fame. Throughout the world, everyone knows exactly who you are, even if they couldn't say exactly which one, and I'd imagine that must be a pretty daunting prospect on occasion.

Posh: Like now, whenever I just walk into a television studio, all the cameras are on me, and then they put a microphone near me, and the microphone picks up every word I say, and then it's all broadcast on television into the homes of millions and millions of people and sometimes I just wish I could be left alone for a change, like I wish I could just sit here in a studio and no one would bother me with questions. Sometimes I just wish I could be totally unanimous again.

Parky: And after all a year's a helluva long time to wait, isn't it? But for the time being do you and David ever manage as it were to live what could be described an ordinary life in a sense?

Posh: We're both just really ornry peepaw. Okay, we might have a bit of extra cash, but we don't let it change us, like we've still got our heads firmly on the ground, we're still really normaw, like we just sit round in the evening watching *EastEnders* like everyone else, and just because we can afford to pay the real actors to perform it live in our sitting room I don't see that makes us any different from anyone else.

Parky: There's one question the whole world is itching to ask, and that's – when's the new Bananarama album out?

Posh: At the moment, I'm writing my own album –

Parky: A solo album?! Great! I remember when I last interviewed the late, great Tony Bennett he also was writing a new alb—

Posh: And I'm writing all my own songs. It's like magic. They just come to me like that, generally when I'm like listening to the radio. Yesterday I wrote one I called 'Do You Know the Way to San José?' then another called 'Say A Little Prayer' and tomorrow I'm writing one called 'Son of A Preacherman'. They just sort of flow out, it's like someone else was writing them, some like higher being.

Parky: Smashing. And you'll be singing them all solo?

Posh: Yup. I'll have backing singers and that, but I'll be definitely like joining in quite a bit on the days I'm in the studio. Hopeflee.

Parky: Finally, the question on everybody's lips: we know you from your press image, and we know you from the telly and from the record, but, tell me – who's the *real* Emma Bunton?

Posh: I'm just someone who wants to live a normaw life with my husband and my baby and not have everyone following me about who isn't part of my accredited camera crew. I don't ask to be on television, you know.

Parky: Cheers. Now it only remains for me to—

Posh: Shall I come back next week with David and the baby? I could if you want?

Parky: Ladies and Gentlemen, a big thanks and farewell to Victoria Principal!

There Yego: A Day with Tony Blackburn (1994)

Dad a dad a da did a, dad a dad a da did a, dad a dad a da di do di do. Gonna knock on your door, dad a did a, do di di do do do. As I entered his studio at Capital Gold at 8.00 in the morning, Tony Blackburn (Toe-neee Black-buuurrrn) was singing along, headphones on, as happy as Larry. The record came to an end. 'Now let's take a look at what the WEATHER'S doing' he said, 'WEATHERWISE, it's a really GLORIOUS morning.'

A phone-in competition was coming up. 'It's Neil DIAMOND Day here on the *Tony BLACKBURN Show*'. To win a Neil Diamond video, listeners had to name the Neil Diamond song. 'Sweeeeeet Caroliiiiine' went the chorus, over and over again. The correct answer was: 'Sweet Caroline'. The lines were jammed. 'Okay, Valerie, when you pick up the line to Tony, let's have a nice bright HELLO!' said the organiser.

'Once again, we're having far too much FUN for our own good,' enthused Tony, as the record came to an end, 'but that's the way we are! There yego!'

Valerie came from Margate.

'Margate – that's by the seaside, isn't it? So you'll be having a bit of a paddle today, Valerie? There yego! Nice to have someone by the seaside! Congratulations to Valerie, there.'

Next came a pre-recorded jingle for Capital Gold's lunchtime show. 'Hi – David HAMILTON here . . . Don't forget to join me for lunch – come on, have a NIBBLE.'

While 'Dock of the Bay' was playing ('Rub-bub-bubby-da-rub-a-bub-bub') Tony Blackburn told me why he has always liked the breakfast slot. 'It's quite a UNIQUE time of the day, really,' he explained. The record came to an end. '29 minutes past 8, CAPITAL GOLD time,' he said. 'And WEATHERWISE, it's another BEEE-OOODIVUL day, with the temperature at 77 CAPITAL GOLD degrees.'

While he was enthusing into the microphone about the weather, I noticed that Tony Blackburn has an almost orangey complexion. A lot of showbusiness celebrities have this almost orangey complexion. It is as if their sun is not ours, or as if they sunbathe by moonlight. It is one of the clearest signs that they are different from us.

'And now it's back to 1970 on the station that's never forgotten GREAT music!' said Tony, and 'Love Grows Where My Rosemary Goes' ('Love GROWS la la la la la GOES') by Edison Lighthouse came on. Meanwhile Kenny Everett walked in, eating a banana. Kenny Everett, it was revealed not long ago, is HIV positive. He asked me why I was bothering to write about Tony Blackburn. I said that it was his thirtieth anniversary as a disc jockey. 'Funnily enough,' chipped in Tony, 'as you get OLDER, there are more things to CELEBRATE, aren't there?'

'Like friends dying off,' muttered Kenny, taking a bite of his banana.

There was a pause. Tony kept smiling. 'Mr Happy!' he said, with a laugh. 'Spread a little JOY!' The newsreader came in. 'Funny thing about newsreaders,' observed Tony, still smiling. 'They always come in at the last minute.'

'Have a great CAPITAL GOLD day! Thanks for listening! And see you TOMORROW!' At the end of his show, Tony packed his large collection of jingles away into a cupboard. 'What was the name of that dog that used to bark on your show?' I asked him, wondering if the 'WOOF WOOF' that used to wake me up in the morning was still around. My wife and I had been arguing over the dog's name the night before. She had maintained that he was called 'Adolfo'. Though I found this hard to believe, I had failed to come up with a better alternative.

'Arnold,' answered Tony, 'but the Beeb wouldn't let me take him with me. Anyway, he'd be thirty years old by now – so maybe it's JUST as WELL!'

Tony Blackburn's laugh operates as if through the agency of a delay mechanism. If he makes a joke, he signals it by pausing for three seconds and then laughing, so that the previous joke should really read, 'Anyway, he'd be thirty years old by now – so maybe it's JUST as WELL (1–2–3) fnurr fnurr fnurr!!!!'

As we left Capital, I sensed Tony Blackburn was in the process of winding down after his breakfast show. It reminded me of watching the air go out of a balloon: gradually, his laughter became less emphatic and the exclamation marks ceased to hover over the end of each sentence. On air, everything he said would end with a punch and a wave of boundless enthusiasm. Now, almost everything tailed away, and sentences would close with a mumbled phrase such as, 'Yeah, quite nice really I suppose.'

We left Capital and got into his car, a slim black Cadillac. 'It was actually very reasonable. Very reasonable indeed,' he said. How much did it cost? 'Do you know, I can't remember. No, I really can't remember exactly to be honest.' Cars are important to Tony. Aged twenty-six, he had appeared at his old school, Millfield. 'As a showbiz celebrity I had the accessories to match,' he reveals in his autobiography, 'an E-type jag, and a gorgeous bunny girl in the shortest mini-skirt ever invented.' When he proposed to his first wife, Tessa Wyatt, he said, 'In my life, I wanted to be the top disc jockey and I am. I wanted an E-type Jaguar and I have one and I want you, and of course I'll get you.'

In the Cadillac, Tony started to talk about what a great guy Noel Edmonds is. As the day progressed, this was to emerge as one of his major themes. 'Noel's a really great guy. You can't help but admire a guy like Noel,' he said. Yet things between them were not always so happy. Delving into his 1985 autobiography, *Tony Blackburn – The Living Legend*, I discovered that their relationship had got off to a shaky start a few years before when Tony had heard Noel's audition tape for Radio Luxembourg. 'He was cracking jokes the way I did but not very well and so I said, "There's only room for one of us to tell stupid jokes and I've cornered the market." I was joking but unfortunately he thought I was serious and I think he was hurt . . . that incident characterised our relationship which never became warm. I didn't blame Noel for taking over my place on the breakfast show. But I wouldn't be human if I didn't admit that for a time I resented him. I found Noel rather cool and difficult to get on with . . .'

Later in the book, Tony reveals how he fell out once more with Noel on a Radio 1 Roadshow in Weston-super-Mare. 'I was very upset when Noel Edmonds booby-trapped Mike Read's hotel room. Noel unscrewed the bed and the doors and the phone but that didn't bother me. He also locked some chickens in the bathroom to give Mike a shock when he opened the door. I tried to stop him but I was looked on as a kill-joy. I packed my bags and returned to London in disgust.'

Fifteen years later, Noel has become a multi-millionaire businessman and television personality. Tony Blackburn remains a disc jockey, now on Capital Gold. Oddly enough, for the last two series Noel has regularly invited Tony as a special guest on to his top-rated television show, *Noel's House Party*. Each week, the smiling Tony is ritually humiliated. Driving through London on the way to Tony's own show on a satellite shopping channel called QVC ('Quality, Value and – errr, lemme see, what's the C stand for?') Tony Blackburn told me how he made it all up with Noel. ('Convenience – that's it!')

On the very first *House Party* in which Tony was a guest, the script required Noel slam the front door in Tony's face. 'And Noel slammed it very, very hard INDEED, right in my face. So after the show, I went up to Noel, and I said, "Noel, I get the FEELING you've been wanting to do that for a LONG TIME, am I right?" And he said, "yes". And do you know, Craig, from that moment on we were the best of friends!' Tony smiled at the fond memory. And then after a long pause, he added, 'He's a great guy!'

QVC goes out live all day. Its formula is simple. The presenters show the viewers about ten or so household products an hour, and get very excited about how useful they are around the home. The viewers then phone a number and pay for these household products by credit card. Before he goes on air, Tony takes care to study the products he will be selling.

'Good God!' he said to his fellow presenter, a bubbly woman called Julia, picking up a pair of awkward-looking spectacles. 'What are they for?' He pulled one section out, creating a ramshackle binocular effect. 'That must be the focus!' He placed them on his face. 'Oh, yeah – amazing! And it comes in a pouch! And it's got a nose support!' I watched Tony as his enthusiasm for the product grew and grew. 'The power of binoculars and the convenience of spectacles,' he said, 'and actually also very good for the theatre – beeoodivul.' The next product along, The Chickie Egg Boiler, was a plastic chicken with a removable top. 'So you put the water in there, and then you set the timer and then you boil your egg – that's actually very clever.' Feeling like a spoilsport, I pointed out that a saucepan performs the very same function. Tony gave the matter some thought. 'Yes,' he said, 'I suppose you could be right there. In a way. Great!'

Through a tie press ('that's really quite good'), a rechargeable torch ('yes, I quite like that') and an antique coffee grinder ('quite a good idea, that') to a decoy security camera ('no, it doesn't actually work, but that's what makes it cost-effective which is quite good'), Tony exercised his enthusiasm. 'I find it an exciting channel to work for because I've always had a great belief in satellite television.' And he is very much a gadget man himself. His own wristwatch, he explained, can even open his garage doors.

Tony went off to change. For his Capital Gold show, he had been wearing a floral denim shirt and Wrangler's. For QVC, he changed into slacks, a smarter shirt and a mauve zip-up jacket, all newly pressed. He also wears a gold bracelet on his wrist and a gold necklace. His hair is scrupulously black and sits, neatly parted, a little oddly on his head, though this may be just because the top of his head seems to be flat, rather than curved, so that the hair that drifts over his forehead falls at an unusual angle of 90 degrees. His teeth are very white, his eyes strangely bloodshot, his fingernails heavily and unevenly bitten, as if by an aggressive dog.

By the time the cameras had started to roll, Tony Blackburn was charged up once more, and the mumbled 'quites' were replaced by cheery 'verys'. The first product for Tony and Julia to sell in their mock-up studio kitchen was an alarm clock which goes cock-a-doodle-doo.

Tony: Has anyone noticed at home that Julia has TIME on her HANDS. Fnurr! Fnurr!

Julia: I hope you're not going to be like this for an hour!

Tony: Fnurr! Fnurr! It had to be said! Fnurr! Fnurr! The next product was a Metric Conversion Calculator.

Julia: And it's only 11.49.

Tony: That's AMAZING value, isn't it? This really is TERRIFIC.

The third product was a Corby Tie Press. Julia was holding a demonstration tie, ready to be pressed.

Tony: You're a bit TIED UP at the moment! Fnurr! Fnurr! Actually, seriously, I do wear a lot of ties, and it is annoying when they crease, so . . .

The fourth product was the magnifying glasses.

Tony: We've been having a lot of fun with these!

Julia: Tony, you've never looked better!

Tony: Fnurr! Fnurr! Seriously, though, if you go to the theatre you often have to pay 20p – well, why not save money? I mean they REALLY ARE SENSIBLE!

Producer: If someone asked me to the theatre and I wore those, it'd be my first and last date.

The fifth product was the Chickie Egg Boiler.

Tony: You've got to make eating fun really, haven't you? I think it's a GREAT idea!

And the sixth was an Adjustable Can Opener. Sadly –

Tony: Now this isn't actually working!

– the Adjustable Can Opener failed to open the can, merely tearing its label off.

Tony: Something not quite right here, which is a shame, because this usually works absolutely BEEEOOODIVULLY, I've used it many times. Quite often, for instance, I've cut my hand on these things, but this device stops that.

The can remained stalwartly unopened.

Tony: So, there yego – that's something really worth having there!

After the show, Tony and Julia bounced up to the producer. Tony was very keen to know how the products were selling. The producer said that they were going very well. 'That's good, that's good,' said Tony, 'because it's such a lovely morning outside'.

Actually, judging by the monitor on the producer's desk, sales had been slow. Next to the Chickie Egg Boiler, for instance, were the words 'Quantity in Stock: 44. Quantity remaining: 42'. And the Adjustable Can Opener had sold 0.

Our next stop was Birmingham, where Tony Blackburn was due to appear as a guest on *Pebble Mill*. In the Cadillac, he spoke of how he sees himself.

'I hate the term disc jockey. I look upon myself more as a salesman. A salesman of the air. You see, I see myself as a product that I'm marketing, and that's why QVC fits in so beeodivully. I've always been seen as more radio than television. I still love radio but I'm very, very fond of TV now.' He pauses, then adds, 'No, I'm very, very fond of TV now. Very fond of TV.' Over the course of our day together, I noticed that many of his replies came to an end in this way, with the repetition, slightly quieter, of the sentence that has come before, rather in the way that the pop singles fade out.

'I'm very fond of TV now. On radio, the people have become harder, whereas television has a lot of nice people. Yes, I'd go so far as to say that television people are nicer than radio people. Of the two, television people are probably the nicer.'

'Nice' is probably the key adjective in Tony Blackburn's off-air vocabulary, just as 'terrific' and 'beeodivul' are the key adjectives of his on-air vocabulary. He always found the Beatles 'very nice', for instance, and he explained to me that on the one occasion when he met Robert Maxwell (backstage as fellow guests on *Through the Keyhole*) 'To be honest, I didn't get the impression he was a very nice man.'

I asked him whether there was anyone he had met in the world of pop who he didn't find very nice. He thought for a while. 'I had slight trouble with Mott the Hoople,' he replied. What was wrong with them? 'I thought they were a bit conceited, to be honest. I always think it's a shame when things go to their heads.' But what did they do wrong? 'I used to take the mickey out of the spoken bit in "All the Young Dudes", and the guy objected to it. I said to him, okay, I won't play it if that's how you feel, and he said, you don't have any say in it, and I said well in actual fact I do. So I didn't play "All the Young Dudes" for three weeks. That lost them a few sales.'

I asked Tony Blackburn who he personally liked in the world of pop. 'I always got on well with Richard and Karen Carpenter, and Neil Sedaka's a very nice guy. Most of the people I've met have been very pleasant, very pleasant, really. Just Mott the Hoople stand out in my mind. And Noddy Holder's a terribly nice guy. The Searchers are very nice, for instance – they're doing very well at the moment, you know. And Gene Pitney's another nice guy,' he said.

I said I had read somewhere that Gene Pitney now had a leisure complex.

'Really?' he said, looking a little bemused.

Later, it occurred to me that he had misunderstood what I had said, and that he had imagined that a leisure complex, like an inferiority complex, was some sort of psychological disorder.

The mobile telephone purred. 'Has it? Great!' he said. 'That'll really be something to look forward to!' It was his wife, he said.

She had been watching him a couple of weeks ago on QVC, and on the strength of his salesmanship had ordered a twenty-piece cookware set. She was just ringing him to tell him it had arrived.

'But what is a "cookware set"?' I asked.

'It's quite a bargain actually,' he replied.

'But what is it.'

'Well, if, say, you had just made yourself a sandwich, you can put your sandwich in it.'

Other members of his family had also ordered products after watching Blackburn selling them on QVC. His sister had ordered a Country and Western CD set ('and I never even knew she likes Country and Western') and his mother had ordered a non-drip steam iron for going away with.

'We were talking about who you liked in pop.'

'When we at Radio 1, we weren't that close, but now I think Noel Edmonds is a very, very nice guy. He's got a great capacity to learn scripts, you know. Give him quite a long thirty-second script and he'll have learnt it in seconds. And he's a very good businessman, Noel. He's got his head on his shoulders, very happily married and things.'

'Who are your close friends?'

'Sorry?'

'Who are your close friends?'

It struck me that he had never thought of people in such terms before.

'You say close friends . . . Well, David Hamilton was my best man, so I suppose he must be.' Another pause. 'There's no one I'd call a best friend.' Pause. 'No one I'd call a great friend.'

'Who was at your wedding?'

'Most of the Capital Gold people. And my family. And that was about it, really.'

'Have you been on *This Is Your Life*?'

'Yes – about two years ago.'

'Who did they have on?'

'Well, David Hamilton of course was there. And Marty Wilde. And Pete Murray. I've always been a great fan of Pete

Murray. And Anne Aston from the *Golden Shot*. Remember her? I hadn't seen her in ages.'

I asked him whether he kept up with any of his contemporaries from Millfield. He hadn't kept up with any of them, but over the years he had bumped into three or four. 'The only ones I've met have been terrific failures, actually,' he added.

Tony Blackburn is closest to his mother and his sister, who live together in Poole, where Tony grew up. The only time during our day together when I felt sure Blackburn was not performing – was not simply saying what he thought would sound best – was when he spoke of his sister Jackie, who is disabled. 'I've got a great deal of admiration for my sister,' he said, his head tilted to one side. 'She had great pain in her life. And that's altered my whole attitude to life. It's made me a lot less tolerant of people. For instance, I want to go up to hooligans and say, "You're so lucky – why don't you do something useful for a change?" I'll never forgive the way the Conservatives behaved over that Disability Bill. It was disgraceful. Absolutely disgraceful. I'll never forgive them for that.'

He has a son, Simon, by his famously ill-fated marriage to Tessa Wyatt. Simon is now twenty-one, and reading for a business studies degree. 'He's always kept it a secret from the other students that he's my son, but they know now.' His comical-tragical attempts to win Tessa Wyatt back over the air have now entered popular mythology, like the ski-jumps of Eddie the Eagle. When she left him in 1976, Blackburn at first said nothing in public, but then one morning on Radio 1 he played 'We've Thrown It All Away' by R. and J. Stone and dedicated it to 'the person who will always be very special to me'. He followed it with Peter and Gordon's 'A World Without Love'. 'That should have been enough,' he later recalled, 'but once the dam of my misery broke I found I couldn't stop.'

But his second wife, Debbie, is embarrassed by this strange chapter, and Tony has now learnt reticence. 'To be honest with you,' he told me, 'I think I went slightly off my trolley.'

He first met Debbie in 1976 when he was starring as Buttons in *Cinderella* at Palmers Green, and she was in the chorus line. Singing 'Tie a Yellow Ribbon', they danced together on stage around an old oak tree. Over a decade later, they met again. She, of course, remembered him, but he didn't actually remember her. Nevertheless, romance blossomed.

'She's the first person I've ever been out with who doesn't play those stupid games – you know, they flirt with someone in front of you. But she's not like that. Terrific really. Smashing. At the moment, it's just tremendous.' Pause. 'It just worries me that it won't go on.'

Arriving at Pebble Mill ('We've kept a lovely place for you, Tony,' said the car park attendant), we were met by three male autograph-hunters with something of a Diane Arbus air about them. 'Could we have an autograph, Tony?' 'Could we just take a photo, Tony?' 'Thanks, Tony!' Every time Tony Blackburn is recognised by a member of the public, he seems to gain extra energy. I had noticed this earlier, when we stopped at a garage to put some more petrol in the Cadillac. He had walked to the pay desk in a slightly weary manner, but through the windows of the car and the garage office, I noticed him engaged in an animated conversation with the cashier, and he had returned to the car with a new spring in his step. 'Did she recognise you?' I had asked him, as he pressed his seat belt into its slot. 'Yes!' he had replied. 'Fnurr! Fnurr!'

There were three hours to go until the programme was recorded, but Tony was at ease amidst the bustle of television, smiling broadly and exchanging merry quips about the weather with everyone he passed. An unusual number of people seemed to have bumped into him before, somewhere.

'You probably won't remember me, Tony, but years ago, and we're going back years now, you did a singing session here for Radio 2.'

'Sure, I remember that.'

'Well, I was the bandleader then.'

'I reckon that ruined my singing career! Fnurr! Fnurr!'

'Sorry?'

'I reckon that ruined my singing career! Fnurr! Fnurr!'

Tony admitted to me that he has a bad memory for faces. 'I can't even remember my own face sometimes. Hur! Hur!' But over the years he has developed a means of transferring from radio into real life his speedy impression of intimacy.

'Hi Tony! I work for Pebble Mill now, so I thought I'd just pop up to say hello!'

'Hi! Er. So do you live round here now?'

As we were sitting around at Pebble Mill, chomping some BBC sandwiches, Richard O'Brien, the creator of the *Rocky Horror Show* and a fellow-guest on the programme, strode up to Tony and introduced himself.

'Tony,' he said, somehow lending a gently satirical lilt to the word 'Tony', 'way back in 1965, before you were a disc jockey, even, when we were both just starting out, we found ourselves on a tube together going from Oxford Circus to Earls Court. And on that journey, you told me all your plans and hopes for the future. And we said goodbye to one another at Earls Court Station, and we've never met since.'

Tony looked a little defensive, as if he might be being sent up, but he managed to emit a cautious beam. 'Is that so?' he said. 'That's amazing!'

Later, when Tony was away in make-up, I asked Richard O'Brien about their chance encounter thirty years ago. 'He did most of the talking,' he recalled, 'and I couldn't work out where he was coming from.'

'And how come you remembered Tony Blackburn but he didn't remember you?'

'I imagine it's because I'm rather more *alert* than Tony,' replied O'Brien. And everyone in the room began to laugh.

Tony Blackburn emerged from his dressing room in a new outfit, his third of the day. He was wearing a pinky-beige jacket ('nice colour, isn't it?'), neatly pressed trousers and a clean white shirt with a zip rather than buttons. It was on a day preceding a rail strike, and I was beginning to think that I would have to catch a train home before I had witnessed Tony's scheduled eight-minute performance on Pebble Mill. With time running out, I was beginning to wonder whether there was some vital question I hadn't answered.

'Are you religious?'

'I can't stand organised religion, actually. It's one of those things I quite hate. I mean, I don't see why the Pope should be closer to God than I am.' He thought for a moment. 'But I've always felt that something guides me. I don't see why there shouldn't be a life after death. But I hope it's not different from this one. You see, I quite like broadcasting and I might not come back as a broadcaster.'

Checking out the studio, Tony noticed a crease in his pinky-beige jacket. A pleasant woman from the BBC whisked the jacket away and ironed out the crease before bringing it back to him with a smile. Tony thanked her. 'You know QVC, the new shopping channel?' he asked her. 'Well, we do a very good steam iron at a very reasonable price. Does yours squirt water?'

'Yes!'

'Ah. Well, there yego. Lovely.'

I told Tony that I thought I'd better go now, as I was worried about getting caught up in the strike. As we shook hands, for a split second I thought he looked almost desolate, as if part of his apparatus for the day was set to vanish into thin air. At one point in our drive to Birmingham, the news had come on the radio, and he had turned it down. 'I always think to myself that after I've gone, the newscaster will say, Tony Blackburn died today. He opened up Radio 1, he was on a pirate ship. And now the weather. And that's it really, isn't it?' he had remarked.

On my way home, I tried to imagine what Tony Blackburn would be like all alone, driving back in his car unobserved, or by himself the next day in his house. He had told me that his hobby was sunbathing ('Do you do much sunbathing, Craig?') but this was not much help. What would he think? How would he behave? I found it impossible to summon up an image of

Pop

Tony Blackburn without an audience, without a camera or a microphone. Who knows? Perhaps when he closes the door behind him, away from the do-do-di-do of his fan-tas-tic life, he breathes a sigh of relief, closes his eyes, and evaporates into the ether.

The
Conservatives

Wallace Arnold: The First Time Ever I Saw Her Face

The first time ever I saw her face, she struck me as nothing very remarkable. Quite the opposite: a timid little matron in early middle age, her mittened hands clutching anxiously at her third-class railway ticket, a thermos of PG Tips cradled at her side. She sat all alone, her lips moving silently up and down, up and down, as she devoured her morning copy of the *Daily Telegraph*.

It was at some point in the early 1960s. We were travelling to a Conservative conference in Blackpool at the time. I was, of course, travelling first class, but I spied this mousy figure through the connecting window of our carriages, and pointed her out to my travelling companions. 'Do look!' I said, and they all craned their necks to peer through the window. 'You'll never believe it, but she is a newly elected Conservative Member of Parliament!'

Needless to say, they all roared with good-natured laughter at the very idea that this Mrs Mopp figure, clad, as I remember, in housecoat, pink fluffy slippers, ill-darned socks and hairnet, should be their representative at Westminster. 'It's really too priceless, Wallace!' chortled Lady Diana Cooper, the then Minister for Transport, resplendent in the ballgown in which she always travelled, 'Do let's ask her to join us! It would be too killing for words!'

I volunteered for the task. Putting my head around the door of third class, I warbled out my invitation. 'Ahem! Ahem! We were wondering if you would care to join us for a light luncheon – nothing too exotic, I assure you!'

The lady thanked me kindly, finished her boiled sweetie, adjusted her housecoat, tottered through into first class and, with a murmured 'thank you kindly', took up her place next to Dame Edith Sitwell, the then Under-Secretary for Health and Social Security. And this was how we came to be lunching with a little-known MP called Mrs Margaret Thatcher, though I rather doubt whether, at the time, we even knew her name, or were sufficiently interested afterwards to bother to discover it. Was she wearing Wellington boots beneath her house-coat? I rather think so, though obviously we were all too polite to draw attention to them at the time.

To the best of my recollection, the whole meal passed without her saying a word. The impression she gave was that she lacked the social confidence to dare to open her mouth. Even when the saintly Cecil Beaton (at that time, Secretary of State for Wales) tried to 'bring her out' by asking her whether she kept racing pigeons, the poor little woman barely looked up from her single portion of Heinz Cream of Tomato soup.

Once she had finished her luncheon, I suggested, as tactfully as possible, that she might feel more comfortable in the long run by returning to her third-class carriage and leaving the rest of us to enjoy a more sophisticated political discussion over a glass of port and a slice or two of halfway-decent Stilton. As we bundled her back to her place, Mr John Aspinall, President of the Board of Trade, presciently announced that he had been mighty impressed by her. Did we know, he wondered, whether she might be prepared to do a little bit of light dusting for him on those days when Parliament wasn't sitting?

Twenty years on, my goodness, how things had changed! This dowdy little woman had now been reborn as a modern-day Boadicea, rescuing our beleaguered nation from the feathered bed of sloth, greed and apathy into which it had sunk its grizzled head. The trades unions (dread phrase!) had been defeated, the miners routed, the Falklands reclaimed, the wets brought to their knees, unilateralism crushed, communism obliterated, Keynes humiliated and all alien creeds put firmly in their place. Three cheers for Margaret! Those of us in the Conservative Party bowed in supplication to her as the greatest peacetime leader of this, or any, century. Hail, bright goddess! Hail, oh beauteous saviour!

The other day, while sitting comfortably in a 125 train, a group of us were celebrating these outstanding achievements when, quite by chance, who should I see in the next carriage but – yes! – Lady Thatcher herself, all alone, reading her *Daily Telegraph*, her lips moving this way and that. She seemed strangely solitary there, as she clutched her ticket anxiously in her mittened hands. 'Oh Lord!' I whispered to the assembled company. 'It's Margaret! Do you think we should ask her to join us?'

The others looked down at their plates, and after a bit of umming and erring, we all decided that, for her own good, the poor woman would probably prefer to be left alone with her funny little thoughts and memories. For good or ill, time moves on. These days, if we invited her to our table she would simply have nothing to say.

4,250 Days

On 30 October 1987, Alan Clark was sitting in his bedroom in the British Embassy in Santiago, writing up his diary. 'I was thinking – a totally wasted day; then, with a start, how many more days have I got left? Two thousand? Three thousand at the most. Each one is more significant, and more important, than its predecessor.'

We now know that this estimate was far too gloomy. In fact, he had around 4250 days left, and since those days included the publication of his diaries, his consequent emergence as a celebrity, his retirement as an MP, then, five years later, his re-election, a television series and a history of the Conservative Party, they might indeed be said to have been the most significant and most important of his life.

Though people remember his *Diaries* for their jokes and their jauntiness, their insults and their ogling, re-reading them now, what strikes one is how threaded they are with intimations of mortality. Whenever he looks in the mirror, he grimly catalogues an increase in jowls and wonders how long he has to go. Throughout the book, the ghosts of the First World War hover, so that at times it seems as though that era, with its disillusion and destruction, is his spiritual home. 'I can get carried back to the summer of 1914,' he writes, 'or worse, the year following, when the telegrams started to arrive thick and fast, pedalled up the drives of the great houses by sly sideways-looking postmen, and Kipling lost his only son at Loos.'

To me, it is the 'sly, sideways-looking postmen' in that

301

beautiful sentence that lend it its peculiar strength. At first, the image seems comical: postmen on bicycles always bring to mind Ealing comedies, and those sideways-looking figures suggest something crafty and scheming and Terry-Thomas-ish. But then you think of the sorrow contained in the envelopes in their sacks, and you realise why the poor postmen are looking sideways, and you picture their slow pedals up the long drive, and at that moment the grief of Kipling, and of so many other parents, hits you all the harder.

On 21 October 1990, Alan Clark hosts a Bloomsbury evening at Saltwood, and ends it – as unpredictably as ever – with tears in his eyes after a performance by Eileen Atkins of Virginia Woolf's *A Room of One's Own*. Before the event, he has made a little speech of welcome, 'fraudulently and bogusly referring to my father's death from a falling tree. What mischievous impulse made me do this? Pure Roger Irrelevant. I did just manage to keep a straight face, although William, from the far end of the room, gave me an odd look.'

It is this strange intertwining of the solemn and the silly (and the way Clark finds them grudgingly reliant upon each other, like Siamese twins) that makes his *Diaries* so mesmerising. Most of the victims – David Mellor ('everyone loathes him'), King Hussein of Jordan ('oily little runt'), David Penhalligon ('with his demi-bogus vowels'), Nigel Lawson ('There is a suspicious henna tinge to his hair – is he tinting, or rinsing?') etc, etc – are already up to their heads in the sands of our collective amnesia, but, like great drama, Clark's *Diaries* seem destined to grow all the more powerful with the evaporation of their subjects.

On Tuesday, when Alan Clark's death was finally announced, Tony Benn popped up on all the news programmes saying that he should be remembered as a serious historian and passionate animal rights campaigner, rather than as a frivolous diarist. This would, I suspect, have pleased Clark, who spent his life toing and froing between the straight face and the smirk, but who could never shake off his attraction to the glint of gravitas. Yet he never really trusted either: his silly side would always be lurking, ready to slip a banana skin in front of his serious side, and in turn his serious side would grow touchy and pompous if ever his silly side began hogging the limelight.

In 1997, I went to a party he held on the terrace of the House of Commons to celebrate his return to Westminster. To my surprise, it was full of some of the most gruesome celebrities in London – tanned TV talk-show hosts, swaggering tabloid columnists, Andrew Neil, Eve Pollard, Jeffrey Archer, the lot. The only person I could see who might have been an old friend of Clark was Sir Robert Rhodes James. At first, I wondered if it was all some sort of joke – how many grotesques can you fit on one terrace? – and then I realised with a jolt that if it was a joke then I must be part of it. 'Why isn't Michael Winner here?' I tipsily asked Clark when he sashayed up to me to say hello. He looked taken aback. 'Why do you ask?' he said. 'Because every other awful person in London is here,' I replied. Oddly enough, he then admitted that he had indeed invited Michael Winner, but that he had already accepted an invitation to a West End premiere.

I still don't know whether that guest list was a joke. Perhaps it wasn't. Like many with sensitive antennae for vulgarity in others, Alan Clark was unusually vulgar himself. One need only think of his ostentatious delight in his own wealth, his flash old cars with their personalised number plates, his insatiable love of gossip and his camp chorus-line walk, as though he were endlessly auditioning for a spot on *The Black and White Minstrels Show*. Even those few issues on which he chose to be holier-than-thou (blood sports, animal rights) were somehow ill-fitting and naff.

But it is precisely this push-me-pull-you aspect of Clark's vision that made it so appealing. Tony Benn was obviously being altruistic when he attempted to sieve through the life of Alan Clark for signs of high seriousness, but in doing so he was reducing him to the size and shape of any other po-faced MP. When Clark was just being purely serious – attempting to gain Mrs Thatcher's support for his Fur Labelling bill, slogging his way through his history of the Conservative Party – he became as commonplace as a ventriloquist without a dummy.

It was his consciousness of death that was the fuel of his frivolity. 'Everything in politics is so instant,' he once said to Michael Cockrell, sitting on top of a hill at his Highland estate. 'But here you can realise we are all just grains of sand.' His *Diaries* are serious precisely because they are so hopelessly irresponsible, with what Benn would see as his frivolous side observing his 'serious' side with a godlike separation. He is thus able to view his workaday self, grubbing away in the hope of advancement, with wry detachment, rather like the anaesthetised patient on the operating table enjoying an out-of-body experience, floating above his inert body with a grin.

Thus, his rejected petition to Mrs Thatcher to push through his Fur Labelling Order may have been just another two-a-penny example of the dashed hopes of a junior minister, but his *description* of the same event is both hilarious and charged with meaning. Tony Benn, on the other hand, is a diarist who can never view himself from above. The *Benn Diaries* are the record of a man washed along by events, all the while imagining himself to be steering them. With more detachment – more silliness, if you like – how much more true they might have been!

Why I Am Best Placed To Reunite the Tory Party

I do not need to underline the seriousness of the Conservative defeat last week. It was deeply humbling. But we must learn to take pride in the way we have been deeply humbled.

I was deeply hurt by the loss of so many of my friends and colleagues, among them the Defence Secretary, or Former Defence Secretary, as he is now. He would so love to have been writing this article for himself. But now he cannot. It grieves me greatly that he is now in the political wilderness. It must be deeply humbling.

But this is not a time to look back. It is a time to move on. But before we move on, we must look back. Because only by looking on can we move back.

As a party, we must learn from our mistakes. We must not be afraid to take a long, hard look at where we went wrong.

The Conservative Party can be tremendously proud of its achievements over the past eighteen years of government. In fact, we did nothing wrong, nothing wrong at all.

So why did the electorate put their cross in so many wrong boxes? There is one reason, and one reason alone. Poor eyesight, leading to poor eye-to-hand co-ordination. Our decision to abolish free eye tests has cost our party dear in this election. We must not let it cost us another.

The Conservatives

The task before us is daunting, but far from daunting. Although Labour won a famous victory, it attracted fewer votes than we did in 1992, and by any normal standards cannot really be said to have won at all. Conservative support in key areas – a key village just outside Tiverton, a key hamlet near Godalming, the key north-west corner of Smith Square – held strong. We fought an excellent campaign, which showed up the empty promises of Tony Blair for what they were. If it were not for the unscrupulous Labour media machine, the country would not be aware that the Conservatives have in fact scored a thumping victory, with MPs well into triple figures, policy reviews never more vigorous, and some of the best-loved members of the Cabinet still with their own seats.

What sort of Conservative Party do I hope to lead? We must not become a narrow party. Quite the opposite. We must become a wide party, very, very wide, eight, nine, even ten foot wide at its widest point, and up to twice as long.

We must tackle the European issue head-on. And there is only one way to tackle the European issue head-on: we must have the boldness, courage and humility to remember what Winston Churchill once said: 'Never do today what you can put off until tomorrow.'

During the past five years, the British people have grown sick and tired of our divisions over Europe. The values which unite us on Europe are far more important than the issues which divide us. Our party is unanimous on three crucial areas. First, Paris is the capital of France, and should remain so. Second, spaghetti can be perfectly enjoyable when taken in moderation. Third, Britain is an island, surrounded by sea. Yes. These are the areas of agreement upon which to build in the years ahead.

Crucially, we need to make people feel good about being Conservative. It is time to re-establish the connections between what we believe, what we believe we believe, what we believe the British people believe we believe, and what we need to believe if the British people need to believe that we believe what we believe they believe. It's as simple as that.

I believe I am best placed to reunite, rebuild, renew, repossess and regurgitate the Conservative Party. I was born in Britain as a child. After a brief period as a British teenager I became a British adult. And a British adult I shall always remain.

If elected leader, I promise to visit every Conservative Association in the country. And if they fail to elect me leader, I promise to visit them twice.

We must carry our message of freedom to those places which no longer wish to hear it: Scotland, Wales, the Midlands, the South, the West, the East and the North. Not forgetting all our major cities. I will lead the party not from the back or from the middle but from the front, weather permitting. I will initiate a sweeping review of policy, holding fast to our most deeply held beliefs while never being afraid to jettison them if need be.

I was a loyal member of the last government. Silently, I argued in and out of Cabinet against everything that now appears deeply humbling.

I believe John Major earned the respect and sympathy of the British people for the courage with which he dithered and the enormous dignity he brought to the task of caving in. But the time has come for a new brand of leadership. The party is crying out for a leader of my age, height and build, a leader who in many ways looks just like me. I am the only candidate who fits this description; and these are precisely the qualities which I now offer the party.

I offer energy, enthusiasm and an ability to communicate with all types of people, if I really have to. The party needs someone who is prepared to think afresh, someone who has been arguing these very same fresh new beliefs constantly in and out of government for the past twenty years.

My ministerial experience has taught me one thing above all: never be afraid to stick up for your convictions unless it is wiser not to. This is the belief that animates my resolve that fuels my values that consolidates my conviction that reinforces my belief. And one thing is certain. With me as its leader, no party has ever been better placed to transform itself into the natural party of Opposition.

Political Conjugations

I am a character
You are a loose canon
He is a drunk

I am urbane
You lack the common touch
He is a snob

I built up a sound financial base to ensure my future
independence
You sailed pretty close to the wind
He lined his pockets

I am a raconteur
You tend to go on a bit
He never knows when to stop

I am much loved
You are part of the furniture
Isn't he dead?

Mine was an error of judgement
Yours was a Greek tragedy
His was a disgraceful episode

This Is Craig Brown

I am a senior backbencher
You are an excellent constituency MP
Who on earth is *he*?

I am helpful
You are available
He is rent-a-quote

I once met Jack Kennedy
You once met Robert Kennedy
He once met Ted Kennedy

I am ebullient
You are jovial
He is obese

I am up-and-coming
You are ambitious
He is on the make

I am a safe pair of hands
You lack punch
He is a crashing bore

I am a bit of a dandy
You aren't married
He is a security risk

I engage in frank discussion
You enjoy a bit of a gossip
He runs down close colleagues

I am my own man
You are their own man
No one listens to *him*

The Conservatives

I have a colourful home life
You have a complicated home life
He forgot to use a condom

I remain loyal to my leader
You toe the party line
He is cannon-fodder

I stood up to the woman
You stood up for the woman
He let the woman walk all over him

I am a reassuring figure
You are larger-than-life
He is fat

I just want to finish what I am saying
You are having difficulty getting your point across
He won't let anyone get a word in edgeways

I am a wit
You are a lightweight
He is an alcoholic

I like to make my views clear
You like to make your views known
He likes the sound of his own voice

I am a procedural expert
You are never afraid to make a point of order
He is a pedant

I make a brave stand
You are not afraid to rock the boat
He is a troublemaker

This Is Craig Brown

I am a good listener
You use your words sparingly
He never has anything to say

I am highly intelligent
You are an intellectual
He is too clever by half

I speak their language
You make a real effort
He dumbs down

I engage in cut-and-thrust
You make a habit of interrupting
He never lets anyone get a word in edgeways

My point bears constant repetition
You have made your point perfectly clear
He goes on and on

I am a man of vision
You are a man of strong views
He looks dreadful in those new specs

I communicate
You spin
He leaks

I look to the future
You carry on as best you can
He buries his head in the sand

I say what I mean
You are outspoken
He is a loose canon

The Conservatives

I relished fresh challenges in industry
You wanted to spend more time with your family
He simply wasn't up to it

I continue to support the Government from the backbenches
You look after your constituents' interests
He is still very bitter

I am a statesman
You have an estate
He is an estate agent

I speak my mind
You speak his mind
He has nothing to say

I speak up for the silent majority
You play to the gallery
He descends to the gutter

I have a hinterland
You have a record collection
He has a colour TV

My wife is a saint
Your wife is standing by you
His wife is long-suffering

Wallace Arnold: Europe – The Case Against

It won't end there, let's be in no doubt about that. Far from it: they'll go on and on and on and on until they've spat us out of their garlicky mouths and ground this once-great nation into the dust.

Where was I? Ah, yes. Chin up, Wallace. Wipe those tears away. Big blow. And again. Deep breath. All better now. I am writing, of course, about our 'friends' (please note the inverted commas – as you may have guessed, I am no stranger to irony!!) in the EUC (European Uneconomic Community – I jest!). In the past, they have sorely tried one's patience with their absurd and priggish rulings and strictures, but new twin rulings take the proverbial biscuit.

First of all, let's recap on just a few of the past misdeeds of the paper-pushers of Brussels. As my old chauffeur, Richard Littlejohn, would say: you couldn't make it up!

In 1982, they passed a law forbidding the age-old inclusion of rabbit-dung in the traditional Cornish pasty. A year later, when a Padstow butcher was discovered harbouring a hundredweight of rabbits' droppings in his back parlour beneath a giant pastry casing, he was summarily fined £100 and forbidden from repeating the offence.

In 1988, two upstanding women, pillars of their local

community in the picture-postcard town of Petworth, West Sussex, were fined £250 apiece for chaining a passing black man to their living-room floor and forcing him to perform household tasks. 'No one had the common decency to tell us that slavery had been abolished,' complained Mrs Deirdre Cunningham, fifty-eight, to the sympathetic magistrate. 'This whole European thing is getting out of hand.'

In 1991, a retired civil servant from Shropshire, whose house was valued at £250,000 and who had worked hard all his life to send both his daughters through public school, was admonished by magistrates for taking a bullwhip to a beggar with dirty fingernails, thus contravening a ruling laid down by the European Court of Human Rights. It later emerged that the beggar was a quarter French!

In 1995, a Yorkshire mattress company was fined £500 and given a caution for filling its mattresses not with the recommended poor quality 'Eurolining' (!) but with dead ferrets – even though dead ferrets have been the traditional Yorkshire mattress-filling for over 500 years.

For over 600 years, an ancient statue of the proud people of the Isle of Man has decreed that any child between the age of eight and fifteen years of age caught stealing over two apples from any store or tree in or around the capital city of Douglas shall face a public beheading in the main square. These colourful events – no more than two or three a year – afforded the honest townsfolk a touch of pageantry to lend meaning to their otherwise routine lives. But now the executions are to be summarily stopped, by order of the so-called European Court of Human Rights – with disastrous consequences for the honest apple-growers of Douglas.

Five separate incidents, five further examples of the dread Euroboot stamping hard on the fingers of good old British individuality. And this week has brought news of two more examples of Eurolunacy. First, the Brussels bureaucrats have withdrawn the basic and inalienable right of every living Briton to carry the head of Her Majesty the Queen on his or her banknotes. Second, they have withdrawn the right of any adult to admonish a child by bringing out the strap and giving him a sound beating.

Walking through the House of Commons last week, I was upset to find my old friend and quaffing partner Mr John Redwood visibly distressed by the currency news, the tears pouring down his narrow cheeks as he sobbed 'Why, Wallace? Why? Why? Why?' Like me, John is a patriot: in the Redwood household, there is a franking machine situated by the main door to ensure that Her Majesty's profile is automatically stamped on all items brought in and out of the building, including bananas, pre-cooked meats, towels, pillowcases, electrical goods, hosiery, footwear, haberdashery and assorted skincare products.

And out on College Green, I heard a repetitive banging noise and chanced upon the shattered figure of Sir Teddy Taylor, knocking his pate against the ancient stone wall. It was the ban on corporal punishment that seemed to upset him the most. 'The writing's on the wall, Wallace,' he informed me. 'Next they'll say we're not allowed to take our machetes to troublesome teenagers and that the British bobby is to be forbidden from fibbing in court.' Sad days, indeed: and where will they end?

*

Will Mr Postie ever forgive me? Since penning my remarkable polemic against the EUC (or European Uneconomic (!!) Community) the week before last, I have received sackfuls of mail from distraught readers wondering where the dread Euroboot will stamp next, many telling tales of great British institutions and traditions brought to their knees by the Brussels bureaucrats.

Wake up Britain! A Mr R.D. Harvey from Bristol informs me that new EEC regulations outlaw the flying of the Union Jack in public places. 'When I last visited Paris,' Mr Harvey begins, 'I brought with me, as I always do, the Union Jack, 10 foot by 14 foot, that my grandfather sewed entirely from sails he had stealthily removed from boats in friends' bottles.

The Conservatives

'Yet when I parked my Hillman Sunbeam across just one lane of traffic in the Champs Elysees in order to fly my flag from a 20-foot balsa-wood pole attached to its roof, I was stopped by an irate and abusive French *gendarme*. Upon closer questioning, he informed me in no uncertain terms that it was – and I quote – "against the law" – to stop the traffic in the Champs Elysees in order to trumpet's one's pride in being British. Has it really come to this, Wallace? Are we to stand back and watch as our national identity is trampled underfoot?'

Distressing news, indeed. I, too, have first-hand experience of the French distaste for Things British. Just six months ago, I found myself dining in an expensive French restaurant outside Lyons (where, incidentally, I had been misled into believing I might find a good old-fashioned Lyons Corner House). Surveying the menu – written, needless to say, entirely in French! – I was horrified to find no mention of The Great British Banger. I summoned the head waiter (you've guessed it: a Frenchman!) and complained of the omission. 'Does – your larder,' I said, speaking very, very slowly, so that he couldn't claim not to understand me, '– not – run – to – a – guaranteed – 12 per cent – Wall's – Pork – Sausage? Eh? Eh? Speak up, man!'

On hearing that I was after a decent banger, the head waiter trotted off to his kitchen and returned with what he described, with an over-familiar kiss of his thumb and forefingers, as a Toulouse sausage. Taking my courage in both hands, I sliced the object clean in half and peered slowly inside: to my horror, it contained everything but the kitchen sink. 'Mr Wall would never permit his sausages to look like that!' I howled in outrage. 'Why, this so-called Toulouse sausage looks as if it's been made out of a pig! Away with it, man!'

Others of my correspondents have been similarly affronted by the jackbooted invasion of the Eurocrats into the foothills of our national diet. Mr Dribble, for thirty years a family butcher in Basingstoke, Hants, writes in to tell me that, following the visit of a Euro-health inspector to his premises last June, he has now received a missive telling him in no uncertain terms that, under threat of forced closure, he may no longer entertain his loyal customers by biting the heads off ducks, chickens, quails or rabbits – even though there is nothing remotely cruel about the practice, since he has always taken great care first to stun the animal with a perfectly aimed blow from his fist. 'It's the animals I feel most sorry for,' adds the genial Mr Dribble. 'I was like a father to them.'

And the Euro-horrors continue, even threatening our religious devotions. Mrs P. Robertson from Ashford in Kent, a lifelong churchgoer and devoted mother of four, writes to tell me what happened when she accompanied her local church congregation – five in all, two of them tone-deaf but the others blessed with a singular passion for the first few lines of 'All Things Bright and Beautiful' – on a tour of the cathedrals of the Rhine. 'We thought the Germans would welcome a surprise rendition of a Great British Hymn during moments when their own services went all silent,' says Mrs Robertson, 'but instead they blocked their ears – and some even ran screaming from the churches. Never have I experienced such Euro-ingratitude!'

Finally, I must alert you to the terrible tale told by Mr J. McCord of West Fife. For the past thirty-five years, come rain or shine, he has been taking tourists on fishing expeditions around the Western Isles. With only three fatalities a year (and mostly children at that) he is rightly proud of his impressive safety record. But now the EEC are insisting that his boats carry expensive notices alerting passengers to the holes in the floor – a further financial burden on an already hard-pressed business. Hard to believe – but, alas, all too true. Do keep sending me these outrageous tales of Eurolunacy. I plan to deliver them personally to Number 10 early in the New Year – if said address still exists, that is!

*

So. Even. The Danes. Have turned.

The words simply. Will not. Come out.

Oh, my God.

Deep breath, Wallace, deep breath. I am, to borrow an expression from our footballing fraternity, 'choked up'.

The Conservatives

I fear it is up to those of us who love our country – no sin, surely, even in this day and age? – to fight, fight, and fight again to uphold those values we as a nation most cherish. Warm beer. Boarding schools. Shoveha'penny. Low wages for the underpaid. Kellogg's Corn Flakes. The common cold. The short sharp shock. The Royal Family. Morris dancers. Higher penalties for those who simply cannot cope. Crosse and Blackwell. Black Rod. Bowyer's Great British Bangers. The cold shower. National Car Parks. Bernard Matthew's Turkey Roast. The musicals of Andrew Lloyd Webber. Sanatogen. Pay and display. Now Wash Your Hands. And it is up to all of us to warn the doubters of what Maastricht really means. To this end, I plan an occasional series, 'The Disagreeable Europe of Wallace Arnold' to warn of the terrors set to befall us with the Maastricht Treaty.

Clause XV11 (para 9): This is the famous 'Forcible Circumcision' Clause which will bring Britain into line with the European health and safety laws. Every British male over the age of eighteen must be circumcised by a foreign doctor with a blunt instrument – or stand to lose his car licence. The discarded foreskins will then be delivered straight to one of the European sausage factories attached to all the major European teaching hospitals, for what the Maastricht legislators euphemistically term 'product recycling'.

Clause XX111 (para 32): In the 'Readjustment of Linguistic Anomalies' section, over a thousand of our most splendid British words and phrases will be banned by the Brussels bureaucrat. I will be dealing with quite a few of these over the coming weeks, but none more painful to readers of the quality press than the compulsory use of the word 'toilet', and the consequent banning of marvellous old English words such as 'loo' 'latrine' 'gents' 'lavatory' or – my personal favourite – 'the little boy's room'. Can one imagine a man of the distinction of, say, Sir Peregrine Worsthorne being forced to say, 'I'm just off to the toilet' or 'Could you tell me the way to the toilet?' or 'I have just been to the toilet'? The very idea makes one shudder – yet that is the prospect with which we are faced, if Maastricht is signed.

This Is Craig Brown

The Domestic Animal Chapter: This widely overlooked chapter rules that a) cats, b) dogs and c) goldfish will be outlawed throughout the community. Henceforth, the only animals permitted in British households will be the gecko, the adder, the earwig, and a variety of poisonous insects, with the single exception of the dog, but only if it has been officially diagnosed as being in the final grip of rabies. This will mean that HM the Queen will no longer be seen with that delightful array of corgis trailing behind her. Instead, at the end of each of her leads will be a deathwatch beetle: hardly the same thing at all.

Subsection V1: The infamous Subsection V1, introduced by Italy in the late 1980s, demands that domestic servants and all employees in the hotel and catering trades must swear their allegiance to the Pope. Further to this, all washing machines used on British commercial premises must be filled with at least one (1) serving of incense for each rinse, in addition to the regular detergent. Employers of over twelve (12) persons must make provision for high mass to be conducted on the premises very third Wednesday in the month, with Benediction on alternate Fridays. These strictures will also apply to the entire British Rail operation. A qualified priest will occupy the buffet car on all long-distance journeys, available for blessings and light confessions. Soft drinks, snacks and refreshments must henceforth be purchased prior to the start of each journey from the designated station kiosks.

Clause X1X, section 8: In accordance with subsection B (16), the Maastricht Agreement makes compulsory the kissing of gentlemen by other gentlemen as a normal greeting in offices, factories and other places of work. If, say, I were to enter the good offices of the *Independent* for high-powered round-table discussions with my old colleague and quaffing partner Mr Andreas Whittam-Smith (dread words!) on the subject of acquisitions and mergers, I would be obliged by the treaty to give him a thorough kiss – the more vulgar might even term it a full-blown 'snog' – before getting down to business. This is, of course, what they have been obliged to do for some time now on the Continent, where up to 23 per cent of any working

319

day is taken up with the forcible exchange of saliva; but is it really a practice we wish to see established over here? Frankly, I think not, and my little friend Andreas agrees with me.

The European Toilet Act (1992): I have already explained in some detail how Maastricht will force all Britons, including Sir Peregrine Worsthorne, to refer to the lavatory, loo or what-have-you by the single word 'toilet'. But the oft-o'erlooked European Toilet Act (1992) makes it clear that this is only the tip of the all-too-proverbial iceberg. To bring British public conveniences into line with those of our European neighbours, the European Toilet Act (1992) declares that – and I translate – 'all public toilets in the Community are to be inspected regularly to check that they are in possession of a) Two (large) spiders and/beetles beneath the seat b) a pool – minimum depth 2cm – of unnamed liquid around the base and c) a door which flies open at the moment of maximum embarrassment. Failure to comply will be met with draconian fines, perhaps even imprisonment.

Clause X, paragraph vii. To demonstrate the sheer bloody-minded lunacy of this particular (or none-too-particular!) clause, might I recount an anecdote concerning a visit to my local hostelry, The Dead Dog and Maggot, only last week? The landlord, Reg, a fellow pipe-smoker and all-round decent chap, had just been paid a flying visit by a crack-squad of officials from the Department of Health. To his utter astonishment, they insisted that his excellent 'Ploughman's Lunches' did not comply with European Health Standards. 'And why not, prithee?' said Reg, taking a good old puff on his trusty pipe. The officials had the sheer nerve to say they objected to the mixture of tobacco and phlegm that formed a coating over the pickle in the Ploughman's Lunch. 'But there's nowt wrong with that,' protested Reg. 'It came from me own mouth, fresh this morning!' Flying in the face of such evidence, they issued Reg with a Gestapo-style warning: no phlegm in future, or the pub closes.

Extraordinary – yet this is the grim world in which we shall find ourselves, if ever the Maastricht Treaty is signed. Beware, Britons, Beware!

I'm Backing Britain

In this first draft of his speech to the Centre for Policy Studies, *'Who Am I and What Am I Doing Here?', the Rt Hon William Hague MP, Leader of the Conservative Party, addresses the question of British identity, posing such important questions as 'Where Has It Gone?', 'Where Did You Last See It?' and 'But Didn't You Have It Last?'*

I want to talk to you about Britain. Britain at the cusp of a new millennium. And, like all cusp – tea cusp or coffee cusp – this one has to hold water. And let me assure you of this. We are in hot water. And we are in it deep.

Britain now. A Britain of bustling cities, thriving communities, a British countryside full of crops that are growing day and night, a British coastline full to the brim with well-salted sea. A Britain of new technologies, ambitious businesses and tremendously exciting arts opportunities. *Chariots of Fire*. *Cats*. And that one with the girl from *The Larkins*.

And I want to talk to you about the British people. A very public people – and at the same time intensely private. A mature people, full of youthful zest. A philanthropic people who believe you don't get something for nothing. A tolerant, outward-looking, multi-ethnic people who simply can't abide being told what to do by a bunch of foreigners who have no right to stick their noses into other people's business.

A people with a strong sense of who we are and where we have got to and where we have come from in order to get where we have got to. A people who know we have got to where we are not by stopping and asking the way but by carrying on in a straight line in the hope that we will get there in the end. A people confident of ourselves. A people not afraid, upon sighting a pedestrian, to stop the car and give him directions.

My speech today has two purposes. The first is to show that as a people, the British both is and are literate. The third is to show that we are numerate. And the sixth is to get in touch with the identity of the British people. Who am I? Who are you? And who the giddy heck is he?

It is my profoundest belief that if the Conservative Party is not in touch with the identity of the British people then it cannot be authentically Conservative. And it is my second most profound belief that to know what it is to be Conservative, you must know what it means to be British. To be Conservative means to be British. But what does it mean to be British? Yes, it means to be Conservative.

Over the past year, we have been Listening to Britain. In a series of meetings up and down this great country of ours, Conservative MPs have been turning up in their hundreds to listen to what an ordinary, decent Briton has to say. And now that he has at last finished speaking, let me tell him this. Yes, thank you, we've got the message. The message has been coming through loud and clear. If we've heard it once, we've heard it a thousand times. You can stop speaking now. I said, you can stop speaking now. And if we want your advice, we'll ask for it.

I want to talk to you about The British Way. The British Way for the Twenty-First Century. It is time for the Conservative Party to rise to the challenge, take a great leap into the future, grasp the nettle while the iron's hot, and step forward with our backs to the wheel and both feet firmly on the ground.

We want a modern, British approach to all that the new century has to offer. But first we must be clear what being British is – and why it matters. When we talk about the British, we are talking about more than just the Scottish, English and

Welsh. There's the Isle of Man, for instance. Anglesey. Eigg. Guernsey. Gibraltar. Maidenhead. Cornwall can be lovely at this time of year. But we must remember to wrap up well.

Together, we are a nation of small, close-knit families. Few other families are so close. And few other families are such knits. Our British individualism expresses itself in many forms. We like staying in. And we like to go out. We like chatting to other people. And we like a bit of time to ourselves. We like to go on holiday. But after a while it's always nice to be home. We like roaring log fires. But we appreciate the convenience of a fully integrated central heating system. We work hard. But we're not afraid to put our feet up. We are a nation of eccentrics. And we have a healthy distrust for those who go out of their way to be different. We want to stand on our own two feet. And we appreciate a bit of a leg-up. We are Conservative to the core. And we vote for New Labour.

The Labour Party would have us believe that British history began in 1997. Wrong. King Alfred and the Cakes. Good Queen Bess. The Battle of Waterloo. Dunkirk. These all took place under the last Conservative government.

The Conservative Party must offer the people an alternative to New Labour's so-called Third Way: a British Way founded on the experiences of the British people. The British people do not want The Turkish Way or The French Way. Those ways may be all right for the Turkish and the Frenchish. But they're not all right for the British.

Conservatives must embrace Britain as it is today and as it will be tomorrow, not as it was yesterday morning, nor as it might be at lunchtime the day after tomorrow. Not just the sleepy villages, cock-fighting, friendly vicars, cricket on summer lawns, kiddies up chimneys, warm ale, headless bodies in leather suitcases and the novels of Scott and Austen that have always been Britain. But also the modern, brassy Britain, the Britain where thousands flock to the Notting Hill Carnival in baseball caps and smart/casual wear to exchange pleasantries with the local coppers, the Britain which likes to jive to the latest top tunes from the hit parade, the Britain which gives three cheers to Bobby Moore and the boys for their magnificent victory in the World Cup, the Britain which declares loud and clear, 'I'm Backing Britain!' before hopping into its Hillman Minx for a smashing night out in front of the colour TV.

The future is very exciting. The future is what will happen next. For all its undoubted qualities, the past has already happened. And it's not going to happen again. The present is not the past, but nor is it the future. Statistics show it's somewhere in between.

I'm hugely optimistic for the future. The world is at our feet. But I'm also deeply pessimistic. It's high time the world got off our feet and left us to our own devices. Mr Blair is holding a dagger to the heart of what it is to be British. If he is left unchecked, he will drive it right through that heart, over and over again, in a frenzy of murder and mayhem.

A dismembered Britain, a Britain on a pathologist's slab, a Britain awaiting identification by close relatives. Is that what we want? Is that really The British Way?

Wallace Arnold: Not a Good Day

1 May 1997. Not a good day for the Conservative Party, I regret to say. I know this only too well, as some two weeks previously the estimable John Major had placed me in charge of our Conservative victory celebrations. I had spent the day sellotaping brightly coloured balloons to the walls of Smith Square, preparing the jellies and the fancy cakes, hiring the song-and-dance troupe and the hypnotist, lining up the crackers, putting John through his paces in rehearsing his victory speech and generally making sure everything was shipshape for a tremendous bash.

And a tremendous bash is, I fear, exactly what we were given. Throughout the day, Dr Mawhinney had been cock-a-hoop. 'We've walloped 'em!' he would chuckle, 'Yes – we've given that Mr Blair a bloody nose he certainly won't be forgetting in a hurry!' But as the results began to trickle in, Dr Mawhinney's grin began to falter. At first, he was desperately 'upbeat' (dread word!). 'Guildford's no indication at all!' he said, as the first results came through. 'Surrey's always been a Stalinist heartland.' But when the news of Mr Portillo's defeat filtered through, even the good doctor began to realise things had gone pear-shaped.

His reaction to defeat was, I suppose, all too predictable in a man so highly strung. He went straight to his desk, pulled out a long, thin pin, and went around each and every office popping all the brightly coloured balloons in what can only have been described as a fit of real temper. 'We don't need these crackers any more!' he said, flinging them out of the window of Smith Square on to the waiting cameramen. 'And you can tell that lot to go hang themselves!' he bellowed, pointing coarsely at the assembled company of Black and White Minstrels who were at that point in the midst of rehearsing a spirited rendition of 'The Yellow Rose of Texas'.

By 3.00 in the morning, the balloons had all been popped, the jellies and fancy cakes binned, the crackers defenestrated, the Minstrels sent packing. John Major's victory speech lay crumpled in the wagger-pagger and the press and television people had all moved on to the Labour Party's gaudy, ill-mannered celebrations in the Festival Hall. Senior Ministers were arriving in their dribs and drabs to pay their last respects to an abandoned administration. I am not much given to 'atmosphere', but in retrospect I feel pretty sure I sensed a note of disappointment in the building.

'Ding-Dong!' It was the doorbell! 'Whoever it is, tell them to go take a running jump!' said Dr Mawhinney, pounding his head in rage and despair. I unlatched the front door of Smith Square. 'Hi!' said a beaming figure. 'I believe you were expecting me!'

'You believed wrongly,' I snapped. 'Name?'

'Paul McKenna,' he replied. 'Stage hypnotist. You hired me for the victory celebrations. Regrettably, there was no cancellation agreement.'

'I suppose you'd better come in,' I sighed.

I led Mr McKenna through to the main room where most of those who had, until a few hours ago, constituted Her Majesty's Government now sat around, dishevelled and dejected.

'Who the bloody hell are—' began Dr Mawhinney, staring into McKenna's piercing eyes, purple-faced with rage. But then, all of a sudden, his face took on a serene, almost benevolent expression, and he emitted what sounded to my ears like the purr of a kitten.

'You are feeling sleeee-peeeeeey,' said McKenna. 'When I click my fingers, you will do whatever I saaaaaay!' He then clicked his fingers, and all the assembled Ministers sprung swiftly to attention.

For the first twenty minutes or so, McKenna put them through assorted high jinks. Michael Howard was made to dance the can-can in his sauciest manner, Virginia Bottomley quacked like a duck, Michael Heseltine began to sing the praises of the Millennium Dome, and, yelling 'Get it on' and strumming an invisible guitar, poor William Waldegrave gave every impression of believing he was the late Marc Bolan. Meanwhile, John Major was prancing about in a tutu, Kenneth Clarke, having convinced himself he was a Twix bar, had begun to chew his own right hand, and the young William Hague, cigar between his teeth, was repeating 'We shall fight them on the beaches . . .' over and over again.

'And when I click my fingers,' said McKenna, warming to his task, 'you will all go into a deep, deep sleep for the next ten years.' And with that he clicked his fingers and exited. At the time, one thought it all good fun. But could this tomfoolery have had some more lasting effect? One does hope not.

There's a Good Baby

What would you do to get on telly? And once on telly, what wouldn't you do? Earlier this week, I just happened, ahem, ahem, to be watching an ITV documentary called *Vice – the Sex Trade*. A prostitute called Leila, married to a man in computers, was entertaining a client in her front room. He was a caterer from Surrey called Rick, quite portly, in his forties, with a goatee beard.

All went well until Leila began taking off Rick's clothes. At this stage, I imagined the cameras would stop whirring when she got down to his underpants, and when they didn't I imagined that a discreetly positioned potted plant would block out the view, and when it didn't I imagined there would at least be an ad-break and when there wasn't I began to thank goodness I wasn't a major shareholder in Surrey catering.

In the old days, faced with something untoward on the box, an adult would leap up and say, 'I think *The Black and White Minstrels* are on the other side.' But these days I am the adult, and my curiosity is unfettered. I didn't know where to look, so I looked even harder at the television.

First, the naked Rick (or 'my baby' as Leila called him) was washed and powdered, then he was placed in an XL nappy ('we had a bit of an accident last time, didn't we?') and then he was breast-fed and winded ('there's a good baby') and cradled by Leila. From the look of it, there was a remote-control camera in the room and the film crew were huddled around a monitor in a van parked out the back. But Rick must have been aware that he would soon be parading his secret fantasy before millions of viewers.

So why did he go through with it? It couldn't have been the money. His appearance fee might have been in the upper hundreds, but I doubt it was much more. Being a caterer, perhaps he imagined that this was how TV chefs get their big break, and that a five-minute slot on *Vice – The Sex Trade* might prove an invaluable springboard for a guest appearance on *Ready Steady Cook*. Perhaps he felt he was striking a blow for the liberation of sexual infantilists the world over, and that Mothercare would soon have no alternative but to open an adults-only section. But I suspect that the real reason he agreed to appear was not far removed from the reason the rest of us agreed to watch. Television induces a deep schizophrenia in both the watcher and the watched: on the one hand, we think to ourselves that we are not really watching, and on the other hand, they think to themselves that they are not really appearing.

If you had asked me that morning whether I would care to spend my evening sitting in the corner of a prostitute's bedroom watching a Surrey caterer being breast-fed in his nappies, I would have been most affronted. 'What sort of person do you take me for?' I would have yelled as I grabbed you by the collar and frogmarched you to the door. Yet that is exactly how I spent my evening, with just a thin glass screen separating me from reality. I would guess that much the same level of double-think was going on in the mind of the Surrey caterer: on one level, he knew that he was being filmed, but on another level he was able to imagine that he wasn't.

Anyone who has been on television, from the most dumb-struck participant on *Kilroy* to a benighted serial-presenter like Sir David Frost, knows that the experience is at the same time both real and unreal. A chirpy young call girl on the same documentary, obviously revelling in being on camera, confided that her parents didn't know what she got up to. Yet she was far from stupid: deep down, she would have known that her secret would be out the moment it was broadcast. But for those few minutes, she was a TV star, and the rest of her life was an illusion.

The attraction of being on the small screen is undeniable and virtually irresistible. Even when I am queuing in my local Victoria Wine, I find my eyes straying up towards the small black and white security screen. 'Oooh! That's me!' I think, and I am unnaturally gratified to find myself duplicated, even in this humble arena. And I bet Sir David Frost likes to sneak a look at himself on these shop screens: television does not quench the yearning to appear on it, but inflames it, so that the television personality feels fully alive only when the studio monitor has his face on it. And we are all guilty: I remember a producer of *This Is Your Life* saying he never had to worry about guests from any walk of life failing to arrive at the studio on time: the lure of being on telly carried its own guarantee.

One of the strangest places in the world is surely the Green Room of a live TV magazine programme, where everyone awaits their turn before being led into the studio. A few months ago, I was on *This Morning with Richard and Judy*. (Even writing that sentence gives me a warm glow. In fact, though they still appeared in the title, the real Richard and Judy were on holiday, and had been deftly replaced by pretenders to their title). In the Green Room, the various studio guests gingerly sipped coffee and stared in silence at the telly screen, beamed live from the studio along the corridor. There was a chef, an agony aunt, the actress Imogen Stubbs, a waitress, a taxi driver, a clairvoyant, some sort of fashion expert and me. In the corner nearest the door sat a burly, bald-headed man. 'What do you do?' I asked him. 'I'm a former football hooligan,' he replied.

The odd thing about that Green Room was that, though everyone watched their fellow guests as they appeared on the screen, none of them displayed the faintest interest in each other in the flesh. Even when a troupe of male models clad only in lime-green posing-pouches marched out of the studio and into that Green Room, no one gave them a second glance. We all preferred them on telly. Life, I concluded, is far less interesting than television, even when the two are divided only by a corridor.

I have a friend who envies anyone who has ever been on television. She believes that in future scientists may be able to resurrect the dead from the TV images they have left behind. She hasn't yet worked out whether this resurrection will be restricted to those parts of the body once exhibited on screen. But there is certainly a danger that newscasters, say, will be revived only from the waist up, and that to move about they will have to place what remains of their bodies on skateboards, manoeuvring themselves around with their hands. Perhaps we are now in the realm of science fiction, but the image is apt. One is permitted on television only in a simplified and bisected form, stoked by temporary amnesia: the expert forgets he has doubts, the personality forgets he lacks personality, the victim forgets he has self-control, the prostitute forgets she's a daughter, and, in the delirium of the telly brothel, the man in nappies forgets that, one it's all over, he'll somehow have to go on being a caterer in Surrey.

Bel Littlejohn: I Fell in Love with a Chicken

Accessibility is my watchword. As I can't say too often to my clients in the media, you might have created the greatest work of art of all time in the world ever, but if less than two million poor sods get to see it, what's the bloody point, then, love?

I have a helluva lot of time for one of our most valued clients, the lovely Michael Jackson of Channel 4. His old boss at the Beeb, Sir John Birt, taught him to keep the following flow chart in his head at all times: C + A = B, or, in laymen's terms, Credibility Plus Accessibility Equals Buzz.

Credibility is a word that needs no explanation from me. It's the bedrock of broadcasting, and let's hope it remains that way. Broadly speaking, it means 'what you can get away with'. But accessibility is a more complicated animal, incorporating a lot of highly innovative, diverse and relevant concepts in an over-all structure of programming values. Pulled out of the air, words Michael and I associate with accessibility include 'partnership with the audience', 'strong language', 'clitoris', 'prostitution', 'widespread concern', 'Thailand', 'respon-sibility', 'Courtney Love', 'dildo', 'penis', 'cunnilingus', and 'talking frankly'. After all, we're all grown-ups.

With major new Channel 4 series on church architecture

This Is Craig Brown

(*Women Who Make Love In The Confessional: An Investigation*), zoology (*I Fell in Love with a Chicken*) and birdwatching (*As Nature Intended: Twitching in the Nude with Bill Oddie*), we have a highly innovative and accessible spring season of documentaries upcoming. Meanwhile, our drama schedules have never looked stronger, never more relevant. For instance, our keynote drama series *Brookside* will continue to hold a mirror up to society, with hard-hitting storylines exploring the changing role of women in society (Beverly enters the twilight world of prostitution), personal fulfilment (Linda explores her sexuality in the shower with Chairman), psychological challenges (Darren's D-I-Y sex-change ends in tears) and man's relationship with nature (things take a turn for the worse when Frank is caught by Louise with a distraught hamster concealed in his underwear).

Major new drama on Channel 4 includes the six-part series *Scrubbers*. Set in a Tyneside strip-club, it is a no-holds-barred indictment of a male-dominated world, with full-frontal nudity, lengthy hand-held close-ups of naked breasts, strong language and a number of disturbing shots of all-over body massage that may offend some viewers. Fulfilling our commitment to quality broadcasting, we will also premiere a striking new production of Ibsen's *A Doll's House*, with Samantha Janus as the doll.

Small wonder, then, that with the re-invigoration of Channel 4 behind us, my company 'Bel and Frendz' has been approached by the lovely Greg Dyke to work our magic on the BBC schedules. 'You've got a massive 98 per cent brand recognition, Greg,' I told him, straight up, when he checked into our intensive two-day media workshop last weekend, 'and that's something to build on. On the other hand, we have a downside: viewers have told us that the BBC is still "authoritative", "intelligent", "principled" and – I hate to say it, Greg – "decent". And that translates as *stuffy, old-fashioned, irrelevant and inaccessible*. Yes, Greg, we have a problem on our hands.'

But Greg's a quick learner, and it didn't take him long to

work out that the best way forward is to build on our assets. This means directing additional resources to re-branding some of our existing programmes. The autumn schedules are still in a process of formulation, but I'm delighted to say we have already approached Graham Norton to replace Joan Bakewell as the presenter of our prestige religious documentary series, *The Heart of the Matter*. Filming on the first two programmes, *The Church of England – Should Female Vicars Go Topless?* and *A Spiritual Buzz: The Role of the Vibrator in Christianity* will begin in late June.

Other progs to get a makeover include Delia Smith's *How to Slag Out* in which Delia lets her hair down on a Club 18–30 holiday with half a bottle of rum and a whole range of fun recipes involving bananas and pineapple rings; also old favourites like *Blue Peter*, in which, for the first time ever Peter himself will appear – and viewers will be able to find out exactly why they call him 'Blue'!!!! Meanwhile, the cut and thrust of contemporary politics will continue to be covered by much-loved series such as *Question Time* jointly chaired by David Dimbleby and Ulrika Jonsson, with the introduction of a one-item-of-clothing forfeit for every hesitation, repetition or deviation. Stuffy? No. Accessible? Yes. And that's the way – uh-huh, uh-huh – I like it!

Bel Littlejohn: How Does it Feel?

My daytime talk show, *Bel!* is now in its tenth year, can you believe it. It's won accolades throughout the industry and beyond. Only last year, I stepped up to receive a 'Golden Heart' award from the Bulimia Society at a twelve-course gala meal held outside Jane Asher's cake shop, and I've twice won the Caring Presenter of the Year Award from the Society of Manic Depressives, though sadly on both occasions the dinner had been cancelled at the last minute owing to indisposition.

Of course, when *Bel!* was first broadcast, way back in March 1989, we were pioneers, so we had to tread very, very carefully indeed. It's easy to forget it, but at that time the problems we tackled were truly ground-breaking – 'My Pocket Has a Hole In It', 'My Mother-in-Law Is a Vegetarian', 'My Son Received Two Parking Tickets in a Month and I'm Up To My Neck in Housework', 'My Boyfriend Has a Slight Lisp', 'I Find It Quite Difficult to Open Milk Cartons'. Yet by today's standards they probably seem tame.

It was in the early 1990s that we began to expand our remit. Competition in the shape of my good friends Kilroy and Esther, bless them, was beginning to breathe down our necks, and frankly the prog. was in danger of becoming stale. For instance, we had covered the problem of hip replacements on fourteen separate programmes, from every conceivable angle – 'My Girlfriend's Had a Hip Replacement' (August '89), 'My

Boyfriend's Had a Hip Replacement' (June, '90), 'My Mother's Still Waiting for a Hip Replacement' (November '90), 'My Sister Doesn't Need a Hip Replacement' (January '91), etc, etc – and there was a definite feeling around the production office that the time had come to move on.

Frankly, we wanted a lot more pain. Turning our eyes to the competition, we realised that, statistically speaking, Kilroy was achieving one guest in tears every third programme. We resolved to achieve a proportion of one in two within the space of the next three months. For the first prog of the new series, 'My Hip Replacement is Causing Me Slight Pain', we experimented with recreating that pain for the cameras. Out of shot, I would surreptitiously kick the hips of the guests – caringly but firmly – and the viewer was thus able to empathise with their pain. By the end of the first week, our major show, 'My Doggy Has Just Been Shot Dead by a TV Researcher' had received no fewer than four guests in tears and one in a full-scale nervous breakdown. We had grabbed the headlines, the ratings had soared, and we were over the proverbial moon. But ratings aren't everything: as our press release made clear, we were all proud to have confronted a major problem facing many ordinary people in our society, and we called on government to press ahead urgently with legislation to make sure that nothing like this ever happened again.

From that moment on, the *Bel!* programme led the way. With my hand-held mike clutched compassionately to my chest, I would rush from cross-dresser ('How does it *feel*?') to serial-adulterer ('Tell me, how does it *feel*?') and back again via racist hooligan ('Sorry, but I've got to ask you: how exactly does it *feel*?'), determined to confront all the major issues in a sympathetic fashion.

We never shied from controversy. In September, 1993, we hit the headlines after screening a special programme in which, with great compassion, we tackled disability head-on. A blind man, a deaf man and a mute man were featured live. To help them overcome their nerves, bless them, our lovely researcher, Sue, took them to one side just before the programme began.

Sue mentioned to the blind guy that the mute guy had been making rude gestures in his direction, then she told the deaf guy that the blind guy had been saying nasty things behind his back, and finally she confided to the mute guy that the deaf guy had just about had enough of his whispering campaign. Within minutes, we had a full-scale on-screen fight on our hands as they confronted the demons in themselves. 'Hey! Guys, guys! Break it up!' I urged, but sadly I was holding the mike away from my mouth at the time. Our rating were the best ever, and I ended with an urgent and compassionate plea to the government to call a halt to battles raging within the disabled community. But on the crest of a wave, a new and terrible threat appeared: the fraud. I'll be back after the break.

Nothing Worth Watching: The Memoirs of Marmaduke Hussey

CHAPTER ONE: THE FIRST CHAPTER

It's a funny old world, isn't it? Which makes one all the more grateful one is in charge of it.

One evening, I was warming my slippers in front of the log fire when I turned to my wife.

'There's a funny sort of ringing in my ears,' I complained.

'It's the telephone, Duke,' she explained.

'But why on earth would anyone put a telephone in my ears?' I countered.

She passed me the receiver. Someone was talking on the other end. For the life of me I couldn't hear a word he was saying.

'Put the telephone to your ears, Dukie, and you'll be able to hear him,' my wife, who is tremendously up to speed on these matters, advised.

It was the Home Secretary calling. Douglas Hurd was my godson, and still ran the occasional errand for me.

'Oh, Dukie, how would you like to be in charge of the BBC?' he asked.

'BBC?' I said. '. . . Remind me.'

'Broadcasting. Radio, telly, that sort of hoodjamaflip.'

'To be perfectly frank, Douglas,' I said, 'I've got absolutely no use for a telly. I mean, where would one put it?'

'But you don't have to *buy* a television, Dukie – you just have to be in *charge* of it.'

'You've convinced me,' I said, and went to sleep.

CHAPTER TWO: THE NEXT CHAPTER

'Is there anything I need to know about the BBC?' I asked my deputy chairman.

He was obviously impressed. He rightly sensed that I would leave no stone unturned in my bid to get on top of things.

'Anything good on the box tonight?' I said, flicking through the *Radio Times*. It was a phrase I had picked up at a top-level briefing the day before. Mastering the technical language was half the battle won.

Taken aback by my command of the essentials, he told me that there wasn't much on at all. 'Then I think we both deserve a jolly good lunch,' I replied, reserving a table for two at the Berkeley Grill.

A few weeks later, I had already mastered the basics of television. It came on when you pressed the little button on the bottom left, and you switched 'channels' by pressing the little buttons to the right. To turn the sound up, one looked to the 'vol' button – but this was purely voluntary, as the name suggested.

CHAPTER THREE: THE STORY CONTINUES

Over many years, I have learnt that there is no point in being in charge if you can't fire someone. But who wasn't pulling his weight? The BBC was a self-indulgent organisation, filled with people entertaining friends and family at the licence-payers' expense. To put a stop to this cavalier behaviour, I needed top-class advice. So I invited my son-in-law, my wife, my nephew, my godson and my old nanny (who was by now Chancellor to the Duchy of Lancaster) out to a really first-rate lunch at the BBC table at Claridges.

By the end of that magnificent repast, we were at our wit's end over who to fire. 'I know,' said the head waiter, a marvellous old character with a great deal of wisdom in that head of his. 'Why not fire the Director-General?'

I left the fellow a handsome tip that day, before asking for a receipt.

I returned to the BBC knowing what I had to do. The Director-General had shown every sign of taking me for a fool. Little did he realise this was a cunning ploy. I have always enjoyed being thought an utter fool. It is a brilliant double-bluff: I am far more stupid than they think.

My rule for these difficult situations has always been the same. Be clear, decisive and fast – but for goodness sake to nothing if half of you thinks that might be better in the long run.

CHAPTER FOUR: AN END TO WORDS

The departing Director-General was a man of great personal charm and immense ability, but with one fatal flaw: he was the sort of person one simply couldn't help firing. Once I had done the deed, I felt I had earned a jolly good lunch. Over roast partridge with all the trimmings, I mentioned to Arnold Goodman that I had just fired the D-G.

'Now you'll have to appoint another one,' he commented over a second helping of lemon meringue pie.

This came as a bolt from the blue. Who on earth would fit the bill? My wife was busy getting to grips with her needlepoint. My nephew had moved from the treasury to take over the National Theatre. And my old nanny was still finding her feet as First Admiral of the Fleet.

The Deputy D-G was known to be a stuffed shirt, lacking any sort of vision. He struck me as just the sort of man we needed. I appointed him at once. Like all my decisions, it was one I was to live to regret.

CHAPTER FIVE: SOME MEMORABLE CALVES LIVER

I had been Chairman of the BBC for two months when I arranged to meet Douglas Hurd at an excellent little restaurant in Ebury Street. I was only too well aware that there would be some tough negotiations ahead.

'Now, Douglas,' I said, 'first things first.'

Douglas paused. 'Agreed,' he replied. I breathed a secret sigh of relief. If he had stuck in his heels at this stage and demanded that second things be first, or – worse – first things be second, I might have faced a lot of tough bargaining. But even before the soup had arrived, he had conceded everything I had been holding out for! I decided to press ahead with further demands.

'Douglas,' I continued, 'I want to just clear with you the conditions of this lunch. These are my demands. I suggest we talk to one another, occasionally placing food in our own mouths until we have finished what is on our plates and it is time to go. What say you?'

He agreed without a murmur. My strategy had paid off. I was running rings around the Government! Of course, many of my critics had put me down as some sort of 'Thatcher placeman'. Nothing could have been further from the truth. As Chairman, it was my job to fight the BBC's cause against the Government well into the first course of any meal. After that, I would see which way the wind blew. But one thing was absolutely vital: I had to safeguard the BBC from Government cutbacks.

'Tell me, Ducky,' said Douglas.

'Dukie.' I believe in standing firm.

'Tell me, Dukie, exactly how strapped for cash is the BBC?'

At that point, my main course arrived – a delicious dish of calves liver with rosemary. I felt it was time to make a concession. 'There are rivers of gold running through the corridors of Broadcasting House,' I said, washing it all down with a decent claret. 'Don't give it a thought, Douglas. I say, this liver really is top hole.'

The rest of our meal went swimmingly. Sticking strictly to my pre-arranged tactics, I agreed to reduce the output of the BBC over a period of five years to a hospital radio service in the Leicestershire area. In return, Douglas would reduce our licence fee to something more manageable, and I would replace our Managing Director with someone more incompetent. I told

Douglas I had heard that we may be able to attract Basil Brush, the up-and-coming glove-puppet, to fill the post. Brush had a reputation for being hands-on, I observed. Douglas nodded approvingly.

At this point I judged it strategic to order a *tarte tatin*. Douglas gazed on admiringly. Like Margaret Thatcher, he respected those who were prepared to take a stand.

CHAPTER SIX: ARMAGNAC TO FINISH

'It's the general sloppiness of the BBC I find so hard to stomach,' I said, licking my napkin and dabbing at some cream on my tie. 'Not to mention the complacency.' I leant back in my chair, slipped off my shoes and gave myself a well-earned pat on the back. Not for the first time, I was putting my head above the parapet, placing a gun to my head and steadfastly refusing to duck. I may have been strengthened in my resolve by a couple of glasses of whisky.

The *tarte tatin* proved quite excellent. If I had any lingering concerns, I couldn't for the life of me remember them. Instead, I stood firm.

'I demand an answer, Douglas.'

'But how can I?' he remonstrated. 'You haven't asked a question.'

'Are you saying I haven't asked a question?' I countered.

'Well, you have now.'

I had him exactly where I wanted him. I had been at this game for years and knew how to handle it. 'Then what was it, Douglas? What was the question I asked?'

It soon became clear he had no idea.

CHAPTER SEVEN: AFTERNOON TEA BECKONS

Lunchtime gave way to teatime. 'I think we might just manage a few sandwiches,' I observed, cautiously. Douglas was in total agreement. Over years in negotiation, I have found that a sandwich affords a welcome bridge between one meal and the next.

I had reached the final stage of my game plan. I was more

determined than ever to push ahead with my plans for change. The D-G wanted to change too slowly; his Deputy wanted to change too fast. But I was determined to steer a middle course. 'It's audacious but it might just work,' I confided to Douglas, as I signalled to the waiter for a scone. 'We must plough ahead with *no change at all*!'

Bel Littlejohn: The Freedom to Censor

AS an artist (maybe even – who knows? – a great artist, or so the experts tell me) I have long been at the forefront of the campaign for total freedom of speech, within acceptable limits. Censorship? It should be banned.

Can it really be over a quarter of a century since I first made my name as a key witness for the defence in the *Oz* trials? My appearance in court certainly made an impact. I boldly spoke up for the three defendants' inalienable right to place a giant penis on the figure of Rupert Bear for the special schoolkids edition of *Oz*. 'I regard that penis as one of the most powerful and beautiful statements in the whole of twentieth-century literature,' I said, going on to describe it as 'a touching and very moving testament to the glory of a child's sexuality'. Within days, I had become one of the most sought-after experts in the whole field of anti-oppression, telephoned day and night by senior producers of radio and television programmes desperate for my tough and uncompromising views.

What a year 1971 was! The next month, I was back in the media spotlight again, this time bravely defending Sam Peckinpah's controversial movie *Straw Dogs* from the insensitive scissors of the censors. In just one week, I was on three separate programmes, including Ken Tynan's *Lunchbox*, vociferously defending that famous scene in which Susan George is sexually assaulted by four nameless villagers. 'To my mind,' I said, 'It's one of the most powerful and moving scenes in the entire history of twentieth-century film. What Peckinpah is showing us, surely, is not just some sort of "mindless rape", but rather a metaphor, even a paradigm, and arguably even a symbol for the direction in which our post-Imperial society is going. It's shocking, yes – but then rape *is* shocking.'

And on BBC 1's *Nationwide* with Michael Barratt, I bitterly attacked those who claimed cinema could in any way influence the actions of viewers. 'No one in their right mind would think that!' I argued eloquently, defending freedom of expression against an old person who had been wheeled on by the National Viewers and Listeners Association to spout the usual geriatric rubbish. 'And frankly you have no right to say it.'

It was just a few months later that Stanley Kubrick's great masterpiece *A Clockwork Orange* was released, accompanied by the all-too-predictable calls for it to be banned. On a *Late Night Line Up* panel of experts with Sir Gerald Nabarro, Lord Patrick Lichfield and Leapy Lee, I singled out for particular praise the scene where Malcolm McDowell repeatedly kicks the crippled old man in the face while – and this was a brilliant touch by a master craftsman – simultaneously performing 'I'm Singing' in the Rain'. 'For me,' I said, 'this is one of the most powerful and sensitive moments in twentieth-century cinema. For Kubrick, that kick is not only a symbol and a metaphor but also a stunning indictment. Surely what he is really saying is that the old man stands for a worn-out, crippled Britain, which is being kicked aside by something new and vibrant and modern and, to me at any rate, very, very exciting.'

Twenty-seven years on, and I'm still known as our most passionate defender of freedom of expression, often appearing on *Talk Radio* at 3am to put forward my views. If anything, I've grown even more determined to preserve free speech from those who seek to undermine it. For instance, on the *Today* programme only yesterday I was passionately defending the rights of those of us who are sick to death of the gratuitous sexism rampant in television's salacious *Baywatch*. 'By focusing solely on women as sexual creatures, the makers of this disgraceful programme are helping to create a society in which it is impossible for a woman to walk down a street without fear of assault. It is a wholly cynical attack on the essential freedoms for which I have fought throughout my life. Frankly, it should not be allowed on our screens.'

I am also, of course, a leading light in CAOSS, the Campaign Against On-Screen Smoking. I see it as our duty to safeguard future generations from being prey to one of the most extensive abuses of freedom of expression in our history, namely the glamorisation of harmful tobacco by Hollywood. Next month, I will be handing a petition to my good friend Chris Smith calling for a total ban on films and television programmes containing scenes involving the smoking of all tobacco products. But I don't want any medals for it. After all, someone's got to defend the multi-national assault on free speech, so it might as well be me.

Wallace Arnold: Remembering Esther

Unhappy days, indeed. For twenty-one good-hearted years, Esther and her highly polished young men have had us in fits with their doughty mix of journalistic endeavour, wit, sunshine and old-fashioned British fun (incidentally, that's a word you don't hear much these days).

Twenty-one years . . . ah, memories! Who can forget those hilariously appropriate names such as Mr BARBER, the hairdresser (or 'barber'!!) from Teddington? Equally amusing were Mrs BROWN, who helped in a sun-lamp shop in East Molseley, Mr SPENDER, the tax collector from Manchester and – if you can believe it! – Miss WHITE the laundress from Potters Bar. Priceless, one and all.

And still alive in the memory are those marvellously ordinary old women, rich in Cockney character, high spirits and honest-to-goodness stupidity, whom Esther would somehow chance upon during her delightfully light-hearted consumer-tests in the streets of London. For me, the star was that splendid old dear who, when Esther handed her something gooey to taste, quipped, 'Gorblimey, Esther, it tastes like cat's droppings!!!' – only to be informed that this was exactly what it was! Say what you like about Esther but she was always prepared to let ordinary, everyday, normal, working-class (let's be frank, in many ways thoroughly boring) people have their say on prime-time television – the only condition being that they had to swallow something disgusting before-hand!

The contests, too, were an absolute must, full of healthy British jocularity, particularly the famous 'Root Vegetable' competitions, in which, as far as I can remember, each of the presenters sat behind his – or her! – desk and we, the audience, had to guess whether they more closely resembled a carrot, parsnip or other root vegetable. And – on a more serious note! – let's never allow ourselves to forget some of the admirable campaigns championed by Esther and her hard-working crew. For instance, after a 52-year-old mother-of-three from Penge mistook a chain-saw for a banana, receiving severe cuts to the mouth and chin, Esther campaigned for years on end to have all chain-saws sold in Great Britain and Northern Ireland clearly labelled 'Unsuitable for Eating'.

When this proved unsuccessful, she launched a secondary *That's Life!* campaign – equally doughty – to urge the Government to label all bananas unsuitable for cutting hedges. 'A great many people – some of them senior citizens, others hard of hearing – are going to face grave disappointment this year when they come to cut their hedges only to discover that their brand-new banana is simply not up to the job,' she sighed. I'm happy to report that the present Government has at last sat up and taken notice, and that the Citizen's Charter will carry provision for the labelling of all bananas, including those used in fruit salads, milk-shakes, 'splits' and the like, and that a Bananawatch Line is at this very moment being set up for those who experience any sort of trouble with bananas and/or citrus fruits. Well done, Esther!

On a more personal note, a large number of what one might call 'ordinary folk' know Wallace Arnold not as a scrivener, raconteur or political philosopher but as the immensely lovable 'personality' whose presence adorned the *That's Life!* team from 1977–81, offering viewers the benefit of his deliciously offbeat view of the world. After a particularly poignant piece about the unscrupulous behaviour of one salesman or another – resulting, if we were lucky, in the loss of the life-savings of a recently widowed OAP – Esther would turn to me with one of her wry, quizzical looks and say, 'Wallace?!'

'Thank you kindly, Esther,' I would reply from a sedentary position on my famous leather sofa. I would then greatly amuse the audience with priceless *bon mots* concerning the aforementioned appropriate names of professional folk. 'I hear tell,' I would say, 'of a bank manager from Ilford who delights in the name of Mr BANK.' Allowing time for the laughter to die down, I would then quip 'Let us hope Mr BANK gets to the BANK on time!!' Result? Collapse of audience! Rosy memories, soon to be rendered obsolete, like so much else, by the mirthless moguls of the BBC.

Wallace Arnold: Starting the Week

I was, of course, the original presenter of *Start the Week*, when Uncle Dickie Baker (forgive me, Richard!) was parading around his nursery school in shorts and sun hat. At that time young Melvyn was still sucking on his HB, wondering whether to stick around in Cumbria and write about real people and their real problems, hopes, fears, despairs and triumphs or whether to hot-foot it to London to rub shoulders with the Bee Gees.

The format was rather different in those early days. Only those who had attended one of our major public schools were permitted into the studio, though from time to time one or two others did somehow manage to slip through the net. For instance, we had a sworn affidavit from the agent representing Mr Sid James, the light comedy actor, that he had been to Eton but I smelt a rat when he began 'goosing' (dread activity!) Dame Margaret Rutherford beneath the studio round table, accompanying his actions with loud kissing sounds and the brash encomium, 'Cwor, you got a nice pair of hoodjamaflips there, love – oi! oi!' On closer investigation, we unearthed documents which proved conclusively that Mr James had not been to Eton at all, but to Harrow: a very different kettle of fish.

But by and large, all went swimmingly. From time to time, Lord Reith would drop into the studio to announce improvements to the schedules: fewer programmes in the mornings, for instance, or a complete crackdown on ordinary members of the public telephoning in with their half-baked opinions on this, that and the other.

But time moves on, and at some point in the mid-sixties Richard Baker arrived on the scene with his easy manner, his Afro haircut, his slinky tie-dye 'grandad' T-shirt and his mauve loon-pants, only too willing to speak in the absurd 'hip' jargon of the day. At first, he was employed as my assistant presenter, but soon his little contributions – a halfway-intelligent question here, an on-air compliment to myself there – had snowballed into lead questions and full-scale monologues; before long I had effectively been elbowed into playing second fiddle.

'Hoots mon!' he would greet each new guest in the trendy argot of the day. 'Have you got a light, boy?' Sure enough, his catchphrase took off, leaving my own – 'Good morning to our listeners, if any' – looking lame by comparison. By the beginning of the summer of '68, Richard had moved into the studio, lock, stock and barrel, and I had been given my marching orders, with the modest consolation of an offer to act as holiday replacement for the presenter of the shipping forecast.

Within little more than a decade, the biter was himself bit. Richard was judged old hat, and along came the thrusting young Melvyn Bragg, determined to drag his concerns about arts funding and exciting new directions in science into the kitchens of every home in the land. 'And I have with me this morning a major scientist with a book out, a major expert on major developments in Eastern Europe, a major young novelist whose most recent book has been described by more than one major critic as both provocative and disturbing and I am also joined by my little helper, a major young woman from a broadsheet newspaper,' became his catchphrase. As catchphrases go, it did not prove all that catchy, but who was I to judge? I had by now been summarily transferred to *Stop the Week*, in which I shared my best anecdotes about household chores with my fellow panellists Laurie Taylor, Denis Nilsen, Godfrey Smith and Ann Leslie and our resident chairman, Robert Robinson.

And now, a decade on, they have nobbled Bragg. And not only nobbled him, but enobled him too (I jest!): determined to get him off the air, Messrs Birt and Co have arranged for his immediate transfer to the House of Lords, where he can stop, start, and continue the week to his heart's content, but with the added bonus that for once the rest of us will not be expected to listen to him. I imagine the ambitious Bragg will soon have risen to become Speaker, no doubt cutting down the week's sittings to fifty minutes every Monday morning, with permission to speak only granted to those plugging new books and TV series.

But what next for our old friend *Start the Week*? Rumours have been flying this way and that as to who will be its next presenter. An O-level in charm is a necessary qualification for the job: accordingly, some say David Montgomery, others Gerald Kaufman, still others Harold Pinter. May I disabuse them? Anxious to lend a little weight and bottom to the programme, the DG has asked Yours Truly to apply. I fancy it is time the nation's travel schedules stretched to a trip down Memory Lane. With so much else that is new, young and modern, is it not time for something a little more urbane, a little more civilised?

Bel Littlejohn: My Week in the Arts

Saturday: Sue and I go to see the cult *American Beauty*. We're literally knocked backwards by it. 'It's a subtle yet ultimately harrowing dissection of the angst at the very heart of the American dream,' says Sue over a delicious glass of New Zealand Chardonnay afterwards. I agree with her: it's a movie that has that rare ability to make you stop and think about your own life. An absolute must.

Sunday: Geoff drags me round the Ruskin exhibition at the Tate. Talk about Victorian! The guy was obviously an anal-retentive, and boy does it show: he can't paint for toffee, and his critical judgements are all couched in the most hoity-toity toffee-nosed windbaggery bound up with sexual repression. So much so that I wanted to shout, 'Get a life!' After this, Tate Modern will prove a real breath of fresh air.

Monday: To dinner with Janet Street-Porter, bless her. She gets a bee in her proverbial bonnet, arguing that the Oscar-winning *American Beauty* is grossly overrated, presenting a stilted, clichéd, dated view of American life. The subject changes to contemporary comedy. Janet says that Ali G is 'simply to die for' and we all agree that *The League of Gentlemen* is a tour de force.

Tuesday: At a working lunch with Channel 4, I say that their new Wednesday night late-evening schedule is 'in danger of looking a bit stuffy and up-your-arse – a bit like the Ruskin exhibition at the Tate!' Michael Jackson replies that he found Ruskin at the Tate one of the most intellectually stimulating exhibitions he's seen all year, that Ruskin has one helluva lot to tell us at the start of a new millennium, and that he's an artist and critic who transcends his time in so many ways, not least the cutting-edge democratic quality of his prose style and his totally unrepressed energy, probably sexual in origin. I nod agreement. We both also agree that *The League of Gentlemen* is a step forward in British satire. 'Almost up to the level of Ali G,' says Michael.

Wednesday: In the morning, I bump into Sue and she asks me what I've been up to. I tell her I've been to the Ruskin exhibition at the Tate. She asks what it's like, so I tell her it's worth seeing because it raises a lot of interesting questions. Last night, she saw *The Beach*. She says it isn't nearly as good as the book, and Leonardo diCaprio must take a lot of the blame.

Over lunch with Geoff, he says I must go and see *The Beach*. 'It's so much better than the book and diCaprio is a total knock out,' he adds. He says he hasn't seen *American Beauty* yet. I tell him that, after all that Oscar hype, it turned out to be a bit of a disappointment, and that it really doesn't have anything new to say. I tell him that he must see *The League of Gentlemen*. 'Everyone says it's the new Ali G,' I say. 'Not that racist crap,' he says, before taking a hard look at the bottle of wine we are drinking. 'I'm getting a bit sick of New Zealand Chardonnay, to be honest,' he says. 'It's been over-hyped.'

Thursday: Gillian in the office says she's thinking of going to *The Beach* this evening. I say I've heard it's much better than the book and that diCaprio steals the show, but that, frankly, compared to the book it's not up to much and that diCaprio is, arguably, out of his depth. 'But do, I beg you, go and see the Ruskin show at the Tate,' I tell her. 'It really knocked me backwards. The guy's just so . . . *upfront.*'

In my lunchbreak, I put on the CD Walkman and listen to the new Oasis. It's every bit as good as they say it is – the first great rock album of the new millennium. In the evening, I meet up with Marcelle and we try to think of something we want to see.

'We could always stay in and watch television,' I say. '*League of Gentlemen* is on tonight.' Marcelle says she finds it offensive: men dressing up as women and distorting their faces is not her idea of comedy, she adds. 'Is it me,' I ask, 'or are there one helluva lot of overrated things doing the rounds? I mean, the way everyone goes on about New Zealand Chardonnay, for instance!' In the end, we decide to go to *Magnolia*. It's a real tour de force – brilliantly inventive and wholly original. It knocks us backwards. 'To me, it was a subtle yet ultimately harrowing dissection of the angst at the very heart of the American dream,' I say.

Friday: American Beauty has picked up yet more awards. Just shows what hype can do! In the office, Gillian sees the new Oasis CD on my desk. 'What's it like?' she asks, adding, 'Everyone's saying it's total crap.' I tell her I haven't heard it yet. She says she killed herself laughing at *League of Gentlemen* the other night. I say, I'm very sorry, I simply can't see what's so funny about it. 'Like Ruskin, they basically just don't like women,' I say, 'but have you seen *Magnolia* yet?' Gillian replies that it's not a patch on *American Beauty*. Overall, I agree with Gillian.

Problems
and
Crises

Gore Vidal's
September 11 Diary

Well how about that, I thought, as I flicked on the television in order to observe the aeroplanes making their way with such un-American precision into the World Trade Center. Or, as my grandmother in Oklahoma might have said, 'Jist watch dat cookie crumble.'

How about that, indeed. Needless to say, the world's media, in what we are still pleased to describe, in our sweetly innocent way, as the Land of the Free, were anxious for my thoughts on the matter. So for the rest of that nondescript mid-September day I sat in a geranium-filled garden *en Italie*, the blustery breeze playing havoc with my hair, attempting to explain by satellite the true meaning of what had just occurred to an American population now largely subliterate.

Am I going too fast for you? I have long worn the mantle of Unofficial Historian to the United States of Amnesia [sic!] and I regard it as an essential part of my position to explain the inner workings of that ungainly continent to its sluggish and frequently slack-buttocked but not entirely unreceptive peoples. Of course, there is a danger that by listening they might actually learn something, and thus present a grave danger to a government which, with its allies in the tobacco industry, asks nothing of its noble citizens other than to, in the resonant words of that ill-shaven archbore Richard Milhous Nixon, 'put up and shut up'. But that particular peril is one they must learn, as F. Delano Roosevelt, once said, to live with.

In the past six months alone, I have devoted many precious screen minutes (costing me a small fortune in the appropriate cosmetics, bills never wholly repaid by the Great Broadcasting Institutions of Our Sacred Land) to passing on to my fellow Americans the information that their sacred President Jack Kennedy met his untimely demise not from a lone gunman but at the hands of his wife Jackie, of blessed memory, who had, of course, been armed and trained by a consortium jointly headed by Mr Aristotle Onassis and Mr Fidel Castro, under the day-to-day direction of the American Tobacco Lobby, headed by your very own Duke Philip of Edinburgh, whose connections with J. Edgar Hoover and his ivory-tinkling sidekick Noel Coward are already well established.

'It should ne'er be forgotten,' I informed the ostentatiously feminine Diane Sawyer when I appeared on the top-rated *60 Minutes*, 'that the whiskery Mr Osama bin Laden is, of course, a senior backstage figure in the Disney Corporation.'

This, it seemed, was news to the white-toothed Miss Sawyer, who was also, it emerged, blissfully unaware that the far-from-dead Elvis Aaron Presley has now donned a beard and head-dress and is living in a luxury cave somewhere near Kabul under the direct command of the Taliban and their flat-footed apparatchiks in the CIA.

A brief lesson in history, if I may be so bold. The so-called Twin Towers was, of course, in fact the Triple Towers, the existence of the third tower being kept from the Great American Public by their government for what are euphemistically known in those high-falutin' circles as 'security reasons'.

It was the virtually unknown Third Tower – where, back in 1966, the infamous moon landings had been secretly staged and filmed under the direction of our old friend Mr Walt Disney – that was, of course, the true target of the 'terrorist' assault, for here it was that your own Prince Edward, fifth son of Queen Elizabeth II and a full colonel in the SAS, was training the heavily disguised yeti, who had entered America under a false name, clean shaven and wearing a fedora, to mount an all-out attack on the city of Beirut.

Doggedly, and with the natural good manners of my Texan forebears, I attempted to talk Ms Sawyer and her eager if saddeningly odiferous viewers step by step through their own history, a lesson my poor, dear second-cousin George W. Bush has been only too keen to avoid.

Most of my horny-handed fellow-citizens – the majority happy to believe in the somewhat spartan, indeed positively cocktail-free paradise offered by a nondescript beard-and-sandals Jewish woodworker – remain unaware that the United States of America was formed in ancient Egypt, under the aegis of the Ford Corporation, who had recently completed the construction of their fifth pyramid, in which they were to install a series of listening devices. Kidnapped, as predicted by Nostradamus, by a series of unidentified flying objects, after a brief sojourn in the Bermuda Triangle our ancestors were to settle in America under the beady, lightly mascaraed eyes of the gaunt prig Abraham Lincoln, operating under direct orders from King George III.

And so to me. History now leaps ahead a century or twain, until we arrive, with the keenest anticipation, at my own birth, most elegantly executed by all accounts. A meticulous dresser, I immediately eschewed the nappy proffered by my nursemaid, holding out for a miniature handmade suit from Brookes Brothers (then, of course, a leading front for the CIA under our old friend Randolph Hearst).

Are you still with me, or am I too knowledgeable for you? To resume: I am not now in daily contact with the much-maligned Osama bin Laden, though I have, in the past, found him an amusing, if restless and somewhat picky, dining companion. Having examined all the evidence, I find that he currently shares his cave with our old friend Miss Monica Lewinsky, who, of course, once placed dear old Ronnie Reagan in such a sticky position. Between the two of them they are apparently planning to sell arms to the Loch Ness monster, which is now in residence in Cuba. But that, as my great-aunt Wallis Simpson would say, is another story . . .

Wallace Arnold Chews the Cud

I need hardly say that the present veal furore has upset me most terribly. Call me sensitive, but ever since I was a child, I have had a soft spot for little calves, the more succulent the better.

As Motoring and Food Editor of the late lamented *Punch* magazine throughout the 1970s, I was forever trumpeting the tender delights of veal (see my much-lauded culinary series 'Veal I Never! The Lighter Side of Serving Calf', *Punch* issues 32, 349–52, 355 with illustrations by Barry Appleby). As a dish, veal has long been subject to the ups and downs of gastronomic fashion, but I have always maintained that it is the perfect food for every occasion. Indeed, while on a motoring holiday through the Dordogne in '78 with Sir Harold Acton and Dame Barbara Cartland, I made a point of keeping a calf tethered to the rear mudguard, so that we could help ourselves to a thin slice whenever that great demon Mr Peckish came knocking at the door.

Being readers of the *Independent on Sunday*, I suppose you will wish to tackle some of the weightier moral problems arising from this complex issue. Is there, you may well be asking yourselves, anything a civilised person should *not* permit himself to nibble? This dilemma first entered my life in 1972, after I found myself boarding an aeroplane to cross the Andes for my acclaimed 'Arnold in the Andes' series in the

Telegraph magazine. Quite to my surprise, the aeroplane soon plummeted into the mountainside, leaving just seventeen survivors, among whom W. Arnold was one. The story of the other sixteen is recorded by Piers Paul Read in *Alive* (1974), but after he had persistently refused to retitle it *Arnold Alive* I withdrew all permission to include my own tale in the book, and so I found myself ruthlessly excluded.

A shame, because my own tale is, as always, well worth telling. As luck would have it, I had landed bang next to a large hamper chock-a-block with packed lunches. This proved perfectly sufficient to see me through the ten weeks we spent in those frosty climes waiting to be rescued, though I had to exercise discretion in keeping its presence from the other fellows, or they might have wanted the odd nibble. The moral dilemma that faced me then was all too vivid: when he is really up against it, is it acceptable for a member of the English upper classes to eat peanut butter sandwiches? In the comfort of home, such a course of action would of course have been unthinkable. Here, peanut butter is quite rightly considered beyond the pale, but things were different out there in the nippy Andes. By week five, closeted away with my secret hamper while, in the distance, lots of little South Americans looked at one another with ravenous eyes, I found myself succumbing to the lure of the peanut butter. And – yes – before long I had downed those ghastly sandwiches, one and all.

Chin up, Wallace, chin up. It was three years after my rescue before I confessed to anyone of what I had consumed out there. Soon, the rumour spread around the Garrick that I had eaten peanut butter, and I found myself shunned by friend and foe alike. 'You're not really telling me that there was no decent veal available?' protested an old friend. Ever since that day, I have taken a calf in a crate with me wheresoever I travel. Indeed, I write this very article sitting in the crate-laden Arnold office suite in Canary Wharf, the lowing of tender young calves ringing in my ears, my mouth a-water.

Distasteful? Hardly. Personally, I believe it to be a sign of good manners to eat whatever is placed in front of one, be it beast, fish or fowl. Only the other week, I found myself sitting in an empty room come elevenses, the old stomach on the rumble once more. Empty, that is, but for a birdcage containing a parrot and a budgerigar. I eyed the pair of them. 'No, I really mustn't – I mustn't be so greedy,' I told myself, so I just had the parrot.

Frankly, I draw the line at goldfish (too moist) and hamster (too hairy) but I have a soft spot for mole, which compares favourably with lightly sauteed guinea pig. It grieves me deeply that my old friend and quaffing partner William (or Vealyham – I jest!!!) Waldegrave is up to his neck in it from rent-a-mob. I have stuck my knife and fork into many a juicy calf while ambling around his estate, and would be loathe to see 'em go. If the Almighty had not wished man to eat of the animal, He would surely have made vegetables much tastier.

*

If ever there was a valuable piece of advice given to me by Great Grandfather Arnold all those years ago as he sucked on his Old Scrag, it was most surely this: Never Trust a Boffin. And the truth of this richly Arnoldian aphorism was never made more plain to me than this week, as I perused with astonishment the assorted eggheads holding forth in the newspapers on the subject of bovine spongiform (dread gibberish!).

I have been an enthusiastic beef eater all my life. Morning, noon, and night, houseguests in Chateau Arnold find that assorted cuts of beef, beef and more beef are freely available: roast rib on the television in the drawing room, chump in the servant's quarters, a chilled consommé with parsley and cream in the toothmugs in all the bathrooms, perfect little pats of steak tartare on the pillows in the guest bedrooms and, for our American cousins, good big rissoles next to the floral soaps in the shower rack . . .

Never a day goes by without a tasty good bit of beef slipping its merry way down the Arnold throat. I start the day with a goodly wodge of beef dripping poured daintily – but with all due generosity! – over my Scott's Porridge Oats. When I am feeling really naughty (!) I then treat myself to another spoonful (or three!) in my breakfast cup of Earl Grey, and jolly good it is too. And so to elevenses, where a simple Penguin chocolate biscuit can be greatly enhanced by the addition of a few slices of lightly roasted beef plus oodles of horseradish and a pinch of nutmeg.

Come luncheon, I tend to fall back on that great British standby: a decent joint of beef. This must, perforce, be served rare, or 'still kicking' as my grandmother would call it. It has been said that a gentleman who manages to conclude his luncheon without a sizeable splash of blood on his necktie is no gentleman at all. Personally, I end my own luncheons looking rather as if Mr Jackson Pollock has just paid a lightning visit, and my friends are well used to the spectacle of my good self parading along the streets of London come the afternoon with little flecks of blood and gristle attached to my jacket, to be devoured a few minutes later, as an essential part of a light afternoon tea.

For dinner, I tend to favour a little more beef. As a first course, I acquaint my stomach with a couple of dainty beef vol-au-vents on a bed of lightly curried beef, to be followed by a delicious beef goulash, Olde English Beef stew or beef curry, depending upon mood, with a goodly slab of Mr Wall's ice cream plus a couple of spoonfuls of beef jelly as a pud. For my savoury, I tend to favour something a little lighter: a minute steak, perhaps, or a decent piece of tongue, or a lightly poached oxtail with a cheese sauce. And last of all, in deference to the health lobby, I occasionally manage a lettuce leaf with my steaming hot mug of Bovril.

Marvellous! But now the politically motivated scare-mongers seem determined to spread their home-grown variety of rumour, gossip and innuendo. Yet the fact remains that though this may afford them some amoosement, it is highly destructive to our national dish. They claim that bovine spongiform encephalopathy (dread mooouthful) may well transfer to human beings. But this is, at best, a moooot point. Personally, I have found no sign whatsoever, either in myself or in my close friends, that the consumption of beef products results in any form of human moootation.

To celebrate our continued allegiance to beef, a groooop of us gathered at the Beefsteak Club on Thursday last to hear Mr Douglas Hogg produce a generous toast to the bull and cow. I have to say, it was moosic to my ears, and when he sat down he acknowledged our applause with a snort and wave of his hoof. The delightful performance of our second guest, Mr John Selwyn Gummer, was equally memooorable. Gummer brought along his dear daughter. Cordelia, I need hardly say, has never looked more healthy or happy, wagging her tail from left to right throughout the speeches.

The big guns of the BSE lobby are, as you see, somewhat short of amooonition. My body and brain will continue to be oiled by beef for many mooonths yet, regardless of the scaremooongers, who I don't believe for one moooment. Mad cow disease, forsooth! The very mention of such an absurdity makes me want to lie on my back and wiggle my legs, front and back, in the air. In short, something mooost be done.

The Fayed Book of Unexplained Mysteries

WHO KILLED JFK?

President Kenny he very very nice man, he good man, he personal friend, he love shop Harrods when he in town. I tell him, John, I tell him, you take envelope from Uncle Mohamed, you order your American people buy luxury items, household goods, electrical products, ladies clothing, cashmere, the lot, only from Harrods, we fix cut-price deal, very good?

I say to him one day, I say, Johnny, I say, who this bloody LBJ breathin' down your neck? He bad people, I say, he shifty, he up no good, he go after your job, he no human, he garbage, he even garbager than garbage, he garbagest garbage in the world, you want loyal number two, you need lifer-than-large stand-upping gentleman, you need Uncle Mohamed, what you say ten thousand cash, no, twelve thousand plus luxury executive hamper, and al Fayed be your Vice-Pres, okay?

That morning in Dallas, JFK he agree. He tell me personally, I have many witnesses so you no call me bloody liar, FKJ he say 'You right, Mohamed. I get rid LBso-calledJ. With you my Vice-President, we go far, with my looks and your shirts we dream ticket.'

Then KJF he set off licking lips into limo with pretty wife and picnic hamper in back, gobblin' down rich fruit cake like no tomorrow. But LBJ is seethin', he no want Mohamed to take job, he say that job mine, and he pay crook called Grassy Noel to get own back on JFK. And when limo passes, Grassy Noel shoot President Kenny through head, so poor Mohamed never make Vice-President. Is disgrace, I tell you, is complete disgrace.

IS THE LOCH NESS MONSTER REAL?

Of course Nessie real, Nessie very close personal friend, we do good business together, why you say he no real, you stupid, you know nothin', you shaddup, okay?

His real name is Loch Ness al Monster, he very old family, very smart, very prestige, top quality. But the Establishment, they no like him, they spread rumour Nessie no real, they attempt suppress him, they scared what he knowing. Prince Philip, he saying, 'Nessie no bloody existing.' But Philip jealousy: he think Queen would rather be marry to Nessie, she make him Prince Nessie, they live happy ever after, Prince Philip hoppin' mad. He scream, 'I never want hear no more about this bloody Nessie,' and he get MI5, MI6, MI7, MI8, the lot, to organise massive bloody cover-up, but they no fool al Fayed, okay?

WHAT IS THE MEANING BEHIND THE LYRICS OF 'AMERICAN PIE'?

Silly question, is answer obvious. Homage to Mohamed al Fayed. 'Buy, buy, miss American Pie'. Harrods sale now on, you got to get off backside okay and buy, buy very quick or you miss delicious Harrods American Pie available fresh baked in world famous Food Hall while stocks last hurry hurry hurry. What about other lyrics, you say, okay, you want know, I tell you. 'Drove my chevy to the levee but the levee was dry'. Why chauffeur bloody drive there then? What he bloody playing at? Who wants drive millions of miles to levee to find levee is dry? Imbecile, he should be checking before start journey. He kind of human being who have no dignity, he nothing for me, he not human, he ape, I have no business with this man, no wonder music die if he in charge that day.

WHO REALLY WROTE THE PLAYS COMMONLY ATTRIBUTED TO 'WILLIAM SHAKESPEARE'?

Measure for Measure? Don't tell me *Measure for Measure*. Measure for Measure is garbage, I say playwright know nothing of business. I give you measure, you give me two measure in return, we do business, okay. I give you measure, you give me one measure, we no way do business, what you talkin' is total rubbish, you get out of my store or I call security and have you be prosecuted. *Measure for Two Measure* much more better name. *Hamlet*. Huh. Who want bloody hamlet, I want town or city, I no want piddley no-good rotten hamlet, who want couple barns and old ruin, only imbecile, I offer good money, you give me luxury executive-style mansions, retail facilities, health club, the lot, or I take my business elsewhere and you take your bloody hamlet with you.

But Shakespeare very prestige name, very first-class product, my friend, he no write garbage, he quality writer, he contribute many millions to country. I tell you this, my good friend Lord Jeffrey Archer, he wrote Shakespeare, he tell me one day, Mohamed, he say, he say, Mohamed, I never tell anyone this before and I never this tell anyone again, but you man of honour, Mohamed, you man of principle, you keep good secret, you no tell no one: I, Lord Jeffrey Archer is writing plays of so-called fuggin William Shakespeare, I shave head and grow beard and write with quill, they bit wordy but they bring in good money, no wonder they jealous, the lah-di-dah so-called bloody critics. So I send him hamper and envelope to calm him down, because Mohamed generous man, Mohamed want everybody being rich and happy.

WHO KILLED COCK ROBIN?

'I,' said the sparrow, 'with my bow and arrow. I killed Cock Robin.' You got proof? You show me proof! This sparrow, he just bird, two wings, beak, chirpy-chirpy, he no one, so what he know about bows and arrows? You ever see sparrow holdin' bow and arrow, my friend? Impossible! The feathers, they get completely in way, all bloody fluff everywhere, how you get grip of bow?! See, this sparrow, he just a bloody patsy, he set up by Establishment. I am know exactly what happening. High-up enemies of Cock Robin, they get him carry can, while they laugh in our faces, is true.

Trust me. I proof, I have signed statement from my loyal trusted and well-paid employee, Mr Fly. '"Who saw him die?" "I," says the Fly. "With my very very big eye, I saw him die." Cock Robin was killed by the Blair Government working in conjunction with the Royal Family, MI5 and the Tory Party. And his dying wish, expressed only to me, was that Mr al Fayed must be granted a British passport. Signed A. Fly.'

Now, you telling me Mr Fly made this up? You callin' him dirty filthy liar? You very rude person, you sinking in corruption, you garbage. But maybe we come to deal. We do business. You scratch my back, and – how you say? – I scratch mine.

Bel Littlejohn: Coping with Crises

As an award-winning columnist, I know better than most just how much mental stamina, personal discipline and sheer common sense it takes to do the job properly. In one's private life, things may be going up the pan or down the shoot, but your faithful readers, bless 'em, will still be turning to you for a sane, balanced view on national and international affairs.

It's been one of those weeks. After I had given her the benefit of my hard-won advice on how to maintain a tidy desk, Trish, my lovely, lovely secretary decided out of the blue to venture forth to pastures new, and good luck to her – even if it does mean she's left a trail of abandoned paperwork behind her and sadly can expect no future recommendation from yours truly!!! I mean – *really*!

Things have been scarcely less chaotic at home. While I was distracted by news of my son's upsetting decision to abandon the Grateful Dead in order to support the Tory 'Keep the Pound' van on its tour round the country, I forgot to close the hamster cage. The result? The hamster ate the goldfish and the hamster was itself eaten by the cat, which choked to death as a consequence. Seconds later, my guy, who has campaigned with Anita Roddick and myself for the past seven years against the testing of beauty products on animals, rang to say he was leaving me to set up a factory in the West Country for putting false eyelashes on rabbits. Meanwhile, my daughter's pregnant by the deputy lead singer of Prodergy, the Prodigy tribute band operating in Swansea and surrounding areas.

As I say, it's been one of those weeks when one thanks God for the Prozac. But you – my loyal readers (and thank you in advance for those lovely supporting letters you'll send me) – will still be wanting my usual guidance on where to stand on the major topics of the week. So I put all the pressures of my personal life behind me, and focus, clearly and calmly, on the key issues.

For example, should all those passengers in the Boeing 727 hijacked last week be returned to Afghanistan? As I pointed out in my *Guardian* leader at the time, this is a sensitive issue, and one which the Home Secretary would do well to ponder long and hard, for the number of people in American prisons is now at two million, and rising: with David Bowie set to be a father again at the ripe old age of fifty-three, we as a society must determine for how long the expansion of the Murdoch empire into the Internet is a development with which we can remain comfortable.

As London Fashion Week gathers steam, proving once again that British designers are among the best in the world, it seems perfectly possible that Robert Mugabe will be forced to release his shaky grip on the reins of power in Zimbabwe. But where will this leave Sam Mendes? Will he accomplish the impossible and become the first foreign director to scoop a Best Director Oscar with his own very first movie? From where I'm sitting (huddled up below the kitchen sink, for warmth and pro-tection) it's a decision that's very much in the hands of Edith Cresson, whose continued persecution suggests that, whatever Senator John McCain may have us believe, old-fashioned misogyny is alive and kicking among the senior Roman Catholic hierarchy.

Whither the Dome? Is fundamental change the only way forward – or does it simply need a little tweaking on the public relations front? Were Jorg Haider to visit Britain, would he be permitted to visit the Dome unescorted – and how would this effect Clause 28? This is the question I am addressing when the doorbell rings. It is a messenger from my publishers with the proofs of my next book, the latest in my *Coping with . . .* series. Previous books in the series have included *Coping with Modern Italian Cookery* and *Coping with a Living Parent*, but my editor firmly believes that the new one, *Coping with Problem Skin, Your New Wok and the Impending World Economic Crises on Less Than £25 a Day* will appeal to a larger readership than ever before.

Six hours later, I finish correcting the proofs, take my dirty clothes to the washing machine, wind the knob round to Rapid Wash and press the Start button. I look down at my right hand. I am still clutching my dirty clothes. This can only mean one thing: my proofs are on Rapid Wash, there's nothing I can do about it until the cycle's over, and I still haven't come up with a firm opinion on the future of the Dome. What is a fair minimum wage, is Leonardo diCaprio losing his popular appeal, is Vladimir Putin a threat to BSE – and does baking soda mixed with a splash of water make a more effective form of scouring powder than many of the commercial brands? These are all problems I hope to solve in the coming weeks, with your help help help help help help help, help, help, help

The Complete Works of William Shakespeare for Telephone: Romeo and Juliet (46-Hour Version)

Romeo: She speaks. O, speak again bright angel; for thou art
As glorious to this night, being o'er my head,
As is a winged messenger of heaven
Unto the white upturned wond'ring eyes
Of mortals that fall back to gaze on him
When he bestrides the lazy-passing clouds
And sails upon the bosom of the air.
Juliet: O Romeo, Romeo, wherefore art thou Romeo?
Helpline: Thank you for calling our
Customer services helpline. If
You wish to continue, please
Press your start-button twice.
Juliet: O Romeo, Romeo, wherefore—?
Helpline: For further assistance, press button three.
Juliet: O Romeo, Romeo, wherefore art thou Romeo?
Helpline: Welcome to our customer
Hotline. Please note that your call

Problems and Crises

May be monitored and/ or
Recorded in order to help us
Improve our quality control for
Customer-related services. If
Your enquiry concerns consumer
Whereabouts, please press five now.
Juliet: O Romeo, Romeo, wherefore art—?
Helpline: Thank you for pressing five.
Please select from one of the following
Options. For home and office, please
Press one. For business, please
Press two. For parts and warranty, please
Press three. For customer care, please
Press four. For technical support please
Press five. For tickets and booking information, please
Press six. For further information please
Stay on the line.
Juliet: O Romeo, Romeo, where—
Helpline: To hear the same message again, please
Press eight.
Juliet: O Romeo, Ro—
Helpline: To hear the same message again, please
Press eight.
Juliet: O Ro—
Stevie Wonder: Ah jist caw do say Ah lurve yue
I jist caw do say ah love is drue-ue-ue-ue
I jist caw do –
Helpline: Thank you for calling our customer
Hotline. Please hold. A representative
Will be with you shortly.
If you have any query regarding
Outstanding information, please press four. If—
Juliet: O Romeo, Romeo, wherefore art thou Romeo?
Helpline: You are being held in a queue. Please
Hold and one of our operators will
Deal with your enquiry shortly.
Thank you for calling our

This Is Craig Brown

Information hotline. Should you require
Further information, why not visit our
Website at doubleyoudoubleyoudoubleyou
Dot Hotline DotUK. You are now being transferred
To our customer satisfaction team.
Phil Collins: Ah kihn fee lit car min in the yair
To-narght, wo law, wo law, Ah kin fee lit –
Helpline: Thank you for calling customer satisfaction.
If you require further satisfaction,
Please press nine. If you are already
Satisfied, please press—
Juliet: O Romeo, Romeo, wherefore art thou Romeo?
Deny thy father and refuse thy name,
Or If thou wilt not, be but sworn my love,
And I'll no longer be a—
Helpline: For details of our customer care priority
Club, please press six. To help us enhance
The quality of the customer care, please
Press three. Welcome to the country's
Leading customer care helpline. We aim to
Provide a comprehensive service
For all your communication needs.
For further information concerning
Our friendly and efficient
Service, please press button two.
Juliet: O Ro—
Helpline: Thank you for calling our
Customer services helpline. If
You wish to continue, please
Press you star-button twice.
Nurse: O, me, O me, my child, my only life!
Revive, look up, or I will die with thee.
Help, help! Ring the helpline!

Bel Littlejohn: Men in Crisis

Drained just isn't the word. It's been a totally draining experience. In fact I've never felt so drained. It makes me wish I'd been on a journalist draining scheme, just so I'd know how to cope.

I'm talking, of course, about my new book, *Half-Cocked: Men in Crisis*. For the past seven years, I have been talking to all kinds of men. Tall men. Short men. Medium-sized men. Men who wear neckties. Men in open-necked collars. I was even introduced to one man, in an alley in Brooklyn, who was wearing a cravat. I have been talking to men with one eye. Men with two eyes. Men in trainers. Men in shoes. Men in sandals. Famous men with two eyes but without trainers. Unknown men with sandals but with only one eye. The lot. And I've been asking them a simple question they've never, ever been asked before: *Why do you feel so very, very angry and miserable – is it because, deep down, you are so utterly worthless?*

No one had ever taken the trouble to ask men that question before. What I found on what I call my listening tour was a feeling of supreme irrelevance among them. 'Why do you feel so totally irrelevant?' I would say, before adding, 'Next please!' By the way they'd slouch out of the station, I'd intuit a profound sense of anger and disaffection, as though they were feeling ignored by a society that had once primed them to feel important.

We have changed fundamentally from a society that produced a fundamentally changing culture to a society that produced a culture of fundamental change. The difference, I discovered, was fundamental. And what of the men who were left behind? To understand what all men *really thought*, I made it my mission to talk to some of the most fundamentally stupid men still alive on this planet. To find out what modern man really thought of women, I listened to what half a dozen serial rapists from a high-security prison in Colorado had to tell me. And to find out what modern man really thought about concepts such as the uses of structuralism in a post-modernist age, I turned to leading Hollywood movie star Keanu Reeves, with whom I enjoyed an exclusive ten-minute interview.

I even managed to locate an educationally subnormal 310lb kleptomaniac from Nebraska to advise me on the limits of changing concepts of masculinity within the context of local communities in decline. Only by uncovering the dashed hopes and expectations within the most fundamentally daft men in the world would I be able to come to terms with the full severity of the crisis facing modern man.

Unlike his daft father, today's daft man grew up without any sense of pride. Where his father might once have marched off proudly to die in a war that had not yet been scheduled, today's daft man had to be content with falling flat on his face after an accident arising from a genetically modified banana skin. Today's man wears a baseball cap the wrong way round. He sings the latest Sloop Doggy Dog number to himself without really understanding the lyrics. He is unemployable because he has lost all sense of self-esteem resulting from wearing trousers many sizes too big for him. His fingernails are rarely clean. And in the basement of his modest clapboard house situated just off the main street in an unassuming mid-American town there lie three partially charred, semi-clad corpses. They have been there three months now, the victims of modern man's unquenchable desire to regain his domination over his environment. I initially uncovered this horrifying trend by visiting death row and talking to a man who is widely regarded as the most unpleasant human being in Montana.

It's crucial for society not simply to denounce but to figure out what the hell's going on. Men speak with their mouths full. They kick stones in the street. They challenge old ladies to arm-wrestling competitions on the top of double-decker buses – and then leap off without paying their fares. *Why are men like this?* Or – to put it another way – *this like men are why?*

It all goes back to space travel. When I talked with men who grew up in the shadow of space travel, they all heard me tell them the same thing. For them, space was a bitter disappointment. Despite all their masculine hopes, the moon had turned out to be a depressing environment, approachable only by cramped and noisy rocket, and with no male infrastructure to speak of: there was no baseball park on the moon, for instance, and little or no opportunity for date-rape or male bonding.

Men are in crisis. You don't believe me? Pick one at random. Take Rick, for instance.

Rick lives in North Somerset. Rick is a zoophile. That's to say, Rick is sexually attracted to animals – farmyard animals, mainly, but also the more voluptuous breeds of fish (salmon, sea bass, squid – though not octopus – 'They're all hands,' he says). Unlike many other zoophiles, however, he is not particularly attracted to horses, finding them too overtly flirtatious, too 'fast'. He prefers the more subtle, less 'in-your-face' looks of a duck, say, or a well-groomed goose. For a few months in the late 1980s, he even dated a hen. 'But it didn't work out,' he says, with an air of regret. 'She just wasn't a nest-builder'.

I spoke at length to Rick over a period of six months while researching my new book, *Half-Cocked: Men in Crisis* (Chatto and Windus). Only by listening to ordinary men like Rick could I hope to understand the crisis facing men in the new millennium.

A computer programmer, Rick enjoys the finer things of life. His four-bedroom home sports an impressive collection of the light classics on CD, as well as the complete Sting back catalogue, which, he reveals, was his Christmas present, the year before last, to a much-loved hamster. A keen gourmet,

Rick cites his chief relaxation as 'eating out': he can often be spotted entertaining a special friend – sometimes a Jack Russell, more often a llama – in an intimate Michelin-starred restaurant in Minehead. His zoophilia has even seen him featured on Channel 4 – with the promise of his own show early in the new year.

A pretty average – you might even say ordinary – kind of guy then, with a lifestyle which would be the envy of many. So by understanding Rick, we should be able to understand every man on this deeply troubled planet of ours. For behind Rick's easy-going exterior lies a very real sense of betrayal. And Rick's crisis is the crisis of modern man. Unless we face up to their pain, we'll never find out what the hell's going on. You see, after months of cross-questioning it emerged that Rick – happy, regular, ordinary, home-loving Rick – is deeply disillusioned. 'I am a man in pain,' he says, 'I've got all the farmyard animals I could wish for, but there are no wars to fight, technology is usurping my manhood, and the Internet is no replacement for a true community. So my masculinity feels betrayed. If it wasn't for the animals, my hopes would be dashed.'

Rick doesn't have many close friends, but one of them is Dick, who lives just fifteen miles away as the crow flies – or as it would fly, if Rick wasn't enjoying a quiet evening of early Phil Collins videos with her over a tray-supper from the River Café Cookbook. Outwardly, Rick's friend Dick enjoys a lifestyle that would be the envy of many a high-achieving male. He lives in a luxury executive maisonette within each reach of a high-profile shopping complex. He keeps in shape with regular games of squash at a prestige members-only sports club. He is married to high-flying public relations consultant Jane, who has just negotiated an impressive three-year contract with the second biggest sportswear manufacturers in Taunton.

Yet Dick is a man in pain.

Eighteen months ago, approaching half-time in a game of squash, a ball passed through his open mouth and disappeared. 'There was no problem about getting another ball,' Dick claims. 'They're relatively inexpensive, and the sports club has its own shop, open from 8.00am to 8.00pm every day including Sundays.' But, on deeper probing over a three-month period, he admits that the original squash ball, travelling at an odd angle, is now permanently lodged somewhere to the back of his nose. 'I am a man in pain,' he confesses, 'yet another victim of the crisis facing men in the run-up to the twenty-first century.'

Rick's friend Dick has a friend called Nick. Nick's sick, but he won't tell Vic because Vic's worried about Mick. And Mick is a man in crisis.

Outwardly, Mick is your average family man. Four-door saloon, mortgage, holidays abroad, top job in the pharmaceutical industry. But inside, he's hurting. 'In his headlong pursuit of society's goals, my father abandoned me to an image-based, commercial-ruled world for which traditional forms of masculine self-image left me wholly unprepared,' confesses Mick. Happily, he is able to cope with his personal crisis by setting aside two or three hours each day to make detailed plans for visiting local shopping malls with an armoury of dangerous weapons.

Three men: a disillusioned zoophile, a man with a squash ball up his nose and a gun fanatic. One male crisis. For God's sake, let's do something about them – and fast.

Wallace Arnold: The Garrick Cottage Hospital

My old Great Granny Arnold was a unique source of wisdom. 'It's an unwise man,' she would often find cause to say, 'who puts three biscuits in his mouth at the same time.' That's a lesson that has helped me through thick and thin. And so is another of her familiar mottoes. 'If a man is going to wear a sock,' she would say as she puffed at that old pipe of hers, 'he'll find it best worn on his foot.'

But it is to another of Great Granny Arnold's marvellous old mottoes that I turn today. 'You know, young Wallace,' she would murmur while gently nibbling on one of her choicest lumps of coal, 'if ever a man is offered the heart of a pig or the kidney of a monkey, he would be a perfect fool to refuse.'

These words came wafting back to me as I read of the all-too predictable 'outcry' (dread word!) that greeted the news that hearts and kidneys from some of our most illustrious pigs are to wing their way into human beings. Needless to say, I allowed myself a quiet Arnoldian chuckle at the story, for some of my dearest friends and admirers have been walking around for years with the organs of animals happily keeping their bodies going.

For a while now, it has been something of a fad among the *cognoscenti* to pep themselves up a little when times are low by nipping down to the small cottage hospital situated on the third floor of the Garrick for a quick organ transplant. Sometimes, they would insist on bringing their own donor along with them – a chicken, perhaps, or a cock pheasant – but more often than not they would be perfectly content to browse through the animals in the Garrick's own collection, under the expert guidance of the club's very own general practitioner.

Any mid-to-heavy smoker in search of a fresh pair of lungs need look no further than the Garrick's masterly selection of kangaroos, bred in captivity but given a good run around the Covent Garden area by trained experts for up to two hours a day, thrice weekly. When the time comes, these are then used as a profitable source of lungs for senior Garrick Club members. A member can be having a pre-prandial drink in the Smoking Room and be plucked from his seat by a skilled surgeon, only to be returned before the middle of the main course, fighting fit and with a fresh pair of kangaroo lungs. Lord Wyatt of Weevil is probably the most prominent Garrick member to sport such lungs. Few would be able to spot the difference, though, on reflection, Woodrow's habit of taking great hops towards the cold table while furiously shadow-boxing the air may well be a tell-tale sign.

Other animals have proved just as invaluable. Ferrets have provided many members with a marvellous new set of eye-brows, at once more flexible, bushier and more severe than their own. Sir Kingsley Amis opted for an eyebrow-transplant only last week, to tie in with the publication of his latest novel. I note with some amusement that many interviewers have commented on the gruffness of his facial expressions without ever guessing that he owes it all to a couple of ferrets.

Such success stories from the Garrick Cottage Hospital are legion. Not so very long ago, my old quaffing partner and fellow scrivener Paul Johnson opted to have his vocal chords given a good going-over by the in-house Garrick GP after one or two of his closest friends had complained they were unable to understand a word he said. After a thorough examination with the stethoscope, the aforesaid GP sent out for a bull terrier and recommended an immediate transplant. The operation was a total success. Paul is now speaking at full pitch, though he sometimes complains that the wearing of the obligatory muzzle in parks, recreation grounds and other public places is highly inconvenient.

One final example of this extraordinary breakthrough in medical science. Only last week, my very dear friend Lord Rees-Mogg popped into the Garrick asking for something for his head. Quick off the mark, the Garrick doctor sat William on his couch and opened the door marked 'Livestock'. Just in time for afternoon tea, William emerged from the surgery sporting the head of a Muscovy duck. Ever since then, his weekly column in *The Times* has improved considerably, enlivened by a lively about-turn on Europe. As my old great-grandmother Arnold used to observe as she sat there scratching her left wing, 'No man has a right to call himself a duck until he can quack.'

Jimmy Young Welcomes Osama Bin Laden

Hello there! And a very warm welcome to the JY Col in your numero uno favorito magazinato! So what's he talking about, I *hear you ask* – what's Our Jimbo on about now? Good question, as you might say! Well, the answer is that I've been asked to write the diary for the Eye of Le Private fame, *would you believe,* so hold on to your horses everyone – both in this country and *suwer le continong* – and orft we jolly well go!

On a more serious note, I've never had a lot of time for so-called 'satire'. I may be sticking my neck out here – if you'll *pardonnez-mois my Francais!* – but to me it lacks warmth. I can take it or leave it, to be honest – but I'd never turn down the chance to lend a bit of the old JY magic to a magazine down on its luck-luck-lucky-luck, to coin a phrase! But first, let's hear this, from your friend and mine – it's over to you, Mister Phil Collins!

* * *

Today, I had that highly controversial figure Mister Osama bin Laden on the line! *Now there's a name to conjure with!* Like him or loathe him, there's certainly no ignoring the fellow!
JY: And a very good JY morning to you, Osama!
O-b-L: Good morning, Jimmy.
JY: And a warm welcome to today's JY prog! Now, Osama, I

know a lot of our listeners will be wondering how the weather is, out there in deepest Afghanistan?

O-b-L: Not too bad, thank you, Jimmy.

JY: Super! Now, 'Osama' – there's a name to conjure with! Tell me, Osama, how *did* you come by a name like that?

O-b-L: My father he give it me, Jim, when I was born.

JY: Lovely, now a number of our listeners have rung in with *question-nez*, for you, Osama – like Mr Geoffrey Bishop from Edgbaston, who says, 'What I want to know, Jim, is how this character can justify swanning around the world, blowing places up, causing untold mayhem, and so on and so forth? Hasn't he got better things to do, Jim?' Over to you, Osama!

O-b-L: Thanks, Jimmy. Is the word of the Prophet. Is Holy War. Death to the Infidel.

JY: Fair enough, Osama! Can't argue with that! It takes all sorts – of that there's no denying! And we'll hear more from Osama – after this from Miss Sandy Shaw!

* * *

The second half of my interview with Osama brought out a warmer, softer side to a man who usually likes to keep it well hidden, for reasons of his *own-io*!

JY: . . . And a Mrs Susan Worth from Orpington in Kent – lovely part of the country – has e-mailed us to say, 'The one thing that gets on my wick, Jim, is that beard of his! What *does* he look like, Jim? I can't for the life of me think why he needs it that bushy! Has the chap never heard of a razor!?'

O-b-L: Is my religion, Jim.

JY: Super! And there's something that's puzzling Mr Arthur Wickham who lives up Shrewsbury way. Arthur says, 'I don't like the sound of this Taliban lot at all, Jim. They've simply got no business setting off their bombs. They may like living in caves, but the rest of us like our creature comforts. Perhaps you'd ask your guest, Jim, to put that in his pipe and smoke it.' Well, point taken, Arthur, and an awful lot of our listeners have raised that point about your cave, Osama. It must get dreadfully chilly as the nights draw in, doesn't it? Time to get our old friend Mr Blow the Blow-Heater out, *nessy-pas*?

O-b-L: My cave is my—

JY: Sorry, Osama, going to have to cut you off there! Best of luck for the future! And now it's Cliff Richard (now there's a name to conjure with!) to take us up to news time, after which we have our consumer expert, Barry, asking the *questionne* on everyone's lips: 'Toilet Ducks – Just How Effective Really Are They?', not to *mentionez* our regular all-round cookery expert Roger telling us how to get the most out of Sausage Appreciation Week . . .

* * *

There's frankly been a lot of nonsense written these past few weeks on the 'JY To Hang Up His Headphones' front. They say there've been whispers from on high that I've grown a bit long in the tooth. Take it from Jimbo, nothing could be further from the truth! It's speculation I first heard, ooh, years ago. I'd just finished chatting to our then medical correspondent, the lovely Florence Nightingale (*now there's a name to conjure with!*) on tips for how to cope with whooping cough when I look in the *Illustrated London News* and what do I see but talk of my *impending retire-mioso*!

My trick for survival? Keep it tip-top-topical! We've had them all on the show – Charlie Chaplin, George Formby, Mr Gladstone, Lord Kitchener, King George V and his lovely wife Queen Mary, Martin Boorman, Tommy Steele, Dorothy L. Sayers, Marie Curie, Rudolf Valentino, Rudyard Kipling, Mrs Beeton and, more recently, Sir Anthony Eden. I think they've all been attracted by my courteous, easy-going style. I'd hate to single any of them out for praise – frankly, once you've met one, you've met 'em all – but my personal favourite would have to be Chairman Mao Tse-Tung – now there's a name to conjure with!

I'll never forget it. What an extraordinary character he turned out to be, full of the most tremendous stories of purging his enemies, not to mention a truly great ability to laugh at himself! We slotted him in between Petula Clark and something very pleasant from the New Seekers –

JY: Mrs Katherine Haines from Teddington – lovely part of the country – has just called in to say she's not best pleased with your Cultural Revolution. 'So what's all this Cultural Revolution nonsense, Jim?' says Kathy. 'Sounds like more of your common-or-garden *Chinese mumbo-jumbo* to me! It's high time those politicians climbed off their high horses!' What say you to Mrs H, then, Chairman M? Sorry, I'll have to stop you there, to hear this, the latest Numero Uno from the New Seekers, after which Raymondo poses that all-important question 'What's the recipe today, Jim?' and so *orft we jolly well go*. TTFN! TTFE!

Grub
Street

Happy Birthday, *Private Eye*

Boasting to a child is always a mistake. At breakfast on Wednesday, I bragged to my nine-year-old son, with the pride of a regular contributor, that *Private Eye* had just published its thousandth issue.

'So?' he replied with a sneer. '*Beano*'s on its three thousandth.'

The comparison was fair enough. The two magazines – or perhaps one should say the two comics – have much in common. Both deal in jokes. Both glorify mischief at the expense of responsibility. Both demonise the adult world, so that, on a blind-tasting, it would be hard to tell the difference between, say, Quelchy of the Bash Street Kids and Alistair Campbell, or Sir Jimmy Goldsmith and Dennis the Menace's slipper-wielding dad. Both magazines relish nicknames: indeed, as far as I know the real names of the Bash Street Kids have never been disclosed, while in his heyday, Sir James could boast a good half-dozen, including Sir Jams, Sir James Goldfinger and Sir Jammy Fishpaste.

Both are printed on very cheap paper, reinforcing the frisson of there being something a little *samizdat* about them. Both are uniquely and inescapably British: even in the USA, there is no equivalent of *Private Eye*, and American comics consist either of superheroes battling for word peace or cutesy, kooky kids who end up telling their moms just how much they really, really love them.

And both *Beano* and *Private Eye* consist of what is generally thought to be 'schoolboy humour'. 'The public-school boys who ran the *Eye* never grew up,' wrote one of the magazine's severest critics over a decade ago. '. . . They still offer obscenity, scurrility and libel, which may appeal especially to the younger reader, but over twenty-five years there has been a surfeit of it. Enough is enough . . . It is funny, too often, at someone else's expense.'

This particular critic was the late Robert Maxwell (aka the Bouncing Czech and Cap'n Bob), writing in 1986, after winning £55,000 in libel damages from *Private Eye*. Since then, Maxwell's reputation has taken a plunge, but this is no reason not to take his criticisms on board, as it were.

Schoolboyish or not? Certainly, when I first started reading *Private Eye*, I was a thirteen-year-old schoolboy (only two or three years out of *Beano*, I now realise). Looking back on those first issues that I read, I feel slightly bemused by what they could have meant to me. The cast list is as weird and wonderful, not to mention as incomprehensible, as *The Faerie Queene*. Allan 'Plug Em' Hall, Lady Magnesia Freelove, Peter Jaybotham, Pirhana Teeth Stevens, Alan Watneys, Yvonne, Perishing Worthless, Glenda Slagg, Lunchtime O'Booze: who were all those bizarre hobgoblins, and why was I, a thirteen-year-old schoolboy with no knowledge of their real-life counterparts, so endlessly fascinated by them?

Looking through *Private Eye*'s 250th issue, dated Friday 16 July 1971 – roughly the moment I signed on as a reader – I feel at a similar remove from these characters, many of them now dead or forgotten, as I must have felt then, yet their names still possess the same magnetic power.

In the 'Grovel' column, the short-sighted political editor of *The Times* is reported as having approached a woman at a party thrown by Norman St John Stevas. 'And what is a sweet young thing like you doing at a party like this?' he purred in her ear, only to be informed that the lady he was addressing was Princess Margaret. In the 'TV Topics' column by Lunchtime O'Views, a repeat of the disparaged *The First Churchills* series is held up as evidence of 'the depths of mediocrity to which the BBC has sunk'.

A correspondent on the letters page writes in to congratulate Mr Auberon Waugh on his observation that 'Grocer' Heath's habit of defecating in public while on board *Morning Cleoud* [sic] may be a sign of incipient megalomania, citing Louis XIV and Cardinal Wolsey as earlier examples of this syndrome. A Heath cartoon depicts a couple watching Robin Day chairing a Common Market debate on television. 'If we go in,' says the husband, 'at least there won't be any more programmes about whether we should or not.'

The adolescent schoolboy tends to see grown-ups as gargoyles. It is a way of viewing the all-powerful adult world that makes it at the same time more grotesque and easier to fathom. *Private Eye* offers, as Maxwell suggested, a schoolboy vision, but it is a vision that springs from the same source as *Alice in Wonderland* and Punch and Judy and the poems of Edward Lear. And *Private Eye*'s particular genius has been to shape an alternative universe so mesmerising that its real-life victims seem ineluctably drawn into it, gradually meta-morphising into their own caricatures. All those toytown characters I read about as a schoolboy in the seventies – Stonehouse, Thorpe, Nixon, Goldsmith, Kagan, the Dirty Digger – now seem ever more closely to resemble the images created for them by *Private Eye*. And even poor old Robert Maxwell will be remembered not, I suspect, as the benevolent international powerbroker he was so keen to become, but as the essentially ludicrous Cap'n Bob, the Bouncing Czech.

In this way, *Private Eye* resembles a magical doll's house in which the schoolboy's movement of each doll is eerily replicated in the real world beyond. Thus, Tony Blair is becoming increasingly like the happy-clappy control-freak vicar of the 'St Albion Parish News' column, and those who have seen Denis and Margaret Thatcher recently tell me that they now appear to be enacting their roles direct from the 'Dear Bill' column.

When John Major first became Prime Minister, I remember

thinking that this time *Private Eye* had got it wrong, and that his caricature as a gawky Adrian Mole figure would never stand the test of time. I sensed that within a few months of being in Number 10, he would surely acquire a gravitas and *savoir faire* that would render his Mole-ish persona redundant. But no – he, too, was doomed to be shaped by satire; by the end of his term he seemed every bit as awkward and unsuitable as he had at the beginning.

Along with the forces of conservatism, one of Mr Blair's particular targets over the past year (particularly in relation to – ho, ho, – the Millennium Dome) has been those he describes as 'the cynics'. Let us hope that the 1000th issue of *Private Eye* gives him cause to reflect that cynicism has never been so buoyant. In fact, it is a sport at which we British truly excel. Happy Birthday, *Private Eye*.

Tina Brown: The Selected TACK! Magazine Editorials:

August *1999. Issue 1:* It opens at the Tribeca Grill. Harvey Weinstein has just finished his second surf 'n' turf and he's busy chewing on a couple of bread rolls, waiting for his main course to arrive.

He tells me the time is ripe for a new magazine, one that combines exclusive interviews with Leonardo diCaprio in swimming pants with world-class authors like Camille Paglia tackling high-culture issues like 'Is Jane Austen the next Heidi Fleiss?'

Before Harvey finishes spreading the peanut butter on his fifth roll, I have given him an emphatic 'Yes!!!' I had been content – and proud – editing the *New Yorker* for six years. But we were running low on sufficiently prolific serial killers to profile in depth. We were already scraping the barrel with guys who had dismembered less than half a dozen victims *in total*. Short of commissioning some more killings – a high-cost business – the time had come to move on.

Harvey wants, in short, a radical new magazine. It's a great idea: he wants a PORTABLE magazine, a magazine that can be moved from one room to another, a magazine full of words to look at and pictures to read. He wants a magazine that stops the disconnect between our literary and domestic culture by getting, like, Top Homemaker Martha Stewart to write on the use of the apostrophe in the works of sex-obsessed genius Vladimir Nabokov, or doyen celebrity serial killer PAR EXCELLENCE Charles Manson to tell all about how to make that truly scrumptious Thanksgiving Loaf just like Mom used to bake it.

But what to call our baby? We fell in and out of love with a parade of titles. GARBAGE sounded too earthy, CAMEMBERT too cheesy, and VOGUE had already been taken.

Then – *TACK!*

From the moment we saw that logo on page one we knew it was right. Somehow, it conveyed the idea of an intimate gun pointed between the ears of the American conversation.

And so – hey, y'all! – meet the team who'll be bringing their top talents to the *TACK!* party! All the way from sun-soaked Iraq, we welcome as Contributing Editor high-octane ever-controversial Gatsbyesque dictator-about-town Saddam Hussein, who argues that at long last the moustache is back. We also offer an up-close look at top presidential contender, feisty maverick Dan Quayle, and in his profile of feisty Brit actress Liz Hurley, prestige novelist Paul Theroux takes a long, hard look at what he calls 'the maverick duality of Ms Hurley's breasts'.

Enjoy!

December 1999, Issue 5: The velocity of the blast-off has been wonderfully disconcerting. *TACK!* magazine is right up there sailing high in the sky – even though some of the ground staff have been literally burnt to a crisp! Whoops! That'll teach 'em to stand too close!! But fallout from a launch is perfectly natural: we are indebted to the memory of those junior astronauts who sadly neglected to close their doors firmly and pack a parachute.

When super-slender movie mogul Harvey Weinstein invited me out to lunch this month, rolled out the red carpet and treated me to whatever I wanted from the $12-and-under menu at our top-rated local VIP sandwich bar, he wanted to know about the changes I was planning to make to *TACK!* magazine.

I was glad to explain that – such has been the enormous success of *TACK!* magazine – we have decided to change everything about it. Out go the dull typeface, duller photos and even duller articles – and in comes one of the most exciting magazines any of the remaining staff will see in the remainder of their lifetimes!

So, here goes, contents-wise: Gatsbyesque maverick high-flier Al Gore speaks with candor about his Great Defining Moment – the day he decided to go on doing roughly the same as he's been doing up to now. We ponder whether seventies celebrity kidnap victim Patty Hearst will be a suitable bride for England's lifestyle supremo Prince William. And kudos-filled movie maverick Oliver Stone asks this month's Big Question – IS CHE GUEVARA STILL ALIVE?

Stone has gathered unsettling evidence to suggest that Che shaved his beard, entered the Catholic Church, put on weight – and successfully morphed a life change to become international prestige high-flying pontiff, Pope John Paul II. Played in Stone's top-grossing new Miramax movie by Gatsbyesque chameleon Robin Williams, Che is portrayed as kooky and madcap but with a great big beautiful heart, filled to overflowing with treasured childhood dreams.

What these stories have in common is what *TACK!* is all about: intimacy – that thrilling, spine-tingling moment when you call in an exciting young writer to tell him – or her – that their desk is needed for someone even younger and more exciting.

Enjoy!

March 2000, Issue 8: Yessiree! We're riding the crest of a wave in our top-of-the-range private jet with both feet firmly on the ground!

When we launched *TACK!* we hoped to contribute to the synergy between the magazine and movies. So when svelte Gatsbyesque movie mogul Harvey Weinstein treated me to lunch at top-rated international restaurant McDonald's on 5th

Avenue last month, I found it hard to contain my yip-diggety-dawg excitement.

'You eat all you want, Tina,' said fast-paced maverick Harvey, seen by many as the natural successor to Italy-based painter and man-about-town Michelangelo, 'I'll be eating someplace else. I have someone important to see.'

So it was over a masterly Fillet-O-Fish in an oven-baked bun complimented by a Diet Coke served in an eco-friendly designer paper cup that I first heard Harvey's exciting new plans for mega-movie cross-fertilisation.

'Hey, I've got a real swell idea for a movie from the pages of *TACK!*' he said, pocketing a bundle of my French fries for his cab journey.

'You HAVE?' I gasped in delight as he finished squeezing the ketchup into his pocket.

'You ever seen that great movie *Titanic*?' he said. 'I'm thinking of a land-based sequel set on a magazine. Hey, whaddya think of *Tinatic* as a title?'

'Oh Harvey!' I said. 'You always have the BEST ideas!'

Enjoy!

July 2002, Issue 25: When we launched *TACK!* we made it plain we would publish only pieces that reflect our passion for literary quality, scholarship, intrinsic news values, nudity and serial killers. Elsewhere in this issue, we present feisty Dr Henry Kissinger as you've never seen him before – wearing bottle-thick spectacles, crinkly hair and a dark suit, eyeing up a B-list actress. On the medical front, we grab a VIP front-row seat in an operating theatre, welcoming you along to sit back and enjoy the ride while a top heart surgeon rides the cardiogram roller-coaster of medical thrills and spills – only to have an elderly patient die on him.

There's more glamour, too, as Donald Trump's girlfriend Malania Knauss proves she cares as much about brains as beauty when she asks hirsute maverick and archipelago-go trendsetter Alexander Solzhenitsyn for his very own Top Ten Raunchy Reads for browzing poolside with a mint julep this summer. And elsewhere Dr Ruth encourages maverick actor Rupert Everett to pour out his heart on how he feels Jon Bon Jovi is coming to terms with feisty Sarah Jessica Parker's latest multi-million dollar landmark role as Hillary Clinton in the new top-selling Miramax movie based on the life of maverick screen actress Demi Moore.

This month, we at *TACK!* have copied multi-millionaire model and intellectual Kate Moss and rethought our design. We've gone for the sleeker, leaner, shorter look favoured by this season's cutting-edge postage stamps. We know our sophisticated readers will prefer smaller pages, and fewer of them.

And who can blame 'em?

Enjoy!

February 2002, Final Issue: Our story closes this month, in the epicentre of an exclusive queue at a top-rated open-air soup kitchen on fashionably Bohemian Skid Row. Maverick visionary and skinny mogul Harvey Weinstein has just dropped me out of his limousine on his way to exclusive VIP eater the Tribeca Grill.

Harvey has come up with a great idea. He thinks the time is ripe for a total change. 'You know what I want, Tina?' he says, as the in-car microwave tings to tell him that his salmon is now poached, buttered and ready to eat. 'I want TACK! to be the type of magazine they don't produce any more.'

'Great idea, Harvey!!!' I enthuse to this pencil-thin international genius. 'But how do we turn it into the type of magazine they don't produce any more?'

'You wanna know how we do it, Tina? I tell you how we do it! WE DON'T PRODUCE IT ANY MORE!'

The more I think about closing down a great new magazine from scratch, the more enamoured I become of the idea. Its absence would contribute to the vitality of our nation's news-stands.

So at long last we have reached our destination. We remain on course to achieve the most brilliantly successful closedown in magazine history. As Harvey's limo recedes into the distance, and I stand here waving, I reach for my mixed vegetable soup and look around for Bill and Hillary, Donald and Malania, Demi and Arnold and Leonardo and Gwyneth and Tom – but they are all BRILLIANTLY ABSENT.

TACK! magazine is already a legend, and like all legends – from maverick VIP new-age forest-dweller Robin Hood to feisty Gatsbyesque Santa Claus – something tells me it never really existed.

Great!! CIAO!!

And – Enjoy!

Bel Littlejohn: How to Be Humorous

If you want that humorous Sideways Look At Life – well, you know on whose door to knock! Though best known through my pieces in the *Guardian* as a serious writer, over the years I have also built up something of a reputation in the realm of what used to be known as 'women's magazines' as a quirky, irreverent and hilarious commentator on the Perils and Pitfalls of Family Life.

The most recent of these off-the-wall (off-my-trolley, more like!) pieces are soon to be collected in a volume rejoicing in the title, *How Was It For Me?!*, companions to my earlier, well-loved and much-thumbed tomes *Me and My Five Pairs of Hands!* (1987) and *Excuse Me While I Collapse In a Heap!* (1973), along with my celebrated compendium of the roller-coaster ride that is parenthood, *Of Nappies, Naughtiness – and Oodles of Love* (1991), memorably described by the lovely Esther Rantzen in *Coping Woman* magazine as 'truly a must-read for all those with irrepressible little bundles of energy, bless 'em'.

Over the years, our very own Postman Pat has worn out many a thick sole delivering a positive tidal wave of hand-written missives from lovely, lovely readers on to our hard-pressed doormat, many of them asking me for my advice on How to Pen a Humorous Column – and Stay Sane!! So I'd like to take this opportunity to pass on any handy tips to All You Aspirant Humorists Out There – and, as we all know, if you can't laugh at the (metaphorical) banana skins of everyday life – well, you'll find yourself reaching for the Kleenex, and creating a Niagara Falls with those hard-pressed tear-ducts of yours! So, all aboard for 6 Handy Hints for Penning a Light-Hearted Column – and here goes!

1) *Employ Capital Letters to Heighten The Comic Effect.* Combine this with Handy Nicknames and it comes in particularly useful when conjuring up a word-picture concerning the hilarious comings and goings in your immediate family, with particular reference to The Firstborn, Elder Daughter, Him Indoors, His Nibs, Himself, Long-Suffering Moggie, etc.

2) *Laugh at Yourself – and The World Will Laugh With You!* If you've ever burnt that special-occasion cake just when the vicar was coming round – or ended up with your skirt tucked into the back of your tights at that all-important company 'do' – don't worry, it's a disaster that's sure to tickle the readers' ribs when they Read All About It in your hard-pressed column!!

3) *Deliver Some Home-'Pun' Wisdom!* The 'pun' or 'play on words' is one of the great sources of the contemporary chuckle – a sure way to tickle the funny-bone of even the most po-faced reader! And my new column in my old mate Eve Pollard's smashing new *Aura* magazine even has a title with a pun in it – 'Bel Letters', if you will! But just remember – the 'pun' is mightier than the sword!

4) *The English Language Includes Some Highly Amusing Words of the Lengthy Variety for your Delectation and Delightification!* Even the most humdrum of household chores can be turned into chucklesome *hors d'oeuvres* by recourse to words and phrases that some might describe as long-winded – or even a tad eccentric!! For instance, I once memorably described my hair, on one particularly hard-pressed morning (!) as 'looking more like the proverbial bird's nest, though with none of that ornithological dwelling's wholly admirable pride in its appearance'. Result? Collapse of stout readers!

5) *Develop Some Catchphrases – Particularly Those of the Common-or-Garden Conversational Variety!* Personally, I try to include the catchphrase 'Eat your heart out' in all my columns, as in 'Eat

your heart our, Liz Hurley!' or 'Eat your heart our, Cherie Blair!' Also, never forget to temper your perfect (!) prose with colloquialisms – for instance, I always call Will Shakespeare 'The Bearded Bard', and my own good self 'Yours Truly'. And it's sure to make your readers chuckle if you call your fellow women 'La So-and-So', eg La Rantzen, La Feltz, La Halliwell, etcetera, etcetera.

6) *Men!!!!* The mainstay of any sideways look at life! My ex, Vic, was a constant ingredient in my light-hearted 'Count Me Out' column for *Cosmo* magazine in the 1970s, with memorable columns including 'The Joy of Sox', concerning his habit of wearing the same smelly socks for days on end, 'My Nose-Pickin' Pardna' about his penchant for stuffing his index finger up his nose, and 'Size Isn't Everything – or Is It?' about his shortcomings in the Basement Department (!). Vic upped and left at the height of the column's success in 1979 (I still don't know why) but at least I managed to get six months' worth of columns out of it, later published as *That's Blokes For You!!*

On the Rocks with Bel Littlejohn

'You look so happy' friends would say. I didn't like to disillusion them, but I would quietly point them in the direction of my article for that week's *Observer*, headed 'On The Rocks' and subtitled 'Bel Littlejohn's deeply moving and poignant account of a marriage made in hell'. It was only a matter of time before Don came across it – but we struggled on.

To be honest, married life had occasional glimpses of laughter and sunshine. I remember one day bursting into fits of giggles when Don stubbed his toe on the side of a table, and I'll never forget how once, sometime early that April, Don seemed to laugh, though he wouldn't tell me what about. It was only when, hours later, I pushed open a door, only to find a pot of treacle on my head, that I began to put two and two together.

Hurtling along the M25, I pressed my foot on the brake and found it severed. It was at that moment that I began to suspect that my husband's love of practical jokes might mask a streak of cruelty. In retrospect, the experts might claim I repeatedly stabbed him with that carving knife as some sort of psychological 'revenge', but at the time it just seemed a normal thing to do. Our marriage might be having its ups and downs, but the two of us were more determined than ever to keep it going, at least until we had finished writing about it.

'You've ruined everything!' I screamed. Don had inadvertently (a word he was to use a lot in our marriage) knocked a teacup off the table.

The teacup had fallen headlong on to the head of our cat, which in a fearful panic had leapt on to the table, knocking over a dish holding a range of novelty marbles. Leaning forward to pick up the smashed teacup, Don had caught his left foot on a marble and fallen head first on to the trolley holding our twenty-four-piece dinner service, a wedding gift from his parents. The trolley slid forward and smashed into an occasional table on which was displayed my beloved collection of decorative glassware.

'Thanks a lot! Thanks a bloody lot!' I yelled, brandishing a pair of kitchen scissors and rushing at him with a speed born of a healthy low-fat diet. But at the last moment, he had inadvertently (that word again!) moved out of the way, causing me to trip and the kitchen scissors to lodge in our brand-new Habitat beanbag, spilling thousands of little foam balls all over the floor.

Call it sixth sense, call it what you will, but looking back, it must have been around this time that I first began to suspect there might be something wrong with our marriage.

My cuttings book informs me that, a few days later, I wrote an article for the *Observer* about our sex life ('When He Can't Get It Up'). It was intended as an informed and dispassionate discussion about the problems faced by any married couple, and I even protected Don's identity by changing his name. 'Whenever I look at the pitiful state of my naked husband Nod,' I began the second paragraph, 'I know that, yet again, it's going to be *Newsnight*, a cup of cocoa and a Picador classic.'

All responsible journalism, you might have thought. But not Don. Oh no: Don considered it an invasion of privacy. 'And what are you doing now?' he snapped. 'Just taking notes,' I replied, scribbling p-r-i-v-a-c-y on to my pad, 'I've got an article to do tomorrow, *remember*?'

Christmas Day. We should have been so happy but I sensed that something was, well, not quite right. It must have been the way he had moved the upright piano, barricaded himself into the spare bedroom, and was now refusing to come out. 'Don?' I said. 'Don, what are you doing in there?' No reply. My mind turned to the turkey with all the trimmings that was coming along nicely in the oven downstairs. 'So what am I going to do with your Christmas lunch, Don?' I asked. Again, no reply. In the end, I was left with no alternative. I carved the turkey wafer thin, squashed the sprouts, and slid the whole lot under his door. He could have the gravy later. Some Happy Christmas that turned out to be.

Boxing Day. In the beginning, we had communicated directly. Now, things were becoming more complicated. I muddled through in O-level Spanish, while he attended evening classes in semaphore. There is a photograph of the two of us at this time, still trying to make a go of it. We are in the kitchen together. To all intents and purposes, it should be a scene of domestic bliss. But if you look carefully, you can see he is holding two semaphore flags. Look a bit closer, and you'll see that the message he is communicating is 'Mayday! Mayday!' Meanwhile, I am looking the other way, my face buried in the leftovers of the Christmas pudding, desperate, once again, to find some sort of consolation in food.

As January turned to February, I filled my *Observer* column with things I wouldn't have confided to my best friend. My piece of February 14th (how ironic that date seems now!) was headed 'I Think He Might Be Having It Off With a Trollop'. With the benefit of hindsight, I can see it hints that we were drifting apart. To the outside world, our marriage was perfect. But by now the two of us, and any *Observer* readers, knew we were living a lie.

Don was changing before my very eyes. Of course, when I first met him I must have noticed that his teeth were very sharp, his skin unusually scaly and that he had the beginnings of a powerful tail sticking out of his back. Often he would wait, stock still, for days on end, observing my movements while I fetched myself another cup of coffee. I thought nothing of it at the time. It was only now that I began to realise that he had turned into a crocodile. Should I call the RSPCA? Or send away for a blow-pipe? Then it came to me. Everything was perfect. Me and the crocodile. The crocodile and me. Yes! I would turn us into a circus.

The video says it all. I watch it, over and over again. Over and over and over again. Over. And Over. And over. And. Over. Again.

It should have been so beautiful – our break-up, I mean. I was late with my deadline, so I had already written the first half of it in advance. 'I can't live with you – and I can't live without you,' I had me down as saying.

'Oh, Bel, Bel, Bel, Bel, Bel,' I had Don saying (or, to be more accurate, Nod, as I called him in the column). 'You won't find another fool like me, babe. It's a heartache, nothing but a heartache. I love you love you love me too love I love you love me love.' And then he would break down, sobbing like a broken reed.

But it all had to go wrong, didn't it? Rather than take notes during the final scene – I'm sorry, but these columns demand you play life as though it were for real – I had set up a video camera. 'Ding-Dong!' The doorbell went, and I switched the video to REC. Looking back at the video now, I watch things fall apart, all over again.

'Hi!' I say.

'Hi,' says Don. Just like him to leave out the exclamation mark, leaving me to do the work. I decided then and there not to put it in when I wrote it up, just to show him how it feels to live with someone who's so bloody *understated*.

'So!' I say.

'So . . .' says Don.

'*Could you please stop repeating everything I say?*' I say. He had always been a control freak, and part of his control freakery was to try and make it look as if I was the control freak, setting an agenda which he would then be 'forced' to follow. When in fact it was quite the opposite.

'What do you mean – "could you please stop repeating everything I say"?' he says.

'There – you just did it again!'

'Did it again? Did what again?'

'That!'

'That?'

We were getting nowhere and fast. At this point, the phone rings. It's a researcher from *Woman's Hour*. She says they're doing a three-minute slot on the modern break-up and could I come on?

Watching this moment on the video, I can see Don in the background, idly leafing through an old column of mine in the *Guardian*. I wrote it shortly after our honeymoon. It was about his annoying habit of breaking wind in bed. Selfishly, he was upset by it at the time, saying it was private – private!! Yet here he was, re-reading it!

'When do you need me?' I whisper to the researcher on the other end of the phone. 'It's just that – well – we haven't quite broken up yet.'

The researcher says they'll have to send a cab for me in twenty-five minutes, and that my fellow guest is Erica Jong, my mega-heroine.

'Done!' I whisper into the phone. I hang up, and turn to Don. 'Let's get this thing over,' I say.

'Over?' he says. 'This thing?'

Then the video shows me rushing across the room to switch on the radio. I have just remembered that the interview I recorded the day before is going out live on GLR. Behind me, Don, always unsettled by the idea of a woman more successful than himself, is visibly disconcerted.

'. . . and now we turn to top *Guardian* columnist Bel Littlejohn,' says the interviewer. 'Well, Bel, you've been to hell and back in the last few weeks – and now, according to this week's column, you're planning to leave your husband. When are you going to do it, exactly?'

'Hey!' interrupts Don, ever the control freak, ever trying to frustrate my career.

'Sssshhhh!' I say. 'I'm on the radio.'

From the radio comes the sound of me saying I'll be telling

Don today. 'Brave lady,' says the disc jockey, 'and now pin back your lugholes for this, the latest from Chris de Burgh.'

I switch it off. I know that look of Don's. It says, *Boo, hoo. I'm so hurt. And don't expect me to congratulate you on your brilliant performance on the radio just now, 'cos frankly I'm too wound up in myself.*

I decide to ignore him. I've got my own life to lead.

'Don,' I say, 'I've gotta rush. Speed-read last week's *Guardian* and you'll know why I'm leaving you. And read next week's for my emotional farewell. Ciao!'

And with that I rush out of the house, and out of his life. The video then shows Don leaping in the air, doing a double thumbs-up to the mirror and shouting 'Yes!' The bastard. The bloody, bloody bastard. I make a note to write about it soonest.

The Diary of Max Clifford

Have you ever seen a tot in tears, a poorly tot of three or four years of age – in tears? Well, I have. It cuts me up, it really does. There's only one word for it. *Shattered*. And whenever I see a poorly tot with great big tears rolling down her tender little cheeks, I say to myself, *'Never will I allow a tot to suffer like this.'* And with that, I lift the phone, call a top editor and provide him with an exclusive scoop concerning an MP's three-in-a-bed kinky love-romp for 120K up front. By destroying a reputation, I'm putting something back into society – doing my bit to make this world a better place. And when I see those tears dry, and a lovely, sunny smile lighting up the face of that very, very special little tot, well, it makes it all worthwhile, it really does. Have you ever seen a tot smile, a tot of three or four years of age really *smiling*? Have you? Believe me, it's one of the most beautiful sights in the world, it really is.

My good friends and clients Alan and Judith Kilshaw are very tot-minded too. And they love two tiny tots in particular very, very much. Is that a crime? Not in my book it's not. So I was delighted to help steer Alan and Judith and improve their public perception. 'If you want to bring ordinary decent folk round to your point of view, Judith,' I told her, 'then you've got to dye your hair blonde, behave erratically, and scream obscenities in court.' Well, it did the trick. I've already got the Kilshaws on to top-rating shows like *Kilroy* and *Richard and*

Judy, and of course *Oprah* in the States – and we've got high hopes for a recording contract come the autumn, and publishers are showing a lot of interest in *The Official Kilshaw Babycare Manual*. Believe me, Alan and Judith are going to be mega, and we're talking both sides of the Atlantic. I could do for them what I did for Mandy Allwood. Remember her? IVF lady. Eight lovely tots on the way. Exclusive rights worldwide. Sadly, the tots all passed away. Broke my heart. So now when I'm advising Alan and Judith Kilshaw, I'm not doing it for Max Clifford. No, I'm doing it for the Allwood lots, bless their little hearts. Well, you've got to put something back, haven't you?

Don't get me wrong. I've got the greatest respect for the Beatles. Lovely guys, nice tunes, flogged a few copies, even if it's not quite so many as they claim. Fair enough. I'm not knocking them. But let's not kid ourselves. I was their publicist when they meant zilch. And believe me it was an uphill struggle to put them on the map. But with my talent and their push, we just about succeeded. I've been called the Fifth Beatle, but that's not a phrase in my vocabulary. I was more like the Second or Third Beatle. Elvis, too. When I first made his acquaintance, Elvis looked terrible, sang rotten. But with my help he conquered the world. Rudolf Nureyev, Francis Bacon, Frank Sinatra, Pablo Picasso, Winston Churchill – ever heard of them? These people didn't just appear out of nowhere, you know. They came to me and said, Max, they said, we've got the talent, you've got the contacts. Nelson Mandela, he was another. When he first came to me, he was a total unknown. I said to him, look, Nelson, do yourself a favour, check into prison for a couple of decades, check out again, then put on a fancy shirt and keep smiling. Fast-forward to the year 2001, Nelson's a major public figure with a worldwide reputation for integrity – and that's something we can build on.

It's not something I talk about to my friends outside the media, but I'm secretly a very very religious bloke. I hate to see a tot in tears. There's an old lady down our road – I really wouldn't like to see anyone hurling abuse at her and making her life a misery. I pray a lot, and I'm not embarrassed to admit it. Well, you've got to put something back, haven't you? And sometimes when I'm talking to Jesus, I say, Look, mate, we've got to do something about the old image. I'm not knocking the Pope, he's done some great things for your image in his time, but he's stuck in the past. Beards are a turn-off, and no one cares for the whole scars-and-loincloth look any more. Ditch the cross, mate, get yourself a shave, a haircut and a decent suit, and we'll see what we can do for you. You've heard of Denise van Outen? Lovely lady, Denise. When she first came to me she was on the check out at Sainsbury's. She said to me Max, I want to be a star. And the rest is history. Well, I think Denise could be persuaded to be seen out and about with you, Jesus. You'd give her the gravitas, she'd give you the glamour. Cross-fertilisation, that's the name of the game.

Dear, oh, dear. Sophie's come a cropper. Still, I can't shed too many tears. To be honest, it's the hypocrisy that gets up my nose. If she insists on telling fibs for clients and mixing with all sorts of unsavoury types and talking to the press and acting all holier-than-thou, well, she's only got what was coming to her. It's the pomposity of these toffee-nosed types that sticks in my gullet. The way they act as though they're doing the public a service. And that's why it's my duty to expose them. No doubt about it – I'm doing the public a service.

Charlie Manson? Lovely guy, top talent, great future. He phoned me from the penitentiary last July, said this is the way I see it, Max, I like what you've done for the profiles of your A list clientele O.J. Simpson, Tony Martin and the Stephen Lawrence suspects, now I want you to work the same magic on me. Okay, the guy might've murdered some people in the past. But you could say the same about Hitler. Look, I know the guy, I know what a decent, gentle human being he is, not pompous at all. Never voted Tory in his life. And Charlie would hate to see a tot in tears. I tell you, he'll be the new Ann Robinson –

especially after my friends in the press get to hear what I have on *her*. Meanwhile, O.J.'s lined up for his own talk show, Tony Martin, bless him, is set to be the public face of Bernard Matthews's Norfolk Turkey Roasts, and the Stephen Lawrence lads are set to be the biggest boyband since the Beatles. And if my hard work stops the tears from trickling down the cheeks of just one tot, or prevents just one old lady being roundly abused by a masked gunman, believe me, it'll've all been worthwhile. Cheers!

Wallace Arnold Looks Ahead

Among the greatest of life's pleasures I count settling down to a goodly jar of Best Bitter with my old friend and quaffing partner Lord (if you will!) Rees-Mogg.

I have known William since way back, and for the past two decades I have been a regular summer guest for picnics aboard his delightful yacht, *Vesuvius*. William is, as you might imagine, an excellent skipper, though perhaps best when safely in dock. Of course, there is bound to be the occasional mishap, and our last voyage proved no exception. 'My own balance of expectation leads me to veer strongly towards the belief that we shall be sighting land in over four hours,' he intoned just before the yacht went smack into the White Cliffs of Dover. But I am happy to say that William took it on the chin. 'As one who has long held to the belief that the yacht was about to go straight into the White Cliffs of Dover,' he purred, with a knowing smile playing over his fine features, 'I must confess to a little satisfaction that my prophecies have held so steady.'

We imbibe together in a friendly hostelry maybe twice a year, contentedly chewing over the fat of the previous six months. One such quaffing session took place in the mid-seventies, shortly after William had advanced his career by predicting that the so-called 'Watergate' scandal would, in his judgement, soon blow over. It was a bright summer's day, yet William arrived positively sweltering in three woolly jumpers, an overcoat, ear-muffs, balaclava and sou'wester. 'Though I recognise the strength of the claims of those who maintain that this is a sunny day,' he explained, 'on balance, I find myself more and more convinced that it will end in a fearful blizzard of a type this country has not known for at least half a century.'

As the sun poured through the window, William explained through his balaclava how he had arrived at this diagnosis. 'When visiting my kitchen, I occasionally find cause to open a cupboard, particularly when the staff are away. You know, of course, what a "cupboard" is, Wallace? It's a compartment, generally used for storage, often containing shelves. Well, this morning I ventured to open one such cupboard, only to find, to my amazement, that it was quite literally *covered* in ice and snow. This I understood at once to mean that our civilisation was heading for an imminent ice age, and that is why I am so attired.'

'Forgive me, William,' quoth Arnold, 'but might it not have been a *refrigerator* into which you peered?'

'A what?' replied William. Realising that a 'refrigerator' was not within his frame of reference, I decided to change tack, and he was soon expounding merrily on the absolute impossibility of a woman becoming Prime Minister before the turn of the century, sweat pouring off his spectacle frames and on to his overcoat.

During another such convivial get-together in early 1966, we found ourselves drawn into a pub conversation concerning the England World Cup squad. As luck would have it, William turned out to be something of an expert on the matter. 'On reflection,' declared William, 'and with the greatest possible regret, for I have a great deal of respect for Mr Robert – or "Bobby" – Moore, I am afraid to say that, in my considered judgement, they are unlikely to make it through the qualifying round.'

He then applied himself to an assessment of each member of the squad. Martin Peters, he maintained, had a 'good third-class intellect rather than a lower second-class one' while Nobby Stiles, 'though reasonably gifted with the manipulation of a football' had, it pained him to say, 'a mind of no very great profundity, a middling fourth-class intellect rather than a bottom-class third, with scant knowledge of Locke or even Mill'.

And so to Tuesday last, when William and I discussed the vexed issue of religion over a Dry Martini at White's. 'In my experience,' he said, 'God has no very great knowledge of international affairs, and He is sometimes let down by an unbecoming impulsiveness in matters geographical.' William then took a nibble of a peanut, 'Nevertheless, I would say He has a decent second-class mind: an ideal administrator, if no very great leader.'

'Incidentally,' he whispered, 'I have come to one very firm conclusion.'

'And what is that, pray, William?' quoth I.

An agitated look came into this eye. 'The End of the World is Nigh!'

'Would that give us time for a little light luncheon?' I asked, a little perturbed.

'Maybe!'

'Bit of pud? Welsh Rarebit? Coffee? Decent port?'

His eyes lit up. 'On second thoughts,' he said, 'I'll have lunch first, and prepare for the end later. One should never be over-hasty, eh, Wallace?'

'Indeed not,' I said, adding encouragingly, 'cheer up, William – it may never happen,' before guiding him into the dining room.

The Other Craig Brown

'Craig Brown is today exposed as a vile bigot and love cheat,' said the *News of the World* two Sundays ago. Since then, it has been a bad fortnight not only for that Craig Brown but for all Craig Browns.

For a good thirty years, I lived happily in the belief that I was the only Craig Brown on the planet. There have always been a lot of Browns, of course, but in the late 1950s, when I was born, Craig was still an unusual name.

Aged ten, I had heard of only two other Craigs, both slightly famous. I felt an obscure kinship with them, building up their importance in my mind, thinking that their greater glory would in some way reflect downwards on me. One was Craig Beedlove, who broke a land-speed record, I forget which, at some point in the 1950s. The other was Craig Douglas, who had enjoyed a number one hit record, 'Only Sixteen' when I was two years old, but whose last record 'Town Crier' achieved only a disappointing thirty-sixth place in the chart in 1963, when I was six. At some point in the mid-sixties, I remember feeling a preternatural pride when I read that Craig Douglas was the all-American voice singing 'Gets right to the heart of the waaaarrsshh!' every night on the TV commercial for Daz (or was it Omo?).

A few weeks ago, leafing through an excellent new encyclopaedia of forgotten pop stars called *Whatever Happened To . . .?*, I found myself looking him up. I felt a pang of disappointment when I discovered that his real name was not

418

Craig Douglas but Terence Perkins, and that he had been born not in America but in the Isle of Wight.

Right up until the mid-1970s, people would ask me to repeat my Christian name, and then to spell it. This made me feel special, and one up on both my younger brothers – James, who had to share his whole name with the sexually charged soul-singer, and David, who had to share his not only with a cricketer but also with a make of tractor.

It was the late Peter Cook who first alerted me, at some point in the late 1980s, to the fact that there was another Craig Brown on the horizon. This one was, he said, the coach for Celtic. I found this slightly upsetting, but guessed that this other Craig Brown would soon disappear into obscurity. Peter Cook had himself been alert to doppelgängers since receiving his biggest-ever envelope from a press cuttings agency and feeling that his career was on the upturn, only to discover that every single article was about Peter Cook, the recently arrested Cambridge Rapist.

My guess proved wrong: each year the other Craig Brown grew more and more illustrious, moving from coach to trainer to team manager, and then to the top job of manager of Scotland. Irritatingly, he was now not only far better known than me but better liked too. Despite the daily mentions of this other Craig Brown, one's name is so bound up with one's sense of identity that I found it took a very long time to get used to the idea of sharing mine with someone else. I remember once turning on Radio 4's *Today* programme and hearing that the people of Aberdeen had called for a statue of Craig Brown to be erected in their main square. For a brief moment ('But this is extraordinary – I've only been to Aberdeen once in my life!') I genuinely thought they meant me. Such split-second disappointments were soon to become part of my daily life.

During the World Cup, the other Craig Brown would pop up on the television news, giving predictions, expressing delight or disappointment. He seemed a cheery sort, and reassuringly dull. I had often felt sorry for a young TV AM news reporter called Paul Newman, and even for the poet John Wain, their perfectly worthy lives dwarfed by their more glamorous counterparts, but I at least felt confident that this would not be my lot. As a child, I had muddled in my mind the TV conjuror David Nixon with President Richard Nixon, first believing them to be one and the same person – a US President who regularly made the effort to turn up on *The Cilla Black Show* to perform tricks with foam-rubber balls and lengths of rope. Later, when I realised that they were two entirely different people, I felt sorry for President Nixon for being stuck in his dull job, with no hope of appearing on *Cilla*.

The other Craig Brown loomed larger and larger. While the World Cup was on, people on the other end of the phone would ask me for my name and then reply, 'How many goals have the team scored today then, ha ha ha!?!' adding, 'I suppose you get that all the time, ha ha ha!!' My agent once sent me a letter from an advertising agency, asking me how much money I would need to appear in a series of TV advertisements for a Scottish supermarket chain. I used to write about food, so I tried to convince myself that they meant this Craig Brown and not that Craig Brown, but in the end I had to admit that it must be a mistake, and wave goodbye to the free money.

Such muddle-ups are not uncommon. Roy Plomley once invited Alistair Maclean to appear on *Desert Island Discs*. In line with Plomley's usual procedure, the two men had met for lunch in the Garrick before the recording. Over coffee, Maclean asked Plomley to explain why he of all people had been chosen as a castaway. 'But you're one of our most popular novelists, Alistair, and several of your books have been filmed,' Plomley had replied, 'so you're an obvious choice.' Alas, it emerged that this particular Alistair Maclean was not the novelist at all, but a leading light in the Forestry Commission.

Before long, I began to feel peevish towards the other Craig Brown for subsuming my identity. This resentment came to a head when, compiling a book of journalism, I asked the *Telegraph* library to look up some old articles of mine on their computer. The reply came back that there were thousands of references to Craig Brown, most of them involving football, and that there was now no way to separate the football manager from the journalist.

I am not alone in my dilemma. What of Alan Clark the MP and Allan Clarke, the lead singer with the Hollies? Does the MP find himself avalanched with requests to play Sixties Revival nights? There are at least three Robin Cooks, one of them a Foreign Secretary and two of them novelists, one recently deceased. There is the Peter Townend who was social editor of the *Tatler*, the Peter Townsend who was Princess Margaret's great love, and the Peter Townshend who was the leader of the Who.

Add to this four Michael Jacksons – the portly wine and beer writer, the neo-Caucasian pop star, the TV mogul and the general – two left-wing journalists, both called Duncan Campbell, three Michael Whites – one the political editor of the *Guardian*, one an opera critic, the other an impresario – three John Lloyds (director, journalist, tennis player), two Jack Joneses (crooner and trades unionist), two Michael Fishes (sixties fashion designer and TV weatherman), two Ted Heaths (danceband leader and ex-Prime Minister), two David Mellors (kitchen designer and ex-MP) and two Richard Bakers (serial rapist and veteran broadcaster) and you are left with a frightful muddle as the identity of each merges into the other. 'Not *the* Mr Slazenger?' an elderly friend of mine said upon being introduced to the film director John Schlesinger. 'Oh, but I swear by your tennis balls!'

'Bigot Brown Faces The Axe' ran the *Daily Mirror*'s headline on the Monday after the scandal broke. So far, the other Craig Brown appears to be hanging on. I hope he survives. I have now come to think that, in some strange way, we depend upon each other. For all Craig Browns everywhere, it's time to sink or swim.

Bel Littlejohn: Woody and I

He seemed delighted to see me again. 'Woody!' I said as his lovely, lovely PR lady ushered me into his hotel suite. 'How *are* you! Long time no see!'

I had flown to New York especially to interview Woody Allen. I gave him a great big hug, which seemed to please him greatly, then took off my coat (the Big Apple can be pretty cold at this time of year!!), set up my tape and reached for my handy list of Qs and As.

'Woody!' I said again, unable to contain my enthusiasm. 'Great to see you! You're looking great!' My delight in his company seemed to please him, so I reminded him of our last meeting. Twelve years ago, on an evening in autumn (or 'Fall'), I had sat with Woody on a table of twenty-five or thirty people in a downtown jazz eaterie. I was down one end, and Woody down the other, but I had sensed, even then, a strong empathy between us.

In retrospect, I now see that we were both trapped in fickle, doomed relationships, and we were searching for something else, something free of the constraints we had previously set ourselves. And, of course, we both shared a kooky sense of humour (!), both enjoying depicting ourselves as the hard-pressed underdog in rib-tickling tales of mayhem and madness. And was there not also a bond of underlying melancholy between us? Did we not both try as hard as we

422

could to present a happy face to the world – even if inside we were hurting?

Anyway, it had been an unforgettable evening, and as I leant forward in my seat and stretched my neck to see how Woody was doing, right up the other end of the table, I had somehow known – don't ask me how – that it wouldn't be all that long before our paths crossed again.

Call it chance. Call it serendipity. Call it what you will. But just twelve years later, here I was again, in Woody's New York apartment, this time to formally interview my old friend for the *Guardian*. 'Remember the last time we met, Woody! Do you remember!?!' I began to laugh at the memory of that totally madcap evening, which ended in both of us going our separate ways. 'Still crazy after all these years, right, Woody?!?!' I added, with a delightful little laugh which somehow reminded me, heaven knows why, of Diane Keaton as Annie Hall.

After a morning of stiff, formal interviews with complete strangers Woody seemed delighted by the more light-hearted, carefree approach of an old friend. I sensed, too, an 'us-against-them' camaraderie developing between us: it was as though we had both had it up to here with the pressure on the person interviewing and the person interviewed to be seen as 'on opposite sides of the wall', and we were both determined to experiment with a more relaxed, cross-fertilising approach.

'You were wearing jeans the last time we saw each other!' I said. 'And I see you're wearing jeans again today! Snap!' I couldn't help but laugh at this. Woody seemed pleased. From the look of him, he was impressed by my almost photographic memory, so I couldn't stop myself from extrapolating further.

'Now let me see,' I said. 'What was I wearing? Don't tell me! Yes! I know! I was wearing jeans too, can you believe it! Serendipity! Then I had my favourite silk shirt, a sort of mauvy-purply colour, with bell sleeves, and a favourite old jean-jacket, and some expensive new boots I had bought the day before from that shop on 5th Avenue, what'd'you call it?'

Pausing to look back on that momentous day, I began to worry that perhaps I had been a shade under-dressed, but then

I thought of Woody – never the smartest person at the best of times! – and, after emitting another of my famous 'Annie Hall' laughs, I began to relax, and I felt that Woody did too.

First question. 'Soooo, Woody!' I said, taking off my coat and looking him straight in the eye. 'What've you been up to since we last met!?! How's tricks?' But before he answered, I decided to make the whole thing a lot less confrontational by telling him what I myself had been doing – the award-winning *Guardian* column, my romantic history (don't!), the successful PR agency, my involvement with New Labour, my links, both personal and professional, with some of the top names in the British film industry, including David Puttnam. 'So, as you can imagine, Woody, it's been a roller-coaster – but it's been a helluva lot of fun!' I concluded. Woody seemed pleased.

Sadly, at that moment the lovely PR lady put her head round the door, saying there was somebody else for Woody to see. Just our luck! Oh, well, lah-di-dah – as Annie Hall would say! After another marvellous meeting, I packed my tape recorder away, gave Woody a great big farewell hug, and promised to come and see him again before too long. And you know what? Woody seemed pleased.

The Diary of Dominick Dunne

There's no actress I'd rather sit next to at dinner than Joan Collins, whose second husband, bearded Victorian novelist Wilkie, was an old friend of mine from way back, and whose sixth husband, rock star Phil, is to appear at glamorous Queen Elizabeth II's jubilee celebrations in her prestigious parkside London mansion Buckingham Palace, and I had that great pleasure at the top-rated exclusive upmarket Le Cuiller Gras restaurant on Park Avenue when Joan was in New York recently to launch her fabulous new range of high-quality scent 'Odeur du Corps'.

Joan put her gorgeously wrinkled hand on my shoulder and whispered deep into my ear, 'Dominick, I have to talk to you.' As she was telling me something truly astonishing about the certain involvement in the O.J. Simpson case of AWOL moustachioed English aristo Lord Lucan, which I agreed not to pass on, down the far end of our table Snow White, the deeply unhappy ageing two-bit hooker and former Disney starlet, now married to multi-billionaire plastics supreme triple-face-lifted 87-year-old Vernon D. Vernon Jr, slumped into her cheese soufflé from a shot to the head. No, the news was not good for 57-year-old thrice-married former call girl Snow White: she was stone dead.

It was a horrible sight, White's lifeless face slap in the middle of an otherwise perfect cheese soufflé. 'She's let herself go,' whispered Joan. The autopsy report was later to confirm this view: the impact of falling into the soufflé had fatally smeared Snow White's make-up, so her face had to be retouched at considerable expense to her estate for her glamorous internment in Forest Lawn attended by media mogul Barry Diller whose four-part mini-series *Kennedy* starring Leonard Nimoy as the one-time President who faked his own assassination, costars Angie Dickinson, who was once married to my late wife's grandfather's god-daughter's first husband's agent, who once famously rented a Malibu beach-apartment from the late Telly Savalas.

Consummate professionals, the waiters cleared away Snow White's corpse in no time at all, resetting her place for my old friend Elizabeth Taylor, who sadly is often late, though not as late as her former husband, tragically drunk now dead Richard Burton. But even as the conversation turned to the much-touted romance between Michael Jackson and Rose Kennedy – Rose's death is rumoured not to be a barrier – I found myself troubled by that bullet to the back of Snow White's head.

Two minutes after her demise, people were saying that White had been committing suicide for years, that it was the kind of hey-look-at-me whistle-while-you-work attention-grabbing thing she would happily do three times a day just so long as someone was watching. It was just like her, they said, to position a high-velocity shotgun fifteen yards away and, via an intricate web of invisible wires, secretly pull the trigger just to embarrass her fellow-guests.

As the second course came round, everybody in that restaurant had forgotten the woman who had lain slumped in her soufflé only ten minutes before. The late Snow White's masterly public relations agent, Cyrus J. Bandana, highly practised in these affairs, explained to me later that the last thing his late client would have wanted was to upset the dinner party ('I know she'll be DEVASTATED not writing a thank-you card before doing away with herself'). So he had taken the matter in hand, discreetly scooping her corpse from the table and placing it neatly in the laundry-chute until the exclusive fifty-five dollar apiece topflight European liqueurs were being served on the architect-designed balcony with its luxurious parkside views, overlooking an exclusive apartment once rented by Larry King from my old friend Gloria Vanderbilt.

All was not what it seemed – or so it seemed: or was it? I looked round the dining table, sifting suspects. Down the far end, there were seats vacated by lowlife former colleagues of Snow White from those days when she was still big. The emptiness of those seats suggested to me they had been vacated. I was later told by someone who knew someone who was told by someone who knew someone who knew what really happened that these two former colleagues – Sneezy and Dopey – had in fact retired to the restroom to indulge their seedy drug habits.

Three days later, I was phoned by Lynn Witch of Houston and the South of France, who is a personal friend of the royal family of Monaco and whose sister Wicked worked on the top-grossing dwarf movie with Snow. 'I wouldn't say this to anyone else,' she told me, 'but it's an open secret that Sneezy and Dopey wear stack heels.'

But it was Prince Charming who aroused my deepest suspicions. He had once had his pick of all the most beautiful and famous women in Hollywood. A stormy first marriage to Goldilocks ended in an acrimonious divorce in which three different bears were cited. This was followed by a disastrous second marriage to busty lowlife former child star Big Red Riding-hood. A third marriage, this one to Sleeping Beauty, collapsed amidst allegations that she had cleaned out Charming's medicine cabinet before slipping into a coma. But those days were past. He was now scraping a living in two-bit roles in straight-to-video mini-series – and his fourth wife, Snow White lay dead in a soufflé.

I had known Charming for thirty years – I first met him with the third wife of Frank Sinatra, whose fourth husband was twice-married to the sixth wife of the first husband of his former wife – but I never trusted him an inch. It was the little things that did it for me. The furtive, sneaky way he blinked his eyes. His appallingly second-rate toupee. That habit he had of clicking his knuckles. They all convinced me he was the true murderer of Snow White.

Let's, for the sake of argument, say the stories going the rounds aren't true, that Charming isn't a former top-ranking Nazi who gets his depraved kicks by dressing in leather and clubbing baby seals to death with a $40,000 silver hammer from Tiffany's. It's still a sign of the smarmy public feeling he has created that such degrading stories continue to cling to him.

Postscript: I was later contacted by Charming's dental hygienist. She told me he gave up flossing in late May or early June 2001 – exactly a year before the brutal murder of his fifth wife. Coincidence?

I don't think so.

Wallace Arnold: Forty Years of Today

'And here is your newsreader, Brian Perkins . . .' Delicious phrase! One strives to be on top of the news at all times. Is the *Financial Times* index rising or falling? How are the foreign wars doing? Has the Secretary of State for Hoojamaflip made a major gaffe again? Any new earthquakes? And what of rising crime?

I am an inveterate news buff, tuning in my wireless on the hour every hour for the very latest in national and international crises. And I may say that sitting back and listening to the news, with its varied and nutritious diet of disasters, upsets, wars, massacres, disputes and tragedies, has kept me cheerful through many a personal crisis. For instance, back in the mid-eighties, when my country seat had burnt to a crisp after a misaimed puff on my trusty pipe, and my long-running column 'The Voice of Tradition' was being axed by the *Daily Mail* for being too old-fashioned, and I was experiencing something of a severe nervous breakdown (dread phrase!), I could always turn to the very latest news of atrocities in Afghanistan and Iran to cheer myself up.

And over the past forty years, the *Today* programme on the Home Service has proved my most trusty companion, supplying me with a marvellously lively balance of disaster whenever times are low. Happy Birthday, *Today* – and I am delighted to hear that the Powers That Be (!) are extending your airtime by a further forty-five minutes every morning! Well done!

Of course, when the *Today* programme first took to the air, way back in 1957, it was given just fifteen minutes a week on a very occasional basis, and this would always have to include a cookery slot, two hymns, a children's story and three shipping forecasts. In those days, there was comparatively little news. Indeed, for just over a week in 1958, between 7 July and 15 July, nothing at all happened anywhere in the world, and the *Today* team – at that time consisting of Jack de Manio, June Whitfield and Tommy Reilly on the harmonica – were given the full eight days off, to do with as they wished.

In fact, virtually nothing happened throughout the second half of the 1950s, allowing the resident Home Service newscaster full rein to pursue a second, highly successful career as a soft drinks manufacturer in the East Midlands. Of course, every now and then there was an outbreak of news, and the *Today* team would feel duty-bound to convene in order to pass on any relevant information to the dedicated listener. For instance, when Fidel Castro took charge of Cuba back in 1958, Jack de Manio interviewed him 'live' down the telephone about how he achieved quite such a magnificent beard, June Whitfield set a Fidel Castro anagram competition, and the weather-forecaster predicted – wrongly, as it emerged – that for the next twenty-four hours Cuba would be experiencing scattered showers with sunny intervals.

It was in late 1960, with the onset of the *Lady Chatterley's Lover* trial, that news really started to come into its own. There was no going back: the Bay of Pigs, Profumo, the Berlin Wall, the First Man in Space, the Great Train Robbery, the Beatles – the *Today* programme was expanded from occasional to weekly, from weekly to daily, from fifteen minutes to thirty and then to the full hour. Yet still they found it difficult to cope with the sheer quantity of news. 'I don't mind telling listeners that I've been absolutely run off my feet today,' complained Jack de Manio on the day of Kennedy's assassination, 'and I very much hope the relevant authorities give Mr Lee Harvey Oswald a jolly good dressing down.'

This Is Craig Brown

I myself joined the *Today* team surprisingly late, in 1973, when the volume of news coming in each day had become almost too overwhelming for one programme to manage. Every morning when we arrived at the office, great stacks of news would be there to greet us, often clogging up the doorway, and even, on occasion, spreading into the corridor. We tried to sift through it all, of course, broadcasting the important items and filing away anything less important for use in a few weeks' time. But every now and then an oversight would occur: news of the wedding of Princess Anne to Captain Mark Phillips was broadcast a full six weeks after it had happened, and, as far as I know, we completely forgot to inform our listeners of the unfortunate resignation of President Nixon, which coincided with the Chelsea Flower Show.

Alas such blips were the inevitable result of such a massive increase in the news, which now arrived almost hourly, carried in huge container lorries. No doubt the bureaucrats who seem to run the BBC these days would describe our approach as 'unprofessional' (dread word!). But I wonder if we have really gained much from jettisoning our easy-going, gentlemanly approach to the news for a more exhausting – and exhaustive! – topicality?

Anyway, we rushed through the backlog as fast as we possibly could, with little loss to our authority. It must have been in the February of '73 that I was given the singularly happy task of announcing England's 1966 World Cup victory to a delighted audience. By late 1975 we were virtually up to date, and all the 1974 General Election results had been broadcast, though a few complaints trickled through in 1977 when our producer suddenly realised that, by some unfortunate oversight, we had entirely forgotten to inform listeners of Harold Macmillan's resignation some fifteen years before.

Of course, those were the days before the ill-mannered and cut-throat approach to the cross-questioning of VIPs had been introduced by the likes of Paxman and Co. It was always my opinion that one could extract far more from a politician or world statesman through relaxed chat, peppered with amusing anecdotes and easy-going chinwaggery. For instance, when General Idi Amin came into the studio for a major interview in mid-1975, I managed to set him very much at ease with a few gentle ruminations on the English climate.

'General,' I began, lighting my trusty pipe with a few well-timed puffs, 'I imagine that the weather here is a little more chilly than it is in the country from which you hail!'

'Uganda,' he replied.

'Really?' I said. 'Well, that's a very long way away. Did you fly?'

'Yes, indeed.'

'Comfortable flight? Much turbulence?'

'Very comfortable.'

'Excellent news!' By this time, the General was eating out of the palm of my hand, so I judged the time appropriate to ask him one or two rather more tricky questions.

'General,' I began, in my most commanding voice. I fancy he tensed in his chair, crossing and uncrossing his legs so that the array of medals upon his chest were set a-jingle. 'General, in 1969, the pocket-sized chanteuse Lulu stormed to victory in the Eurovision Song Contest. The winning number subsequently went to number one in the British charts. What was its title?'

The General looked back at me blank-faced. I could tell the poor fellow was baffled! 'I'm going to have to rush you, General!' I said.

'I – I – I –' he stuttered – but it was too late.

'Sorry, General!' I said, pressing my palm hard upon the nodule of the studio bell. 'The correct answer was, of course, 'Boom Bang-a-Bang'. I should think you're kicking yourself, ha ha – am I right?'

Tremendous fun, and much more agreeable than ruthless inquisitions on such personal details as government policy. Yet today such a prying and impertinent line of interrogation is the norm, the light-hearted general knowledge question a thing of the past. Happily, I maintain some contact with the show through my popular appearances presenting *Thought for the Day*. I am the acknowledged master of the topical homily.

'Good morning' I say, 'I see fish are in the news again. And let's never forget that fish are sea-creatures, never happier than when swimming about. A bit like us, really. Goodbye!'

I then exit swiftly from the studio, leaving Messrs Naughtie and Humphreys alone with their abusive clipboards. And now *Today* is to be extended by a further three-quarters of an hour. One would hope the time will be filled with a little light music, a few gardening tips, or a pleasant stroll down Memory Lane with Uncle Bill Deedes. But one fears the very worst.

England,
my
England

Looking Down on England

A minute or two before your aeroplane is set to land, or a minute or two after it has taken off, just at that moment when everyone else on the plane is busily sucking their boiled sweets, or pretending to concentrate on an in-flight magazine, or staring straight ahead, all sensible people will be looking out of the window, voraciously taking in the view of the land below.

It is like an out-of-body experience, for your body has quite literally left the world behind. The buildings and countryside that, only minutes ago, defined your idea of yourself and your position in the world are suddenly reduced to toytown size. Cars scooting hither and thither down below seem foolish in their urgency; human activity seems footling in comparison with the never-ending landscape upon which it takes place. Sometimes, I am even seized with the supernatural belief that, if I look long and hard enough, I will catch sight of myself scurrying about unawares.

I was able to relieve these vivid sensations – and even the odd stab of vertigo – as I looked through this huge, awe-inspiring photographic atlas of England.* Here, in one heavy volume, is the whole country seen from 5,500 feet up in the sky: every house on every street, every wood and every

* *England: The Photographic Atlas* (HarperCollins)

factory, every golf course, every stream and every meadow.

The scale gets bigger and smaller. Most areas are presented on a scale of 1:36000, so that with the naked eye one can see trees but not cars, but in key cities the scale is magnified to 1:4500, so that one can make out cars and boats and even the tiny pin-pricks of individual people. This will appeal to the voyeuristic element in us all, even if it will not wholly satisfying it: how one yearns for a scale of, say, 1:20, so that, hovering above Salisbury, one would be able to take a jolly good look at Sir Edward Heath enjoying a pina colada on his sun-lounger in his garden in the Cathedral Close, or, zooming in over Beckingham Palace, one could see Mr and Mrs Beckham playing topless croquet or having a blazing row, or possibly both.

Like Borges's ideal map of the world (scale 1:1), this is probably asking too much. Nevertheless, *England: The Photographic Atlas* contains many revelations, especially if you have the patience to give it time. At first glance, it may seem much of a muchness, the aerial photograph of the countryside around Tonbridge in Kent appearing almost identical to the aerial photograph of the countryside around Keyworth in Nottinghamshire, and so on. But the more you look, the more you see, and the more differences shine out, every field a different shade and shape, every group of fields forming a different pattern.

There are beautiful patterns everywhere, all overlooked by traditional maps: a nest of Vs in the water as a boat makes its way up the Tyne, a man-made semi-circle divided by diagonal lines on the eerie coastal area of Orfordness in Suffolk, the spider's web of paths in Hyde Park, the rocks in Cumbria and the Yorkshire Dales creating a swirling effect, as though the paper has been marbleised, the beautiful crescents and circles in the midst of great cities like Bath and Winchester. There are pages and pages of fields (one of the uplifting effects of the book is the way it shows that England is still predominantly a green and pleasant land) yet the patterns that emerge from them are all subtly different, and often astounding: the area where Cambridgeshire borders on Lincolnshire, flat and unexciting when one passes through it on foot, is like the most brilliant Cubist painting from the air, its various quadrilaterals criss-crossing and intermingling to dynamic effect.

Most peculiar of all are the patterns created by golf courses, the fairways stretching out over the landscape like wonky fingers. A thousand years from now, will archaeologists pore over these pages, wondering what on earth these fingers were for? And will they conclude that these were religious sites, with their Mecca in the Sunningdale area, all created by primitive man to satisfy his spiritual lust? And will they be wrong?

Many sites that are dull and ugly viewed from the ground become unexpectedly beautiful viewed from above: for instance, the thick smoke pumping out of towers around Leeds gives that area of the map an Impressionistic feel, as though an artist has just used his thumb to create a smudge. Ipswich, which is in reality a dump, looks perfectly pleasant from the air, the full sweep of its river setting suddenly released from the hideous buildings that imprison it.

And the opposite is true, too: aerial views flatten everything, so that the tallest and most magnificent buildings and the highest hills and most beautiful downs are here squashed into the background: London's Canary Wharf, for instance, is virtually invisible, and Ely Cathedral which, in real life, dominates the landscape of the Fens for miles around, becomes very hard to locate. The great white dome of Sizewell B Nuclear Power Station, which looms creepily over my own area of the Suffolk coast, is rendered scarcely bigger than a full stop. Meanwhile, the sublimely beautiful Malvern Hills are squashed as flat as Norfolk.

Roads, disproportionately enlarged in most other atlases for the convenience of the motorist, are here rendered back into their proper place, so skinny as to be barely visible. Even Surrey, which has the reputation as a built-up suburb of London, appears bountifully green: years ago, I read that it had more trees than any other county, and the aerial maps seem to confirm this. It is sad, though, that the country's railway lines are too narrow to make any sort of mark on the landscape: try as I might, I could not spot a single train.

The glory of *England: The Photographic Atlas* lies in the way that it makes you see things with fresh eyes. The English have, over the past fifty years, developed an inferiority complex about their own land, preferring to look abroad for a sense of wonderment. Familiarity has bred contempt. But this book should make us wonder anew at places we have taken for granted: it is time we started feeling the same sense of excitement about the extraordinary union of man and nature that has given us Portsmouth Harbour as we already feel about far more humdrum Continental ports.

Of course, one's immediate impulse is to look up the places one knows best. But even here, there are surprises. For instance, a long time ago I spent a year of my life in a university hall of residence in Bristol. Throughout that year, I kept hearing that there were tennis courts, but, being a student, never quite mustered the energy or the curiosity to find out where they were. Twenty-three years later, turning to page 100, map reference C3, I realise with a start that all that time they were just fifty yards from my bedroom.

This atlas offers few favours to the Royal Family. Looking at London, I was struck by what a vast area is covered by the Buckingham Palace Gardens – almost as big as St James's Park – and I was left wondering, a trifle peevishly, whether the Queen really needs all that space for her corgis.

Elsewhere, one or two things have changed since 1999, when most of the photographs were taken. London's Millennium Wheel is pictured prior to elevation, still on its side. Back in my neck of the woods, the thrilling new pier at Southwold is pictured still in its infancy. Here and there, some little thing indicates motion – near Godalming, you can spot a plane in flight, and Beachy Head is awash with surf and foam. But for the most part, surprisingly little has changed in a hundred years: England remains forever England, captured for all time in this book, as if by magic.

The Duke of Devonshire's A–Z of Englishness

A is for ancestors. I am thinking in particular of the 7th Duke, the Marquess of Nuneaton, who held many of the very highest offices of state by dint of his magisterial moustaches, and of whom it was said he never ventured beyond his drive without a flowerpot on his head. A natural conservative, as Home Secretary he placed an immediate ban on the new-fangled device known as the fire extinguisher, which, he declared in his deliciously languid drawl, was 'most disagreeable'. Sadly, during the long heatwave of '23 his flowerpot caught fire and the blaze soon spread to his moustaches, but, true to his word, he refused an extinguisher to the very end. **A** is also for Antarctic. Frightfully chilly, or so they say.

B is for Basingstoke. Not a town one has chosen to visit all that often, I fear.

C is for chess. I have to be careful here, but the knight is, quite frankly, an awfully *common* piece, forever jumping sideways at the last minute, like a cat on a hot tin roof, whatever that may be. Pawns are dreadfully dreary, too, don't you think? I suspect they come from Basingstoke.

D is for Debo. She's a woman, of course, but I've always admired that in a wife.

E is for enema. My great-aunt Enema gave her name to the famous medical procedure. Extraordinary lady. Whenever she used to stay at Chatsworth, she would turf all our gubbins and bric-a-brac out through the back door.

F is for fish. Fish are so very English, don't you think? My ancestor, the 4th Duke, was half-fish on his mother's side. They say he had her fingers. She was one of the Smoked Salmons of Gloucestershire. Her beautiful pink complexion was often remarked upon. I have nothing against fish, which is not to say one would want one's daughter to marry one. Of course, as an Englishman one must always save all fish bones. Bound together with a decent bit of string and sellotaped to the ceiling, they make excellent television aerials.

G is for galoshes. No English gentleman should ever wear his galoshes to a masked ball, unless the ballroom has first been flooded to make him feel more at home.

H is for halo. St John the Baptist was an ancestor of mine. He was supposed to have taken religion rather seriously, but they say he did awfully well. I myself have never spent a great deal of time in the wilderness. It doesn't greatly appeal.

I is for irreplaceable. I once mistook a Ming dynasty teapot for a clay pigeon. To my great sorrow, it was irreplaceable.

J is for Jockey Club. Racing is tremendously important to the English. There is no more democratic institution than the Jockey Club. It's open to absolutely everyone in racing. Except for the jockeys, of course.

K is for Rudyard Kipling. 'If' is the most marvellous poem, full of good sense. If I should die, think only this, that and the other. Some corner of a foreign land. You be a mango, my son. Et cetera. Memorable.

L is for lawn tennis. If we're conjuring up the perfect English scene, can we do better than to sit out in the sunshine, drinking squash, sucking strawbugs and watching the girls in their short skirts as they bend right over for a low volley? Well done, girls! Well done, indeed!

M is for Mitford, a very English family. My wife Debo is a Mitford. Then – let me see – there was Decca, the record producer; Becca, who played at Wimbledon; Necca the nymphomaniac; Mecca, who toyed with becoming a Muslim, and Pecca, the pioneering anorexic.

N is for nuisance. Hats can be the most dreadful nuisance if worn on anywhere but the head.

O is for Oxford marmalade (always pronounced Maw-maw-lad). Since time immemorial, the Cavendishes have spread their marmalade on the bottom of their toast. I adhere to this family tradition but I regret to say the marmalade does not always adhere to the toast. More often than not, it prefers to fall on one's chin or one's bib, and when replaced on one's plate it tends to stick to it. For this reason, we mix our Oxford marmalade with a little glue – Gripfix or Uhu – and that seems to do the trick, though it ruins the taste. **O** is also for orphan. Orphan is not a word in my vocabulary. I prefer to do things seldom, if at all.

P is for Pinter. Harold has quite a number of bees in his bonnet, poor fellow. Did he grow up in Basingstoke, perhaps? I rather think he must have done. But Antonia is a second-cousin on my mother's side, so we are pleased to have the two of them over for tea. One tries to show an interest in the theatre, of course. I once told him how much I had enjoyed an amusing little play called *The Birthday Suit*, and I wondered if he had had anything to do with it? He looked a little broody, then told Antonia to get her coat, it was time for offs. Oh dear. Did I put my foot in it?

Q is for queen, who, in half a century, hasn't put a foot wrong. An absolute treasure. She is sometimes good enough to drop in on Chatsworth to 'help out' when our regular staff are away on their hols.

R is for Reading. Oddly enough, I passed through it once on the way to Wiltshire.

S is for Spam. We don't grow it here, but I'm told it's marvellous for filling in holes in walls and so forth.

T is for torture. I once spent three days without my valet, Henry. Imagine having to walk around with one's shoelaces untied for three days! One kept tripping over.

U is for Uncle Harold (Macmillan). He was a remarkable character. He had the most agreeable manners, and would never stab someone in the back without making a beautiful apology beforehand.

V is for V-neck. Invented by the 6th Duke, who had grown sick to death of staggering around, blind as a bat, in a jersey without a hole in its top.

W is for Walthamstow. The family owns Walthamstow, though I've never been able to locate it on a map.

X is for xenophobia. Such a silly business. Some of our most loyal staff are foreign. And the Italians are good at singing.

Y is for yell. The English gentleman never yells; he employs someone to yell for him.

Z is for Zeus. A cousin on my mother's side; by all accounts quite a character, if a mite Greek.

Who Murdered Ffelicity, Lady Delboy?

The *sun will never set on books about the English in Africa. This past week alone has seen the publication of* Child of Happy Valley *by Juanita Carberry and* The Africa House *by Christina Lamb. In this exclusive extract from* The Fly-by-Nights of Thika, *we ask – Who really murdered Ffelicity, Lady Delboy?*

As the merciless African sun beat down upon the corpse of his young wife, Lord Delboy, feeling a little tiddly after his final gin-and-it before breakfast, reloaded his revolver, lashed his riding-crop against the buttocks of his faithful manservant, M'mble, and roared, 'How many more times do I have to tell you to clear up all corpses before breakfast! Take this, you lazy native swine!'

He had found his wife at the foot of the stairs, lying face down in a sea of old fruits, nuts and vegetables. How had she ended up in this pickle? His mind travelled back to the events of the night before. Cocktails, arguments, cocktails, arguments, cocktails, cocktails and more cocktails. Followed by an argument or two. It had been an evening like any other. And then – oh, the shame of it! – he had grown so drunk, so very, very drunk, that he had ended up in bed with *his own wife*.

At first, as he had fallen into the bed, he had imagined that

Ffelicity had grown an extra set of legs, one batch hairier than the other. Why hadn't the silly woman listened to him when he'd warned her off those trips to the witch doctor? But then he had spotted a pair of goggles and a windblown scarf thrown higgledy-piggledy on to the floor, and he knew then and there that those extra legs belonged to another man: the dashing air-ace Johnny Sunbeam, damn him!

Delboy had married Ffelicity when he was pushing sixty-five and she was little more than a child. She had insisted that her teddy bear be best man. But, wishing to establish his authority from the very start, Delboy had foiled her plan, plying Teddy with drink and introducing him to a roomful of rag-dolls, before gently closing the door behind him and tip-toeing away. The last they'd heard of Teddy was that he had eloped to the South of France with a legless doll. He now spent his days hanging around the clip-joints of Marseilles, half the bear he used to be, drink in one hand, cigarette in the other, desperately trying to impress the locals by boasting of his close friendship with Winnie the Pooh.

Ffelicity had never forgiven Delboy for this dirty trick. In moments of desolation, Delboy would take their wedding photographs out of the bin, dust them down, and sit staring at them for hours, tears trickling between the whiskers on his cheeks. They were an unusual couple – he, bald, red-faced and fat, clad in full military regalia, she a child of barely sixteen summers, a gin bottle just visible in her train.

In moments of depression, Delboy wondered why on earth he had ever given up his commission to come to this god-forsaken land in the first place. He had arrived with a dream of creating the biggest ice-cube farm in the world, but the climate had proved unsuitable. A puddle the size of a lake was all that was left to remind him of those far-off days of ice and hope.

The first fifty years had been something of a struggle. One project after another had crashed to the ground. The first year, he had attempted to set up a hospital in the jungle for manic-depressives, staffed only by hyenas. But the constant screech of laughter had served only to deepen the patients' gloom, and numbers had dropped to zero. Other projects, too, had proved unfeasible – a throat clinic for giraffes, a swamp-side shop selling human bags and shoes to crocodiles, a finishing school to teach cheetahs fair play: all had come to nothing.

On his seventieth birthday, Delboy had been staring bankruptcy in the face. But by a stroke of good luck, his elderly millionairess non-swimming spinster Aunt Ddaphne, out in Africa for the celebrations, had tripped over an outstretched foot into a pool of man-eating cod, and in two strokes – a frantic burst of breast-stroke, followed by a brief stab at crawl – the estate had been saved.

'Bwana! Bwana!' The cry of M'stake pierced the air. Delboy checked his watch. It was that time of day when a servant runs from the lake to report that one of the guests, dizzy from too much sun, has toppled into the open jaws of Emily the crocodile. A smile lit up his face. Emily had been like a wife to him these ten years past. It emerged that M'stake had chanced upon Ffelicity's corpse, and – the lazy good-for-nothing – wanted to know if this meant he was excused having to lay her place for breakfast.

Word of Ffelicity's death soon spread around the British community. 'Deary me,' Floppy Withers said upon hearing the news, 'does that mean she won't be joining us for mah-jong tomorrow? It really is too *dreary* of her.' Clarence the Lion stared back at her, cross-eyed. For two decades now, Floppy had been one of the greatest characters in the whole of Africa. Tales of her eccentricities were legion: her habit of changing not only before, but also during dinner; her insistence upon parachuting into cocktail parties from her biplane, even when they were held in conservatories, not to mention her increasing faith in the wisdom of witch doctors. 'Cold feet will come to he who is without a hat,' she would whisper to fellow-partygoers as she scurried past, Margharita in hand.

'Dreadful nuisance – the police are insisting upon poking their noses into Ffelicity's murder. As if it's any of their business!' Delboy barked at Bunny Rackstraw over a Gin Sling and a boiled egg. At that moment, M'mble approached on his camel to tell them Inspector Chip O'Sholder from the Mounted Police had arrived, seeking to ask them a few questions. 'Show him into the drawing room,' snapped Delboy, feeling in his pocket for his lucky swastika.

Inspector O'Sholder surveyed the drawing room, his lips curling with distaste. 'Something tells me the parties you hold in this room are not simply a matter of chats and *drinki-poohs* eeh-bah-gum,' he said, his northern origins still just detectable, in moments of stress, beneath five long years of elocution.

'How dare you cast aspersions, you common little whipper-snapper!' replied Delboy, reaching for his horsewhip. 'I'll see you're reported to my friend the Governor-General of New South Wales when next he's in Africa! Whatever makes you think my parties are not above board? Well?! Spit it out!'

Inspector O'Sholder's gaze turned slowly towards the ceiling. Delboy's eyes followed suit. Hanging from the main chandelier were three ladies' brassieres. And one man's. Delboy coughed. 'They're to ward off evil spirits,' he spluttered. 'The native has so much to teach us, wouldn't you agree? Drink, Inspector?'

Beyond the wood-panelled room, the jungle writhed in untamed torment, the mute, leaf-encrusted witness of the events of the night before. The sweat tumbled from his brow as he rang for M'mble to smoke some extra cigarettes for him. Oh, Godalming, Godalming, he thought, why did I ever leave you?

Bel Littlejohn: Bel's Britain

Who are we? What are we doing here? Where have we come form? Where are we going? And who's that over there? These are just a few of the questions that have obsessed me these past five years as I travelled this country in search of disturbingly honest answers for my new book, *Bel's Britain* by Bel Littlejohn (Canongate).

Who am I? Who are you? Are we nearly there yet? When are we going back? What's the time? How do we get to where we have just been when we haven't even got to where we wanted to go? In writing my book over these past six years, I have been literally desperate to find major solutions for all these vital questions that we as a country have been facing for as long as anyone can remember. Where did you last see it? Is that someone at the door? What time did they ask us for? Did you see what she was wearing? Can I come too?

Big questions. Demanding big, big answers. The British as a people have lost sense of who they – we – really are. In the old days, we had a highly developed sense of our national identity. Historians tell us that the men wore bowler hats and the women sipped tea with their little fingers crooked outwards. Their talk was mostly of the weather, but in controlled situations would also cover who would be having the next dance but one.

But times have changed. Another big question. What do we

think of when we think of Britain? Here's a list, off the top of my head. The acrid smell of urine in lifts. Overcooked cabbage. Bernard Manning and David Mellor. The F word. Drunks throwing up on the Northern Line. Bent coppers. Robert Kilroy-Silk. Pop-Tarts.

Neil Hamilton. Smashed lager bottles in the street. Violent attacks in beauty spots. Trespassers Will Be Prosecuted. Alphabetti Spaghetti. Shell-suits on Senior Citizens. Six Killed In Motorway Pile-Up. Big Macs.

Welsh seagulls caught in mammoth oil slicks. Tug-of-Love Tots. Greasy hair. Crusts from bacon, lettuce and tomato sandwiches floating in British Rail toilets. Road rage. Football hooligans with rings through their lips.

Little Chefs. Burst tyres. Manic depression. Sexual discrimination. Chewing gum stuck to the sole of your left shoe. A pile of dirty dishes standing unwashed in the sink for three days without being touched by A N Other even though he knows it's his bloody turn. The Emma Thompson video you never quite got round to watching still not returned to Blockbuster after six days and who's fault is that. Your elderly mother, still alive, sitting on a fortune but refusing to downsize to sheltered housing.

A half-eaten tin of Crosse and Blackwell Baked Beans gathering mould in the fridge. The coffee stain on the living-room carpet, 2ft 6in × 3ft 4in. The doorbell on the blink. The father of your child demanding his complete collection of Pink Floyd CDs back, plus the lime-green bean-bag and the remaining bottles of sleeping pills.

Not exactly a happy list, is it? Not exactly a list suggesting a people at ease with itself, a people proud of its past and comfortable with its present and striding into its future with confidence, now is it? For Christ's sake, let's not kid ourselves we're happy. And I didn't even mention the used Band-Aid hanging from the underside of the seat on the Number 73 bus, the dead sparrow beneath the rusting slide in the Kentish Town playground, the pair of unclaimed soiled knickers in the P&O Lost Property at Dover or the pool of congealed vomit in the entrance to the Newcastle disco at 3.00am on a Tuesday morning. Yup. This is Britain on a wet October morning in the year AD 1998.

And it's not a pretty sight.

So. What the hell happened to us?

Over the past seven years, I've been scouring the country for people to tell me where we went wrong. As you'd expect, I've done one helluva lot of listening. I've listened to a serial killer in Broadmoor. I've listened to two drugs barons in Sydmonton. I've listened to three paranoid psychopaths in Glasgow, four convicted sex perverts in Somerset and five under-age arsonists in Tyne and Wear. I've listened to the 56-year-old man employed to scoop up the used condoms from the mud beneath the arches of a Lancashire viaduct. And I've listened to the pathetic bleatings of a middle-aged guy as he screams abuse down the phone to a leading woman columnist.

It's been quite a journey, my voyage into the very heart of modern Britain. But it's been a pleasure – and a pleasure I look forward to sharing with you in the days, weeks, months, and years ahead. Stay tuned.

The Fayed Guide to the Season

Royal *Ascot:* You get smart suit, smart Harrods tailsuit, on special offer to you my friend, ten per cent off, okay, no, I like you, make that seven and half, nice top suit with tails, top hat, bow-tie, plus-fours, the lot okay? You need top hat, right, for into putting your hidden camera, your clothes-circus TV camera, so you able to see your nosey-toffed enemy when he trying creeps up on you from behind your back. All snobs at Ascot they wear security camera in top hats, what else point of wearing top hat? You need tails too, my friend, Mohamed tell you, you need tails – how else you tie up your assassin after you have trapping him with your top hat? Plus sawn-off carnation in butty-hole for extra safety, right? One sniff – enemy kaput.

Which horse you betting on? I have tip you good: at Ascot, never bet on greyhound, my friend. They kidding you, greyhound not horse, greyhound is dog. No hope against horse, no way, my friend – horsey win every time. How jockey, even midget jockey, gonna sit on greyhound? No way! Jockey's legs is drag along ground. He weigh greyhound down, greyhound out of puff, bloody jockey on back, no way is greyhound running well. So, six horses, call that half-dozen to you my friend – which you betting on? I tell you, free tip from Mohamed – you wait til after race is finish, my friend – then you betting on *horse that is won.*

England, My England

Wimbledon: British Establishment of all homos, the lot. Why else they pay good money to sit down watching two guys in shorty trousers to running up down, up down and grunty-grunty for hours at end, eh? You tell me that, my friend. Fifteen love. Thirty love. Love all. Change ends. Is bloody disgusting. Major, Blair, Duke of Edinburgh, they all at it, I got witnesses.

But Wimbledon very posh, very grand, no riff-raff, nothing but best, VIP treatment, nice glass bubbly, strawberry, sand, cream, the lot. Is well-known fact, very well-known fact, Mohamed al Fayed win Wimbledon when young man, al Fayed is world champing, al Fayed is beat all. But Establishment, all homos, you know, they is jealousing, they have conspiracying do Mohamed down, they strike al Fayed name from all Wimbledon records, so believe me, I done Wimble, I no Wimbledoing no more, no way my friend, the snobs and homos they go stuffing themselves.

The Royal Academy Summer Exhibition: Millions pictures. Everywhere you look. Houses. Properties. Peoples. Towns. Villages. Even animals, they even having pictures of your cats and dogs. Is the Establishment snoops at work, see? M15, M16, M25 – so many government spies they build own road for them now. They are taking all year to have invade the privacy, gather information on our personal privacy – then what they do, they put it on walls for all to snoop at in so-called Royal Academy.

Is rubbish exhibit. Al Fayed art collection the best, top-tip VIP artists, no garbage. Al Fayed's favourite artist? Is an Impressionist, makes big impression on clients. His name? Money. Clawed Money. Great big canvasses, pricey colours, lot rich oil paint, beautiful frames, very expensive, nothing but best. Civilisation – you want Civilisation? I own it. I give you Civilisation, my friend, but for price. Rembrandt, Picasso, Turner – they very dear personal VIP friends of Mohamed, they work for Mohamed, I get them sign new paintings for you, how many Rembrandts you want? Rembrandt, he want very much help. But is costing you very much.

The Henley Regatta: You know why they call it Henley Regatta? No? I tell you. Name after multi-murdering English King Henley VIII. That no way to treat wives, rest your head here my dear, whoops my axe it slip, what shame, you lost your head in bucket, weep weep, now I marry my girlfriend, okay? That no way to behave. How English letting him get away I want to know – and then they naming Regatta after this crook like he some kind of VIP.

Henley Regatta very crowding, so many people, women, homos, the lot, all chatter-chatter, so everyone want getting away fast as poss but I tell you my friend no one can getting away because so many traffic is all jam. So what they do? Only escape is on water – so clever ones, they give two fingers to Establishment, yes, they hire skinny boats and make getaway fast possible by river, so they no having to chatter-chatter and eat bloody strawberries no more.

Glyndebourne: Special offer Harrods nicpic hamper, lots exclusive goodies, champagne, chutney, ginger, the lot, you are taking to Glyndebourne for beautiful nicpic on top-class luxury lawn outside, is beautiful: cut-glass, table, chairs, candles, butler, believe me, good as sitting inside. But then *dingdong-dingdong* great loud pierce-earring bell is having going and everyone made get up, chop-chip, chop-chip and march into big hall, sit down on hard seats, no butler, no champagne, no cut-glass, and watch for hours while fat man in ladies tights is yelling at fat ladies in totally out-of-fashion ballgowns and the fat ladies yell back and you are having think, 'Where my bloody VIP prestige nicpic, what I doing in here no eating, no drinking, no nothing, when could be enjoy sit downing outside, you call this democracy?'

You know what? Is Establishment MI5 conspiracy, they against al Fayed, against Harrods, against the ordinary people enjoying their nic-pics, so when they see ordinary people sitting happy with Harrods hampers outside, they give Prince Philip top-secret signal and he press button and bell goes *dingdongdingdong* and ordinary people's evenings is ruined and Establishment they have done bloody wrecking it all. I got witnesses, okay?

The Badminton Horse Trials: I want knowing this – what those horses ever done wrong, eh? You tell me that. Like al Fayed, this poor, ordinary horses totally not guilty, they innocent – so you tell me please, why they in Badminton Horse Trials? Okay, so they be eating too much grass, they neigh, they always swish their bloody tails, they big teeth always chomping – but is no crime! Why Tony Blair and his boyfriends make it a crime, that's what al Fayed want to know? Is conspiracy, my friend. You have my word as nobleman. Should be Princess Anne and Establishment hoity-toits at Badminton Trial, sending to prison for many years with no food, no hampers, nothing. Then Badminton would be Notsobadminton. Is joke. Is Mohamed joke. Why you no bloody laugh? I pay you laugh, you laugh or I sue, okay?

Have You Paid and Displayed?

Have you read any good countryside lately? I only ask because there are now so many signs pointing out what you can and can't do in the countryside – bossy signs, explanatory signs, forbidding signs, advising signs, demanding signs, pointing signs, boasting signs, signs thanking you, signs welcoming you, signs telling you what to do with your dog, signs telling you what to do with your car, signs telling you where to visit, what to do, where to put you car before you shop, where to shop, where to put your litter after you've shopped, signs to heritage sites, signs to camp sites, signs to swimming pools, ruins, picnic sites, and shopping malls – that it is often very hard to see past them to the countryside itself.

> I think that I shall never see
> A billboard lovely as a tree
> Perhaps, unless the billboards fall
> I'll never see a tree at all

– Ogden Nash once wrote of America. In Britain, one need only substitute the words 'council sign' for 'billboard', and the ditty retains all its potency.

My own small town on the Suffolk coast seems to give birth to a new sign every day, almost as though it were on a fertility pill. Most of these signs are to do with the parking or non-parking of cars, though on the coast road, within sight of the sea, there is a bizarre sign with an arrow which simply says, 'BEACH'. It can't be long now before there is a council sign popping out of the sea itself every fifty yards saying 'SEA', and from then on there will be no stopping them: by law, every field will have to bear a sign with a council log, saying 'FIELD' and every cow a large sticker saying 'COW'. The sky may prove difficult, though barrage balloons saying 'SKY' and 'CLOUDS' would remain well within the council's budget, with special emergency balloons for 'RAINBOW' and 'SUDDEN DOWN-POUR'.

Virtually every town around us is now equipped with a vast brown sign, fifteen feet high, headed HISTORIC MARKET TOWN. What joy to be an unhistoric market town, and fall through the net! Near us, the town of Woodbridge, perfectly historic in its unassuming way, is termed not HISTORIC MARKET TOWN but HISTORIC RIVERSIDE TOWN, with its facilities ('TIDE MILL – MUSEUM – SWIMMING POOL – THEATRE') dutifully listed. I doubt there has ever been anyone who, zipping past Woodbridge on the A12, has seen the sign, screeched to a halt and rejoiced to himself, 'A tide mill in an historic riverside town! Just what I was after!'

Once inside these historic towns, there are further signs, many of them pointing out what is already easily visible. Thus, a town on a hill crowned with a castle or a cathedral inevitably displays signs with arrows saying 'HISTORIC CASTLE' or 'HISTORIC CATHEDRAL', for those with eyes untrained in recognising battlements or steeples. The writer Candida Lycett-Green reserves particular contempt for the people who put up the signs along the A34 saying 'THE RIDGEWAY'. 'The Ridgeway is the oldest road in Europe,' she says. 'It was made immediately after the ice age. Why do they suddenly have to behave as though no one has noticed it before?'

'HAVE YOU PAID AND DISPLAYED?' strike me as five of the most irritating words in the English language, easily on a par with 'NOW WASH YOUR HANDS' and 'THANK YOU FOR NOT SMOKING'. A few hundred yards from my house, on a previously unblemished piece of bleak Suffolk coastline, full of rare plants and rarer birdlife, 'HAVE YOU PAID AND DISPLAYED?' signs, tinged with bright nursery green stand looking proudly out at their new domain. Six months ago, this was just a rough space where those who wished to park their cars did so. But such freedom of choice is anathema to councils. First, they bring in the tarmackers, then the white-liners. Then, to justify the expense of the tarmac and the white lines and to force people into their lovely new car park, they paint double yellow lines up and down all the neighbouring roads. And then – oh bliss! – the notices! Not only 'HAVE YOU PAID AND DISPLAYED?' but 'CAR PARK' and 'CARS ONLY' and 'EXIT' and 'NO EXIT' and then lots of little signs saying 'NO PARKING ON GRASS VERGES'.

And each sign breeds yet more signs. After all, you cannot have a PAY AND DISPLAY machine without also having another sign giving all the charges (4 hours 30p, Over 4 hours, 60p) and yet another sign listing those exempt from the charges in the first sign (DISABLED PARKING: first three hours free. Thereafter normal charges apply). Before long, other sign-planters want to muscle in on the original signs, so that a large sticker saying 'POLICE WARNING. MOTORISTS! DON'T LEAVE YOUR VALUABLES IN YOUR CAR. CRIME. TOGETHER WE'LL CRACK IT' is pasted on to the second sign.

Within our pretty town, there are sites which were always used as places to park cars, and which never caused anyone any bother. But in the past few months they have been ambushed by large and ungainly signs, with a slightly toytown feel, as if purchased for remedial purposes from the Early Learning Centre, all topped with the logo of the Suffolk Coastal District Council. They announce that these are now official council car parks. These signs have to be large because the moment you write 'CAR PARK' you have to make space for all the hoo-haa that comes with it: maximum periods of parking, excess charges for improper use, permitted and unpermitted vehicles, disclaimers of liability and so on and so forth. All this carry-on for an area that remains, as it has always been, a free car park (though it now has a maximum 18-hour waiting period, just in case some of the elderly residents have begun to feel at ease). 'THIS CAR PARK IS REGULARLY SUPERVISED' reads another sign, meaning that the town now has a full-time parking-warden, whose presence is the product of all these new signs.

I am told that in Ireland there is a sign in the middle of nowhere that simply says 'DO NOT THROW STONES AT THIS SIGN'. Other signs photographed by readers and sent into *Private Eye* over the years include 'GO BACK. YOU ARE GOING THE WRONG WAY', 'CAUTION. VEHICLES MUST NOT ENTER THIS SHED WHEN THE DOORS ARE CLOSED. BY ORDER' 'NO PARKING THIS SIDE SUNDAY MONDAY TUESDAY WEDNESDAY THURSDAY FRIDAY SATURDAY' and a splendid seaside sign, 'WARNING TO ALL SEAGULLS. SWIMMING IN RED WATER IS STRICTLY PROHIBITED'.

On Thursday, friends telephoned from Marlborough telling me that the *Marlborough Gazette and Herald* had run a report in which councillors described the old signs saying just 'Marlborough' as 'a disgrace to the town'. The councillors wished to spend £150 a sign updating them to include the news that Marlborough is now twinned with Gunjur in the Gambia. They then received the go-ahead to get the replacement signs 'designed on a computer'.

Are councillors in Gunjur in the Gambia agitating for new signs to trumpet their twinning with Marlborough? I suspect not. Signs are a peculiarly British disease, the result of too many bureaucrats overseeing too little Empire. It may well be that Britons never ever, ever shall be slaves, but it can't be long before we are obliged to carry signs making it clear that this is the case (for exemptions see reverse).

Wallace Arnold: An English Education

Methinks she doth protest too much! My somewhat catty colleague, Miss (Msss!) Ann Wilson has penned a characteristically contrary column in which she suggested that the traditional English public school was in some ways 'racist' (dread accusation!).

'Pull the other one, Ann!' I wanted to scream. 'It has the proverbial bells on!' Ann's experience at Rugby in the sixties was greatly at odds with my own experience at Rugby in the forties. As my *Who's Who* entry makes quite clear, I spent most of my schooldays at Basters' Academy for Young Gentlemen, and I continue to rejoice in my position as an Old Basterd. But English and languages were thought of as sissy at Basters, which specialised in the more manly pursuits of mathematics and bloodsports, so my parents (woolly liberals, alas) had me sent on day release to Rugby, where one or two of the more effeminate schoolmasters were believed to have a smattering of Shakespeare up their sleeves.

Ah, memories, memories! I look back on the time I spent at Rugby as one of innocent joy. Every morning, I would knock on the door of the Headmaster's office. After a couple of minutes in which I would listen to keys being turned and doors unbolted, I would be met by the Head Matron, a retired Sergeant Major who had been forced to change sex after being dealt a particularly rotten hand in a game of forfeits at some point in the mid-1930s. The Head Matron would then strip-search me, forcing my buttocks apart with a pair of household pliers on the off-chance of discovering a spanner, a jemmy, a packet of Capstan or a half-bottle of Teacher's. If none were found, she would bid me forward with a gentle pat of her fully-licensed cattle-prod.

Oh, balmy days of innocence and hope! I would then make my way to the Junior Gymnasium, where a small selection of Eskimos would be chained to the climbing-bars. Lesser public schools dealt in the bullying of Jews, Blacks, Indians and what-have-you, but at Rugby this outdated practice was always considered wishy-washy and absurdly generalised. For this reason, a dozen Eskimos would be hired each year for the young gentlemen of the school to taunt and poke at our own discretion.

'Esky! Esky! Get back to your igloo, Esky!' we would chant while the poor Esquimos writhed and squirmed. Every now and then, one of us would have a word with the Headmaster about borrowing the school polar bear costume, and, fully dressed up, we would then enter the gym making polar bear noises – only to frighten the young Eskys out of their proverbial wits!

No doubt the 'caring' professions (!!!!) would accuse us of 'racism' or even 'bullying'. What nonsense! To my certain knowledge, not a single Eskimo ever complained (although they were gagged during daylight hours, one of them could easily have lifted an unchained toe in protest) and in many ways they enjoyed the full run of the school, save in those areas – chapel, dormitories, open spaces, classrooms, dining halls – covered by the very neat and straightforward 'Noli Esquimare' notices.

Card-carrying left-wingers such as Ann Wilson love nothing more than to wring their hands over modish worries such as 'racism' 'sexual abuse' and 'bullying in the classroom'. But I have practised each and every one of them and I can honestly say they never did me any harm. No doubt Ann also sees fit to fuss her silly little head over the so-called barbarities of the fagging system. Yet I spent three years as a fag at Basters' Academy ('Come on, the Basters! Baste up, baste up, and baste the ball!'), working for a succession of fagmasters (Dr Brian Mawhinney, Michael Winner, Derry Irvine) who were to gain great distinction in later life, and I found it immensely character-forming.

Winner, for instance, would often produce a sawn-off shotgun to back up his demands for a slice of lightly buttered toast with a smattering of Gentleman's Relish. (In fact, his well-known moving-picture *Death Wish III* was based on his own experience as a fagmaster at Basters' Academy, and is still honoured with an annual showing for the juniors on Founders' Day). And as the years have gone by, I have come to realise that, contrary to all the received liberal 'wisdom' (!), armed force can be an effective and appropriate accompaniment to any halfway-reasonable demand on our time.

So put that in your pipe and smoke it, Ann! And let me add this. By betraying the public school spirit in your column, you have revealed yourself as nothing more than a worthless little squit. You're a worthless little squit, Ann! What are you? Yes – a worthless little squit! Go on, say it, Ann – SAY IT!

Wallace Arnold: A Very English Christmas

What one might delight in describing as an 'elite gang' of us had foregathered in the snug bar of the Garrick Club for a pre-Christmas noggin: Sir Robin Day and Lord Woodrow Wyatt, both hot from panto, the former still clad in the fetching mauve tights of Puss in Boots, the latter sporting the traditional polka-dot one-piece of Widow Twankey; Sir Terry Worsthorne, fresh from a successful season of magic and fun at the De La Warr Pavilion, Bexhill; and Sir Kingsley Amis, following a disappointing season as Writer-in-Residence at the Battered Wives' Centre in Harlow. 'What I want to know,' I said, downing my Famous Grouse, 'is whatever happened to the true message of Christmas? I'll tell you what happened to it! I'll tell you! It has been lost beneath a barrage of presents, fancy lights, party games and banjos in church! And it's about time we regained that true message, that's what I always say!'

'Hear! Hear!' quothed the others, as we ordered the next round.

'But tell that to the modern so-called "Church Leaders",' barked Woodrow, 'and they wouldn't understand a word of it! It's all lovey-dovey goody-two-shoes stuff these days – and not a thought for the true meaning of Christmas!'

Just as we were all humming our agreement, the most

peculiar thing occurred: who should walk into the bar, without so much as a 'by your leave', but

a) a young woman, quite unashamedly pregnant
b) her heavily bearded male 'companion', swarthy and unsmiling – and frankly looking a mite Jewish (!), dressed in what looked like last year's laundry and
c) a blessed donkey!!!

Needless to say, our conversation came to an abrupt halt. As George the Barman was temporarily out of the room on a mercy-dash to the cellars, I stepped forth to 'do the honours'. 'Ahem,' I intoned. 'Ahem – may I introduce myself, I don't believe we've met? – Wallace Arnold, Scrivener Extraordinaire! How do you do? Always a pleasure to welcome a new member and his lady wife – erm – you *are* a new member, I take it, and this *is* your lady wife?'

Through a series of grunts and hand signs, it soon emerged that – as I had, of course, expected all along – he was no more a member of the Garrick Club than I was the son of Adam. As to whether or not the young lady was his wife, thanks awfully but I would prefer not to hazard a guess. 'Who the hell are *they*? – "New Age Travellers", I suppose!' quipped Woodrow, with a convivial chuckle, quite loud enough for the gloomy couple to overhear.

'Committed sandal-wearers both, I fear!' quoth Kingers. 'And what's all this bloody shawl nonsense, eh? Given the choice of one of 'em, I'd probably go for the donkey!!'

'Sorry, old fruits – but on your bikes, as friend Norman would say!' chipped in Sir Robin, as the laughter died down, stroking his extravagant 'Puss in Boots' whiskers with his customary worldliness.

But it was not going to be quite as easy to get rid of the 'tiresome trio' as we might have expected, for at that point old Beardie started to blather about how they needed shelter as his wife was expecting. 'Expecting what?' I chuckled good-naturedly. 'A kick up the backside?'

Amidst the roars of laughter, Terry Worsthorne began to hold forth about single parent families ('excessively tiresome –

particularly at Christmas, which frankly to me seems to have lost its true meaning') while Woodrow wondered out loud whether the Garrick chef might not be able to make a halfway decent casserole out of the donkey. 'I'm sorry,' I said to the hairy couple, taking command of the situation, 'but there is absolutely no accommodation available at the Garrick, the fairer sex are allowed in only when accompanied by members and unless the lot of you piss off out of here within the minute, I'll be calling upon the services of the local constabulary!'

'Out! Out! Out!' The five of us then began to chant good-humouredly to the magnificent old tune of 'Adeste Fidelis'. At last, the penny seemed to drop, and the unkempt trio descended the main staircase back out on to the streets, whence they had issued and whither they belonged.

'Whatever happened to the good old Authorised Version?' I asked, as the hub-bub died down. 'Of course, I read it avidly, but I sometimes worry that, for the younger generation brought up on the ghastly modern translations, the true message of Christmas will be lost.'

'Ghastly,' the others all agreed, 'simply ghastly.'

The Night Train

(with apologies to W.H. Auden)

This is the Night Train crossing the Border,
Air conditioning out of order

Windows sealed, atmosphere muggy,
Outside breezy, inside fuggy

Seats for the rich, straps for the poor
Everyone else stuffed up by the door

'We apologise for the sudden halt
We'd like to remind you it's all Railtrack's fault'

This is the Night Train re-crossing the Border
Forward lever out of order

'Ladies and Gentlemen, no cause for concern
In eight miles time, we'll attempt to turn

'Why not try a microwaved Pasty
Or our new Spongiburger, naughty but nasty'

Coffee for the rich, crisps for the poor
With a sudden lurch, they're all over the floor

Hissing noisily, horribly crammed
Deary me! The sliding door's jammed

England, My England

This is the Night Train re-re-crossing the Border
Toilets temporarily out of order

'Ladies are requested to cross their legs
Gentlemen advised to purchase pegs

'Customers are requested to remain at ease
If you still feel desperate, try crossing your knees'

Leaves busy growing, dreaming of the day
They can fall on the line causing major delay

Cows staring at passengers all asleep
Think to themselves 'They're just like sheep'

This is the Night Train re-re-re-crossing the Border
Signals and points all out of order

'No time of arrival billed as yet –
So why not try our new filled baguette?'

Groans of defiance, sighs of despair
Hands clenched in anger or pulling out hair,

Passengers demanding information
On times of arrival at their destination
Executives bursting with curses and moans
Fishing in pockets for their mobile phones
Calls to the secretary: 'Cancel that meeting!'
Calls to the conference: 'Rearrange that seating!'
Calls to the PA: 'Reschedule my life!'
Calls to the colleagues and calls to the wife,
Calls to the Operator: 'I demand compensation!'
Calls to the mistress in a huff at the station.
Moans from the oldies ('Disgraceful, innit?')
Threats to the kiddies ('Stop that this minute!')
Abuse from hooligans, harrumphs from commuters

This Is Craig Brown

Tapping out grievances on personal computers:
'Never again . . . prepared to do battle . . .
Absolute outrage . . . herded like cattle'
At last! The Conductor, braving the squeeze
'When will we get there?' 'Don't ask! Tickets please!'

This is the Night Train, re-re-re-re-crossing the Border
Overhead lighting out of order

Arrival delayed until 15.22
So why not try our Pizza Vindaloo?

Or a tasty Masala, buy-two-get-one-free –
Or a piping hot beverage, spilt straight on your knee?

This is the Night Train, re-re-re-re-re-crossing the border
Whoops! We're clean off the rails! Apologies in order!

Owing to derailment, we suggest you alight
And if you run fast, you'll be home Monday night.